Chinese Philosophy

A Reader

James A. Ryan

Gratefully dedicated to my teachers:

Paul Groner
Alan J. Berkowitz (*in memoriam*)
John Knoblock (*in memoriam*)

They taught me how to read Classical Chinese texts.

Contents

Preface

Beginning in 1997 and over the course of the years in which I taught college courses in Chinese philosophy, I translated several of the classic Chinese texts for my students to read. The number of these translations grew, and I decided to compile a reader. I hoped to put something into people's hands which would give them as much pleasure and be of as much use as Wing-tsit Chan's *A Sourcebook in Chinese Philosophy* (Princeton: Princeton University Press, 1963) was to me when I was a young man in the 1980s.

My plan for the book was to provide a deep introduction to major texts, with enough material for a two-semester course in Chinese philosophy, all in only a single volume of not more than five hundred pages. I therefore chose the seven key classical Chinese philosophers, plus three key topics from Tang and Song Buddhism. I left out Neo-Confucianism, as well as various philosophers of earlier periods, such as the egoist Yang Zhu and the philosopher of science Wang Chong. Readers who have mastered the texts in this volume can seek out the rest of Chinese philosophy afterwards.

I also wanted to provide introductory essays to the material which would be not only informative but also opinionated and argumentative. I have decided that as long as the translations are accurate, it is okay for the introductory essays and footnotes to take issue and argue over points made in the texts. Take the things I say with a grain of salt. If you are a professor using this textbook for a course, I would be delighted if you will be happy enough with the translations to use the book again and even more delighted if you will frequently, semester after semester, provide devastating refutation of my points in your lectures. If you are reading this book on your own, outside of a college course, then please keep in mind that I could be wrong in the things I say. Just concentrate on the texts themselves, rather than my commentary.

I am deeply grateful to Ming-wood Liu (Minghuo Liao) for graciously providing helpful criticism of chapters 8 and 9. I am indebted to Nicholaos Jones for his insightful criticisms of my translation of Fazang's passage on the ten coins. I am very grateful to my wife, Suzanne Ryan, for her editorial assistance and her support and patience. I am responsible for any errors and shortcomings which remain in this book.

Introduction

This reader gives you a selection of the most important texts in Chinese philosophy from the period beginning around 500 B.C.E. and ending about 1000 C.E. It begins with the Confucian and Daoist[1] classics of Confucius, Laozi, Zhuangzi, Mencius, and Xunzi, the very early moral argumentation of Mozi, and the totalitarian philosophy of Han Feizi. These seven chapters bring us to about 200 B.C.E. The final three chapters contain readings in Buddhist texts of the period running from 400 C.E. to about 1000 C.E. These include the Madhyamaka philosopher Sengzhao, the Huayan philosopher Fazang, the widely influential text *The Awakening of Faith*, a Zen text recounting the sayings of the Tang Dynasty monk Huangbo, as well as a short passage from the record of Huangbo's student, Linji. I think that if you read these texts carefully, you will become well-versed in Chinese philosophy. This is especially true if you also spend some time with the lists of suggested additional readings found at the end of each chapter.

Each chapter begins with my introduction to its texts. You needn't read these introductions. You may simply read these classic texts themselves – the "readings" - and skip over my introductions to them. It is these readings which are important, not my words. However, what I have to say might help you understand the readings and give you some food for thought about them. So, you may wish to read them either before or after you've read the readings. I have also provided footnotes wherever I thought a reader might benefit from explanations from either myself or from one of the Chinese philosophers themselves.

---

[1] This is the newer *pinyin* transliteration of the term. "Taoist" is also still in use after many decades.

It is at this point that I might be expected to provide a lengthy and general introduction to Chinese philosophy and its historical background. However, I don't have very many general things to say about these things. It is the particulars that I think are interesting, and I am eager to get straight to the readings themselves without further ado. Nevertheless, we should first take a view of the terrain from 50,000 feet.

At the beginning of the first of the two periods we will study, China emerged in the middle of the Fifth Century B.C.E. from the period of the early Zhou Dynasty, which was widely thought to be unified and relatively peaceful and harmonious, into a period disunity and war among a handful of states aptly named the Warring States Period (403-221 B.C.E.) Perhaps war and the loss of fragile and valuable components of civilization cause people to reflect on the nature of reality, the importance and means of preserving moral and political values, and the ways of knowing these things. It may be that hardship spurs philosophical endeavors of metaphysics, ethics and epistemology. In any event, it is in this period that we see Confucian philosophers develop deep insights into the nature of morality and the virtues, the Mohists offer an alternative moral view in some of the earliest argumentative essays in world history, and the Daoists create a theory of the natural "Way" of things. All of these were meant to be not only true philosophical theories but also sets of principles and patterns of living by which human life could be given political stability and satisfactory meaning. We also see, at the end of this period, a more cynical view of matters in thinkers such as Han Feizi, according to whom the solution to war and instability was brutal and total control by a centralized power. All of these streams of thought, with the exception of the Mohist, which went largely ignored for the last two millennia, were part of the fabric of Chinese civilization for thousands of years afterwards – at least until much of it was destroyed in the late Twentieth Century, when the fragility of civilization became all too evident again.[2] Very frequently in these streams of philosophical thought the Way (*dao* – or "Tao" as it has often been spelled in English) is referred to as a sort of axis of thought. One has to be careful not to overstate this or to make it seem as though the term "Way" was singular and unambiguous for Chinese philosophers of this period, but it seems that in the philosophy of this period there was a great emphasis on the importance of holding to the natural way things are and ought to be. Finally, at the end of this period, the hegemony of the Qin Dynasty began, which was deeply influenced by political views espoused by Han Feizi, bringing an end to much of the conflict.

Our second period, the six centuries beginning in 400 C.E., sees the creation of Chinese Buddhism and Chinese Buddhist philosophy. This is the story of China's first deep encounter with another civilization, that of India, and it was so deep that China imbibed and embraced the religion and philosophy of a major component of this civilization: Buddhism. During the First Millennium C.E., Chinese went to India, learned the languages of Buddhism, such as Sanskrit, obtained and brought home Buddhist texts, and proceeded to translate and understand them to the best of their abilities, forming monasteries and schools of Buddhist thought and integrating the religion fully into Chinese society. What is interesting here is rise of Chinese forms of Buddhist philosophy, such as Huayan and Chan.[3] There is more to this

---

[2] If you have little knowledge of the Cultural Revolution, let me give you the gist of it. One of my Chinese teachers, a woman born in 1965 who taught me Mandarin in the mid-1990s in Beijing, told me that when she was a school girl of about ten years of age, her class teacher gave the class an assignment: write an essay "criticizing Confucius" (*piping Kongzi*). She went home and tried to do the assignment, but realized that she didn't know anything about Confucius. Upset and ashamed, she returned to class the next day and reported to the teacher, "I'm sorry, but I don't know anything about Confucius." Her teacher replied, "That's okay. I don't know anything about Confucius, either."

[3] We have in English the term "Zen" which was borrowed from the Japanese. I will use the Chinese term from which the Japanese term was

4

story than three chapters of a reader can cover, but you will drink deeply of it through several key Chinese texts, including a prominent Chan text. Chan, which by now is well known in the West and which comes to the West via Japan, has its origins in this period. We will study some of these origins closely, along with three other schools of Chinese Buddhist thought.

So much for the view from 50,000 feet. If you want a more detailed overview of Chinese philosophy before proceeding to the readings, please make use of the suggested readings listed below. I could never improve on those introductions. However, I will suggest two things to you before we move on to the readings. The first is that, while of course your first task is to understand what these texts are saying, you also should read critically. Is the philosophy in these texts, aside from whatever historical import it may have, good philosophy? Are the terms clear enough? Are the arguments sound? Are the conclusions non-trivially true? The second bit of advice is for you, if you come to this book with a knowledge of Western philosophy but no knowledge of Chinese philosophy. To study it gives the reader who knows only of Western philosophy an opportunity to see how human beings worked out answers to philosophical questions in a second and largely isolated culture. Such a reader is like an exobiologist discovering life on another planet and comparing it to life on earth. Is it the same? Is it made of cells? Carbon based? Did the life forms evolve by natural selection and by coming up with similar solutions to similar problems? For example, we do see the Confucians and Aristotle developing analyses of the virtues at roughly the same time and in isolation from one another. As a matter of philosophical anthropology, whether Chinese philosophy is almost the same, somewhat different or radically different from Western philosophy, the answer should be fascinating. So, you have two things to look for as you proceed: the intrinsic value of these texts as works of philosophy and

---

derived, in order to keep it clear that we're referring to the Chinese roots of the Buddhist school.

their historical import as testaments to the human mind's philosophical depths.

A technical note: I have not included any Chinese characters here. They are largely clutter on the page to readers who neither read Chinese nor are learning to read it. Given that I have provided the transliteration (in the pinyin spelling system) of many of the key Chinese terms, readers who read Chinese will have no trouble determining which characters the transliterations refer to. Readers who are learning Chinese would perhaps profit from the presence of characters and so they get the short end of the stick. But perhaps those readers can turn lemons into lemonade by learning how to dig the correct characters out of their dictionaries. In addition, in the transliterations of Sanskrit terms I have omitted almost all diacritical marks, as I have found over the decades that they are mainly visual clutter in introductory philosophical texts, being useful only to those who don't need the help. I have abbreviated "Sanskrit" with "skt" and Chinese with "chn."

Suggested Readings

Chai, Chu, and Winberg Chai, *The Story of Chinese Philosophy*, various editions

Cheng, Chung-ying, "Chinese Philosophy: A Characterization," *Inquiry* 14(1971): 113-137

Creel, H. G., *Chinese Thought from Confucius to Mao Tse-tung*, various editions

Fraser, Chris, *Chinese Philosophy: An Introduction* (New York: Columbia University Press, 2016)

Garrett, Mary, "Classical Chinese Conceptions of Argumentation and Persuasion," *Argumentation and Advocacy* 29(1993): 105-115

6

Graham, A. C., *Disputers of the Tao: Philosophical Argument in Ancient China* (New York: Open Court, 1989)

Holloway, Kenneth W., *The Quest for Ecstatic Morality in Early China* (Oxford: Oxford University Press, 2015)

Littlejohn, Ronnie L., *Chinese Philosophy: An Introduction* (London: I.B. Tauris, 2016)

Leong, Wai Chun, "The Semantic Concept of Truth in Pre-Han Chinese Philosophy," *Dao: A Journal of Comparative Philosophy* 14(2015): 55-74

Liu, Wu-chi, *A Short History of Confucian Philosophy*, various editions

Needham, Joseph, *Science in Traditional China* (Cambridge: Harvard University Press, 1981)

Pines, Yuri, *Foundations of Confucian Thought: Intellectual Life in the Chunqiu Period, 722-453 B.C.E.E.* (Honolulu: University of Hawaii Press, 2002)

Schwartz, Benjamin, *The World of Thought in Ancient China* (Cambridge, MA: Belknap Press, 1985)

Shaughnessy, Edward L., *Before Confucius: Studies in the Creation of the Chinese Classics* (Albany: State University of New York Press, 1997)

Van Norden, Bryan W., *Introduction to Classical Chinese Philosophy* (Indianapolis: Hackett, 2011)

Waley, Arthur, *Three Ways of Thought in Ancient China*, various editions

Wu, Genyou, "On the Idea of Freedom and Its Rejection in Chinese Thought and Institutions," *Asian Philosophy* 16(2006): 219–235

Wu, Joseph S., "The Paradoxical Situation of Western Philosophy and the Search for Chinese Wisdom," *Inquiry* 14(1971): 1-18

1

Confucius

Confucius (551 - 479 B.C.E.) was raised in poverty by his widowed mother in the small state of Lu (located in what is now Shandong Province in the eastern part of China). In his early career he held various offices, such as Keeper of the Granaries and Director of Pastures. However, he sought higher office and he wanted to bring the Zhou Dynasty (1027 - 256 B.C.E.), which was in moral and political decline, back to the dignified stature it had enjoyed in its early years. With Lu controlled by the usurping Three Families, Confucius eventually left the state when he was almost fifty years old, choosing to travel in order to seek audience with and give moral counsel to the rulers and ministers of various Chinese states and in order to find and instruct students who might take official posts in various states and help to usher in a moral renaissance. Some of Confucius's students did come to hold office, but the renaissance of the Zhou never came. Confucius's political aspirations failed to come true. Eventually the political climate deteriorated to the point that the term "The Warring States Period" (403-221 B.C.E.) became apt.[4]

Confucius left no essays or books. We have only the record of his pithy sayings, *The Analects* (*Lunyu*), with which to reconstruct his philosophy, and most of this text consists of sayings that were compiled and attributed to Confucius decades or even hundreds of years after his death. Other texts sometimes attributed to Confucius (*Spring and Autumn Annals*, and parts of the *Yijing*) are probably not by his hand.

---

[4] See the book by Annping Chin in this chapter's list of suggested readings for more on the life of Confucius. The name "Confucius" is the Latinization of Kongfuzi ("This Master Kong"). His given name was Qiu. So, he was Kong Qiu. He is also referred to as "Kongzi" ("Master Kong").

A philosopher and an unwitting founder of what evolved into a religion, Confucianism, Confucius was also a great educator. This is to say that he has long been revered as the founder of the value that Chinese have placed on education for the last several thousand years. This is not a diversion for us as we inquire into his philosophy; the reason that he valued education was crucial to his moral philosophy. He thought that education was the means to dignity. "Study" referred to book learning and writing, for Confucius, but it was more than that. His school taught the six traditional Zhou subjects: ritual, music, archery, charioteering, writing, and mathematics. In these endeavors, what the students studied was how to be a good person, a person of virtue, dignity, and cultural refinement. Scientific knowledge was seen as a distraction from the goal of cultivating humane, trusting and impartial motivations, as well as fluency in the traditional ritual forms in which those motivations could be expressed. Thanks to Confucius, China very early in its history strove to make education available to all through national schools. One type of folk hero in China has long been the poverty-stricken scholar, the paradigmatic examples of which were Confucius and his best student, Yan Hui. This figure studies hard to lift himself up into dignity and also to conserve and perpetuate the roots of his civilization.

Because Confucius thought that education was necessary for moral dignity and virtue, he viewed the "barbarian" tribes that surrounded China as morally inferior (though perhaps of equal moral potential to the Chinese.) One might object that one can be uneducated and still be a good person. But Confucius had a rather wide definition of "education" as simply the absorption from others of virtue (*Analects* 1.14, 4.1, 4.17, 7.21).[5] He believed that the rituals of social convention had to be mastered in order for one to count as virtuous.

---

[5] Here and below, I will refer to the *Analects* with only the numbered passages.

The literature studied in Confucius's school consisted mainly of poems and anecdotes that inquired into the nuances of moral character. These texts included the *Odes*, which we will find quoted many times in this reader, and the *Documents*. It has been recognized in the West, of course, that one purpose of reading literature is to discover the human virtues and the foibles to which we are prone and which inhibit our endeavors to achieve the virtues. But the Confucian tradition is particularly keen on this purpose. During the Zhou Dynasty, it was common for diplomats and other government officials to quote passages from the classics in order to make their arguments regarding policy. In this way, they could "keep warm the old and provide understanding of the new" (2.11). The gradual eclipse of this practice by crude arguments from expediency or self-interest was, according to Confucius, part of the cause of China's moral decline.

Confucius therefore sought to reanimate tradition. The creator of Confucianism famously claimed, "I transmit but do not create" (7.1). Tradition was the repository of civilization, including the moral life. It was a set of ritual practices, social hierarchies, and stories, along with an essential core of moral values (2.23), all set forth by ancient geniuses and passed down from the virtuous to the would-be virtuous (5.3). The duty of the educator was to "keep warm the old," in order to facilitate this transmission of the tools of the cultivation of dignity and moral character. Admiring and imbibing this tradition were the only way to the knowledge necessary to lift one above the level of the beasts and barbarians (3.5, 7.20).

The reason for this traditionalism was partly the observation that embracing the conventions and values in question had supposedly enabled the ancient kings to win the mandate of heaven and secure a peaceful and prosperous society. During the early part of the Zhou Dynasty, King Wen (whose name also means "the civilized king") won over the then-corrupted Shang people and returned the empire to harmony. But the tradition was not simply effete pomp and circumstance. King Yu, legendary founder of the Xia Dynasty

c. 2000 B.C.E., out of his deep compassion for his agrarian people and their hardship, devoted himself to developing national irrigation and thereby reigned over a peaceful and prosperous society. Moreover, as far as Confucius knew, there was no alternative to this tradition, besides barbarism; China had not yet come to know of any other advanced civilizations.

Any conservative philosophy needs to embody means of self-criticism. Otherwise, there may be places where its enthusiasm for its cultural inheritance inhibits self-criticism and protects inconsistencies, injustices, and other errors from being weeded out. Confucianism may take this concern into account in the *Analects* and especially in the *Mencius*. You should consider this as you read along and see whether any such account suffices to make for a robust conservative view. Part of the account, sketchy though it is, is the rest of the quote about keeping warm the old: "but understand the new."

Despite his aforementioned claim that he merely transmitted, Confucius did create when he transmitted. He created a moral philosophy, albeit one that merely reflected the facts as they were in his moral tradition. Confucius was the first philosopher to illuminate the central importance of ritual (*li*) in moral life. Whereas ritual might be thought of as a set of rather grand and special affairs, including awesome imperial sacrifices and the rigid political rituals at a ruler's court or in challenges to battle, Confucius showed that the concept stretched much farther down, all the way to the quotidian level of common human interactions. For Confucius, ritual should inhabit almost all of our actions, from our tone of voice, to the straightness of the mat on which we sit (10.1, 10.7). Even a relaxed and carefree demeanor should be assumed only with ritual propriety. Confucius was right. We have grand state ceremonies, at the middle level weddings, graduations, and funerals, and at the mundane the usages of "please," "thank you," handshakes, and opening doors for one another. Confucius shows us that these behaviors, though not obviously purposive are the forms of the moral life.

According to ancient religions the world over, rituals, such as a ritual sacrifice of meat to God, can secure heaven's cooperation with the state or village and maintain the harmony of the cosmos. Confucius's humanistic innovation was to portray ritual as having these effects through its moral and aesthetic power. Grand state ritual inspires awe at the dignity, grace, and beauty of the ruler and thus tends to bring forth people's consent to be governed and to aspire to moral virtue (2.3, 2.20, 4.13, 7.35, 9.13, 11.12, 14.41). Ritual inspires with a sublimely beautiful harmony of people, in which everyone has a role in an event of greater value than any individual's narrow self-interest. Rituals present dignity palpably. The concept of dignity is at once aesthetic and moral, and this is precisely Confucius's insight. He speaks of the ruler keeping his "person correct" (*shen zheng*, 13.6) in order to get things done without having to give orders. This term connotes both rectitude of character and straight posture in body. Morality, in this view, is more than mutual non-interference and prudent cooperation. It is of a higher quality than those values. Thus, Confucius speaks of ritual as preferable to litigation (12.13).

Ritual is something beautiful to which we submit ourselves and lose our individual concerns. It is difficult and requires practice, and the extent to which one has subdued one's self-interest shows through (3.3), as in the weakness of a smile or handshake, two rituals that we partake of every day. In order to bring off a ritual properly, every participant must see the event as having intrinsic aesthetic and moral value. This means that each must see each of the others as of intrinsic value, since each is a part of the ritual. Ritual transforms what would be competition into intrinsically valuable harmony (3.7), instead of abiding by the merely prudential and instrumental concept of morals upheld by, for example, Thomas Hobbes.

This is as it should be. For the prudential concept of morality fails to convince the free rider. If self-interest is the goal, why shouldn't I pretend to follow the rules while cheating others whenever I can do it with impunity? Other philosophers, such as Aristotle, Kant, Hume, and Mill, have offered alternatives to the Hobbesian view, appealing to personal excellence, disinterested reason, or to benevolent sentiments. Confucius's theory might have elements of these. As you will read, it surely contains the Golden Rule that we find reinterpreted in Kant's Categorical Imperative. But Confucianism uniquely appeals to the importance of ritual. The point is that if impartial interests are never beautifully expressed, people lose sight of the fact that they are intrinsic values rather than mere instruments to promote cooperation. Even worse, the youth of a society bereft of ritual would never even get this right idea in the first place. So, Confucius would have these values almost constantly expressed in our interactions. Our actions must therefore meticulously conform to ritual forms.

In sum, ritual is not just an epiphenomena or expression of moral life but also one of its drivers. Ritual is the skill one practices in cultivating moral character. For all his emphasis on form, Confucius is quick to remind us that substance is even more important (3.4, 3.8, 3.12). The humane feelings are the *sine qua non* of ritual, feelings that are necessary to have before one can perfect them. Confucius even advises frugal restraint, in order to avoid an ostentatiousness that might obscure the affective purpose of the ritual.

Confucius's preoccupation with music (7.14, 8.8, 8.15, 9.15, 11.1, 13.3, 14.12) makes sense in connection with his view of ritual. Music is a harmony of behaviors which is beautiful, dignified, and which is an end in itself. Among the players, there are smaller parts and larger ones, but none is a mere means. Music is a way of portraying the intrinsic value of people in a form that doesn't represent something else but rather ecstatically relishes its own being. It also affords representation, as well, with lyrics, which for Confucius were the classical poems telling of moral virtues (3.25). Music is expressive of humane sentiments (3.3) and, as the Confucian text *The Doctrine of the Mean*[6] says, its harmonies are analogous to family unity.

Let us look even more closely at the details of Confucian moral philosophy, namely Confucius's concepts of the virtues. These are the good character traits that reach fulfillment in the rituals: humanity (*ren*)[7], filiality (*xiao*, also translated "filial piety"), good faith (*xin*), loyalty (*zhong*)[8], and reciprocity (*shu*).

According to one of his disciples, Confucius's teaching has "one thread" running through it: loyalty and reciprocity (4.15). However, these are components of what is probably the chief Confucian virtue, humanity. Loyalty, as a technical translation of the Confucian term *zhong*, is the taking of others as ends worthy of respect. Reciprocity is application of the Golden Rule (5.12, 12.2, 15.24). Equally important is good faith, the disposition to trust and to be trustworthy. Confucius says that good faith is basic to personhood (2.22) and to the integrity of the social fabric of any community (12.7, cf. 5.10).

The chief virtue, humanity, is represented by a Chinese character that is a combination of the character for "human being" or "person" and the character for "two." It thus on its face indicates something to do with man being a social being, and it indicates the fulfillment of one's human nature and one's social nature. Humanity is the simple moral sentiment that is extremely easy to have (2.2, 7.30). Yet its mastery, requiring that one subdue oneself in ritual, is extraordinarily difficult (12.1, 12.2) and so elusively ideal that it is impossible to know whether oneself or any other person has achieved it (5.5, 5.8). Although it is a simple feeling, one can hardly maintain it for more than a moment (4.6, 6.7). Humanity is the perfection of

---

[6] The *Doctrine of the Mean* is a text attributed to Confucius's grandson Zisi.

[7] "Humanity" here means "benevolence," not "the human race," although the ambiguity is apt, since it exists in the Chinese. Think of it as "humaneness," which is another reasonable translation of the term.

[8] See Paul Goldin's article on the perils of simply translating this term as "loyalty" in this chapter's list of suggested readings.

all of the other virtues, and its method is to treat others as one would be treated (6.30).

There are several other virtues in *The Analects*, including the general one: virtue (*de*)[9] itself. Also, righteous (*yi*),[10] of particular interest to Mencius, has a role in *The Analects*, as do courage (*yong*) and deference (*rang*). Of particular importance in Confucius and in China is filiality: the loyalty, deference, and respect one gives to one's parents and the elders in one's family. The cultivation of this virtue is the training grounds for human dignity (2.7), as shame before one's parents is the primary stimulus to moral behavior (1.2, 2.6). As *The Doctrine of the Mean* (20.5) would put it, "The relative degrees of affection we ought to feel for our relatives and the relative grades in the honoring of the worthy give rise to the rules of ritual." Famously, *The Great Learning* traced the social harmony of the country to the state, and the latter to the moral wellbeing of the family. In the *Analects*, Confucius says that filiality is each person's way of contributing to the government. It is difficult to overestimate the importance of this virtue in Chinese culture. The ruler's filiality, manifested in rituals devoted to his deceased parents, inspires his onlooking people (1.9, 2.20). His majesty inspires everyone else to the virtue. In demonstrating his great humility, which tempers his awesome power, the majestic ruler serves as an invigorating reminder of the ubiquitous importance of deference.

---

[9] *De* also means "kindness" and, in other contexts, power.

[10] "*Yi*" can refer to either the rightness of an action or to the righteousness of a person who does such actions. In this book, I usually translate it as "rightness" which, while somewhat awkward, nevertheless may be defined as a moral property of actions or people and enables us to avoid the old-fashioned "righteousness" with its unpredictable connotations. As for what the property of the rightness of an action is, it is at least the property shared by all morally permissible actions; it is perhaps also the best of all permissible options for actions (in the sense of "the right thing to do"). Rightness of people, then, is their disposition to choose to do the right thing.

In addition to virtue itself, its cultivation was an important topic for Confucius. According to him, there are two stages in moral self-cultivation. First, there is the initial, youthful incubation of the moral sentiments in filiality and the control of baser lusts. This process required that one dwell in a humane family and community (1.2, 4.1, 5.1, 5.2, 5.3), so that one had moral exemplars. It also required extensive classical literary study in addition to the six traditional subjects, since the classics were the repository and nuanced expression of the forms of virtue of the society. At this stage of cultivation, one's humane sentiments are nurtured while the potentially anti-social desires for status, wealth, and the like are reined in, so that one avoids arrogance, obsequiousness, begrudging, and boasting (1.15, 5.11, 5.26). In the second stage one subjects one's given set of motivations to fine tuning in the rituals. Here the goal is to render that set into a natural fit with what is right, so that one no longer has to restrain any desires but rather easily delights in doing the right thing without reservation (1.15, 2.4, 5.11). The moral substance of a society was transmitted from the virtuous to those aspiring to virtue by means of the strenuous efforts of the aspirants. This was a process of rigorous self-examination in the midst of those who were one's moral superiors (4.17, 9.25) so that one might see how to resemble them ever more closely. It required contemplating one's inner transgressions (4.7, 5.5, 5.22), especially in the presence of one's moral inferiors to whom one is not as dissimilar as one would like to think (7.22). Yet, absorption of moral and cultural forms from literature and moral exemplars, though necessary, was not sufficient (2.15, 9.30).

This depiction of moral self-cultivation offers answers to the question of moral motivation: Why be moral? Since moral action seems to require sacrificing one's self-interest[11]

---

[11] The meaning of the term "self-interest" is not obvious. I take interests to be desires or, at least, the desires one would have were one fully informed of the facts relevant to one's life and given time to reason about them. I take self-interest to be the set of interests one has that are not desires for

for the sake of others, it is difficult to state how one could have a reason to be moral. Confucius suggests that the moral life was more pleasurable (1.1, 6.11) than the pursuit of wealth and power and that the social relationships that require a moral life were essential to happiness (12.5, 6.19). Moral life is so deeply fulfilling that it overwhelms all evil (4.4), including death (4.8, 8.4). In this it seems to assuage any existential anxiety one might otherwise have (9.29). The reason is that in morality one rises above (17.2) the meaningless and bestial level of service to one's lusts (2.7) and participates in a beautiful and dignified ritual that is bigger than one's tiny, humdrum concerns. Of course, Confucius advocated morality as a means to social harmony, as well (1.2, 6.17, 12.7).

Confucius's moral philosophy included a political philosophy. It was monarchical, so if there is anything of value for us modern non-monarchist readers to gain from it, we will have to use our imaginations.

Confucius yearned for a "[true] king," like the ones of the Xia, Shang, and early Zhou dynasties. There were two roles that this figure was needed to play: moral exemplar for and benefactor of the people. In Confucius's view, the people were incapable of attaining moral character without the inspiration of a sage king of supreme virtue. They also were incapable of avoiding famine without central agricultural planning. Confucius makes clear that the moral substance of a society outweighs the value placed on utility (12.7), but he is gravely serious about the ruler's duty to care for the people as though caring for an orphan (8.6) by ensuring sufficiency of food and weaponry (12.7). He exalts King Yu's tireless effort to irrigate China (8.21) and argues that the ruler needs to centralize agricultural planning according to the seasons (1.5) and make government thrifty (1.5, 11.14, 12.9).

---

others' welfare: non-instrumental desires, purely altruistic or benevolent desires for others' welfare. A difficulty comes in the fact that the altruistic desires and the self-interested desires are intimately intertwined in human nature. We are social beings. It may be that the term "self-interest" is quite problematic.

The ruler's burden of playing the exemplar of humanity (8.7) required that he inspire the people to moral aspirations (1.9) by filling them with awe (1.8) at the spectacle of his majesty. The value of the moral standard was to flow from his person in state rituals and to appear in the institutions affected by his appointment of virtuous ministers. As we have noted, just by being correct the ruler would govern. He was to be a still central point towards which the people oriented themselves. Sitting still in perfection, he would just face south - a powerfully simple traditional ritual - so that his subjects would take the ritual north-facing position and orbit the still center, just as all the stars in the heavens circle the Northern Pole Star (2.2). A proper government transforms society from the field of the litigious pushes and pulls of people's conflicting needs into a harmonious orchestration of deferential attitudes founded on the relationship of good faith between the ruler and the ruled.

There is a notion of political legitimacy in Confucius. The ruler derives his right to rule from his moral virtue (1.5, 2.20). Because of it, the people consent to be governed (12.18, 13.4). Confucius also held that the ruler had a duty to command soldiers only if they were educated (13.29, 13.30) and a duty to educate the people (13.9). In addition to the intrinsic moral value of the education, Confucius seems to have had in mind the power to consent that it would bring. Also, there is the peculiarly Confucian concept of political participation, in which each individual's personal moral endeavors played a role in the state. We find this in *The Analects* 2.21 and in a handful of lines that lie at the core of the Chinese heart in *The Great Learning*.[12] The idea is that by

---

[12] *The Great Learning* (*Daxue*), a chapter of the *Book of Ritual* (*Liji*), says, "The ancients who wanted to manifest clear character to the world first governed their states. Desiring to govern their states, they first regulated their families. Desiring to regulate their families they first cultivated themselves. Desiring to cultivate themselves, they first rectify their minds. Desiring to rectify their minds, they would first make their ideas sincere.

contributing to a harmonious family each person would be contributing to a harmonious village, and therefore, ultimately, to a harmonious state. Rocking the boat in response to injustice was not part of Confucius's vision for the common man (1.2). It is difficult to overemphasize the importance of this vision of political participation in Chinese political history, including even the events of the late Twentieth Century.[13] Totalitarianism isn't always or only based on fear. Sometimes it uses moral and aesthetic suasion, as well.

One might object that Confucius's political views are, if not intrinsically unfair to the powerless people, then overly optimistic about the possibility of locating an enlightened king, an optimism even Confucius mournfully forsook in the end. There is also a shortcoming in Confucius's moral philosophy; it isn't critical enough. Confucius "transmitted," but how was he to know whether everything he transmitted was righteous morality? He never even raised the question of how one should go about scrutinizing traditional values in order to discover any bad ones. His moral psychology was keen, and surely much of what he said about moral virtues is interesting and true. But in addition to mimicking traditional moral exemplars, there is also the need to filter out the mistaken and sometimes evil values that they espouse along with the rest. Only after thousands of years are we coming to recognize women's equal rights and to give up the delusion that one's economic class is an essential station in which one must remain. There is nothing in Confucius (though there may be something in Mencius) that accounts for this essential role of self-criticism that morality requires. On the other hand, it may be uncharitable to require of a man laboring to conserve a fragile tradition against the onslaught of brutal tyranny and degradation that he also

---

Desiring to make their ideas sincere, they would first extend their knowledge."

[13] When you read the chapter on Legalism, consider the dual influence of Confucianism and Legalism on Chinese political history. It is as if Confucianism has been the Yang, the obvious, and Legalism the yin, the dark and unnoticed force in Chinese political history.

provide tools for criticizing that tradition's foibles and mistakes.

The Reading

Unfortunately, *The Analects* was compiled when prose was almost unknown China, and we don't have any essays by Confucius that might have explained his points of view in more depth. *The Analects* was compiled by Confucius's disciples and their disciples. Some scholars argue that only Book Four should be taken as authentic, with the rest of the work consisting of sayings of varying degrees of authenticity and faithfulness in letter and spirit to Confucius's views. If you like, consider the text as a blend of Confucius's views and the views of some of his disciples.

The text comprises twenty 'books,' each about three pages each long and containing twenty or so 'chapters' of about three lines each. The books and chapters have little in the way of topical or narrative order. The reading below comprises most of the text: almost all of the first twelve books plus much of the remaining eight books. I have rearranged the order of the chapters according to topic and artificially put them under the topical section headings of virtue, self-cultivation, ritual, political philosophy, and for miscellany. Some chapters speak to more than one topic, but I have placed each under only one heading each. So, you will have to read all of the sections even when you are concerning yourself with only one topic. Treat my artificial rearrangement with suspicion and note that you can always recover the original order by the numbers: "7.18," for example, means book seven, chapter eighteen.

Footnotes identify people when it is important for understanding the passage. Many of them are officials Confucius met during his travels. Also many are Confucius's disciples: Yan Hui, Ran You, Zigong, Zai Yu, Zhonggong, Zilu, Zixia, Ziyou, and You Ruo.

The Analects

The Virtues

1.3   The Master said, "Skillful speech and impressive looks are rarely humane."

1.7   Zixia said, "If one treats the worthy as worthy, if one de-emphasizes the sensual, if one can exhaust one's strength in serving one's parents, if one extends oneself in service of one's ruler, and if in dealing with friends one speaks in good faith, then, even if one is unlearned, I must call such a one learned."

1.10   Ziqin asked Zigong, "When the Master arrives in a country, he always has to hear about its government. Does he seek [the information] out? Or is he given it?" Zigong said, "The Master is warm, nice, respectful, frugal, and deferential, and that is how he gets it. The Master's way of seeking it out is different from others' way of seeking it out, isn't it?"

1.11   The Master said, "While his father is alive, observe his aspirations. When his father is dead, observe his actions. If for three years he makes no changes in the Way[14] of his father, he may be called filial."

1.13   Youzi said, "When one's good faith keeps to what is right, one's word is to be relied upon. When one's respectfulness keeps to the rituals, one keeps away shame and disgrace. If one marries without breaking any family ties, one may lead the clan."

1.14   The Master said, "The gentleman eats without seeking to be full and makes his residence without seeking comfort. He is diligent in affairs and reticent in speech. By associating with those who have the Way, he is corrected by them. He may be said simply to like learning."

1.15   Zigong said, "'When poor, not obsequious, and when rich, not arrogant' - How about that?"

---

[14] "Way" (*Dao*) is the same term that the Daoist school takes as its central concern. Confucius uses it to refer to the moral path for human beings, while the Daoists take it to mean much more than that.

22

The Master said, "Not bad. But it's no match for, 'When poor, joyous, and when rich, enjoying ritual'."

Zigong replied, "The *Odes* says, 'As though cut, filed, carved, and polished'. Is that what you mean?"

The Master said, "Si [Zigong] is really someone with whom one can discuss the *Odes*. When one explains something to him, he knows what comes next."

2.2   The Master said, "The poems in the *Odes* number three hundred. But to sum them up in a sentence: 'Let your thoughts be free of depravity.'"

2.6   Meng Wubo asked about filiality. The Master said, "Let parents have only your falling ill to worry about."[15]

2.7   Ziyou asked about filiality. The Master said, "The 'filiality' of today means that one is able to sustain [one's parents]. But that applies to dogs and horses, both of which one can keep and sustain. If you don't show respect, what's the difference?"[16]

2.8   Zigong asked about filiality. The Master said, "The mien is what is difficult. If, when there are matters to be dealt with, the son takes the burden, and when he has wine and food, the elders eat, then are we to count this as filiality?"

2.9   The Master said, "I can talk all day with [Yan] Hui, and he never disagrees with me - as though he were stupid. But when he withdraws, and I examine his personal conduct, he really has what it takes to show the way. Hui is not stupid."

2.10   The Master said, "Look at how he does things, take note of his purposes, inquire into what gives him repose - how can his personality be hidden?! How?!"

2.11   The Master said, "If one understands the new, while keeping warm the old, one can be a good teacher."

2.12   The Master said, "The gentleman is not a tool."[17]

---

[15] In other words, one should not have any moral failings for one's parents to worry about.

[16] See 2.5 in the section on ritual.

[17] See 5.4 in the miscellaneous section. The same term (*qi*) is translated here as tool, there as implement. The gentleman is not a tool because he has autonomy and moral standards.

2.13   Zigong asked about the gentleman. The Master said, "He first puts his words into action and only afterwards sets them forth as something to be followed."

2.14   The Master said, "The gentleman is impartial and not biased. The small man is biased and not impartial."

2.22   The Master said, "To be human but without good faith - I don't know how one could countenance it. A carriage without the yoking bar, a cart without the yoking bolts - what are they going to use to go?"

2.24   The Master said, "To sacrifice to spirits that aren't one's own is flattery. To see that something is right but not to do it is lack of courage."

3.3   The Master said, "If you are human but not humane, what could ritual be to you? If you are human but not humane, what could music be to you?"

3.20   The Master said, "The Guan Ju: pleasure without lustiness, mournfulness without being damaged."[18]

4.1   The Master said, "Humanity is the place to take your place. If you choose not to dwell in humanity, how can you gain understanding?"[19]

4.2   The Master said, "One who is not humane cannot stand to be deprived for very long and cannot abide long in a pleasant state. The humane find repose in humanity. The knowledgeable profit from humanity."

4.3   The Master said, "Only the humane can like a person or despise a person."

4.4   The Master said, "If you are really intent upon humanity, you will be free of hatred."

4.5   The Master said, "Wealth and rank are what a person desires, but if you can't manage them with the Way, you are not to keep them. Poverty and degradation are what a person dislikes, but if you can't manage them with the Way, you are not to avoid them. If the gentleman does without humanity, how,

---

[18] This section of the *Odes* apparently expressed the right affective harmony, according to Confucius: temperance and moderation.

[19] The last two words are ambiguous and could be translated "become known," or "be recognized" as worthy of government office.

then, does he establish his name? A gentleman does not even for the time of an afternoon meal diverge from humanity. In harried haste, he must stay with it. Falling flat on his face, he must stay with it."

4.6   The Master said, "I've never seen anyone who loved being humane and despised not being humane. Someone who loved being humane, would, for the sake of humanity, not let anything inhumane be added to his person. Is there anyone who can, for one day, apply all his strength to humanity? I've never seen anyone who lacked the strength. Perhaps there are such, but I've never seen one."

4.7   The Master said, "As for people's errors, each is of a certain type. Observe the error and thus come to know [the degree of his] humanity."

4.10   The Master said, "As for the gentleman's attitude towards the world, there is nothing that he is inclined towards or against. He goes with what he takes to be right."

4.11   The Master said, "The gentleman values virtue, but the small man values land. The gentleman values the law, but the small man values special favors.

4.15   The Master said, "Can[20] [Zengzi], my Way has something threading it together." Zengzi said, "Indeed." The Master left, and some students asked, "What was he talking about?" Zengzi said, "The Master's Way is loyalty and reciprocity, and that's all."

4.18   The Master said, "In serving one's parents, admonish them gently. Upon seeing that they intend not to follow you, be respectful and not contrary. Though it tries you, do not be angry."

4.19   The Master said, "While your parents are alive, don't travel far. And if you travel, there must be a destination."[21]

4.20   The Master said, "If for three years one makes no changes from the Way of one's father, one may be called 'filial'."

---

[20] Pronounced "tsan."

[21] There must be a way for one to be contacted in the event of an emergency, such as a parent falling ill.

4.21   The Master said, "You must remember the ages of your parents, on the one hand, with delight, and on the other hand, with melancholy."

4.24   The Master said, "The gentleman prefers to be reticent in speech but prompt in action."

4.25   The Master said, "Virtue isn't lonely. It always has neighbors."

4.26   Ziyou said, "In serving a ruler, to belabor a point leads to one's being humiliated. With friends, to belabor a point leads to estrangement."

5.5   Someone said, "Yong is humane but not articulate." The Master said, "What is the use of being articulate? If you hit people with a glib tongue, you will often be hated by them. I don't know whether or not he is humane, but what is the use of being articulate?"

5.7   The Master said, "If the Way were not being followed and I got on a raft and floated out to sea, the one who would follow me would be You[22] [Zilu], wouldn't it?" Zilu heard of this and was delighted. The Master said, "You - he likes courage more than I do, but he has no discretion."

5.8   Meng Wubo asked, "Is Zilu humane?" The Master said, "I don't know." He asked again. The Master said, "You [Zilu] may be assigned to look after the military taxes of a state of 1,000 chariots. But I don't know that he is humane." "What about Qiu?" The Master said, "Qiu may be employed as a steward of a borough of 1,000 houses or a family of 100 chariots. But I don't know that he is humane." "What about Chi?" The Master said, "Wearing a sash and standing in the court, he may be employed to converse with visitors and guests. But I don't know that he is humane."

5.9   The Master said to Zigong, "Between you and Hui, who is superior?" Zigong replied, "Si [Zigong] - how could he dare to look at Hui? Hui hears one thing and figures out ten from it. Si hears one thing and figures out two from it." The

---

[22] Pronounced "yo."

Master said, "You're not equal to him - you and I both are not equal to him."

5.10 Zai Yu was asleep during the day. The Master said, "Rotten wood cannot be carved. A wall of manure cannot be troweled. In Yu what am I to chastise?"

The Master said, "In the beginning, my approach to people was, having heard their words, to take their actions on good faith. Now my approach to people is, having heard their words, to observe their actions. It is by Yu that I have been given to change in this way."

5.11 The Master said, "I have never seen anyone who is resolute." Someone said, "Shen Cheng." The Master said, "Cheng is lustful. How does he count as resolute?"

5.12 Zigong said, "What I don't desire people to do to me I also desire not to do to them." The Master said, "Si [Zigong], you haven't reached that point."

5.13 Zigong said, "As for the Master's cultural achievements, one can get to hear about them. But when it comes to the Master speaking about human nature and the Way of Heaven, one never gets to hear that."

5.16 The Master said of Zichan that he had the Way of the gentleman in four respects. In carrying himself he was agreeable, in serving superiors he was respectful, in looking after the people he was caring, and in employing the people he was righteous."

5.17 The Master said, "Yan Pingzhong was good at interacting with people. Even after some time he was respectful to them."

5.19 Zizhang asked, "Prime Minister Ziwen held the office of Prime Minister three times but didn't seem to enjoy it. Three times he was deposed but didn't seem to resent it. He always explained for the incoming Prime Minister the previous Prime Minister's government. How does he measure up?"

The Master said, "He was loyal."

"Was he humane?"

"I don't know. How does he count as humane?"

"Cuizi killed the ruler of Qi. Chen Wenzi, though he had ten teams of horses, gave them up and left it. When he reached another state, he said, 'He's like my Lord Cuizi,' and left it. When he reached another state, he again said, 'He's like my Lord Cuizi,' and left it. How does he measure up?"

The Master said, "He was pure."

"Was he humane?"

"I don't know. How does he count as humane?"

5.20   Ji Wenzi thought three times before acting. The Master heard about this and said, "Twice is what is permissible."

5.24   The Master said, "Who says Weisheng Gao was upright? Someone begged vinegar of him, and he begged it of a neighbor in order to give it."

5.27   The Master said, "Is that all? I have yet to see someone who sees his faults and inwardly rebukes himself."

6.4   Zihua had been sent to Qi, and Master Ran [Ran You] asked for some grain for his mother. The Master said, "Give her a half-gallon." He asked for more. The Master said, "Give her five gallons." Master Ran gave her five bushels of grain. The Master said, "When Chi [Zihua] was on his way to Qi he had stocky horses and wore light furs. I was taught that a gentleman helps the desperate but doesn't maintain the wealthy."

6.11   The Master said, "Worthy, indeed, was [Yan] Hui! One bowl of rice, one cup of water, and living in an alley - others couldn't endure such distress. But Hui would not falter in his joy."

6.15   The Master said, "Meng Zhifan didn't boast. Once, when they were retreating, he brought up the rear. When they got back to the city gate, he whipped his horse, saying 'It's not that I dared to stay back. My horse just wouldn't catch up.'"

6.18   The Master said, "When substance outweighs culture, we have boorishness. When culture outweighs substance, we have priggishness. When culture and substance are in harmonious proportion, only then do we have a gentleman."

28

6.20   The Master said, "To be one who knows it is not as good as to be one who likes it. To be one who likes it isn't as good as to be one who takes joy in it."[23]

6.22   Fan Chi asked about wisdom. The Master said, "To work for what is right by the people and to keep ghosts and spirits at a distance by showing them respect - this may be called 'wisdom'." He asked about humanity. The Master said, "The humane put the difficulty first and the gain afterwards. This may be called 'humanity'."

6.23   The Master said, "The wise enjoy the waters. The humane enjoy the mountains. The wise move. The humane are still. The wise are joyful. The humane live long."

6.26   Zai Wo asked, "A humane person, though he is told that in a well is where humanity is, would go after it, wouldn't he?" The Master said, "Why so? The gentleman can be made to go there, but he can't be made to go in. He can be taken advantage of, but he can't be trapped."

6.27   The Master said, "The gentleman, being broadly learned in culture and having restrained himself with ritual, will surely thereby never transgress the bounds, will he?"

6.29   The Master said, "The mean,[24] as a virtue - that is the utmost! Among the people it has been rare for a long time."

6.30   Zigong said, "What about widely giving to the people, and being able to come to the aid of the masses? How does that measure up? May that be called 'humanity'?" The Master said, "Why stop with humanity? Wouldn't it certainly be sageliness? Even a Yao or a Shun[25] would still fret over that. The humane person is one who, desiring to establish himself, establishes others, and desiring himself to succeed, has others succeed."

---

[23] "It" must be the moral Way that Confucius taught.

[24] See *The Doctrine of the Mean* for Confucius's grandson Zisi's explication of the "mean" (*zhongyong,* literally "middle pervasiveness"). It has to do with the equanimity of affect and emotion exhibited by a virtuous character, as opposed to upset or manic emotions which draw the mind away from the natural consistency necessary to virtue.

[25] Two of the ancient sage-kings.

7.11   The Master said to Yan Hui, "When appointed, one is to act. When dismissed, one is to wait in reserve. Only you and I have mastered this." Zilu said, "If Master were leading the three armies, whom would you want with you?" The Master said, "I wouldn't go with someone who wouldn't mind meeting his death wrestling a tiger or swimming across a river. What would be necessary is someone who is circumspect in approaching tasks, who likes to get things done through planning."

8.11   The Master said, "Imagine a person who has talents as fine as those of the Duke of Zhou. If we give him arrogance and niggardliness, then the rest aren't even worth looking at."

8.16   The Master said, "Impetuous, yet not upright, unrefined, yet not earnest, stupid, yet not of good faith - I don't understand such people."

9.27   The Master said, "Dressed in a worn-out silk-padded robe and shamelessly standing there next to those wearing fox and badger furs - that would be You [Zilu], wouldn't it!"

> Not wicked, not seeking anything,
> What does he do that is not good?[26]

Zilu chanted these lines all his life. The Master said, "This Way - what is there worth praising in it?"[27]

9.29   The Master said, "One who knows doesn't become confused, one who is humane doesn't have anxiety, and one who is courageous doesn't fear."

12.2   Zhonggong asked about humanity. The Master said, "When away from home act as though you were receiving an important guest. Command the people as if you were conducting a high sacrifice. What you yourself do not desire do not do to others. In your country there will be no resentment. In

---

[26] A passage from the *Odes*.
[27] Here Zilu's lackadaisical attitude towards ritual propriety in clothing and other facets of life perhaps represents a Daoist streak.

your household there will be no resentment." Zhonggong said, "Although I am not sharp, I would like to work on this lesson."

13.18 The Duke of She told Confucius, "Where I'm from there are upright characters. If a father stole a sheep, the son would testify against him." The Master said, "Where I'm from the upright ones are different from that. The father would protect the son, and the son would protect the father. Uprightness lies in this."

14.4 The Master said, "Someone who has virtue will certainly have something to say. But it isn't necessarily the case that someone who has something to say will have virtue. The humane are certainly courageous. But it isn't necessarily the case that the courageous are humane."

14.6 The Master said, "There are those who are gentlemen but not humane. But there has never been a small person who is humane."

14.7 The Master said, "If you love someone, how could you not work him hard? If you are loyal to someone, how could you not instruct him?"

14.12 Zilu asked about what it is to be a complete person. The Master said, "If one has Zang Wuzhong's knowledge, Meng Gongchuo's freedom from desires, the courage of Zhuangzi of Bian, the varied abilities of Ran You, and if one embellishes this with ritual and music, then one can certainly be taken as a complete person." Then he said, "But why must the complete person of today be like that? If in the face of profit one thinks of what is right, in the face of danger one lays down one's life, and if for agreements made long ago one doesn't forget words that were to last a lifetime, then one certainly may be considered a complete person."

14.31 The Master said, "Someone who doesn't expect to be tricked and doesn't anticipate a lack of good faith, yet recognizes these beforehand - this is a worthy[28], isn't it?"

---

[28] A term frequently used in Confucian texts is "worthy" (*xian*). Although it's somewhat awkward as an English noun here, I have chosen it over "worthy man" in order to keep the translation terse.

14.34 Someone said, "'Repay hostility with kindness'. What about that?" The Master said, "Then, with what will you repay kindness? Repay hostility with uprightness, and repay kindness with kindness."

15.3　The Master said, "Si [Zigong], do you take me as someone who studies many things and memorizes them?" "Yes," he replied, "isn't it so?" The Master said, "No. I use one thing to thread them all together."[29]

15.9　The Master said, "A public servant with a sense of resolve, if he is a humane person, will not injure humanity to save his life, but will in some circumstances kill himself in order to preserve his humanity."

15.18　The Master said, "The gentleman takes rightness as the substance, by ritual puts it into practice, in humility sets it forth, and through good faith completes it. That is a gentleman."

15.22　The Master said, "The gentleman is proud but not contentious. He joins in with social groups but is not cliquish."

15.24　Zigong asked, "Is there a single saying that one could live by for one's whole life?" The Master said, "How about reciprocity? Do not do to others what you yourself would not desire."

15.37　The Master said, "The gentleman is correct, but not artlessly rigid."

17.14　The Master said, "In ancient times, the people had three deficiencies, but today these seem to be no more. The ancients' impetuousness was carelessness. Today's impetuousness is licentiousness. The ancients' conceit was pristineness. Today's conceit is combativeness. The ancients' foolishness was uprightness. Today's foolishness is deviousness."

17.21　Zilu said, "Does the gentleman esteem courage?" The Master said, "For the gentleman, rightness is what is most important. If a gentleman has courage but lacks righteousness, he will cause disorder. If the small man has courage but lacks righteousness, he will commit robbery."

---

[29] See 4.15.

19.2   Zizhang said, "If a person grasps virtue but does not give it wide scope and has good faith in the Way but is not earnest about it, how can we take him as having it? And how can we take him as not having it?"

Moral Self-Cultivation

1.2   Master You said, "Those who are of the type of person who is filial and respectful of elder siblings but likes to oppose superiors are few. No one has ever not liked to oppose superiors but liked to create disorder. The gentleman looks after the roots. When the roots are secure, the Way begins to grow. Filiality and respect for elder siblings - aren't these the roots of humanity?"

1.4   Zengzi said, "I daily perform a threefold examination of myself: In my plans for others, have I been disloyal? In my dealings with friends, have I not acted in good faith? Have I not practiced the transmitted [teachings]?"

1.6   The Master said, "A young man should be filial at home and, when at large, respectful of elders. Earnest and of good faith, he should exude love for everyone but be intimate with the humane. If he has any strength left over, then he is to apply it to the study of culture."

1.8   The Master said, "If a gentleman is not serious, he will not inspire awe. If he studies, he will not be rigid. He is to emphasize loyalty and good faith and to have no friends who are not equal to him. And when he errs, he is not to be afraid to make a change."

2.4   The Master said, "At fifteen I was intent on learning. At thirty I was established. At forty I had no doubts. At fifty I understood the mandate of heaven. At sixty my very ear was responsive to it. At seventy I can follow my heart's desire without missing the mark."

2.15   The Master said, "To study without thinking is stultifying. To think without having studied is haphazard."

4.17 The Master said, "When you see a worthy, think about equaling him. When you see someone who is unworthy, examine yourself inwardly."

4.23 The Master said, "It is not often that one errs in being restrained."

5.3 The Master said of Zijian, "A superior man! Such is he! If Lu had no gentlemen, then where did he get this?"

5.6 The Master bid Qidiao Kai take office. He replied, "I don't yet have good faith enough for that." The Master was pleased.

5.14 When Zilu had gotten a lesson but not yet been able to put it into practice, his only fear was that he would get [another] lesson.

6.12 Ran Qiu [Ran You] said, "It's not that I do not delight in Master's Way. It's just that my strength is insufficient." The Master said, "One whose strength is insufficient breaks down while on the Way. But you're drawing a line right now."

7.6 The Master said, "Set your aspirations on the Way, hold to virtue, rely on humanity, and make diversions into the arts[30]."

7.8 The Master said, "I won't instruct someone who isn't eager. I won't lay things out for someone who isn't searching for the words. If I point out one corner, and he doesn't come back with the other three, I won't repeat myself."

7.17 The Master said, "Give me a number of years more, fifty years to study, and then I could be without major faults."

7.22 The Master said, "If I am walking with three people, there must be a teacher among them for me. I pick out their good points and follow them, their bad points and make changes."

7.28 The Master said, "There definitely are people without knowledge who accomplish things. I don't have that quality. I learn a lot and, selecting the good points from it, I

---

[30] "Arts" include crafts and trades (translated "artisanship" in 9.7.)

34

follow them. I observe a lot and remember it. This is the second best kind of knowledge."

7.29   In the Village of Hu, [the people] wouldn't listen. When a boy got to see the Master, the disciples wondered why. The Master said, "I greet their advances. I don't greet their retreats. Why be so severe? If a person purifies himself[31] in order to come forth, I greet his purity. I don't guarantee what he does when he goes back."

7.30   The Master said, "Is humanity really so remote? I desire to be humane and humanity is right here."

7.36   The Master said, "Extravagance tends toward haughtiness, and parsimony tends toward rigidity. If the alternative is haughtiness, prefer rigidity."

8.10   The Master said, "If you like to be courageous and are repulsed by poverty, then you are out of control. If someone is, although human, not humane, and you are extremely repulsed by him, then you are out of control."

8.8   The Master said, "One is inspired by the *Odes*, established through ritual, and completed by music."

8.17   The Master said, "Study as though you will not reach it, but still fear missing out on it."

9.4   The Master had done away with four things. He didn't hold preconceptions, he wasn't rigid, he wasn't obstinate, and he didn't think only in terms of himself.

9.11   Yan Hui, heaving a sigh, said, "I look up for it, but it's ever higher. I dig into it, but it's ever harder. I look ahead for it, but all of a sudden it's behind. The Master gradually, skillfully leads people on. He broadened me with culture and restrained me with ritual. I want to finish, but I am unable. Having exhausted my capacities, it seems there is something left standing tall. Although I would go after it, I have nothing left with which to do so."

9.16   The Master said, "When one is out, to serve high officials; when at home, to serve father and elder brother; not to

[31] A ritual performed before going to see someone of special worth.

dare not to exert oneself in the affairs of mourning; and not to be troubled by wine - these are no problem for me."

9.19   The Master said, "It is like making a hill. If it's one basketful short of completion and I stop, it is I who stop. It is like leveling the ground. Although I've tossed only one basketful, if I press on, it is I who go forth."

9.20   The Master said, "Someone who doesn't slack off when I have told him something - that was Hui!"

9.21   The Master said of Yan Hui, "What a pity! I could see him progressing, and I never saw him stop."

9.22   The Master said, "There are times when it sprouts but doesn't flower. And there are times when it flowers but doesn't bear fruit."

9.24   The Master said, "Who couldn't assent to the words of a platitude? To change is what is important. Who couldn't be pleased with thoughtfully given words? To interpret them is what is important. To be pleased without interpreting, to assent without changing - there is nothing I can do about such a person."

9.25   The Master said, "Place the most importance on loyalty and good faith. Have no friends that don't measure up to you. If you are at fault, don't shrink from changing."

9.30   The Master said, "You can study together with him, but you still can't pursue the Way with him. Or you can pursue the Way with him, but you still can't establish yourself with him. Or you can establish yourself with him, but you still can't weigh things up with him."

11.16 Zigong asked who was more worthy, Shi (Zizhang) or Shang (Zixia). The Master said, "Shi goes too far, Shang not far enough." He said, "Then Shi is better?" The Master said, "To go too far is no different from not going far enough."

14.30 The Master said, "Don't worry about not being recognized.[32] Worry about your ability."

---

[32] "Recognized" means acknowledged as worthy of government office.

15.16 The Master said, "If you aren't one who says, 'What can be done about it?! What can be done about it?!' then I simply cannot do anything about you."

15.30 The Master said, "Having made a mistake, not to make changes - this is what we really call making a mistake."

(15.31) The Master said, "I once spent a day without eating and a night without sleeping, in order to meditate. There was no benefit. It's not as good as studying."

16.9 Confucius said, "Those who know it from birth are the best. Those who know it through study are the next. Those who study it with difficulty are the next after that. Those who don't study because of the difficulty - the people - are the lowest.

17.2 The Master said, "By nature they are close together. Through practice they are far apart." The Master said, "Only the very smartest and the very stupidest do not change."

19.22 Gongsun Zhao of Wei asked Zigong, "With whom did Confucius study?" Zigong said, "The Way of Kings Wen and Wu has not yet collapsed to the ground. It is in people. Worthies are aware of its greater aspects. Those who aren't worthies are aware of its lesser aspects. There isn't anyone who doesn't have the Way of Wen and Wu within him. With whom didn't the Master study? And, still, what regular teacher did he have?"

Ritual

1.12 Youzi said, "In the practice of rituals, harmony is most important. In the ancient kings' Way, it was cherished. In small and large matters we follow it. If there is a matter in which you reach an impasse, keep harmony in mind and be harmonious. If you don't tie things together with ritual, then it will remain an impasse."

2.5 Mengyizi asked about filiality. The Master said, "Don't act contrary [to the ritual rules]." Fan Chi was driving him somewhere when the Master told him, "Meng Sun asked me about filiality, and I answered, 'Don't act contrary [to the ritual rules]." Fan Chi said, "What did you mean?" The Master replied, "That while alive they are to be served through the rituals and that, upon their death, they are to be buried according to the rituals and sacrificed to according to the rituals."

2.23 Zizhang asked whether ten generations hence could be known about. The Master said, "The Yin took the Xia rituals as its basis. One can tell where it added to and where it subtracted from them. The Zhou took the Yin rituals as a basis. One can tell where it added to and where it subtracted from them. If any others follow after the Zhou, even after one hundred generations one could tell."[33]

3.1 Confucius said of the Ji family, "Eight rows of dancers in their courtyard - if this can be tolerated, what can't be tolerated?"[34]

3.4 Lin Fang asked about the fundamentals of ritual. The Master said, "A good question! For ceremonies, frugality is better than extravagance, while, in grieving, mournfulness is better than being moderate."

3.6 The head of the Ji family [Lin Fang] went to Mt. Tai. The Master said to Ran You, "Can you do something about this?" "I cannot," Ran You replied. The Master said, "Oh! Can you really say that Mt. Tai isn't as smart as Lin Fang?"[35]

3.7 The Master said, "Gentlemen are without contentiousness. If it were ever necessary, it would be in archery, right? But, bowing and yielding, they ascend and descend [the platform], and then take the libation. In contending, they are gentlemen."

3.8 Zixia asked,

---

[33] These are the Xia Dynasty (early 2nd Millennium B.C.E.), the Yin Dynasty (a.k.a "Shang" late 2nd Millennium B.C.E.) and the Zhou Dynasty (1025-256 B.C.E.).

[34] This ritual dance was supposed to be for high rulers only.

[35] Only a high ruler was supposed to go to pay respects to the mountain. Lin Fang had demonstrated an understanding of ritual good enough to know this. Therefore, the mountain would certainly recognize the inappropriateness.

> Beguiling smile, dimples,
> Pretty eyes that shine,
> Plain silk taken and made decorative.[36]

What does it mean?"

The Master said, "The painting is subordinate to the plain silk." Zixia said, "The ritual is secondary?" The Master said, "Shang [Zixia] is one who will pick out implications. Now I can talk about the *Odes* with him."

3.9   The Master said, "The Xia rituals I can talk about, but [the state of] Ji doesn't suffice as an illustration of them. The Yin rituals I can talk about, but [the state of] Song doesn't suffice as an illustration of them. The reason is that the literary records aren't sufficient. If they were sufficient, then I could use them as illustrations."[37]

3.10   The Master said, "At the Di sacrifice, after they're all finished with the libation, I don't want to see it."[38]

3.12   Of "Sacrifice as if present" and "Sacrifice to spirits as if the spirits were present," the Master said, "If I am not present at the sacrifice, it is like not sacrificing at all."[39]

3.13   Wang Sunjia asked, "About 'Paying homage to the southwest corner isn't as good as paying homage to the stove'[40] - what do you say?" The Master said, "It isn't true. If you commit a crime against heaven, there will be no one to pray to."

---

[36] *Odes* 57.

[37] The states of Ji and Song of Confucius's time were the descendants of the Xia and Yin (Shang) dynasties, respectively.

[38] Confucius could not sit through the high ritual poorly done by leaders unworthy of their offices.

[39] Confucius is interpreting the old saying as referring to an earnest presence of mind on the part of the one performing the sacrifice, rather than to belief in spirits.

[40] These are the god (or spirit) of the southwest corner of the house and the god of the stove. The saying means that one ought to pray to the god that could influence the satisfaction of one's lower needs, rather than the god that symbolized more abstract purposes. The saying thus advised that one woo government officials who could benefit one, rather than people who intrinsically deserved respect.

3.15   When the Master entered the Grand Temple, he asked about everything. Someone remarked, "Who says the man of Zou knows the rituals? When he goes into the Grand Temple, he asks about everything." The Master heard this and said, "That's the ritual."[41]

3.17   Zigong wanted to do away with the sacrificing of a sheep in the New Month Ceremony. The Master said, "Si, you treat the sheep as dear. I treat the ritual as dear."

3.18   The Master said, "If you use every ritual in serving your leader, people will take you for a flatterer."

3.19   Duke Ding asked, "When the ruler employs his subjects, and the subjects serve their ruler, how should they go about it?" Confucius answered, "The ruler is to employ the subjects with ritual, and the subjects are to serve the ruler with loyalty."

3.21   Duke Ai asked Zai Wo about altars. Zai Wo answered, "The Xia ruler used pines, the Yin used cypress, and the Zhou used chestnut[42], saying that they would make people tremble." The Master heard about this and said, "Completed deeds one is not to analyze, past deeds one is not to scold, and what is finished one is not to censure."[43]

3.22   The Master said, "Guan Zhong's usefulness is slight."[44] Someone said, "Was Guan Zhong thrifty?" "Guan Zhong had three residences, and in his affairs he did no double duty. How does that amount to thriftiness?" "But did Guan Zhong know the rituals?" "Rulers of states tree in their gates. Guan also treed in his gate. Rulers of states, when they have a meeting between two rulers, have inverted cups. Guan also had

---

[41] Surely the reader can think of contemporary rituals (Chanukah, Easter, for example) in which the participants' refreshing their memories of the protocol itself has become part of ritual.

[42] In Chinese, a homonym with the word for "to tremble."

[43] Apparently Zai Wo thought the Zhou's symbolism oppressive.

[44] "Usefulness" translates "qi" which also means "utensil, tool, vessel." Guan Zhong (7th C. B.C.E.) was a minister to Duke Huan of Qi who took control of the Zhou Dynasty by force, rather than by moral authority.

an inverted cup. If Guan counts as knowing the rituals, then who doesn't know the rituals?"

3.26   The Master said, "To occupy a superior position without being magnanimous, to perform rituals without being respectful, to sit wake without being mournful - how can I countenance these things?"

4.13   The Master said, "If one can use ritual deference to run the country, what problem will there be? But if you cannot use ritual deference to run the country, then what is ritual to you?"

7.9   When the Master had a meal with someone who was in mourning, he never ate his fill.

7.10   On a day on which he had cried, the Master didn't sing.

7.18   What Confucius used proper pronunciation for were the *Odes*, the *Documents*, and maintaining ritual. For all these he used proper pronunciation.

7.31   The Minister of Crime of Chen asked whether the Duke of Zhao understood ritual. Confucius said, "He understood ritual." When Confucius had withdrawn, he bowed to Wuma Qi and had him come forth. He said, "I was taught that a gentleman isn't partisan. Can a gentleman still be partisan? The ruler married a lady of the Wu family and called her the 'Elder Zi of Wu'.[45] If the ruler still understands ritual, then who doesn't understand ritual?" Wuma Qi conveyed this to Confucius. The Master said, "I am fortunate. If I make any mistakes, others always recognize them."

8.2   The Master said, "If you are respectful but don't have the rituals, then you will end up trying too hard. If you are cautious but don't have the rituals, then you will be timid. If you are brave but lack the rituals, then you will be out of control. If you are upright but don't have the rituals, then you will be rude. If the gentleman values his relatives, then the people will be

---

[45] The Duke renamed his wife "Zi", in effort to conceal his impropriety: marrying a woman of his own family name ("Ji").

inspired to humanity. If he doesn't turn his back on his old friends, then the people won't be dissolute."

9.3   The Master said, "A hempen cap is the ritual, but today [they use] a silk one. It's thrifty, and I follow the crowd. To bow below [the ruler's elevated hall] is the ritual, but today they bow on top. That's arrogant. Though it goes against the crowd, I follow [the practice of bowing] below."[46]

9.10   When the Master saw someone in mourning dress, someone in cap and robe for court, or someone who was blind, then upon seeing them, even if they were younger, he always stood up, and if he passed them, he always hurried.

9.12   When the Master was very ill, Zilu had the disciples act as ministers. When the illness was in remission, the Master said, "How long has You [Zilu] been practicing such deceitfulness! To act as though I have ministers when I have no ministers - whom will I fool? Will I fool heaven? Moreover, as for meeting my death in the hands of some ministers, wouldn't it be better to die in the hands of a few disciples? And even if I am made not to get a great funeral, will I be dying on the road?"

10.1   Confucius, when in a village or town, was reserved and straightforward and seemed like someone who couldn't speak. When in an ancestral temple or at court, he was forthcoming in his speech, but careful. At court, in talking with the lower grandees, he was outgoing, and in talking with the higher grandees he was respectfully direct. When the ruler was present, he was humbly deferential and composed.

10.7   He wouldn't sit unless his mat was straight. When the villagers were drinking wine, he would leave after those carrying canes left.

10.11   Once a stable burned down. The Master, upon returning from court, said, "Was anyone hurt?" He didn't ask about the horses.[47]

---

[46] The traditional ritual was to bow before ascending the steps to the ruler's hall.

[47] Clearly, financial loss (horses) is important, but so much less so that asking about it when human safety has just been in question is a ritual impropriety.

10.15 Whenever he went into the Great Temple, he asked about everything.

10.17 When in bed, he didn't lie as a corpse does. When at home, he didn't behave like a guest.

10.18 When he saw someone in mourning attire, even if it was someone well known to him, he always changed his countenance.

11.1 The Master said, "The first to come forward[48] were rustic fellows in regard to ritual and music. The ones who came forward later were gentlemen in regard to ritual and music. But when it comes to how they used them, I follow the ones who came forward first."

11.8 When Yan Hui died, Yan Lu asked for the Master's carriage, in order to use it as a coffin enclosure. The Master said, "Whether he's talented or not, everyone talks about his own son. When Li died, he had a coffin but no coffin enclosure. I did not go on foot, in order to give him a coffin enclosure, because I came right behind the grandees. It wasn't permissible to go on foot."[49]

12.1 Yan Hui asked about humanity. The Master said, "To subdue oneself and return to ritual is to be humane. If for one day a person could subdue himself and return to ritual, the world would count him as humane. To be humane - is it based on oneself or based on others?" Yan Hui said, "Please tell me the details." The Master said, "Do not look at what is contrary to ritual, do not listen to what is contrary to ritual, do not speak what is contrary to ritual, and do not move in a way that is contrary to ritual." Yan Hui said, "Although I am not sharp, I would like to work on this lesson."

17.9 The Master said, "'It's the ritual,' they say. 'It's the ritual,' they say. What do they mean? The jade and the silk? 'That's music,' they say. 'That's music,' they say. Do they mean the bells and drums?"

---

[48] I.e., to seek instruction from Confucius.

[49] Yan Lu: Yan Hui's father. Li: Confucius's son. It was unseemly for people in the procession near the grandees not to go in style.

Political Philosophy

1.5   The Master said, "In leading the Way for a country of one thousand chariots, one is to be reverent in attending to affairs and to be of good faith; one is to be frugal in expenditures and to value the people dearly; and one is to use the people according to the season."

1.9   Zengzi said, "When one shows solicitude towards the end [of one's parents' lives], and one follows up [with sacrifices to them] when they are long gone, then the people's virtue will return to its fullness."

2.1   The Master said, "One who governs with virtue is like the North Star, which stays in its place while the other stars pay homage to it."[50]

2.3   The Master said, "If you lead the Way with laws and keep them in line with sanctions, then the people will avoid these but have no sense of shame. If you lead the Way with virtue and keep them in line with ritual, they will have a sense of shame and also ruliness."

2.19   Duke Ai asked, "What can I do so that the people will submit?" Confucius responded, "Lift up the upright and set them above the crooked, and the people will submit. Lift up the crooked and set them above the upright, and the people will not submit."

2.20   Jikangzi asked about making the people respectful, loyal, and invigorated, and about how to go about it. The Master said, "Look upon them with dignity, and they will be respectful. Be filial and kind, and they will be loyal. Lift up the good and instruct the incompetent, and they will be invigorated."

2.21   Someone said to Confucius, "Why don't you partake in government?"

The Master said, "What does the *Documents* say about filiality? 'Just filiality and fraternity towards siblings contribute

---

[50] Due to the rotation of the earth, the North Star, situated along the axis of the earth above the North Pole, seems to stay still while all of the other stars circle it.

to there being a government.' This is also partaking in government. Why make something of partaking in government?"

3.11 Someone asked to hear an account of the Di sacrifice. The Master said, "I don't know. For someone who knew its account, wouldn't he see his relation to the world as if it were right here?" He pointed to the palm of his hand.

3.2 The Three Families used the *Yong*[51] for clearing away the sacrifice. The Master said, "'With the lords in assistance, the Emperor is awesome.' How could that apply to the hall of the Three Families?"

6.2 Zhongyong [Ran Yong] asked about Zisang Bozi. The Master said, "He is acceptable for being easygoing." Zhonggong said, "To take a stance of respectability and to be easygoing in practice in order to manage the people is surely permissible, right? But to take an easygoing stance and to be easygoing in practice - isn't that too easygoing?" The Master said, "Yong's [Ran Yong] words are true."

6.8 Ji Kangzi asked whether Zhongyou [Zilu] could be assigned to pursue a governmental position. The Master said, "You [Zilu] is decisive. What problem would he have seeking a government position?" He asked whether Si [Zigong] could be assigned to pursue a governmental position. The Master said, "Si is perceptive. What problem would he have seeking a government position?" He asked whether Qiu [Ran You] could be assigned to pursue a governmental position. The Master said, "Qiu is talented. What problem would he have seeking a government position?"

6.9 The Ji family assigned Min Ziqian to be steward of Bi. Min Ziqian said, "Tactfully decline the offer for me. If someone returns for me, then I better go stay on the Wen River."[52]

8.6 Zengzi said, "If he can be entrusted with a small orphan child, if he can be put in charge of a 100-square-li region,

---

[51] A selection from the *Odes*.
[52] The Ji family was not worthy of serving.

if in a great emergency he is not shaken, would he be a gentleman? He would be a gentleman."

8.18   The Master said, "Awesome was Shun and Yu's possessing the empire while being nonchalant about it."

8.21   The Master said, "I find no flaw in King Yu: with meager meals, yet extremely filial to the ghosts and spirits; with poor clothing, yet splendid ceremonial attire; with a humble abode, yet exhausting his energy on irrigation. I find no flaw in Yu."

11.14 The men of Lu were working on the Long Treasury. Min Ziqian said, "Why not restore it? Why must you build anew?"[53] The Master said, "This man doesn't speak much. But when he speaks, he hits the mark."

12.7   Zigong asked about government. The Master said, "Make the food sufficient and the weaponry sufficient, and the people will have good faith in it." Zigong said, "If one absolutely had to give up one of these three, which would be first?" The Master said, "I would give up the weaponry." Zigong said, "If one absolutely had to give up one of these two, which would be first?" The Master said, "I would give up food. Ever since ancient times, everyone has had to die. But a people without good faith will not stand."

12.9   Duke Ai asked of You Ruo, "There was famine this year, and revenues are insufficient. What should I do about it?" You Ruo answered, "Why not take a 10% tax?" The Duke said, "Even 20% wouldn't be enough for me. What good would 10% do?" You Ruo responded, "If the 100 surnames have enough, then with whom will the ruler go wanting? If the 100 surnames are left without enough, then with whom will the ruler share his sufficiency?"

12.11 Duke Jing of Qi asked Confucius about government. Confucius answered, "Let the ruler be a ruler, let ministers be ministers, let fathers be fathers, let sons be sons." The Duke said, "Good! Indeed, if the ruler is not a ruler, then even if there is any grain, will I get any of it to eat?"

---

[53] Min Ziqian advocates a thrifty government.

12.17 Ji Kangzi asked Confucius about government. Confucius answered, "'Govern' means 'correct'. If you lead by being correct, who would dare not to be correct?"

12.18 Ji Kangzi was worried about thieves and asked Confucius about it. Confucius answered, "If you didn't desire things, then even if they would be rewarded for it, they would not steal."

12.22 Fan Chi asked about humanity. The Master said, "It is to love others." He asked about wisdom The Master said, "It is to understand others." Fan Chi didn't grasp the point. The Master said, "Promote the upright and reject the crooked, and you can cause the crooked to become upright." Fan Chi withdrew and went to see Zixia. He said, "I just saw the Master and asked about wisdom. The Master said, 'Promote the upright and reject the crooked, and you can cause the crooked to become upright.' What does that mean?" Zixia said, "What profound words! Shun, having possession of the empire, selected from among the masses and promoted Gao Yao. The inhumane disappeared. Tang, having possession of the empire, selected from among the masses and promoted Yi Yin. The inhumane disappeared."

13.4 Fan Chi asked to be taught farming. The Master said, "I wouldn't be as good as an old farmer." He asked to be taught vegetable gardening. The Master said, "I wouldn't be as good as an old gardener." Fan Chi left. The Master said, "Fan Chi is a small man, indeed!" If their superiors love ritual, then none of the people will dare not to be respectful. If their superiors love what is right, then none of the people will dare not to submit. If their superiors love good faith, then none of the people will dare not to acknowledge facts. If he is like this, then people from all parts will come with their children on their backs. What use does he have for farming?"

13.6 The Master said, "When his person is correct, though he gives no orders, they act. When his person is not correct, then although he gives orders, they don't follow them."

13.9 ...The Master went to Wei with Ran You driving. The Master said, "Look at how numerous the masses are!" Ran

You said, "Now that they are so many, what should one do next?" "Make them rich," the Master said. "Having made them rich," Ran You asked, "what should one do next?" The Master said, "Educate them."

13.12 The Master said, "If there were a [true] king, then in one generation, [everyone would be] humane."

13.29 The Master said, "Only after a good person has taught the people for seven years may they be used to bear arms."

13.30 The Master said, "To send uneducated people to war is to throw them away."

14.41 The Master said, "When their superiors love ritual, the people are easy to command."

15.5 The Master said, "Someone who governed without acting - that was Shun, right? What did he do? All he did was to take a reverent attitude and to face straight south."

15.25 The Master said, "In dealing with people, whom do I blame and whom do I praise? Suppose there is someone whom I've praised. There is a standard for this, and it is the people, they whom the Three Dynasties used to keep their Way upright and put it into action."

15.28 The Master said, "When the masses hate someone, you must take a look at him. When the masses like someone, you must take a look at him."[54]

16.1 ...[The Master said], "If distant people do not submit [to rule], then cultivate culture and virtue, in order to attract them. Having made them come, make them content."

Miscellany

1.1 The Master said, "To study and practice it over time - isn't this surely a pleasure? To have friends come from faraway places - isn't this surely a delight? Not to be indignant when others don't recognize one - isn't this surely to be a gentleman?"

---

[54] In other words, the people's opinion of a minister is prima facie evidence about his worthiness, meriting further inquiry.

48

1.16   The Master said, "Don't be upset that others do not recognize[55] one. Be upset when you don't recognize others."

2.16   The Master said, "To attack from a different premise - this is simply meant to harm someone."[56]

2.17   The Master said, "You [Zilu], shall I instruct you about knowledge? To treat what you know as what you know and what you don't know as what you don't know - that's knowledge."

3.5   The Master said, "The Yi or the Di with a ruler is still not as good as the Xia states without one."[57]

3.16   The Master said, "In archery, we don't emphasize [the piercing of] the leather.[58] Strength is not equally distributed. This is the way of the ancients."

3.23   The Master was talking with the Grand Music Master of Lu, saying, "Here is what may be understood about music. When it begins, it is in unison. As it proceeds it is harmonious, clear, and sustained, through to the finish."

3.24   A boarder guard of Yi asked to be introduced, saying, "When gentlemen come here, I never fail to get to see them." The followers introduced him. When he came out, he said, "Sirs, why are you upset by the misfortunes? The lack of the Way in the world is now old. Heaven will use this Master as a bell ringer."

3.25   The Master said that the *Shao* was perfectly beautiful and perfectly good. He said that the *Wu* was perfectly beautiful but not perfectly good.[59]

4.8   The Master said, "If one hears of the Way in the morning, then it is alright to die that evening."

---

[55] "Recognize" means "notice the worthiness in."
[56] It is simply quarrelsome (and, indeed, fallacious) to object to someone's position on the basis of a mere change in the assumptions of the debate.
[57] The Yi and Di were barbarian tribes. The "Xia" meant "Chinese." Probably Confucius had in mind a cultural superiority, rather than an intrinsic racial superiority.
[58] There was a leather patch on the bull's eye of the target in archery.
[59] These were poems in the *Odes*.

4.9   The Master said, "A public servant who sets his intentions on the Way but is ashamed of bad clothing and bad food is not good enough to hold discussions with."

4.12   The Master said, "If you aim for what is profitable in your actions, there will be a lot of resentment."

4.14   The Master said, "One doesn't worry about not having a position. One worries about that whereby one comes to be established in one. One doesn't worry about not yet being known but seeks to become worth being known."

4.16   The Master said, "The gentleman understands by familiarity with what is right. The small man understands by familiarity with what is profitable."

5.1   The Master said of Gongye Chang that he could be given a wife. Although he had been in shackles, it was not for any crime of his.[60] He gave him his daughter in marriage.

5.2   The Master said of Nan Rong that when the country had the Way he would never be unemployed, and when the country was without the Way he would evade punishment and disgrace. He gave him his elder brother's daughter in marriage.

5.4   Zigong asked, "What am I like?" The Master said, "You are a utensil." Zigong said, "What sort of utensil?" "A jeweled jade vessel," the Master replied.

4.22   The Master said, "The reason that the ancients' words did not come forth is that they were ashamed lest they did not live up to them."

3.14   The Master said, "The Zhou turned to the two dynasties, and how rich its culture! I follow the Zhou."[61]

5.15   Zigong asked, "Kong Wenzi - why was he called 'Wen'?" The Master said, "He was diligent and liked to study. He wasn't ashamed to ask advice from inferiors. That is why they called him 'Wen.'"[62]

---

[60] The social disgrace of criminal punishment was, for Confucius, cancelled when the convict was actually innocent.
[61] The two were the legendary Xia and Shang (Yin).
[62] "Wen" means: literature, culture, achievement, good form and embellishment.

5.22   When the Master was in Chen, he said, "I'll go back! I'll go back!⁶³ The young men of my group are heedless and hasty. With such accomplishments and achievements, they don't know how to tailor them."

5.18   The Master said, "Zang Wenzhong had a house for a giant tortoise with mountains [carved] on its capitals and duckweed [carved] on its beams. What sort of understanding is that?"

5.25   The Master said, "Skillful speech, a compelling countenance, and reverently shuffling feet - Zuoqiu Ming thought these shameful, and I also think them shameful. To conceal resentment and act friendly towards the one who is its object - Zuoqiu Ming thought these shameful, and I also think them shameful."

5.26   While Yan Hui and Zilu were by his side, the Master said, "Let each of you tell of your aspirations." Zilu said, "I desire that, when I share my carriage or horse, or my light clothing or furs with friends, they could wear them out without by being annoyed." Yan Hui said, "I wish not to show off and not to put my works on display."

Zilu said, "I would like to hear Master's aspirations." The Master said, "For the old - to give them comfort, for friends - to show them good faith. For the young - to cherish them."

5.28   The Master said, "In a borough of ten houses, there will certainly be someone as loyal and as much of good faith as I am. But there won't be someone who likes studying as much as I do."

6.3   Duke Ai asked which of the disciples loved learning. Confucius answered, "There was Yan Hui. He loved learning. He didn't take his anger out on anyone. He didn't repeat a mistake. Unfortunately, his allotted years were short, and he died. Today he is gone, and I haven't heard of anyone who loves learning."

---

⁶³ I.e., return to Lu and give up teaching.

6.5   Yuan Si became steward and was given 900 portions of grain. He declined them. The Master said, "Don't. Take them and give them to the local villages and boroughs."

6.6   The Master spoke about Chonggong, saying, "If the offspring of a brindled ox were red and horned, then, though one might not want to use it, would the mountains and rivers reject it?"[64]

6.7   The Master said, "[Yan] Hui! For three months his mind did not depart from humanity. As for the others, they manage it once it a while, and that's all."

6.10   Boniu had a disease. The Master went to see him and, holding his hand through the window, said, "We're losing him. It must be fate. That such a man should have such a disease! That such a man should have such a disease!"

6.17   The Master said, "Who can go outside without going through the door? So, why does no one go by this Way?"

6.13   The Master said to Zixia, "Be the gentlemanly sort of scholar. Don't be the small-man sort of scholar."

6.14   Ziyou was steward of Wucheng. The Master said, "Have you found anyone there?" Ziyou said, "There is Tantai Mieming. He doesn't cut corners, and he doesn't come to my quarters, except on official business."

6.19   The Master said, "A person's being alive is due to uprightness. Without it, being alive can only be due to luck."

6.21   The Master said, "Those who are superior to the average person may discuss what is superior. Those who are inferior to the average person may not discuss what is superior."

6.24   The Master said, "[The state of] Qi, with one adjustment, would reach [the level of] Lu. Lu, with one adjustment, would reach the Way."

6.28   The Master went to see Nanzi. Zilu was not pleased. The Master swore at this, saying, "Whatever I have done wrong - heaven will reject it! Heaven will reject it!"

---

[64] Sacrifice required a red, horned ox. Its poor pedigree shouldn't matter.

7.1   The Master said, "I transmit but do not create. I am of good faith and love the ancients. I would hope to be compared to Old Peng."[65]

7.2   The Master said, "To enlarge my understanding quietly, to study tirelessly, to instruct others without growing weary of it - these are no problem for me."

7.3   The Master said, "Virtue that I don't cultivate, studies that I don't deliberate over, having been taught what is right but being unable to move toward it, and where I am not good to be unable to change - these are my anxieties."

7.4   When the Master was at leisure, he was at ease and light hearted.

7.7   The Master said, "From someone bringing dried meat on up I have never refused to teach anyone."

7.12   The Master said, "If one would obtain wealth and it would be permissible to seek it, then even if it took being the officer who held the whip,[66] I would certainly do it. Since it is not permissible to seek it, I pursue what I love."

7.13   What the Master exercised caution over were fasting, war, and illness.

7.14   When the Master was in Qi he heard the *Shao*, and for three months he didn't recognize the flavor of meat. He said, "I never imagined that the playing of music could reach such a level."

7.16   The Master said, "Eating coarse food, drinking water, bending one's elbow to use it as a pillow - delight is to be found even in these things. But while being unrighteous to get rich and even to gain rank - these to me are like floating clouds."

7.19   The Duke of She asked Zilu about Confucius. Zilu didn't answer. The Master said, "Why didn't you say, 'As a person, he is one who, in his zeal, forgets to eat, in his delight, forgets his anxieties, and who doesn't recognize that old age is on its way'?"

---

[65] This is likely Peng Zu, the Chinese Methuselah. Perhaps Confucius just means that he represents what stands the test of time: tradition.
[66] I.e., a demeaning position.

7.20 The Master said, "I am not someone who was born knowing. I am someone who loves the ancients and seriously inquires into things."

7.21 The Master did not discuss paranormal events, force, [social] disorder, or spiritual beings.

7.24 The Master said, "Disciples, do you think I'm hiding something? I'm hiding nothing from you. There is nothing that I practice that I don't pass on to my disciples. That is my way[67]."

7.25 The Master taught four subjects: literature, conduct, loyalty, and good faith.

7.26 The Master said, "I'm not going to get to see a sage. If only I could get to see someone who is a gentleman, that would do. I'm not going to get to see a good person. If only I could get to see someone who was good, that would do. I'm not going to get to see someone who has constancy. If only I could get to see someone who had constancy,[68] that would do. But when people have not but act as though they have, when they are empty but act as though they were full, when they are oppressed but act as though they were comfortable, it is hard for them to have constancy."

7.27 The Master fished with a line but did not use a net. He shot with a corded arrow but did not shoot at [a bird] at rest.

7.32 When the Master was singing with others, and it was good, he had them repeat it and then make harmonies for it.

7.33 The Master said, "In cultural achievement, no one makes me look like ordinary people. But as for being a gentleman in practice, this is something I have not yet managed."

7.34 The Master said, "As for 'sage' or 'humane', I could never be so presumptuous. However, as for 'aiming for them tirelessly, and instructing others without growing weary of it' - at least this may be said of me."

---

[67] This is not the word "*dao*" but an unrelated term, so I leave it uncapitalized.

[68] I.e., at least a consistent aspiration to moral character.

7.35   The Master was ill. Zilu asked to say a prayer. The Master said, "Is that what is done?" Zilu answered, "That is what is done. The prayer for the dead says, 'Here we pray to the spirits above and below.'" The Master said, "I have been praying for a long time."

7.37   The Master said, "The gentleman is even and composed. The small man is always disconcerted."

7.38   The Master was warm but strict, awe-inspiring but not fierce, respectful but at ease.

8.4   When Zengzi was ill, Meng Jingzi inquired after him. Zengzi said, "When a bird is about to die, its cries are mournful. When a human being is about to die, his words are good...."

8.7   Zengzi said, "A public servant simply must be broad in view and resolute. His responsibilities are heavy and the Way is long. Humanity he takes to be his own responsibility. Is it not heavy? It ends only after death. Is that not long?"

8.9   The Master said, "The people can be made to follow it, but they cannot be made to understand it."

8.15   The Master said, "Music Master Zhi's beginnings, and the *Guan Ju*'s finish - how vast was the sound that filled the ears!"

9.1   The Master seldom spoke of utility, fate, or humanity.

9.2   Someone from the village of Daxiang said, "How great Confucius is! But while his learning is so broad, he has nothing with which to establish his name." The Master heard this and said to his disciples, "What should I take up? Should I take up charioteering? I'll take up charioteering."[69]

9.5   The Master was under threat in Kuang. He said, "After the passing of King Wen, wasn't there still culture here? If heaven had meant to destroy this culture, later mortals wouldn't have managed to get any of this culture. If heaven still doesn't mean to destroy this culture, then what can the people of Kuang do about me?"

---

[69] Sarcasm.

9.6   A Grand Steward asked Zigong, "This Master is a sage, right? Then, why the many abilities?" Zigong said, "Certainly heaven has given him to count as a sage and have many abilities." The Master heard of this and said, "Does the Grand Steward know me? When I was young, I was not well off. Hence the many abilities and lowly jobs. Does the gentleman really have many? Not many."

9.7   Lao said, "The Master said, 'I was not given a try[70]; hence the artisanship.'"

9.8   The Master said, "What knowledge do I have? I have no knowledge. One of the simple folk asks questions me, as though empty-headed. I press on his initial dilemma and do so exhaustively."

9.9   The Master said, "The phoenix hasn't arrived, and the river hasn't produced a diagram.[71] I'm finished!"

9.13   Zigong said, "If you have a beautiful jade, do you wrap it up, box it, and keep it? Or do you seek a good price and sell it?" The Master said, "You sell it! You sell it! I'm someone who is waiting for the price."

9.14   The Master wanted to live among the nine barbarian tribes. Someone said, "They are vulgar. How will you handle it?" The Master said, "If a gentleman dwelt among them, what vulgarity would there be?"

9.15   The Master said, "It was after I had returned from Wei to Lu that the music was set right, the *Songs of Royalty* and *Songs of Praise* each finding its place."

9.17   The Master was by the side of a river when he said, "What passes on is like this! It doesn't stop, day or night."

9.18   The Master said, "I have never seen someone who likes humanity as much as he likes sensuous beauty."

9.23   The Master said, "The younger generation is worthy of respect. How do you know that the next generation will not be as good as today's? When they are forty or fifty and

---

[70] I.e., Confucius was not given high office.
[71] These were auspicious omens. "Diagram" refers to diagrams such as the He Tu numerological diagram.

there is nothing one can learn from them - only then would they not be worth respecting."

9.26   The Master said, "The Three Armies can have their commander taken from them, but an ordinary person cannot have his will taken from him."

9.28   The Master said, "The year grows cold and only then do we realize that the pine and the cypress[72] are the last to fade."

9.31
The cherry flowers
Fluttering about!
How could I not be thinking of you?
Your house is so far away![73]

The Master said, "He hadn't thought of her. Otherwise, what distance would there be?"

11.9   When Yan Hui died, the Master said, "Oh! Heaven is destroying me! Heaven is destroying me!"

11.10   When Yan Hui died, the Master cried for him and was grief-stricken. A disciple said, "The Master is grief-stricken." The Master said, "Is this grief-stricken? If I am not to be grief-stricken for this man, then for whom?"

11.12   Zilu asked about serving ghosts and spirits. The Master said, "If you cannot yet serve people, how can you serve ghosts and spirits?" He said, "May I ask about death?" The Master said, "If you don't understand life, how will you understand death?"

12.5   Sima Niu was melancholy. He said, "Everyone else has brothers, but I am all alone." Zixia said, "I have been taught that life and death are fated, and riches and rank are up to heaven. If a gentleman is reverent and doesn't err, if he is respectful to others and has the rituals, then all the world are his brothers. Why should the gentleman fret over not having brothers?"

---

[72] Symbols of stout moral character.
[73] Possibly a poem from the *Odes* now missing from the existing version.

12.13 Confucius said, "In hearing litigation, I'm the same as everyone else. What is necessary is to make it so that there is no litigation."

13.3 Zilu said, "If the ruler of Wei were to let you run the government, what would you do first?" The Master said, "It would be necessary to rectify names."[74] Zilu said, "Is that what is done? Master pursues a diversion. Why rectification?" The Master said, "You peasant! A gentleman is more tentative towards what he doesn't understand. If names aren't rectified, then speech will not be fitting. If speech is not fitting, then affairs will not be brought to completion. If affairs are not brought to completion, then rituals and music will not flourish. If rituals and music do not flourish, then punishments will not hit the mark. If punishments do not hit the mark, then the people won't have their bearings. Therefore, what the gentleman names something may certainly be spoken. What he says of something may certainly be carried out. In his speech the gentleman is lax about nothing."

15.29 The Master said, "Man can give full scope to the Way, but the Way doesn't give full scope to man."[75]

Suggested Readings

Chen, Li Fu, *The Confucian Way*, Shih Shun Liu, trans., various editions

Cheung, Leo K. C., "The Unification of Dao and Ren in the Analects," *Journal of Chinese Philosophy* 31(2004): 313–327

Chin, Annping, *The Authentic Confucius: A Life of Thought and Politics* (New York: Scribner's, 2007)

---

[74] This is the doctrine of the rectification of names: the establishment of norms for the various roles and moral concepts in use in society. See 12.11.
[75] Perhaps this is a contradiction of the Daoists' transcendental view of the Way.

58

Dawson, Raymond, trans., *The Analects* (Oxford: Oxford University Press, 1993)

Fingarette, Herbert, *Confucius: The Secular as Sacred*, various editions

Goldin, Paul R., "When Zhong Does Not Mean 'Loyalty'," *Dao: A Journal of Comparative Philosophy* 14(2008): 165-174

Ivanhoe, Philip J., *Confucian Moral Self Cultivation* (Indianapolis: Hackett, 2000)

Ivanhoe, Philip J., *Confucian Reflections: Ancient Wisdom for Modern Times* (New York: Routledge, 2013)

Liu, JeeLoo, "Moral Reason, Moral Sentiments and the Realization of Altruism: A Motivational Theory of Altruism," *Asian Philosophy* 22(2012): 93-119

Ryan, James A., "Conservatism and Coherentism in Aristotle, Confucius, and Mencius," *Journal of Chinese Philosophy* 28(2001): 275-284

Sarkissian, Hagop, "Confucius and the Effortless Life of Virtue," *History of Philosophy Quarterly* 27(2010): 1-16

Slingerland, Edward, trans., *Analects: With Selections from Traditional Commentaries* (Indianapolis: Hackett, 2003)

Van Norden, Bryan W., *Confucius and the Analects: New Essays* (New York: Oxford University Press, 2002)

Wong, David B., "Early Confucian Philosophy and the Development of Compassion," *Dao: A Journal of Comparative Philosophy* 14(2015): 157-194

2

Laozi

According to the long tradition fostered by a biography by Sima Qian (145-90 B.C.E.) in his *Record of History* (*Shiji*), Laozi[76] was supposed to have lived during Confucius's (551-479 B.C.E.) time, even meeting Confucius and giving him advice on one occasion. But Sima Qian's biography is an unreliable assemblage of legends. Also, neither the *Mozi*, *The Analects*, nor the *Mencius* mentions Laozi or his book, *The Book of Power and the Way*, and probably they would have mentioned him at least in passing if he had existed. Perhaps most of the text was written by one author, but philological evidence regarding the language of the book supports the belief that many hands wrote it over a period of time approximately two hundred years after Confucius: 350?-250? B.C.E. The oldest version we have is partial and dates to the Fourth Century B.C.E. Nevertheless, we will continue to speak of the authors as "Laozi" for the sake of convenience. This won't inappropriately conceal divergent trains of thought in the text, since the text exhibits a unity of thesis, worldview, and argument. I don't think the diverse trains of thought in it diverge to the point of failing to hang together coherently. You should scrutinize that claim as you read the book, however; perhaps you will find some tensions in the text.

Daoism (a.k.a. "Taoism") is a religion, as well as a philosophy. Its cultural ramifications, from art to martial arts, go well beyond our philosophical concern. It is replete with deities, rituals, mystical metaphysics, myths, and priests. As you will see, Laozi spoke of prolonging life, and there is a long tradition of Daoists searching for eternal life through yogic and

---

[76] "Master Lao" or, since *lao* means old, perhaps "The Old Master" as a penname, whereas his real name was supposedly Li Er or Lao Dan.

alchemical methods. Also, millions of people practice the strangely energizing and relaxing moves of qigong and taiji (a.k.a., "tai chi") in an effort "to concentrate their energy (qi)" and to stay soft and supple, as Laozi advised. While *The Dedaojing* didn't initiate these cultural phenomena by itself, it is the foremost representation of the philosophical movement that did. The work of the Daoist philosopher, Zhuangzi (369-286 B.C.E.), which we will examine in Chapter Four, is at least as good a work of philosophy and is another fundamental work in this tradition.

The *Dedaojing* is a set of eighty-one paragraph-sized chapters, consisting of verse and poetry. The chapters are often short and cryptic. They fall, for the most part, in no argumentatively or explanatorily important order. The text is an amalgam of metaphysics, speculative cosmology, psychology, philosophy of the good life, and political philosophy, in which each of these strands supports the ideas presented in the others in a way that makes it no easy task to tease them apart. It is a challenge for the reader to state just exactly what is being said by the text.

We should begin by taking a look at Laozi's philosophy in broad outline. Afterwards, as you read the text, you can scrutinize each passage in effort to come to an understanding of its views on your own. While the reader's basic interpretive duty looms so large with a text such as this that the task of philosophical criticism may seem to be forgettable for the moment, always keep it in the back of your mind. We should try to evaluate Laozi's philosophy as to whether it is trivial and as to whether it rests on good grounds.

In the book, Laozi devotes more than half of his attention to political philosophy. You will notice this as you read the text, even though perhaps its most profound influence over the ages has been on readers' metaphysical worldviews and on their ideas of the meaning of life, rather than on their political views. Like the Confucian philosophers, Laozi bemoans the perpetual wars and famines of his age and longs for the rule of the ancient sage kings. One view he seems to put forth is that the duty of the ruler is to promote peace and contentment among the people he rules. In many places, Laozi speaks as though the primary concern of the ruler was quite rightly to keep his head on his neck. He sometimes says that taking certain approaches to government that seem attractive to all but the sagely rulers of long ago, such as expanding the state's power or using the country to glorify the ruler and make his life pleasurable, is the wrong path for the ruler to take because they result in strife and contention among the ruler's subjects, which in turn result in the downfall or even the death of the ruler. However, in chapter 70(26)[77] Laozi says that the reason that the ruler should desire to preserve himself and not to take risks in order to glorify himself or the state is that he is the basis of the state. So, it seems that the welfare of the country is the source of the moral obligation that the ruler has to maintain his life and his power. On the other hand, you should always be suspicious of works of political theory that argue for the continued power of a ruler on the grounds that it is good for the welfare of those he rules.

As you read the text, try to discover what Laozi is either assuming or trying to show to be of paramount value in government. He may succumb to bringing in considerations of self-interest in an effort to demonstrate that a moral obligation applies. For example, people sometimes say things such as the following. "Of course, you should give back the wallet. Maybe someday someone will do the same for you."[78] This conflates moral considerations with self-interest. But such appeals to self-interest can show only which course of action is most prudentially rational. They do not suffice to prove moral claims. If *The Dedaojing*'s political thought is indeed an argument about which course of action will keep the ruler alive, then at least that part of the text is not philosophy. But I

---

[77] I will explain this numbering of the text's chapters below.

[78] While this argument might express something important about the impartiality of morality, strictly as an argument it is unsound, since my returning the wallet will have no effect on whether someone does the same for me in the future. I can be a free-rider on the system of morality.

think that you will find that the text is indeed largely a work of political philosophy and upholds a view about how the ruler ought to rule in the moral, and not just the prudential, sense of "ought." You should try to ferret out any such argument for a moral position.

What course of action for rulers is obligatory? It is non-action (*wuwei*). Laozi recommends minimal government and a policy of inactivity on the part of the ruler. At times he means by this literally not acting, but at other times he seems to mean acting naturally (*ziran*), by which he means spontaneously, in the sense of not having deliberately decided an intention (or deliberate purpose) for oneself in the form of a scheme of values.[79] In the latter sense, non-action is action with an important element of the ordinary concept of action missing: intention based on deliberation and decision.

While many actions are so routine and familiar to us that they require no deliberation, many other actions in our daily lives are based on deliberation and decision; this seems essential to human life. Civilization is a creation of much deliberation, decision, and intentional action. It is, in part, a scheme of values: a set of values, relationships amongst them, and techniques for navigating and applying them. (Confucius would have said that this scheme includes character virtues and rituals.) The effects that we have on the world through causing events without first deliberating and forming intentions is similar to the effects that lower animals and even inanimate objects such as falling boulders or raindrops have. It would seem that the actions flowing from higher order cognitive activity are what makes life worthwhile for us. It is these actions that seem to be what we want to call paradigmatically human actions. But Laozi recommends that we reverse this point of view. And he knows that we won't like to call the

---

[79] This is an enormous topic. See the two books by Slingerland and the article by Bruya in this chapter's list of suggested readings. Also see Eugene Herrigel's 1953 book, *Zen in the Art of Archery*, in various editions. You will also find recent books in popular neuroscience which speak of a similar concept called "flow."

lower order, natural (*ziran*), more brute, and nondeliberate actions, "actions." So, Laozi calls this kind of action "non-action." His meaning is ambiguous. It may be too much to say that Laozi would have human beings empty their minds of all thought and be like brute objects, such as uncarved blocks. But as you will read, he does say exactly this! Perhaps his point is that we engage in deliberation over our actions far too much.

Both the literal and the peculiarly Daoist sense of "non-action" are important in the book. When Laozi describes the ruler sitting and not acting in the former, literal sense, he holds that, because of this the people of the ruler's country will behave harmoniously and carry out the business of the state smoothly. Rulers of this sort "do not act, but there is nothing left undone" (11(48)). But Laozi also condones the ruler's "acting without acting," or without in that action implicitly and consciously upholding, recommending and promulgating a set of values. Those values are the substance of higher civilization. And you will see as you read the text that Laozi is a primitivist. He advocates primitive village life, illiteracy, and action only insofar as it flows spontaneously, naturally, and without extended conscious deliberation over the values it promotes. That is the way to peace.

The concept of naturalness is close to that of non-action. When you read the text, consider carefully their distinction and relation. The importance of naturalness to Laozi's philosophy perhaps cannot be overemphasized, since Laozi says that it is the very content of the concept of the Way, which, as we will see below, is certainly one of the most important concepts of the book. He says, "The Way takes naturalness as a model" 69(25). The political viewpoint and the ideal of naturalness are woven together in the text. Laozi means to show all of the following: the Way is the basis of all things (in a sense that we need to explain); naturalness is things' existing and acting in a way that directly and genuinely reflects and spontaneously and uncontrivedly expresses their basis in that larger scheme; and, finally, the only way to social peace and harmony is through the ruler's naturally acting very little and only without consciously enacting a scheme of values. This ability of the ruler is power (*de*) and he obtains it only if he has the Way (*dao.*)

Laozi's concept of power is different from the ordinary contemporary notion of political power. "*De*" may also be translated as "virtue," especially since the etymology of that word includes both the concept of power and the concept of moral virtue.[80] In Confucian texts it is proper to translate it as "virtue" (as we saw in the last two chapters), since it is mainly moral character that concerns Confucians when they apply the term, even when they describe the political ruler. Laozi does seem to think that the ruler who has *de* necessarily has moral virtue. But his main idea in using the term is to mark that quality which gives the ruler the power to harmonize and pacify society, a political virtue which is had by tapping into the power that causes all events, including natural events that have nothing to do with morality or politics. So, I will translate *de* with the term "power" (and in this chapter I won't use that term in its colloquial English sense.)

You will need to figure out just how the ruler maintains power. It may seem simple. Laozi's main point seems to be that the ruler does little or nothing and ostensibly rejects, or at least declines to uphold or to act on, any values. Because he is like this, it thus never occurs to the people to do much more than tend the fields and content themselves with simple activities that, given the absence of an elaborate system of values, come naturally to them. The natural way for human beings, the fate given them by the Way, is quite satisfying and peaceful. Contriving to go further than this causes strife, contention, and unhappiness. If the ruler dabbles in such schemes, then the people will mistakenly assume that the ruler's values hold the meaning of life, and they will act on this assumption with disastrous results.

Laozi's argument is valid if: (a) promoting valuational schemes as guides to action does indeed make society stormy

---

[80] The Latin *virtus* means both power and virtue.

and chaotic and people unhappy; (b) the ruler's example can indeed stop the people from desiring to pursue these schemes; and (c) naturalness in one's life is better than fulfilling any of the values of higher civilization. The last is perhaps the purely philosophical point, whereas the former two are partly psychological claims. As you read the text, piece together Laozi's argument and evaluate it at these and other points. The hectic stress of modern life makes primitivism seem attractive at times. But primitive village life is lived without modern medicine, without technological protections from famine, without any scientific knowledge of the world around one, and without literature. Maybe claim (c) is too subjective to be absolutely true or false. On the other hand, maybe it is simply misleading, since claim (a) is not always true. There may be relatively uncontentious and peaceful ways to go about attempting to satisfy a set of values, and there may be a scheme of values that promotes such peacefulness. If Laozi is right, then no non-primitive society in history has been peaceful and happy or as peaceful and happy as primitivist Daoist society would be. But that doesn't seem likely to be true. Confucius would have argued that there is a complex scheme of values which promotes happiness and peace very well: the traditional values of the former Zhou Dynasty.

We will examine a more strident denunciation of valuational schemes when we read the Daoist Zhuangzi. Note that Laozi does uphold the values of peace, tranquil contentment, and long life. But he seems to argue that any other valuational schemes prevent people's fulfilling these. Perhaps the distinction between the former values and the latter is that we can let the former guide human behavior naturally and unreflectively, while it's impossible to let any other values do so. You should consider, however, whether the kind of beings human beings are makes it natural for us to maintain other valuational distinctions, such as knowledge and ignorance, leisure and toil, adventure, and boredom. Also, you should consider whether peace and tranquility should trump other moral considerations, such as liberty, technological

66

progress, and the avoidance of poverty and hunger. It would seem that they should not.

These questions raise a peculiar conundrum in the notion of the Way. It is the source of all things, the sum total of all the ways in which they exist, move, and are formed. Yet, Laozi thinks that one can be with the Way or not with the Way. But how can a person not be with the Way? How can a thing or person go against its natural way of being and acting? It is difficult to say why we should not believe that whatever a thing does is what is natural for it to do. Laozi bemoans the human-caused famine and war that beset China at his time. But why do those behaviors count as unnatural or not with the Way? When you read Zhuangzi, you might consider whether the roots of Zhuangzi's more stridently anti-valuational stance may be found in this conundrum.

Laozi's suspicion of the drawing and naming of distinctions among things seems to be the important part of this puzzle. It seems that the Way is chaos, non-being, the inchoate totality of energy, and the sum total of forms. As such, it is not a thing but the source of all things. Unlike the cosmological creators found in the myths of most cultures, the Way is also the ways in which it is natural for things to exist, move, act, and be formed. The Way did produce the many things, but for a human being to pursue on her own the making and naming of distinctions inevitably leads her to conceal the chaotic, merged, unified basis of things and to begin to act from that cut-off, orphaned, perspective. To think and act independently of the Way is to act against the natural way for one to act, since the natural way is, after all, a fragment of the Way and thus can't be found separately from it. On the other hand, it might seem that something is wrong with Laozi's view that something can be other than the Way. Why is a deliberately and ornately contrived system of values not the Way? Why is advanced civilization to be deemed contrary to nature? Why should we deem careful deliberation before action unnatural?

There are two more points to consider. Exactly what is Laozi's metaphysical thesis about the Way supposed to be and what is supposed to be interesting about it? If it is just the claim that one can look at the universe as a big inchoate blob of energy and potential forms, then that may be trivial. Millions of philosophically sincere people have taken the idea of the Way to be the most profound metaphysics there is. It may be that the close intertwining of the metaphysics with the philosophy of natural, stress-free non-action has led some to mistake a psychological cathartic effect of the metaphysics for a profundity of the metaphysics itself. On the other hand, Laozi's metaphysical thesis may not be so trivial if, as he says, people do often overlook it, have difficulty recognizing it, and base their values on ignoring it.

You will have some work to do in developing an interpretation of the notion of the Way as you read the text. The political philosophy of the text rests on this metaphysical concept in a way that makes it seem that the political philosophy was Laozi's ultimate purpose in developing the metaphysics. Perhaps which is more important is not so philosophically interesting. In any event, you will have to wrestle with both concepts in developing a critical interpretation of either.

The Reading

Here is the complete text. Much of it is rhyming verse but I have translated it into prose. The traditional chapter numbers are given in parentheses. The book until recently was known as *Daodejing* (a.k.a *Tao-te ching*): *The Book of the Way and Power*. I have placed the chapters in the order of the recently unearthed Mawangdui editions of the text,[81] in which

---

[81] These two editions, buried together in 168 B.C.E. and unearthed in 1973, were probably copied in the early 2nd C. B.C.E., centuries before the standard version in which the *Dao* half of the text precedes the *De* half. I have relied on both of these earlier editions of the text as well as the later

the section on power (below given as Section I: "Power") comes first, rather than second, leaving the section on the Way (below given as "Section II: The Way") to come second. Also, what were traditionally chapters 80, 81, 40, and 25 fall in different places in the Mawangdui ordering. Except in a few instances in which the reader will notice that small groups of two or three consecutive chapters seem to belong together, it is not possible at this time to know what is the most authentic ordering of the chapters. Moreover, there is no fact of the matter if the text was gradually patched together over many years as a mostly unordered aggregate. On the other hand, if "Power" was placed first by all or most of the original author(s), then perhaps they considered the political theme of the text to be the most important point of the book and the part about the Way to be less so. Yet, both halves of the text discuss both power and the Way, so there is no clear division between the two topics. These puzzles are not very important, since we can understand and evaluate the philosophy of the book by reading the chapters in any order.

Here I have made use of the standard version and the earlier Mawangdui and Guodian versions. I have provided in the footnotes some of the comments on the text by Wang Bi (226-249), an important Daoist philosopher whose commentary on the text, *Notes on the Daodejing of Laozi*

---

standard editions. Reconstructing the text is an ongoing project for specialists, especially since more documents, the Guodian *Laozi* slips, which date to the 4th C. B.C.E., were unearthed in 1993. Including only a fraction of the full text, these slips were either excerpted from the already extant full text or were precisely what counted at that time as the full text, which would accumulate additions over the next hundred years until what we count as the full text was buried at the Mawangdui site. For a discussion of these and other archeological issues, see the books by Csikszentmihalyi and Ivanhoe, Henricks, and Lau, as well as Baxter's "Situating the Language of the Lao-tzu: The Probable Date of the Tao-te-ching" in the volume by Livia Kohn listed in this chapter's suggested readings.

(*Laozi Daodejing zhu*), is perhaps the best, and certainly the best known, of any.[82]

The Book of Power and the Way (*Dedaojing*)

Section I: Power *(De)*

1(38). The superior power does not exercise power (*Shang de bu de.*)[83] That is why it has power. The inferior power does not lose hold of power. That is why it lacks power. The superior power does not act or have any intention to act. The superior humanity acts but has no intentions in acting. The superior rightness acts and has intentions in acting.[84] The superior ritual acts and does not obtain a response. It rolls back its sleeves and applies force. Therefore, if one loses the Way, then one resorts to power. If one loses power, then one resorts to humanity. If one loses humanity, then one resorts to rightness. If one loses rightness, then one resorts to ritual. But ritual, being loyalty and trust worn thin, is a cause of disorder. Foreknowledge,[85] being the flower of the Way, is a cause of

[82] On the commentaries of Wang and others see Lynn (1999) and Chan (1991).

[83] The first line of #38 is four characters long: *shang* (superior) *de* (power/virtue) *bu* (not) *de* (power/virtue; or homonym *de*: 'obtain'). Hence the line says literally: "The superior power is not powerful," or "The superior power does not obtain" [i.e. go out and obtain things, make use of itself]. Alternative translations: "...does not make a point of its power," "...does not treat itself as powerful," "...is not a 'power',", "... is not an external power."

[84] I use the terms "rightness" and "humanity" to translate yi and ren. "Righteousness" has possible connotations of arrogance or "self-righteousness" which I want to avoid. "Rightness" is also a technical term in Western ethical theory perfectly suited to the task, even if it's a bit awkward. "Humanity" has the sense of benevolence, and kindness here, rather than meaning the human species. "Humaneness" would also have been a suitable translation.

[85] "Foreknowledge" refers to prognostication and perhaps more scientific methods of predicting natural and social events. Here and in 8(45) Laozi

stupidity. On account of this, the great old hermits abided where it was thick, not where it had worn thin, abided in its fruit, not in its flower. Therefore, they rejected the one and chose the other.

2(39). Of those who attained the one in the past, heaven, by attaining the one, was clear; earth, by attaining the one, was tranquil; spirits, by attaining the one, were divine; valleys, by attaining the one, were full; the myriad things, by attaining the one, came alive; marquises and kings, by attaining the one, acted as leaders of the world.[86] In extending this, heaven, if it didn't limit its clarity, would be in danger of tearing asunder; earth, if it didn't limit its tranquility, would be in danger of splitting; spirits, if they didn't limit their divinity, would be in danger of expiring; valleys, if they didn't limit their fullness, would be in danger of being desolate; the myriad things, if they didn't limit their life, would be in danger of being extinguished; marquises and kings, if they didn't limit their governance, would be in danger of falling.

Therefore, one must be honorable and yet take meanness as one's basis. One must be lofty but take lowliness as a foundation. That is why the marquis and kings called themselves "orphan," "friendless", and "destitute."[87] Is this not taking lowliness as a foundation? Is it not? That is why they, in attaining numerous carriages, still lacked carriages.[88] This is why they did not desire to glow like jade but were lowly like a rock.

---

uses "stupidity" in a purely negative sense, whereas elsewhere in the text he praises it as beneficial (28(65) and 64(20)).

[86] Throughout the translation I translate *tianxia* as "world," it's more literal meaning. It also means "country," "state," or the region ruled by the ruler being advised by the text

[87] As it was standard European royalty used the royal "we," ancient Chinese rulers would use "this humble person" (*guaren*) and similar locutions.

[88] "Numerous carriages" refers to the size and the glory of the state.

3(41). When the best scholars hear of the Way, with diligence they can enact it. When average scholars hear of the Way, some of it is retained and some is lost. When inferior scholars hear of the Way, they have a big laugh at it. If they didn't laugh, what they heard wouldn't deserve to be considered the Way. Therefore, as the *Established Sayings*[89] say, "The bright Way seems dark. The advancing Way seems to recede. The flat Way seems uneven."

The superior power seems vulgar. The purest white seems to be defiled. The broadest power seems inadequate. The most established power seems flimsy. What is genuine and true seems to be spoiled. The greatest square has no corners. The greatest vessel takes longest to complete. The greatest note is a faint sound. The greatest image lacks any form. The Way is hidden and has no name. Thus only the Way is good at beginning and good at completing.

4(40). Reversion[90] is the movement of the Way. Weakness is the use of the Way. The things of the world arise from being. Being arises from nothingness.

5(42). The Dao gave birth to the One, the One to the Two, the Two to the Three, and the Three to the myriad things. The myriad things carry the Yin on their backs, hold the Yang in their arms, using the *chong qi* ethers[91] to achieve harmony. What people most hate is to be an orphan, solitary, or unworthy, yet kings and dukes use these terms to refer to themselves. Some things one enhances by diminishing them and one diminishes by enhancing them. Thus, what others teach I teach after long deliberation: "Those who are brutal

---

[89] Whether there is such a work or Laozi simply meant, "As an established saying says,..." is unclear.
[90] "Reversion" (*fan*) captures the notion of a return to a primordial chaotic state in which things were created.
[91] These are the "central/boiling" (*chong*) material energy (*qi*) created by Yin and Yang in intimate combination, and resulting in the creation of human beings.

72

and violent do not meet with a proper death."[92] I will take this as the first principle of education.

6(43). The softest thing in the world rides on the hardest thing in the world. Non-being enters into what has no openings. This is how I know that non-action has benefits. The teaching of no words, the benefit of non-action - few in the world attain these.

7(44). Fame or one's body - which is dearer? One's body or possessions - which is more valuable? To obtain or to lose - which is more harmful? Hence, holding things too dear entails great expense. Hoarding much entails substantial loss. Therefore, knowing what suffices, one will not be disgraced. Knowing when to stop, one won't be in danger and can thereby last longer.

8(45). A great completion is as if it were[93] lacking; its usefulness is not worn out. A great fullness is as if it were empty. Its usefulness is not used up. Great straightness is as if it were bent. A great completion is as if it fell short.[94] Great cleverness is as if it were inept.

Activity overcomes cold. Tranquility overcomes heat. Clarity and stillness make the world stable.

9(46). When the Way is in the world, then able horses are used for manure. When the Way is not in the world, then war horses are raised in the suburbs.[95] Of crimes none is greater than permitting desires. Of faults, none brings more distress

---

[92] A proper death would seem to be a peaceful death in old age.

[93] In this chapter, "as if it were" is a translation of *ruo*, which might also be rendered "seems to be" or "is partly."

[94] This is the line as the Guodian version has it. Later editions seem to suffer from a copyist's mistake, rendering it as "a great eloquence is as though it were a stutter."

[95] Thus farmers are deprived of the horses they need to grow enough food for the population.

than wanting to gain. Of calamities, none is greater than not knowing what is sufficient. Therefore, the sufficiency of knowing what is sufficient is the eternally sufficient.

10(47). One doesn't go outdoors to know the world. One doesn't look through the window to know the Way of heaven. The farther one goes out, the less one knows. For this reason, the sage knows things without going to them, names things without seeing them, and completes things without acting on them.

11(48). Those who work at[96] their studies increase daily. Those who hear the Way decrease daily, decrease and decrease, until the point of non-action. They do not act, but there is nothing left undone. When you are about to control the world, you are always without things to do. If you get to the point where you have things to do, this will not suffice as a means of controlling the world.

12(49). The sage always lacks a mind. He takes the people's minds as his mind. The good he treats as good. The not good he also treats as good, and he obtains goodness. The trustworthy he treats as trustworthy. The untrustworthy he also treats as trustworthy, and he obtains trustworthiness. For a sage to be in the world is for him to unite with it. He mixes his mind with the world. The hundred clans all keep their ears and eyes fixed on this. The sage treats them all as children.

13(50). One comes out into life and enters into death. The companions of life are thirteen.[97] The companions of

---

[96] "Work at" is a translation of *wei* – "act." So, the phrase more literally is "act upon their studies."

[97] The thirteen are perhaps thirteen major body parts (Han Feizi says, "four limbs and nine orifices"). As we see in 41(76), it would seem that those who cling strongly and rigidly to life thereby move themselves towards becoming 'stiffs,' dead bodies, whose 13 body parts are rigid, while those who are soft and weak in their attitudes toward life stay healthier and more supple.

death are thirteen. But people treat life as life. They move and all arrive at the thirteen of the realm of death. Now why is this so? It is because they treat life as life. For I have heard that one who is good at holding on to life, when going over land, does not avoid rhinoceros or tigers. When charging into an army, he does not wear shells or skins. For the rhinoceros there is no place to thrust its horn. For the tiger there is no place to place its claws. For the soldier there is no place to receive his blade. Now why is this so? It is because for him there is no realm of death.

14(51). The Way produces them, power feeds them, substance shapes them, and capacities complete them. This is why the myriad things revere the Way and value power. As for the revering of the Way and the valuing of Power, while no one rewards them with noble status, they are always done naturally. Therefore, the Way produces them. Power feeds them, grows them, raises them, stabilizes them, ripens them, nourishes them, and protects them. It produces them but does not keep them. It acts for their sake but does not make them dependent. It grows them but does not govern them. This is called "Profound Power."

15(52). The world has a beginning. It is considered the mother of the world. Having attained its mother, through her one can know her children. Having known her children, return and hold to the mother. To the end of life one will face no danger.

Shut off the passages and close the doors; even in the latter days of your life you will not labor. Open the holes and meddle in affairs; you will not reach the latter days of your life.

To perceive the small is called "enlightenment." To hold to the soft is called "strength." Using its rays to return to its brightness, one will not lose one's life to peril. This is called following the constant.

16(53). If I had little knowledge, then in making my way along the Great Way I would fear only going astray. The Great Way is very level, but people like the connecting byways. The court is well kept, the fields are very overgrown with weeds, and the granaries are very empty. The clothes are colorful and embroidered, and sharp swords are worn. People completely satiate themselves with food, and wealth and goods are in surplus. This is known as being the *yu* reedpipe for thieves. It is not at all the Way!

17(54). That which is built well will not be pulled down. That which is cradled well will not be abandoned. A line of descendants will not let the sacrifices and prayers be cut off. Cultivate it in the body, and one's power will be genuine. Cultivate it in the family, and one's power will be in surplus. Cultivate it in the village, and one's power will last long. Cultivate it in the state, and one's power will be abundant. Cultivate it in the world, and one's power will be widespread.

Have each person watch himself. Use the family to watch the family. Use the village to watch the village. Use the country to watch the country. Use the world to watch the world. How do I know that the world is so? By this.

18(55). The one who embodies the thickness of power is comparable to a baby. Neither bees, poisonous insects nor snakes will sting him. Neither birds of prey nor fierce beasts will grab him. His bones are weak and his tissues soft, but his hold is firm. He hasn't known the meeting of male and female, but his penis stirs. It is the peak of his vital essence. He wails all day but does not become hoarse. It is the peak of his harmony. This harmony is called "the constant." To know the constant is called "enlightenment." Attempts to enhance life are called "bad omens." For the mind to force the vital energy is called "the strong."[98]

---

[98] Here "strong" is meant in a negative sense, whereas elsewhere in the text "strong/strength" has a positive sense.

When things in their prime get old, this is called "not the Way." Not being with the Way, they come to an early end.

19(56). One who knows it does not speak. One who speaks of it does not know. He shuts off the passages and closes his doors. He suppresses his ardor and resolves his confusion. He softens the light and becomes one with the dust. This is called "profound unity." Therefore, there is no way to become close to him, and there is no way to separate oneself from him. There is no way to benefit him, and there is no way to harm him. There is no way to ennoble him, and there is no way to demean him. That is why he is the noblest thing in the world.

20(57). "One governs the country with correctness. One uses the military with surprise."[99] But one takes the world by avoiding officiousness. How do I know that it is really so? For the more the world is intimidated by taboos, the more the people are poor. If the people keep many sharp tools, the country will be in turmoil. If the people have more knowledge and skills, oddities will be stirred up. If legal matters are stirred up, there will be many robbers. Therefore, the sage's saying says, "I avoid intentions and the people change themselves. I prefer quietude and the people order themselves. I avoid business and the people make themselves rich. I desire not to desire and the people make themselves into the hunk of wood."[100]

21(58). If the government is muddled and addled, the people will be genuine. If the government is meticulously discriminating, the country will be divided. Calamity is something good fortune requires. Good fortune is something that calamity covers. Who knows its limits? It has no correct

---

[99] These first two slogans Laozi probably offers as lesser alternative slogans to the third, the one Laozi endorses. The rest of the chapter seems to denounce these alternatives. So, I have added "[They say,]".

[100] "*Pu*" means uncarved block of wood, crude, simple, unadorned. It recurs in many chapters (20(57), 59(15), 63(19), 72(28), 76(32), 81(37)).

state. The correct returns to deviation. The good returns to weirdness. Man's perplexity has lasted a long time.[101] Therefore, be square but do not cut. Be pointed but do not pierce. Be straight but not inflexible. Shine but do not be bright.

22(59). In regulating human affairs and serving heaven, nothing compares to being sparing. Simply being sparing is a means of early repair.[102] Early repair is called "accumulating layers of power." If one repeatedly accumulates power, then there is nothing it does not overcome. If there is nothing it does not overcome, then no one knows its limits. If no one knows its limits, then one may possess the country. Possessing the mother of the country, one can last long. This is called making deep the roots and securing the trunk. It is the Way of prolonging life and prolonging one's everlasting gaze [of the ruler facing south].[103]

23(60). Governing a large country is like cooking a small fish.[104] If you manage everything in accordance with the Way, spirits will not become ghosts. If it is not the case that spirits do not become ghosts, then the ghosts will not harm people. If it is not the case that the ghosts do not harm people, then the sage still does not harm them.[105] For if the two do not harm each other, then powers are exchanged and returned between them.

---

[101] Wang Bi (hereafter "WB"): "This says that since the people's confusion, perplexity and loss of the Way have lasted a long time, one can't make them responsible through the controls of correctness and goodness."
[102] I.e., a return to the primordial state of naturalness that occurs before ordinary people's return to it.
[103] Sitting facing south was how a ruler would exhibit authority.
[104] WB: "One doesn't stir it." This is correct. When you fry a fish, if you flip it too much it falls apart in the pan.
[105] The text is ambiguous. "Them" either refers to the ghosts or refers to the people.

78

24(61). A large state is the lower reaches of a river. It is the female of the world, the world's place of intercourse. The female invariably defeats the male with stillness. Being tranquil, she should take the lower place. Therefore, a large country takes over a small one by being beneath the small one. But a small country is taken over by a large one by being beneath the large one. Therefore, one takes over by being lower and the other is taken over by being lower. Therefore, the large country wants only to bring together and support others. The small country wants only to introduce its business to others. So, the two get what they desire, but the large country should be the lower.

25(62). The Way is the flow of things. It is the good person's treasure, and it is what protects the person who is not good. Beautiful words may be used in selling, and honorable actions may be attributed to people. Even things that people do not regard as good - which will be rejected? Therefore, when setting in place the son of heaven or installing the three lords, although you might present jade discs before a four horse team, it is not as good as sitting and offering this. What was the reason the ancients value this? Did they not say, 'Seeking, with this one may attain; having committed crimes, with this one will escape'? Therefore, it is the most valuable of things.

26(63). Act without acting. Take care of business without being busy.[106] Regard as flavorful that which has no flavor.

Treat the small as great and the few as many. Reward resentment with virtue.[107] Plan for difficulties when they are easy. Do the great when it is small. All difficulties are easy in the making. All great things are minute in the making. Therefore, the sage never does the great. That is how he can

---

[106] Or, "Take care of matters without anything being the matter (*shi wushi.*)"

[107] Here "virtue" (*de*) probably has the sense of "kindness." I doubt it has the sense of "power" here.

achieve the great. Treating promises lightly makes one's believers few.[108]

Believing easy things to be many makes one have many difficulties. Therefore, even the sage treats them as difficult. That is why he never has any difficulties.

27(64). Stability is easy to maintain. The unforeseen is easy to plan for.[109] The fragile is easy to divide. The minute is easy to scatter. Act on things before they take place. Govern things before they are disorderly. A tree which fills one's embrace was made from a downy tip. A nine-story pavilion was made from bucketsful of earth. A height of one hundred feet begins from underfoot.[110]

Those who act on something ruin it. Those who cling to something lose it. For this reason the sage does not act. Therefore, he does not ruin and does not cling. Therefore, he does not lose anything. People, in going about their business, always ruin things just as they come to completion. Therefore, it is said, "Being as careful at the end as at the beginning, one will not ruin matters."[111] For this reason the sage desires not to desire and does not value goods that are hard to obtain. He learns how not to learn and returns to what everyone passes by. Therefore, while the sage can promote the myriad things' naturalness, he cannot act.[112]

---

[108] This paragraph is not in the Guodian version and is likely a later addition.

[109] See 26(63).

[110] This line from the earliest versions of the text. In later editions it reads, "A journey of a thousand *li* begins with a single step."

[111] These sentence and the one immediately preceding it are probably a later explanatory gloss of later editions. The two sentences in the Guodian read simply, "In approaching the end of matters, be as careful at the end as at the beginning; you won't ruin matters."

[112] This line is as the Guodian version has it. Other editions have "dare not act" instead of "cannot act" and lack "Therefore, the sage." The line is ambiguous. It could mean that the sage promotes the naturalness of things with a non-active action. Or it could mean that he could do so but does not (or dares not.)

28(65). Those who enacted the way in ancient times used it not to enlighten the people but to make them stupid. The difficulty in ruling the people is due to their knowledge. To master the state with knowledge is a robbery of the state. To master the state without knowledge is power for the state. One who always knows these two also knows types and models. Always to know types and models is called "profound power." Profound power is deep and wide-ranging. It reverts back along with things. It achieves a great accord.[113]

29(66). The reason that rivers and seas are the kings of the one hundred valleys is that they are good at being below them. This is why they can be the kings of the one hundred valleys. Therefore, when the sage desires to be above the people, he must subordinate himself to them in his speech. Desiring to go ahead of the people, he must put himself behind them. Thus, he stays above, but the people do not regard it as weighty. He goes ahead, but the people do not take offense. The world enjoys supporting him and does not tire of him. Is it not due to his uncontentiousness that no one in the world can contend with him?

30(80). Make the state small and the people few. Let there be weapons for ten battalions of one hundred men, and do not use them. Let the people take death seriously and keep far off the thought of emigration. If you have boats and chariots, no one will drive them. If you have shields and spears, no one will take them up. Let the people return to tying rope and using it.[114] Sweeten their food, beautify their clothing, make pleasurable their customs, and secure their dwellings. Although the country overlooks a neighboring country, and the sound of each other's chickens and dogs can be overheard, the

[113] Note the apparent contradiction. The text first eschews knowledge and then extols knowledge.
[114] Tying knots was an ancient way of keeping records, here symbolizing a simple and illiterate lifestyle.

people until old age and death will not come and go between the two.

31(81). True words are not beautiful. Beautiful words are not true. Knowers are not erudite. The erudite do not know. The excellent are not excessive. The excessive are not excellent. The sage has no holdings. Having done for others, he possesses even more. Having given to others, he has even more. Therefore, the Way of heaven is to benefit and not to harm. The Way of man is to act without contending.

32(67). Everyone calls me great, great and incomparable. And it is only in being incomparable that I can be great. Were I comparable, I would long have been tiny. So, I always have three treasures which I guard and treasure. The first is care. The second is frugality. The third is not daring to go ahead of everyone else. Since caring, I can be courageous. Since frugal, I can be magnanimous. Since not daring to go ahead of everyone else, I can be a superior of mature capacity. If one leaves out caring and yet is courageous, leaves out restraint and yet is magnanimous, and leaves out going after and yet goes before, then one will die. So, if one is caring in attacking, then one will overcome, or, in defending, then one will endure. Heaven will fortify one, as if enclosing one in care.

33(68). One who is good as a warrior is not militant. One who is good in battle does not become angry. One who is good at overcoming the enemy does not compete with him. One who is good at using people puts himself below them. This is called "the power of uncontentiousness." It is called "using people." It is called "being worthy of heaven." It is the excellence of the ancients.

34(69). Those who use swords have a saying: "Not daring to play the host, I play the guest. Not daring to advance an inch, I retreat a foot." This is called going without going, rolling up sleeves without showing your arms, grasping without a sword, leading on without an enemy. Of calamities, none is greater than thinking nothing of one's enemy.[115] Thinking nothing of the enemy is close to losing my treasure.[116] Therefore, when swords are crossed and sides are even, the one who feels grief has won.

35(70). My words are very easy to understand and very easy to practice. But no one in the world can understand them, and no one can practice them. Words have an ancestor, and deeds have a lord. Only because these are not understood am I not understood. Those who understand them are few, so I value them. That is why the sage wears coarse wool and holds on to jade underneath.

36(71). To know that one does not know is best. Not to know that one does not know is a flaw. That is why the sage's being flawless is due to his regarding this flaw as a flaw. That is why he is flawless.

37(72). The people's not treating the awesome as awesome means that the greatly awesome is about to arrive. Do not oppress their means of living. Only by being unoppressed do they thereby take themselves to be unoppressed. That is why the sage knows himself without making himself seen and loves himself without thinking of himself as valuable. Therefore, discard the one and take the other.

38(73). When one's bravery tends towards daring, one is killed. When one's bravery tends towards not daring, one lives. Of these two, one is beneficial, the other harmful. The things which heaven hates - who knows its reasons? The way

---

[115] "Thinking nothing of one's opponent" could be translated as "not having an opponent." In either case, the idea is that one shouldn't desire total world domination, since it will bring calamities and, as we see in 74(30), one's own early death.

[116] "My treasure" refers to the philosophy presented in this book.

of heaven is not to fight but to be good at winning, not to speak but to be good at replying, not to be called but to come on one's own. The net of heaven is coarse and yet it does not lose anything.

39(74). If the people are unvarying but do not fear death, then what good is it to use execution to intimidate them? If you make it that the people are unvarying and fear death, and you would take the oddballs and execute them, then who would dare? If the people were unvarying and couldn't help but fear death, then there would always have to be an executioner. But to play the executioner and to kill is to take the place of the head carpenter. And of those who take the place of the head carpenter, very few do not injure their hands.

40(75). People's starvation is due to their having to take out too much tax grain. That is why they starve. The unruliness of the masses is due to their superior's having certain purposes for acting. That is why they are unruly. The people's taking death lightly is due to their seeking the richness of life.[117] That is why they take death lightly. Only those who have no purpose for life are more worthy than those who value life.

41(76). The life of man is soft and weak. In his death he ends up hard and strong. The life of myriad things, plants, and trees is soft and fragile. Their death is withering and drying out. Therefore, it is said, "The hard and strong are the companions of death. The soft, weak, fine, and delicate are the companions of life."

---

[117] This line may be translated "...is due to the intensity of their effort to stay alive." But it wouldn't make sense for someone who takes death lightly to be making an intense effort to stay alive, whereas it would make sense for someone who seeks the gusto of life to take some risks to get it. The idea of this and the previous sentence is that the people ape the ruler when he upholds and acts on a scheme of value, particularly values about what counts as the 'gusto' of life. WB: "This says that the reason the people are depraved and the reason the government is chaotic both lie in the ruler, and not in his subordinates. For the people follow the ruler."

For this reason, if a warrior is strong, he will not win. If a tree is strong it will come to an end. Therefore, the strong and the great are inferior, the soft and the weak superior.

42(77). The Way of heaven is like stretching a bow. The high it presses down. The low it lifts up. Those with surplus it injures. Those with deficiency it repairs. Therefore, the Way of heaven is to injure surplus and to repair deficiency. The Way of man is to injure insufficiency and raise up surplus. Now, who can have surplus and have some to take and to offer to heaven? Only the one having the Way. For this reason the sage acts without having, and achieves results without dwelling on it. Thus is his dislike for being seen as worthy.

43(78). Under heaven nothing is as soft and weak as water. But in attacking the hard and strong, nothing can surpass it. It is due to there being nothing that can replace it that water overcomes the hard, that the weak surpasses the strong. Under heaven none do not know this. But none can practice it. Therefore, the *Sayings of the Sages* says, "To accept the shame of the state is called being the Lord of Millet and Earth. To accept the bad fortune of the state is called being the King of Heaven." Right speech seems like its opposite.

44(79). In the pacification of great resentment, there must be some residual resentment. How can this be taken as good? For this reason the sage holds on to the right hand tally, but does not use it to hold people responsible.[118] Therefore, to have power is to manage tallies. To lack power is to manage tithes.[119] In the Way of heaven, there is no favoritism. It is always with the good man.

---

[118] The tally was a record of a debt, the creditor and debtor each keeping one half. Here we see that though the sagely ruler holds his half, he never makes an issue of the debt with the people.

[119] I.e., to collect debts.

Section II: The Way (*Dao*)

45(1). The way that can be spoken of is not the unvarying Way. The name that can be named is not the unvarying name. Nameless, it is that which started the myriad things. Named, it is the mother of the myriad things. Therefore, be unvaryingly devoid of desires so that you perceive its subtlety.[120] One unvaryingly possessed of desires thereby sees only what he pines for.[121] These two[122] were merged when they came out. Of different names, both are called "more profound than the profound" and "the doorways to all subtleties."

46(2). When everyone in the world knows the beautiful as the beautiful, this is ugly. When they all know the good, this is not good. The mutual creation of having and lacking,[123] the mutual establishment of difficult and easy, the mutual formation of long and short, the mutual filling-in of high and low, the mutual harmonizing of notes and singing, and the mutual accompaniment of before and after - these are constants. Therefore, the sage keeps to non-intentional activities and practices the unspoken teaching. In the functioning of the myriad things he is not the initiator. In 'doing for' he does not make dependent. In achieving success

---

[120] WB: "The subtle is the limit of minuteness. The myriad things begin in minuteness and only then are completed. They begin in nothingness and only then are created. Therefore, always be without desires, empty and vacant. That is how to observe the subtlety of the beginning of things."

[121] One can imagine a 'tunnel vision' caused by desires keeping someone from seeing as much as a person who merely observes the surroundings without looking for anything in particular.

[122] I.e., the Way and the mother.

[123] "Having and lacking" translate *you* and *wu*, which also mean "being" and "non-being."

he doesn't dwell on it. And just because he doesn't dwell on it, it never leaves him. [124]

47(3). Not elevating the worthy will make the people uncontentious. Not treating goods that are difficult to obtain as valuable will make the people not become thieves. Not making the desirable visible will keep the people from being disorderly.[125] Therefore, the governance of the sages empties their minds, fills their stomachs, weakens their will, and strengthens their bones, invariably making the people lack knowledge and lack desire. When they did nothing more than to make those with knowledge not dare to act, nothing was not kept in order.

48(4). The Way is empty. But one can use it without refilling it again. An abyss! It is like the ancestor of the myriad things. It blunts their points, unties their knots, softens their light, and becomes the same as their dust. Fathomless! It seems perhaps to exist.[126] But I don't know whose offspring it is. It resembles the forerunner of the Lord.[127]

---

[124] WB: "He acts by making things the cause. Achievements come from them. If he made the achievements lie in himself, then the achievements could not last long."

[125] Confucians and Mohists advocated elevating the worthy. WB: "If only those of ability are appointed, why elevate them? If only the useful are given rank, what is the point of honoring them? If you would elevate the worthy, show off their names, and reward them beyond what their appointment makes due, then when you do this, people will always complete and even shoot at each other."

[126] Compare *Rig Veda* creation myths. The creator of all things cannot be a thing unless it created itself, a paradoxical option considered by the *Rig Veda* but not by *The Book of Power and the Way*.

[127] The Lord was the Yellow Emperor (*Huangdi*), the legendary ancestor of all people.

49(5). Heaven and earth are not humane.[128] They take the myriad things to be straw dogs.[129] The sage is not humane. He takes the hundred surnames[130] to be straw dogs. The space between heaven and earth - is it not like a bellows? It is empty, but you can't use it up.[131] Move it and more comes out. To hear much and be often exhausted is not as good as holding on to the center.

50(6). The spirit of valleys does not die. It is called the mysterious female. The gate of the mysterious female is called the root of heaven and earth. It barely persists. It seems to exist.[132] Use it and it is not exhausted.

51(7). Heaven is everlasting, earth eternal. The means by which heaven and earth can be everlasting and eternal is that they don't keep life for themselves. That is why they can live long. Therefore, the sage withdraws himself and is first. He puts himself out of the picture and is preserved. Is it not due to his lacking self-interest that he can fulfill self-interest?

52(8). The highest good is like water. Water is good at benefiting the myriad things and does not contend with them. It stays in places that everyone loathes. That is why it

---

[128] This is a rejection of Confucian ideas. WB: "Heaven and earth are natural. They don't act and don't construct, leaving the myriad things to regulate and to order themselves. Thus, they are not humane. The humane must construct and establish, actively changing things. They have compassion, and they act. When they construct, establish and actively change things, things lose their genuineness...and are not sufficient to stand up on their own."

[129] Straw dogs were used in an ancient ritual in which they were trampled to pieces and discarded.

[130] The "hundred surnames" means, roughly, the people of China.

[131] The idea is that the innumerable things and events apparently emerge from the thin air between the sky and the ground.

[132] WB: "If you say that it exists, well, we don't see its form. If you would say it is nothing, well, the myriad things were created by it."

approximates the Way.[133] A dwelling is good for its site. A mind is good for its depth. In giving, it is good to be like heaven. In speech, it is good to be truthful. In governing, order is good. In affairs, ability is good. In action timeliness is good. It is only because one does not contend that one will be without faults.

53(9). When it is upright and you fill it, this is not as good as stopping early.[134] When a current flows against it,[135] you can't preserve it for long. When gold and jade fill the room, none can protect them. If you are arrogant in your nobility and wealth, you yourself will bring on calamity. To withdraw upon achieving the goal - this is the way of heaven.[136]

54(10). In carrying your luminous bodily soul[137] and embracing the one, can you never leave them? In concentrating your *qi* until it is supple, can you be an infant? In refining and cleaning the profound mirror, can you make it have no marks? In loving the people and governing the state, can you be without knowledge? When the gate of heaven opens and closes, can you play the female?[138] When things in all four quarters are clear to you, can you be without knowledge? Give

---

[133] WB: "The Way does not exist, while water exists." [Hence, as a symbol, it only approximates the Way.]

[134] This is alluding to a royal vessel of Zhou times which tipped over when overfilled. Some versions of the text seem to say, "If you let it accumulate until full..." without speaking of "upright." Upright has additional connotations however, namely moral uprightness.

[135] The idea is of something that sticks up, such that a current flows against it. This phrase in later editions reads, "If you pound it to a point...," probably due to a copyist's mistake. See Henricks (2000), p. 79 – 80.

[136] WB: "The four seasons go on, one after the other. When their achievements are complete, they yield." Heaven here also includes the concept of nature.

[137] The *po* soul, as opposed to the *hun* (spiritual soul).

[138] The gate is that from which all things emerged in their creation into which they will return to chaos. Playing the female means passively causing everything else to act, so that, as WB says: "They will submit to you on their own."

birth to them, nourish them. Give birth but do not own. Grow them, but do not rule them. This is called "profound power."

55(11). Thirty spokes in the same hub. Precisely in its emptiness does the usefulness of the wheel exist. Clay is fired to make a pot. Precisely in its emptiness does the usefulness of the clay pot exist. Doors and windows are carved out. Precisely in its emptiness does the usefulness of a room exist. Therefore, while having something real is a benefit, being empty should be considered useful.

56(12). The five colors make a person's eyes go blind. Horse racing and hunting make a person's mind go mad. Goods that are hard to obtain make a person's stride obstructed. The five flavors make a person's mouth dull. The five tones make a person's ears go deaf. Therefore, the government of the sage is for the stomach, not for the eye. Thus, one should leave off the other and keep this.

57(13). Favor I treat as disgrace, as though it were a trap.[139] Honor I treat as greatly troubling, as though my life were at stake.
What does "Favor I treat as disgrace, as though it were a trap" mean? Favor makes one inferior.[140] When one obtains it, it's like being ensnared. When one loses it, it's like being ensnared. This is what "Favor I treat as disgrace, as though it were a snare" means.
What does "Honor I treat as greatly troubling, as though my life were at stake" mean? The reason I would have great troubles is that I have a life. If I didn't have a life, what troubles would I have? That is why to one who places more

---

[139] The Guodian version of the text has "snare" or "trap" here instead of the "alarm" which the other versions have ("...I treat with alarm.") The idea of the passage is that favor and disgrace put one in the control of the one bestowing them.
[140] When you are favored, there are always demands and expectations of your subsequent behavior.

importance on acting for the sake of his own life than on acting for the sake of the world you can entrust the world. To one who is exceedingly careful in employing himself for the sake of the world you can consign the world.[141]

58(14). One looks for it but doesn't see it. It is named "the fine." One listens for it but doesn't hear it. It is named "the faint." One feels for it but doesn't touch it. It is named "the even." The three cannot be completely fathomed. Therefore, they mix and are one. The One - above it is not constrained in largeness, and below its smallness is not limited even to a tiny fraction. On and on! It cannot be named. It returns again to nothingness. This is called "the form of formlessness" and "the image of nothingness." It is called "ethereal and indistinct." Follow it, and you don't see its back. Await it, and you don't see its head. Hold to the Way of the present to manage what exists in the present and to know the ancient beginning. This is called "the thread of the Way."

59(15). The one who was good at acting with the Way in ancient times was fine, sublime, profound and keen. His depth could not be known, and it is just because it could not be known that, were I forced to describe him, I would say, "Hesitant! As though crossing a river in winter. Undecided! As though in fear of all four neighbors. Serious! Like a guest. Crumbling! Like ice melting. Amorphous! Like a hunk of wood. Undifferentiated! Like murk. Vacant! Like a valley." It is murky, but, staying still, it gradually becomes clear. Let it be at peace, so that it can be moved, and it gradually comes to life.

---

[141] This passage might be perplexing at first. The idea is that the desire for power, glory, and wealth lead a ruler to take risks which often result in catastrophe for his own life and for the people he rules. You might say that an even better ruler would be one who values the welfare of the world more than his own life. However, this would be diametrically opposed to the vision of the text, according to which the kingdom needs to be left to its natural state rather than cared for by a busybody who worries about it.

The one who protects this Way doesn't desire to be full. That is why he can wear out yet not need to be renewed.

60(16). Utmost emptiness is the ultimate. Holding to stillness is the heart of it. The myriad things work together, and I thus observe their return.[142] The multitude of things return again to their root. This is "stillness." Stillness is called "to repair to one's fate." To repair to one's fate is to be constant.[143] To know the constant is enlightenment. Not to know the constant is to be frenetic and to be frenetic causes terrible things. To know the constant is to be encompassing. If you are encompassing, then you will be impartial. If impartial, you will be kingly. If kingly, you will be heavenly.[144] If heavenly, you will be with the Way. If you are with the Way, then for all your life you will face no danger.

61(17). As for a great ruler, those below know he exists. To the one next to that they give affection and praise. The one next to that they fear. Those below that they ridicule. With insufficient trust, there will be mistrust. Hesitant! And sparing with words. He finishes tasks and completes affairs, while the hundred clans say, "It was natural for us."

62(18). Therefore, when the great Way is neglected, there will be humanity and rightness.[145] When knowledge and wisdom turn up, there will be great fakery. When the six relations[146] are not in harmony, there will be filiality and

---

[142] "Return" refers to the return of all things to their natural state and/or to original chaos.
[143] WB: "When one repairs to fate, one reaches the constant of nature and fate. Hence, it says 'constant.'"
[144] "Heaven" also refers to nature.
[145] I.e., people will construct schemes of value. WB: "This means that the Way is reified."
[146] I.e., parent-child, elder-younger, husband-wife.

compassion. When the nation is in disorder and chaos, there will be upright ministers.[147]

63(19). "Be rid of sageliness and do away with knowledge, and the people will benefit one hundred-fold. Be rid of humanity and do away with rightness, and the people will return to filiality and compassion. Be rid of skillfulness and do away with profit, and no thieves or robbers will exist."[148] These three sayings, as a text, do not suffice. So, I make it so that they have something to which they connect: Make plainness visible, and embrace the 'hunk of wood.' Lessen self-interest and make desires meager. Be rid of learning, and there will be no anxiety.[149]

64(20). "Yes!" and "No!" - what is the difference between them? Beautiful and ugly - how do we tell the difference between them? One whom people fear cannot but fear them. Recklessness! It never ends.

Everyone is full of joy, as though they were going onto a terrace in Springtime or holding a *tailao* sacrifice.[150] In the face of all this, I am weary and seem to have no place to return. Everyone has plenty. I alone have a lack. I have the mind of an idiot. Stupid! Ordinary people are discriminating. I alone am

---

[147] In this chapter, some of the cultural values Laozi elsewhere eschews as the causes of social ills are here merely symptoms of them. One might argue that he didn't have a clear etiology in mind and that he therefore didn't understand that there will always be social ills which require moral principles and upright ministers. In other words, Laozi's faith in a natural Way was misplaced, and civilization, moral values, law and order need to be purposefully maintained and preserved in order for a society to fare well.
[148] The Guodian edition of the text speaks of getting rid of knowledge and definitions, instead of sageliness and knowledge. It also speaks of getting rid of educational transformation of the people and deliberations, instead of humanity and rightness. So, one might speculate that the Guodian version wasn't intended to be such a sharp attack on Confucian, or more specifically Mencian, moral ideas (humanity and rightness.)
[149] The Guodian version has this sentence at the beginning of 64(20).
[150] A particularly luxuriant sacrifice in which animals of three kinds were consumed.

in a muddle! Inchoate! Like an ocean. Amorphous! As though restless. Everyone has a reason. I am the only one who is doltish and vulgar. My desires alone differ from others'. I value feeding at the mother.

65(21). The content of the power of hollowness simply derives from the Way. The Way, as a thing, is amorphous and inchoate. Inchoate! Amorphous! Inside there are images! Amorphous! Inchoate! Inside there are things. Obscure! Inside is the vital essence! This vital essence is very real. In it there is genuineness. From the present to the past, its name has never gone away. With it we follow the father of all. How do I know all this about the father of all? By this.

66(24). One who blows his own horn doesn't get established. One who shows off goes unnoticed. One who makes himself seen is not clearly apparent. One who brags about himself goes without merits. One who boasts does not endure. From the point of view of the Way, these are "overeating and excess action." Some things are to be despised. That is why the one who has the Way doesn't abide in them.

67(22). If bent, whole. If crooked, correct. If hollow, full. If worn out, new. If of few, then obtaining. If of many, then deluded. Therefore, the sage holds to the One and in that way is the shepherd of the world. He doesn't show himself off and is therefore manifest. He doesn't make himself seen and therefore is clearly apparent. He doesn't brag about himself and therefore has merit. He doesn't boast and can therefore endure. It is only because he does not contend that no one can be his match. This "if bent, whole" that was said of old - what words! Genuine wholeness returns with them.

68(23). To be of few words is to be natural. A whirling wind won't last all morning. A burst of rain won't last all day. Who made these? Heaven and earth, but they cannot last. Isn't this true when it comes to man? Therefore, one who makes the Way his concern is the same as the Way. One who makes it power is the same as power. One who makes it loss is the same as the loss. The one who is the same as power the Way also finds (makes powerful).[151] The one who is the same as loss the Way also makes lost.

69(25). There is something made in chaos, created before heaven and earth. Quiet! Profound! It stands alone and does not change. It can act as the mother of heaven and earth. I don't know its name. I write, "Way."[152] If I had to give it a name, I would say "The Great." "The Great" means "receding." "Receding" means "distant." "Distant" means "returning." The Way is great.

Heaven is great. Earth is great. The king is also great. The country has four great things, and the king is one of them. People take the earth as a model. The earth follows the pattern of heaven. Heaven follows the pattern of the Way. And the Way takes naturalness as a model.

70(26). The heavy is the root of the light. The quiescent is the ruler of the mettlesome. Therefore, the superior man travels all day without getting separated from his baggage. Only when there is a place to rest in a walled-in lodge does he let things go. How can a king of ten thousand chariots treat himself more lightly than he treats the world? If he treats himself lightly, he loses the basis.[153] If mettlesome, he loses his rule.

[151] A play on words. "*De*" means "power" and another Chinese character which is also pronounced "de" which means "attain," "obtain" ("find"). The author means both.
[152] WB: "Names are used to determine forms. The word 'Way' is picked when there is nothing that one does not refer to. It is, among the vague and complete, the broadest of labels that can be uttered."
[153] Since the king is the basis of the country, for the sake of the country he must have utmost concern for his own safety and health.

71(27). A good traveler leaves no tracks. A good speaker has no flaws. A good counter doesn't use calculating tools. A good closer uses no locks, but the door can't be opened. A good tier has no ropes or cords, but the knots can't be untied. Therefore, the sage is always good at saving people and never rejects people. Among things he doesn't reject the valuable. This is called "higher enlightenment." That is why the good person is a teacher of good people. The person who is not good serves as the material for the good person. If one did not honor one's teacher and did not hold one's material dear, then, though knowledgeable, one would go far astray. This is called "sublime essentials."

72(28). Know the male, but hold to the female. Be the valley of the world. If you are the valley of the world, then consistent power will not leave you. When consistent power does not leave you, you will return to infancy. Know the clean, but hold to the disgraced. Be the valley of the world. When you are the valley of the world, consistent power will be in sufficient supply. When consistent power is in sufficient supply, you will return to the hunk of wood. Know the white, but hold to the black. Be the model of the world. When you are the model of the world, your consistent power will not falter. When consistent power does not falter, you will return to the limitless.

When a hunk of wood is split, it is made into tools. When the sage is used, he is made into a head official. But greatness in the making of divisions occurs without carving.

73(29). If you would like to take the world and you take action on it, I can see that you simply won't succeed. The world is a divine utensil,[154] and one cannot take action on it. The actor ruins it. The grasper loses it. Of things some go forth and some follow. Some are hot and some blow cold. Some are strong and some are frail. Some grow and some fall down. That

---

[154] It is the formless Way.

is why the sage gets rid of the extreme, the great, and the extravagant.

74(30). Those who assist the ruler of people mustn't use the military to strengthen themselves. Their deeds would certainly have repercussions. Thorny brambles would grow where their troops stayed.[155] The good ones will achieve the result and no more. They won't seize strength from it. They achieve the result and are not arrogant. They achieve the result and do not boast. They achieve the result and do not brag. They achieve the result, and, since there is nothing they can do about it, they stay where they are. This is called "achieving the result without strengthening oneself."

When things in their prime get old, this is called "not the Way." Not being with the Way, they come to an early end.

75(31). As for the military, it is an instrument of bad omen. Some things hate it.[156] Hence, one who has the Way does not stay around it. When the superior man is at home, he honors the left, but in using the military, he honors the right.[157] Hence, the military is not the instrument of the superior man. The military is an instrument of bad omen. If there is nothing one can do about it and must use it, it is best to be calm and not to think of it as beautiful. To think of it as beautiful is to enjoy the killing of people. And if you enjoy killing people, you cannot fulfill your will in the empire. Therefore, on joyous occasions, one holds up the left. And on occasions of mourning, one holds up the right. That is why the lieutenant stays on the left, while the general stays on the right. This is to say that they stand as they do at a funeral.

---

[155] The Guodian *Laozi* slips do not have this sentence. Perhaps it was a later addition.

[156] The idea seems to be that natural world finds the military repulsive. See 74(30).

[157] The left is a symbol of heaven, yang, and light, while the right is a symbol of earth, yin, and darkness.

76(32). The Way is unvaryingly nameless. It is the hunk of wood and, though it is small, the world does not dare treat it as a functionary. If marquises and kings could hold to it, the myriad things would submit to them. Heaven and earth would come together to let sweet dew fall. No one would order this, but it would spread itself equally. When we begin to make divisions, there are names. When names are there, then one must also know when to stop. Knowing when to stop is how one avoids danger. The Way's place in the world is like a small river valley's relationship to rivers and seas.

77(33). To know about people is to be knowledgeable. Self-knowledge is enlightenment. To conquer others is coerciveness. To conquer oneself is strength. To know what suffices is wealth. To forge ahead is to have will. Not to lose one's place is to last long. To die without being forgotten is long life.

78(34). The Way floats along. It can go left or right. It completes its tasks and takes care of affairs without having a name. The myriad things belong there, but it doesn't act as master. Thus it is invariably without desire. It can be named along with the small. The myriad things belong there, but it doesn't act as master. It can be named along with the great. Therefore, the sage's ability to accomplish the great is due to his not acting the great. That is why he can accomplish the great.

79(35). Hold fast to the great image, and the world will come to you. Coming to you, it will be unharmed, safe, and peaceful. For music and food passing travelers stop. But the Way, put into words, is "Bland!" It has no flavor. Look for it, but there is not enough of it to see. Listen for it, but there is not enough of it to hear. Use it, and you cannot get through it all.

80(36). If you would like to shrink it, you must stretch it out. If you would like to weaken it, you must strengthen it. If you would like to get rid of it, you must stay with it. If you would like to take away from it, you must give to it.[158] This is called "the faint brightness." The soft and weak overcome the hard and strong. Fish should not be taken from the depths. The state's sharp weapons should not be shown to people.

81(37). The Way unvaryingly takes no action.[159] If marquises and kings could hold to it, the myriad things would transform themselves. If, in their transformation, desires come about, suppress them with the nameless hunk of wood. You also must know what suffices. Know it, so that you can be tranquil. The world will stabilize itself.[160]

Suggested Readings

Bai, Tongdong, "How to Rule without Taking Unnatural Actions: A Comparative Study of the Political Philosophy of the Laozi," *Philosophy East & West* 59(2009): 481-502

Bruya, Brian, "Action without Agency and Natural Human Action: Resolving a Double Paradox," in Brian Bruya,

---

[158] Any extreme is unstable and makes the thing which reaches it collapse into the opposite. For example, let a state have land and weapons and it will succumb to inner turmoil and get smaller and weaker.

[159] This is the line in the Guodian edition. Later editions have "The Way is unvaryingly nameless" instead.

[160] These sentences are as the Guodian version as them. Later editions say, "If, in their transformation, desires came about, I would suppress them with the nameless hunk of wood. While suppressing them with the nameless hunk of wood, I would not disgrace them. By not disgracing them, I would quiet them. And the world would correct itself."

ed., *The Philosophical Challenge* from China (Cambridge: MIT Press, 2015)

Chan, Alan K., *Two Visions of the Way: A Study of the Wang Pi and the Ho-Shang Kung Commentaries on the Lao-Tzu* (Abany: State University of New York Press, 1991)

Chan, Alan K., "Wang Bi and the Laozi," *Journal of Chinese Religions* 31(2003): 127–149

Chan, Alan K., "Interpretations of Virtue (De) in Early China," *Journal of Chinese Philosophy* 38(2011): 158–174

Coutinho, Steve, *An Introduction to Daoist Philosophies* (New York: Columbia University Press, 2013)

Coutinho, Steve, "The Abduction of Vagueness: Interpreting the Laozi," *Philosophy East & West* 52(2002): 409-425

Csikszentmihalyi, Mark and Philip J. Ivanhoe, eds., *Religious and Philosophical Aspects of the Laozi* (Abany: State University of New York Press, 1999)

Dorter, Kenneth, "Indeterminacy and Moral Action in Laozi," *Dao: A Journal of Comparative Philosophy* 13(2014): 63-81

Feldt, Alex, "Governing Through the Dao: A Non-Anarchistic Interpretation of the Laozi," *Dao: A Journal of Comparative Philosophy* 9(2010): 323-337

Giles, James, "The Metaphysics of Awareness in the Philosophy of Laozi," *International Philosophical Quarterly* 53(2013): 435-451

Henricks, Robert G., trans., *Lao-Tzu Te-Tao Ching: A New Tranlation Based on the Recently Discovered Ma-Wang-Tui Texts* (New York: Balantine Books, 1989)

Henricks, Robert G., *Lao Tzu's Tao Te Ching: A Translation of the Startling New Documents Found at Guodian* (New York: Columbia University Press, 2000)

Hongkyung, K. I. M., "The Original Compilation of the Laozi: A Contending Theory on its Qin Origin," *Journal of Chinese Philosophy* 34(2007): 613–630

Kohn, Livia, ed., *Lao-Tzu and the Tao-Te-Ching* (Abany: State University of New York Press, 1991)

Lau, D. C., *Tao Te Ching* (London: Penguin 1964)

Lynn, Richard John, trans., *The Classic of the Way and Virtue: A New Translation of the Tao-te Ching of Laozi as Interpreted by Wang Bi* (New York: Columbia University Press, 2004)

Shankman, Steven, "*The Daodejing of Laozi* – Philip J. Ivanhoe; *Dao De Jing: The Book of the Way* – Moss Roberts," *Journal of Chinese Philosophy* 33(2006): 303–308

Slingerland, Edward, *Effortless Action: Wu-wei As Conceptual Metaphor and Spiritual Ideal in Early China* (New York: Oxford University Press, 2007)

Slingerland, Edward, *Trying Not to Try: Ancient China, Modern Science, and the Power of Spontaneity* (New York: Broadway Books, 2015)

Wang, Qingjie, "Heng Dao and Appropriation of Nature - A Hermeneutical Interpretation of Laozi," *Asian Philosophy* 10(2000): 149-163

Wong, Kwok Kui, "Hegel's Criticism of Laozi and its Implications," *Philosophy East & West* 61(2011): 56-79

3

Mozi

You are about to do what few people in human history have done: to take a close look at the *Mozi*. This book, which contains the earliest known argumentative essays in Chinese history and some of the earliest examples of philosophical logic in human history, has so often been ignored that we are lucky that it was not lost one thousand years ago. Study of the book is so young that it is still unsettled how good the moral philosophy it puts forth is. We will take a look at the moral philosophy in this chapter. We will not examine the logic, since even getting a handle on the meaning of the text's chapters on logic is an enormous task which would take us far afield.[161]

Mozi[162] was a philosopher of the mid-Fifth Century B.C.E., probably living just after Confucius and perhaps hailing from the artisan class as a carpenter or wheelwright. The school of Mohism, both a physical school and a school of thought, lasted for about three centuries, splitting into perhaps a dozen sub-schools which gradually added more essays to what would become the *Mozi*. The essays are a record of provocative ideas, in addition to chapters on logic, epistemology, military science, and other topics. These chapters or "books" of the *Mozi* include quotations of Mozi himself, along with writings by members of Mozi's school. For convenience, I will refer to the plurality of authors, including Mozi and his followers, simply as "Mozi."

---

[161] See the books by Hansen and Graham in the suggested readings listed at the end of this chapter. I have also left the *Gongsun Long*, another instance of analytical philosophy of Ancient China, out of this reader. You may want to investigate that text, as well.
[162] Mo Di was his name, hence "Mozi": Master Mo.

What sort of philosopher was Mozi? He was a critic of what he regarded as the poor governance, hypocrisy, and foolish morals of his time. He intended to use philosophical arguments to persuade members of government to improve their governance. He lamented the poor quality of the governance of his times – the war, corruption, and neglect of the needs of the people of the various states. Like Confucius, he put forward the exemplary kings of the earlier Zhou Dynasty in order to illustrate good governance. Like Confucius, Mozi lamented the plight of people suffering under the callousness and ineptness of poor rulers. But there are differences between the two thinkers. In the case of Mozi, we have extended argumentative essays, whereas in the *Analects* we have only pithy summary recommendations for moral and governmental improvement. Some might portray Mozi as something like a populist in the sense of one proclaiming that he is the champion of the interests of the masses in the political sphere. He might also be taken to be a religious fundamentalist, and one might think of him as the first thinker to articulate and uphold something like utilitarianism or at least consequentialism[163] in recorded human history. None of these

---

[163] Utilitarianism is a form of consequentialism, the position that it is the consequences of various actions and policies that determine which action or policy is the right one to choose. Utilitarianism holds that the particular consequence that ought to be maximized is the utility, in other words the production of welfare or happiness. Other forms of consequentialism might recommend that some other factor be maximized by our actions. Perhaps Mozi's conception of welfare is broad enough that he might count as a form of consequentialist but not of the utilitarian sort. Nevertheless, I will call Mozi a utilitarian in what follows.

In general what sort of thing are we doing when we consider whether we ought to embrace utilitarianism? Philosophers have at times decided that people need a normative theory – a theory telling us how to determine right and wrong. Perhaps they have decided this in order to prove that there is a decision-making procedure that is better than whatever way people do use to determine right and wrong. Perhaps they wanted to explain that procedure theoretically and prescribe its use only for difficult cases in which the ordinary ways of deliberation fail determine what is right. In any event, one normative theory philosophers have proposed is

descriptions holds of Confucius. But as descriptions of Mozi, they might be a bit overdrawn. And since Confucius and Laozi were also reform-minded critics of their times with deep

---

consequentialism. Whereas consequentialism stipulates that the right action in any case is the one which has the best consequences, it leaves "best" to be determined by some other theory. If the "best consequences" means the greatest good for the greatest number of people, then this is a utilitarian species of consequentialism.

This theory somewhat plausible. One might be tempted even to say that it is but a truism, a self-evident truth, that one should not act in a manner that has suboptimal consequences. But that would only begs the question. And there are alternative theories which have their own merits. For instance, one might put forth the theory that we ought to cultivate the moral virtues in ourselves, and that the heuristics "do what a virtuous person would" and "in danger, have courage" and the like are enough guidance in moral decision making. And it might turn out that virtuous characters do not take the maximization of utility to be the only consideration in deciding the right course of action. You can place Aristotle and Confucius in this category: those who would say that an analysis of the virtues offers the best normative theory. Alternatively, one might opt for a theory which upholds natural rights as a guide to action. After, all if in certain cases violating rights by, for example, causing severe and undeserved pain and unhappiness to an innocent person, would bring about the happiest consequence for the greatest number of people, then those cases would seem to be devastating refutations of consequentialism. They would count in favor of having a high regard for rights, instead. Moreover, why shouldn't we count adherence to the virtues and respect for rights as components of "the greatest good for the greatest number"? Rights and virtues appear to be important goods. If that is true, then consequentialism is tautologically vacuous, telling us that the right and virtuous thing to do is what results in the most rightness and virtue. So, it isn't clear what sort of guidance consequentialism or utilitarianism gives us which other theories do not. Indeed, anyone can agree that we should take the consequences of possible courses of action into account in deciding what is right. But there appears to be no reason why that is all we should take into account, as consequentialism would have us do. And all that aside, do we really need a normative theory? Is there something wrong with the ordinary moral reasoning people do who do not have a philosophical theory of ethics in tow? Is there a rarified knowledge which philosophers have which should warrant their replacing our ordinary ways of determining what is right with their engineered decision procedures? How would we tell that their decision procedures got the right answer more reliably than our ordinary ways?

religious convictions, one mustn't draw the contrast too sharply between Mozi and other philosophers. It is not yet clear what to make of Mohist moral philosophy. While I don't wish to belabor the point, keep in mind that every other text you read in this book has been scrutinized by, at the very least, thousands of people over the course of the last two millennia. The *Mozi* has not.

Let's consider some concepts that you might find useful in interpreting and criticizing Mozi. Some of them might be useful in that you may apply them to Mohist philosophy. Others might be useful in that you may decide that, contrary to appearances, they should not be applied to it.

Some Concepts You Might
Use in Interpreting Mozi

Mozi's position might be viewed as a sort of religious fundamentalism espousing a radical answer to Confucian traditionalistic conservatism. Mozi wanted to return China to the ancients' obedience to God or heaven, an obedience which he thought was not festooned by the rituals and musical forms which he thought to be too prevalent in his time and which were recommended by Confucians. Mozi's religious stance is relevant to his philosophy. It is integral to his basic philosophical position, which includes something close to a divine command theory, the sort of theory that holds that God's will that people act in accordance with certain moral principles is at least part of what makes those principles the true moral principles.[164] This prominence of religious

---

[164] In other words, what makes an action right is that God commands it, and it is not the case that God commands it because it is right. This is a difficult position to maintain because it entails that whatever God commands is right, including actions which no one can reasonably count as right (such as torturing innocents for fun, for example.) A weaker position in this neck of the theoretical woods is the view that the best guidance we have for discovering what is right is to ask ourselves what God intends. We don't have to assume that it is God's intent that makes right actions right when we accept this view. We need only hold that his will is a marker of

fundamentalism might make Mohist moral philosophy stand apart as somewhat radical. In addition, if Mozi's moral principles hold that one should take only the utility of actions into account and no other traditional moral consideration, then his view is radically anti-conventional and anti-traditionalist and thus of a piece with his anti-conventional religion. In other words, his moral principles suited his religious aspiration to strip away several centuries of traditional religious practice and return to an austere and unembellished way of religion. (In this it would be similar to Laozi's position.)

Mozi might be viewed as a radical egalitarian.[165] He seems to have held that privilege, wealth, socio-economic class differences, and the upper class's inefficient use of money were wrong, while the right principles were the ones that would replace such selfishness with all-encompassing thinking. On this view, social institutions should benefit all the people as much as possible, and those institutions that didn't do that should simply be forsaken. "Forsaken" is a strong word, but it fits the case. Cherished traditions are scorned by the radical egalitarian whenever they seem to be beneficial only to an elite group and to be replaceable by institutions that would

---

what is right. For, being perfectly good, He is a perfectly reliable indicator of what is good. Nevertheless, this position struggles with a grave difficulty, namely how it is we are to discover God's will. As you will see Mozi endeavors to show us how. For more on this, see the article by Yong Li in this chapter's list of suggested readings and read Plato's *Euthyphro*. It may be the Mozi's theory isn't really a divine command theory in that he thinks we ought to look to heaven only as a reliable indicator and exemplar of what is right. You can decide this as you read this chapter's readings and if you use its list of suggested readings.

[165] Egalitarianism is the position that political policies and moral judgment should take everyone's interests equally into account and spread the goods of society equally among them. Another concept, that all people are equal under the moral and political law, is quite different. For an exploration of egalitarianism, see John Kekes, *The Illusions of Egalitarianism* (Ithaca: Cornell University Press, 2007). Radicalism is the view that one's society's moral values must be all or mostly swept away and replaced by a different moral system.

redistribute that surplus benefit evenly across society. More generally, it is quintessentially radical to maintain that any societal institution which does not promote the singular principle of one's ideology should be destroyed. Mozi's utilitarianism would thus be one example of such radicalism.[166]

On the other hand, assigning these positions to Mozi may simply be incorrect. A different reading of him would be that he was a moderate reformer, calling for reduction in wasteful ceremony, the elimination of devastating and unprovoked military attacks, and greater consideration by selfish rulers of the interests of the ruled. Context is important. Mozi was criticizing selfish, wantonly bellicose, and wasteful political regimes and calling them to reform themselves and show more consideration of others. This doesn't make him a radical, an egalitarian, or a utilitarian. Moreover, the fact that Mozi argued strenuously that consequences of policies and actions are extremely important does not make him a consequentialist. Any moral position can take consequences into account. Consequentialism is the view that *only* the consequences count in evaluating the moral status of an action. Does Mozi ever espouse such a strong view in the texts? It isn't obvious that he does.

Some Concepts You Might Use in Criticizing Mozi

As we read and interpret the text, we would like to make sense of it, interpret its positions correctly, and also evaluate its arguments critically. This entails not distorting, strengthening, or exaggerating the position only to refute it afterwards – in other words, not committing the straw-man fallacy. Of course, you have to interpret Mozi's position

---

[166] Not all utilitarian opposition to tradition is genuinely radical. John Stuart Mill's opposition to the oppression of women, for example, was consistent with the core values of the Western tradition. Radicalism opposes this very core and wishes to destroy it and replace it with different values.

correctly before criticizing it, but the following criticisms lie on the horizon, awaiting the possible interpretations of the text and you might want to take them into account. These are criticisms that construe Mozi's view strongly as radical and utilitarian. Can they be successfully rebutted by developing an interpretation of Mozi's view according to which it is weaker than radical utilitarianism or religious fundamentalism? Notice the sense of "strong" and "weak" here. In this context, they mean "more interesting" (and more controversial) and "less interesting" (and less controversial.) An extremely weak claim is one which, if true, would be trivially true. In philosophy, the objective is to develop positions which are warranted and true while also interesting. This is a difficult objective to fulfill. In its two-and-a-half millennia history, philosophy has produced very little in the way of results that are both well-grounded and interesting. Has Mozi produced any such results?

As you read what might count as utilitarianism or consequentialist passages of the *Mozi*, scrutinize the arguments carefully. Notice that Mozi portrays the utilitarian principle that actions and policies ought to maximize the welfare or happiness of the society as identical with the idea of all-encompassingness. This is similar to a move made by utilitarians in modern times in which the utilitarian defines the principle of utility as the very essence of impartiality itself; this would thus pre-emptively refute any counterargument. However, many non-utilitarian systems of value accept that people may look after their own welfare rather than targeting the welfare of society in their actions. These systems of value argue that people have special ties to certain others, such as their families and themselves, which are the focus of moral life. Or they argue that justice requires that we not provide goods to people who do not deserve them and especially not to people who are wicked and deserve punishment rather than goods. Such systems would object to a utilitarian requirement that I spread my property evenly over all members of society. They would appeal to my right to keep my property and give it to whom I like. They would posit that I have no obligation to give any of it to those who do not deserve it. Such non-utilitarian systems can still count as impartial in the sense that anyone in the system is permitted the same rights, as all are equal under the moral law. In other words, such alternative systems of value would simply reject the utilitarian's initial move of analyzing impartiality as entailing the principle of utility.

Mozi might associate any such alternative to his all-encompassingness with "discrimination," in the sense of making arbitrary and morally unwarranted distinctions among people. But it's not obvious that Mozi provides sufficient argument to maintain such an association. It is very difficult for a proponent of utilitarianism or all-encompassingness to show that other moral systems are merely arbitrary and unwarranted in their sanctioning different ways of treating different people. To look after your own children with more care than you give to your neighbor's children isn't discrimination, as long as it is taken to fall under general principles applicable to everybody. In other words, the position that all people may look after their own children with much less regard for the children of others, there is impartial, rather than discriminatory. Discrimination is the employment of morally irrelevant factors as morally relevant reasons. It is the failure to treat everyone equally under the moral law. The concept of discrimination itself doesn't give support for utilitarianism or any of utilitarianism's competitors, for that matter. Furthermore, it isn't clear that it would benefit the world were we to treat our own children just as we do strangers. One might think that such a world would be worse. On the other hand, if Mozi isn't arguing for such a strongly utilitarian position, and he is allowing distinctions in treatment among people, then he would need to show why his position's distinctions are not "discriminations" while competing moral systems' distinctions are. It isn't obvious that he does so. Of course, a utilitarian could argue that certain distinctions are permissible because they promote the general welfare and are thus all-encompassing. For example, a utilitarian might argue that criminals be punished while non-criminals not be punished – a distinction – on the grounds that this benefits the most people possible by discouraging and reducing crime. But such an argument brings us around to the principle of utility again, which is what is at issue.

As you read the text, you might also notice that Mozi argues for his position on the grounds that adopting all-encompassingness would have specific benefits which are obviously very good. He reasons that if everyone thinks all-encompassingly, people will no longer attack innocents in other families or other states. The flaw in this argument is that deeming such acts to be vicious does not commit one to the utilitarian version of impartiality. For example, Confucian values, along with many other alternative views to Mozi's, condemn vicious attacks as stridently as Mozi does. So, the desirability of an end to vicious attacks is not a point in favor of Mozi's moral position.

There is a curious side of Mozi's argument. As you read, notice that the argument seems to be that maximizing benefit is the right principle since doing so would maximize benefit. This is at once a bad and a powerful argument![167] It seems bad in that since the question is whether maximizing benefit is right, being reminded that maximizing benefit maximizes benefit, being a tautology, adds nothing. It certainly doesn't show that maximizing benefit is right unless it begs the question. Still, utilitarians are wont to argue, as Mozi does in "All-Encompassing Concern," as follows.

> All we have to do is to take all-encompassingness as a rule in order to get these benefits. I don't understand how the men of the world can hear about all-encompassingness and think it wrong. What is the reason?

Nevertheless, we might reflect on how we could reject a doctrine that would increase happiness. The answer must be that we hold a moral theory to a second standard: whether it

---

[167] Whalen Lai's article, found in the list of suggested readings at the end of this chapter, is an example of this perspective.

protects rights and other values to which we are deeply committed. Mozi never seems to consider cases in which violating an individual's rights would promote the welfare of society. He never grapples with the ambiguity of "all-encompassing." A society that worries about making as many people happy as it can will tend to trample on the rights of those who are already well off by using them as a mere means to others' happiness. Does all-encompassingness encourage that? Or does it limit the promotion of welfare within the constraints of rights which individuals have not to be used or disregarded by the majority of people? The latter would be the weaker interpretation of all-encompassingness, the former the stronger interpretation. That Mozi doesn't recognize and grapple with this issue is a shortcoming of the text.

There is another curious point in "All-encompassing Concern." Mozi gives the odd argument that since you would trust a philosopher who espoused all-encompassingness to mind your children more than you would trust a moral theorist of another stripe, Mohism's all-encompassingness is morally superior. Consider that. Does the fact that you'd trust Mother Teresa more than you would trust a randomly selected person show that we ought to live as she did or accept her moral theories, whatever they may be? Of course not. The argument is a *non sequitur*. Moral theorists of other stripes are unselfishly concerned with children's welfare. Moreover, a utilitarian might rob your children if they were wealthy, in order to spread their wealth among people who have less than they do. And Mozi would forbid them to enjoy music. So, would you really trust a utilitarian with your children? More generally, radicalism, as an intention to subvert and replace the traditional values we inherit is perhaps better seen as reckless and arrogant, rather than trustworthy. The radical movements of the Twentieth Century resulted in the deaths of over 100 million people, produced very little happiness, and had no respect for human rights. On the other hand, if Mozi isn't arguing for such a strongly utilitarian view but only for the position the people ought to have more regard for others' interests, then, while of course one would choose a babysitter who had regard for others' interests, this doesn't show that Mozi's moral position is superior to any other moral system that favors regard for others' interests. Moreover, if by "all-encompassing concern" Mozi only means that one ought to consider others' interests, then this does not amount to an interesting moral theory. It may be true that one ought to consider others' interests, but it's trivially true as moral theories go.

When scrutinizing Mozi's moral theory, you should look at the big picture in the following sense. What, exactly, is his moral philosophy? How good are the arguments? What are the rhetorical techniques? At many points, for example, in "Against Confucianism," Mozi repeats patterns of speech as though he were trying to brainwash the reader. This technique is not uncommon among radical political leaders. Mozi was not just a philosopher but also the founder of a radical political group. Although the group was militarized, it goes too far to say that they were militant revolutionaries, because they condemned aggressive military action. However, it may not be too far off the mark to say that the group was something of a revolutionary cult, in the pejorative sense of "cult": a movement offering little of value but commanding many followers through charismatic or oppressive means and intending to overthrow good ways of life. This is a radical, anti-traditionalist movement with little basis in sound moral reasoning. Moreover, such groups usually advocate that an elite cognoscenti have totalitarian power over the masses, who would be required to obey them. Perhaps the Mohists were such a group. The history of humanity has many instances of radicals promising, never with proof, that their more "rational" moral system would make society better off if only society's traditional ways of life would be abolished and the radicals put in charge and given total power. In all of the cases in which the radicals manage to seize power, enormous quantities of evil and very little good result.

Two of the essays in this chapter's readings illustrate what might be regarded as the totalitarian thinking of the Mohists. "Going Along with One's Superior" speaks of the centralization of moral authority. It urges inferiors to blow the whistle on the flaws of their superiors, but it gives no indication that what counts as a flaw is anything other than a failure of one's superior to go along with his own superior. It provides no indication that anyone but the supreme ruler is to decide in general what is right. I'm afraid things become even more ominous in Mozi's indictment of his arch rivals, the Confucians. "Against Confucianism" is, it seems, full of lies and mendacious character assassination of the vilest sort. It barely passes as philosophy worth reading by the fact that it indicates how the radical movements view traditional elite groups and their use of resources. But it presages 20th Century authoritarian regimes of the worst sort.[168] Repeated slogans and character assassination were not hard to find in regimes such as the USSR, the People's Republic of China, Nazi Germany, and many others radical regimes. Indeed, such practices are quite common in China and the West today, including in supposedly free societies such as the United States, where Saul Alinsky's principles of character assassination are frequently employed in political affairs.

But, again, should we draw such a strong picture of Mozi as a radical authoritarian? He might be a moderate reformer who praises whistleblowers who expose corruption and gives us a sketch of how to promulgate moral virtues from leader to follower. Was this weaker position the one he intended? Is that weaker position interesting? It may be that therein lies the flaw of the *Mozi*. It never grapples with its own ambiguity. It never defines its own positions precisely enough. One would be forgiven for reading it as a radical, antiestablishment, and revolutionary tract, replete with theocratic and cultish pseudo-religion and character

---

[168] We will see in a later chapter that the philosophy of Han Feizi presages these things, as well.

114

assassination of opposing philosophers. One would also be forgiven for reading it as a moderate work suggesting sensible moral reforms.

Even if the *Mozi* is deeply flawed, it is worth reading. They present interesting early works for the historian of moral philosophy, logic, and epistemology. They map an important part of the terrain of moral and political philosophy very well, whether we wish to dwell on that terrain or not. If they represent the thought of a radical political cult, then from the standpoint of history, they may be some of the first of a very, very bad sort.

The Readings

Below I've included several chapters (called "books") from the *Mozi*: Book 16 "All-Encompassing Concern," Book 4 "Models and Standards," Book 11 "Going Along with One's Superior," Book 27 "Heaven's Intention," and Book 39 "Against Confucianism." The books are numbered according to the standard edition, but I've placed "All-Encompassing Concern" at the beginning since it is important enough to read first. The essays were pieced together and edited, along with editorial comment, by Mozi's students. In some cases it is difficult to tell where Mozi's words leave off and the editors' comments begin; I've had to guess at many points.

Mozi

16. All-Encompassing[169] Concern

The Master Mozi said, "The humane person's task is to promote benefits to the world and to eliminate harms to world." So, at the present time what is the greatest harm to the world? We say that it includes large states attacking small states, large families throwing smaller ones into chaos, the strong robbing the weak, the many assaulting the few, the clever tricking the stupid, and nobles treating the lowly with arrogance. These are harms to the world. Also, the failure of the ruler of people to be kind, the failure of the subjects to be loyal, the failure of fathers to be caring, and the failure of children to be filial - these are harms to the world. Add to this the lowly people of today who take up weapons, blades, poisons, chemicals, water, and fire, in order to plunder and get the better of one another. These are also harms to the world.

We look for a source from which these various harms arise. Whence do they arise? Do they arise from concern for others and benefiting others? We'd have to say that it was not so. Wouldn't we have to say that they arise from hating others and robbing others? If we classify among everything in the world the person who hates others and robs others, is he all-

---

[169] I have not translated this term *jian* as "impartiality," but rendered it more literally as "all-encompassing" or, in its nominal form "all-encompassingness." While awkward, these translations are serviceable and do not mislead. "Inclusive" or "all-inclusive," and "inclusiveness" would also work, but they are slightly burdened by their connotations as buzzwords of the identity politics of our time. "Impartial" and "impartiality" are tempting translations but they are too loaded up with the baggage of Kantian and utilitarian ethics of modern Western philosophy. It may be that Mozi has something like that sort of impartiality in mind, but we should not beg the question by translating it in that way. Similarly, I translate *bie* (literally "differentiating") what Mozi contrasts with "all-encompassing," as "discriminating," rather than the less literal "partial." See note below.

encompassing? Or is he discriminating?[170] We'd have to say that he was discriminating. Hence, isn't it those who discriminate in their interactions who ultimately cause the greatest harms in the world? Therefore, discrimination is wrong.

The Master Mozi said, "One who rejects another's view must have something to offer as a replacement."[171] If one rejects another's view and has nothing to offer as a replacement, this is like adding water to a flood or flames to a fire. Such an argument will simply not be acceptable. Therefore, the Master, Mozi said, "Replace discrimination with all-encompassingness."

But how can one replace discrimination with all-encompassingness? We say that if we treated others' states as our own states, then who would have his country attack another's? What one did for others one would also do for oneself. If we treated others' cities as our own cities, then who would have his city strike another's? What one did for others one would also do for oneself. If we treated others' families as our own family, then who would have his family throw another's into disorder? What one did for others one would also do for oneself.[172] So, if

---

[170] The English word "discriminate" has a variety of senses and connotations. I use it in only one sense here to translate the Chinese *bie* (literally "differentiate"). In late-20th Century United States "discriminate" can mean to do injustice to people because of one's racial bigotry. The term can also mean "discern," in the sense of noticing a difference or of keenly making fine distinctions which might be overlooked by others. I don't mean either of those senses here. I mean by "discriminate" selfishly to leave others out of one's moral deliberations. This might embody a robust view of what it means to fail to be impartial, namely to make a morally irrelevant distinction between one case and another. Perhaps Mozi has such a robust view.

[171] This is an excellent point. Any criticism of a policy A must be deemed inconclusive unless it proposes and argues for an alternative policy B even if B is just the policy of maintaining the status quo. If the criticisms of A are substantial, then it may be concluded that A should not be enacted until B is considered.

[172] The Golden Rule. Here we find reason to see Mozi's concept of all-encompassingness as similar to modern Kantian or utilitarian impartiality, according to which one should entirely abstract oneself from one's particular set of social relationships in conducting moral deliberations. For example, on this view, one should not treat one's own child any better than

countries and cities do not attack or strike one another, and if families do not throw into disorder and rob one another, would these be harms to the world? Or would they be benefits to the world? We must say that they are benefits to the world.

We look for a source from which these various benefits arise. Whence do they arise? Do they arise from hatred and robbery of others? We'd have to say that it was not so. Wouldn't we have to say that they arise from concern for others and benefiting others? If we classify among everything in the world the person who benefits others out of concern for others, is he discriminating or is he all-encompassing? We'd have to say he was all-encompassing. Hence, isn't it those who are all-encompassing in their interactions who ultimately cause the greatest benefits to the world?

Therefore, The Master Mozi said, "All-encompassingness is right," and as mentioned above, the humane person's task is to promote benefit to the world and to eliminate harms to world. Now, one finds the source of the great benefits to the world in all-encompassingness, and one finds the source of great harms to the world in discrimination. Therefore, the Master Mozi's saying that discrimination is wrong and all-encompassingness is right derives from these ideas.

Suppose we really try to promote benefit to the world and to maintain it, and we take all-encompassingness as a standard. Thus, those of keen ears and eyes will see and hear for others, those of strong arms and legs will labor for others, and those who have the Way will in turn teach others. In this way, the elderly without wives will have a way of being supported as they live out

one treats a stranger's child. This is a radical position. A less radical view of impartiality would hold that one should make moral judgements with the understanding that one allows others to act on the same judgments whenever they are in the same circumstances. Thus, one allows others to treat their children better than they treat one's own children, just as one judges that one may take better care of one's own children than one takes of a stranger's children. It isn't clear where Mozi would fall on these issues. Notice that in this passage, Mozi is describing impartial moral reasoning as the implementation of or cognitive way of realizing all-encompassingness (*jian*). This is a good reason not to translate *jian* itself as "impartiality."

their lives. Helpless children without parents will have something to rely on as they grow up. All we have to do is to take all-encompassingness as a rule, in order to get these benefits. I don't understand how the men of the world can hear about all-encompassingness and think it wrong. What is the reason?

Yet, the talk of those who reject all-encompassingnss still won't stop. They'll say, "All-encompassingness is good. However, how can it be put into use?"

The Master Mozi said, "If it were unusable, even I would reject it. Moreover, how can there be something good that cannot be put to use?"[173] Let us take two approaches to this. Suppose that there were two men, and allow that one held to discrimination and one held to all-encompassingness. Thus, the discriminating man's words would be, "How can I treat my companion's person as my person and treat my companion's relatives as my relatives?" Therefore, in thus looking upon his friends, he won't feed them when they are hungry, and he won't clothe them when they are cold. He won't take care of them when they are sick, and he won't bury them when they die. The discriminating man's words are like this and his actions are, too.

The all-encompassing man's words are not like that, nor are his actions. He says, "I've been told that a man of high order in the world will treat his friend's person as his own person and treat his friend's parents as his own parents." Thus, will he be able to become a man of high order in the world. Therefore, in

---

[173] If a moral theory runs counter to human nature, meaning that we cannot be adhere to it, then you might ask what would count as making it the right moral theory, as opposed to another theory which shows human beings the way to develop moral virtues suitable to our nature. If you do accept the theory which runs counter to human nature as the right one, then you must be willing to accept the conclusion that, given our natural inability to comply with that theory, human nature is evil. Let me give you an example. Suppose you were to accept that impartial reasoning requires that we treat the interests of strangers and the interests of ourselves and our loved ones equally in our practical deliberations. Since you cannot adhere to that requirement, you will have to conclude that you are vicious by nature. Would you be willing to accept that you are vicious by nature, or would you review your initial inference for possible fallacies?

thus looking upon his friends, he will feed them when they are hungry, clothe them when they are cold, take care of them when they are sick, and bury them when they die. The all-encompassing man's words are like this, and his actions are, too.

The two men's words mutually deny each other and their actions are opposed. But allow that the two men speak only in good faith and act only if intending to follow through. Given such a harmony of speech and action, like the two halves of a tally, there would be nothing either one spoke that he did not act upon. In that case, I ask you, if there were a wide open region, and someone were to put on armor and a helmet to go off to war, and whether he would live or die could not be predicted; or if a person under a ruler were sent far away to Ba, Yue, Qi or Jing, and whether he would ever come back could not be predicted - in such a case, I ask you, whom will he choose? To whom should he entrust the care of his parents and the maintenance of his wife and children? I think that when it comes to this, nobody is a fool. Even someone who rejects all-encompassingness will always say that trusting the all-encompassing one is right. This is to reject all-encompassingness in speech but to accept it in decision. This is a contradiction between word and action.[174] I don't understand how the men of the world can hear about all-encompassingness and think it wrong. What is the reason?

Yet, the talk of those who reject all-encompassingness still won't stop. They'll say, "The point of view can be used to choose regular people, but it can't be used to choose a ruler." Let's use two approaches to this. Suppose there were two rulers, and that one held to all-encompassingness, while the other held to discrimination. Thus, the discriminating ruler would say, "How can I treat the persons of my myriad subjects as my own person? This radically opposes everyone's inclinations. A person's life on earth lasts for such a short time; it rushes by like galloping horses passing a crack in the wall." Therefore, in thus looking upon his subjects, he wouldn't feed them when they were hungry, and he

---

[174] Is this a good argument that impartiality is the better moral stance?

wouldn't clothe them when they were cold. He wouldn't take care of them when they were sick, and he wouldn't bury them when they died. The discriminating ruler's words would be like this and his actions would be, too.

The all-encompassing ruler's words would not be like that, nor would his actions. He would say, "I've been told that an enlightened ruler always puts the persons of his subjects first and puts his own person second. Only thus can one be an enlightened ruler." Therefore, in thus looking upon his subjects, he would feed them when they were hungry, clothe them when they were cold, take care of them when they were sick, and bury them when they die. The all-encompassing ruler's words would be like this, and his actions would be, too.

The two ruler' words would mutually deny each other and their actions would be opposed. But allow that the two men speak only in good faith and act only if intending to follow through. So, I ask you, suppose that this year there were a plague and more than 10,000 people were suffering from cold and hunger, their bodies already filling the ditches in great numbers. Whom will someone who must choose between the two rulers follow? I think that when it comes to this, nobody is a fool. Even someone opposed to all-encompassing rulers will always say that trusting the all-encompassing one is right. This is to reject all-encompassingness in speech but to accept it in decision. This is a contradiction between word and action. I don't understand how the men of the world can hear about all-encompassingness and think it wrong. What is the reason?

Yet, the talk of those who reject all-encompassingness still won't stop. They'll say, "All-encompassingness is humane and right. However, how can one do it? I'd compare the impossibility of all-encompassingness to picking up Mt. Tai and leaping over a large river. Therefore, all-encompassingness is only to be wished for. How can it be something doable?"

The Master Mozi said, "As for picking up Mt. Tai and leaping over a large river, from ancient times to the present, as long as there have been humans, there has been no one who has done it. But all-encompassing concern for one another and mutual benefiting of one another - these were actually practiced by the four sage kings of ancient times." How do we know these were practiced by the four sage kings of ancient times? The Master Mozi said, "I did not live during their time or hear their voices or see their countenances. I know it by what is written on bamboo and silk, engraved in metal and stone, inscribed on bowls and basins, and passed down to descendants in later generations." The Great Oath says, "King Wen shed light like the sun or the moon, illuminating the four directions and the Western Land." This speaks to the breadth and size of King Wen's all-encompassing concern for the world. It is like the moon and sun shining on the world without any bias. Such was the all-encompassingness of King Wen.[175]

Mozi's sense of all-encompassingness takes King Wen as its model. But it's not only *The Great Oath* that portrays it so. *The Oath of Yu* also follows suit. Yu said,

> All my people, listen to my words. It is not that I, the little child, dare to stir up chaos. It's that worm, the ruler of the Miao, who could use a little of heaven's punishment. Thus, I will lead you, rulers of the various states, to correct the ruler of the Miao.[176]

Yu's correcting the ruler of the Miao was not in effort to increase his wealth or rank, to gain good fortune or blessing, or to please his ears and eyes. It was in order to promote the benefit to the world, and to eliminate harms to the world. Such was the all-encompassingness of Yu.

Mozi's sense of all-encompassingness takes after that of King Yu. But it's not only *The Oath of Yu* that portrays it so. *The Sayings of Tang* also follows suit. Tang said,

> I, the little child, Lu, would use a darkly colored sacrifice to announce to the Lord of Heaven above that the present

---

[175] Does the fact that the sage kings did certain very beneficial things for the people show that utilitarianism as a general policy is practicable?
[176] This text being quoted is now lost.

drought is on my account. I am at fault. I don't know whether my wrong was against high or low. Any good I would not conceal. Any wrong I would not excuse. Judgment rests with the mind of God. If there are faults in my land, they are on my account. If I have faults, these are not on account of my domain.[177]

This says that Tang, revered as the Son of Heaven and having the riches of the world, would nevertheless not hesitate to offer himself as a sacrifice, in order to pray to the Lord and the ghosts and spirits. Such was Tang's all-encompassingness.

Mozi's sense of all-encompassingness takes King Tang as its model. But it's not only *The Oath of Yu* and *The Sayings of Tang* that portray it so. The *Odes of Zhou* also follows suit. The *Odes of Zhou* says,

> The Way of the King is broad, broad,
> Neither biased nor partisan.
> The Way of the King is even, even,
> Neither biased nor partisan.
> Straight as an arrow,
> Smooth as a whetstone.
> The ruler follows it,
> And the small man looks to it.[178]

The quotes we've provided are not meant as just a theory of the Way. In ancient times, when kings Wen and Wu governed, they fairly assigned rewards to the worthy and punishments to the wicked, without being partial to their family members. Such was the all-encompassingness of Wen and Wu.

Mozi's sense of all-encompassingness takes Wen and Wu as its model. I don't understand how the men of the world can hear about all-encompassingness and think it wrong. What is the reason?

---

[177] This text being quoted is now lost.
[178] These lines are today found in *The Odes of Zhou* and the *Documents of Zhou*.

Yet, the talk of those who reject all-encompassingness still won't stop. They'll say, "If one doesn't loyally intend to benefit one's parents, won't this harm one's filiality?" The Master Mozi said, "Let us inquire into the plans that a filial son makes for his parents. Does a filial son, in planning for his parents, want others to have concern for his parents and to benefit them? Or does he prefer that others hate his parents and rob them?"[179] Upon reflection, he wants others to have concern for his parents and to benefit them. This being so, how could one endeavor to achieve this? Should one endeavor to have concern for other's parents and to benefit them, so that others will repay one by having concern for one's parents and benefiting them? Or should one endeavor to hate others' parents and to rob them, so that others will repay one by having concern for one's parents and benefiting them? It must be that one should endeavor to have concern for other's parents and to benefit them, so that others will repay one by having concern for one's parents and benefiting them. Thus, with such mutual filiality among sons, will the results not be unlimited, but only if they endeavor to have concern for other's parents and to benefit them? Or shall we take all the filial sons of the world to be stupid, such that they are not up to the task of doing what is correct?

Let us inquire into the writings of the Former Kings, such as the *Da Ya*, which says,

> Nothing said goes unanswered,
> No kindness unrepaid.
> Throw me a peach,
> I repay it with a plum.[180]

This says that those with concern for others will always see their concern reciprocated, while those who hate others will always see their hatred reciprocated.

---

[179] Here again, Mozi is arguing, quite speciously, that alternative moral theories to his recommend that people hate and rob others' parents!
[180] *Da Ya*, Mao 256.

I don't understand how the men of the world can hear about all-encompassingness and think it wrong. What is the reason? Do they take it to be so difficult that they can't do it? But there have been people who were able to do more difficult things. In the past, King Ling of Jing liked slender waists. During his reign the people of Jing ate no more than one meal a day. They had to rely on a cane to get up, and they had to lean on a wall to walk. Cutting back on one's food was hard to do, but afterwards King Ling was pleased by it. It took no more than a generation for the people to change. For they sought to comply with their superior.

In the past, King Gou Jian of Yue liked bravery. He taught it to his soldiers and subjects for three years. He took their understanding to be insufficient to count as understanding it, so he set fire to a ship and, drumming the troops on, had them advance on it. His troops rushed over the ranks ahead of them, and those who fell to the water and flames were countless. Even at that time, it was only when he didn't drum that they retreated. We can say that the men of Yue were frightened. To commit oneself to the flames is hard to do, but afterwards King Gou Jian was pleased by it. It took no more than a generation for the people to change. For they sought to comply with their superior.

Cutting back on their food, committing oneself to the flames, and wearing rough clothing are the hardest things in the world to do. But afterwards their superiors were pleased. It took no more than a generation for the people to change. Why? Because they sought to comply with their superiors. Now having all-encompassing concern for each other and mutually benefiting each other are so beneficial and easy to do that it's beyond measure. As I see it, it's just that there are no superiors who are pleased by them. If there were superiors who were pleased by them and promoted them with reward and praise and sanctioned them with punishments, then I believe that people would go about having all-encompassing concern for one another and mutually benefiting one another just as fire goes upward and water downwards. It couldn't be stopped anywhere in the world.

Therefore, all-encompassingness is the Way of the sage kings. It is the means by which to bring security to the kings, dukes and other officials. It is the means by which the myriad people can have enough food and clothing. For a gentleman nothing compares to investigating all-encompassingness and striving to practice it. Practicing it makes a ruler kind, a subject loyal, a father compassionate, a son filial, an older brother friendly, and a younger brother respectful. Thus, a gentleman who would be a kind ruler, a loyal subject, a compassionate father, a filial son, a friendly other brother, and a respectful younger brother cannot but practice all-encompassingness. This is the Way of the sage kings and the greatest benefit to the myriad people.

4. Standard Criteria

Mozi said, "No one in the world who pursues a vocation can do without standard criteria. There has never been anyone who, without standard criteria, could have success in his vocation. We could consider officers who act as generals and ministers; they all have standards. We could consider the various artisans in their pursuit of their vocations; they, too, all have standards.

"The various artisans use a carpenters square when they make something square, a compass when they make something round, a cord for a straight line, a level for a cross beam, and a plumb line for something vertical. Not a single skilled or unskilled artisan. They all use these five as standards. The skilled can adhere to them accurately. The unskilled artisan, although they cannot adhere to them accurately, relies on them in order to pursue his vocation; they still make him better. Thus the various artisans in their pursuit of their vocations all have standards by which to make measurements.

"Today the great leader keeps the world in order. The next below him keeps a large state in order. But they do not

126

standards by which to make measurements. This does not compare to the perspicacity of the various artisans.

"This being so, what can they use as standards of order? How would it be if everyone took his parents as the standard? There are many parents in the world, but few are humane. If everyone took his parents as the standard, the standards would not be humane. And if the standard isn't humane, one cannot take it as a standard. How would it be if everyone took his teacher as the standard? There are many teachers in the world, but few are humane. If everyone took his teacher as the standard, the standards would not be humane. And if the standard isn't humane, one cannot take it as a standard. How would it be if everyone took his ruler as the standard? There are many rulers in the world, but few are humane. If everyone took his ruler as the standard, the standards would not be humane. And if the standard isn't humane, one cannot take it as a standard. Therefore, these three - parents, teacher, and ruler - none can be taken as a standard of order.

"This being so, what can they use as standards of order? This is why it is said, 'Nothing compares to taking heaven as the standard.' Its actions are wide-reaching and unselfish. It gives richly but does not exercise its power. Its brilliance continues yet without diminution. Therefore, the sage kings treated it as the standard. Having taken heaven as the standard, one's movements, productions, holdings, and actions must be meted out according to heaven. What heaven likes one does. What heaven does not like one refrains from.

"So, what does heaven like? What does it hate? Heaven certainly likes people's loving one another and benefiting one another and dislikes people's hating one another and harming one another. How do we know that heaven likes people's loving one another and benefiting one another and dislikes people's hating one another and harming one another? By its all-encompassingly loving them and all-encompassingly benefitting them. How do we know that it all-encompassingly loves them and all-encompassingly benefits them? By its all-encompassingly maintaining them and all-encompassingly feeding them.

"Today every single state, great or small, is heaven's land. Every single person, young or old, noble or base, is heaven's subject. This is why everyone fodders the cattle and sheep, feeds the dogs and pigs, and offers measures of wines and grains in order to honor and serve heaven. But this all-encompassingly maintaining them and all-encompassingly feeding them? Heaven honors all-encompassingly maintaining and feeding them. How can one say that it shows that heaven doesn't like people's loving one another and benefiting one another?

"This is why I say, 'Those who love and benefit one another heaven will certainly bring good fortune. Those who hate one another and harm one another heaven will certainly bring calamity.' And I say, 'He who kills an innocent will meet with a bad omen from it.' How can we say that when people kill one another heaven brings them calamity? It is because heaven likes people's loving one another and benefiting one another.

"The sage kings of old – Yu, Tang, Wen, and Wu – all-encompassingly loved the people of the world and therefore honored heaven and served ghosts. They benefited people greatly. So, heaven brought them good fortune and charged them as the sons of heaven. The feudal lords of the world all held them in their esteem and served them.

"The tyrannical kings – Jie, Zhou, You, and Li – all-encompassingly hated the people of the world and therefore reviled heaven and insulted ghosts. They harmed people greatly. So, heaven brought them calamity and caused them to lose their states and households. They died and were humiliated. For generations afterwards, their descendants held them in contempt, and it hasn't stopped even today.

"Therefore, those who met with calamity by doing what is not good – such were Jie, Zhou, You, and Li. Those who met with good fortune by loving people and benefiting people – such were Yu, Tang, Wen, and Wu. There have been those who have met with good fortune by loving people and benefiting people. There have also been those who have met with calamity by hating people and harming people."

128

11. Going Along with One's Superior

Mozi said, "In ancient times, when people were first created and before there were rules or governance, it seems that people differed about righteousness. Thus, with one person there was one form of rightness, with two people, two, and with ten people, ten forms of rightness. The more numerous the people, the more numerous what they said was right. Thus did people accept their own form of rightness and on that basis reject others' forms of rightness, so that when they met they disagreed with one another. Therefore, family members nurtured resentments and hatreds and went their separate ways, unable to be in mutual harmony. Among the people of the world, everyone used water, fire, poisons and toxins to try to injure one another, to the point that those with extra strength couldn't work for others, those with extra goods going bad couldn't share them with others, and those with secret and beneficial ways wouldn't teach them to others. The chaos in the world even resembled the condition of beasts.

Inquiry into the reason for the chaos in the world shows that it arose from the lack of governance and authorities. Therefore, the most able and worthy one in the world was selected and established as the Son of Heaven. The Son of Heaven was established, but took his strength as insufficient and selected the most able and worthy in the world and installed them as the three dukes. The son of heaven and the three dukes having been established, they grasped how wide and large the world was and couldn't clearly discern so easily what was right or wrong, beneficial or harmful for distant and different lands, they divided them into the many provinces and established the various feudal lords and chiefs. After the various feudal lords and chiefs were established, they took their strength to be insufficient and selected the most able and worthy in the world and installed them as supervisors. When the supervisors had been installed, the son of heaven set forth his governance to the people of the world, saying,

Anyone who hears of something good or not good should report it to his superior. Everyone must accept what his superior accepts. Everyone must reject what his superior rejects. If your superior has any faults, then remonstrate with him. And if your subordinate has done good, then recommend him. Those who go along with their superior and don't form parties below shall be rewarded by the superior and praised by subordinates. In any case of hearing of something good or not good but not reporting it to one's superior, of being unable to accept what one's superior accepts, or being unable to reject what ones' superior rejects, or of a superior having a fault for which he goes unremonstrated, or of subordinates forming parties and being unable to go along with their superior - this shall be penalized by the superiors and vilified by the people.

The superiors proceeded with rewards and penalties according to this, investigating thoroughly to be assured that it is done in good faith.

Therefore, a district officer was the most humane man in the district. The district officer set forth his governance to the people of the district, saying,

Anyone who hears of something good or not good should report it to his village officer. Everyone must accept what his village official accepts. Everyone must reject what his village officer rejects. Stop saying things that aren't good and study the good words of the village officer. Stop doing things that aren't good and study the good actions of the village officer.

How, then, could there be disorder in the villages?

Upon inquiry, how did a village come to be governed? The village officer was simply able to make the forms of rightness of the village go along [with his own]. Thus was a village governed. The village officer was the most humane person in the village. The village officer set forth his governance to the people of the village, saying,

Anyone who hears of something good or not good should report it to the provincial officer. Everyone must accept what the provincial officer. Everyone must reject what the provincial officer rejects. Stop saying things that aren't good and study the good words of the provincial officer. Stop doing things that aren't good and study the good actions of the provincial officer.

How, then, will there be any disorder in the province?

Upon inquiry, how do provinces come to be governed? The provincial officer was simply able to make the forms of rightness of the province go along [with his own]. Thus was a province governed. The provincial official was the most humane person in the province. The provincial officer set forth his governance to the people of the province, saying,

Anyone who hears of something good or not good should report it to the Son of Heaven. Everyone must accept what the Son of Heaven accepts. Everyone must reject what the Son of Heaven rejects. Stop saying things that aren't good and study the good words of the Son of Heaven. Stop doing things that aren't good and study the good actions of the Son of Heaven.

How, then, will there be any disorder in the province?

Upon inquiry, how does the world come to be governed? The Son of Heaven was simply able to make the forms of rightness of the province go along [with his own]. Thus was the world governed.

If the people of the world all go along with the Son of Heaven but do not go along with heaven, then disasters will still not be done away with. The gales and deluges, which are so prevalent today, are heaven's way of penalizing the people's failure to go along with heaven. Therefore, Mozi said, "The sage kings of old formulated the five punishments in effort to govern their people. This is like some silk having a main string or a net having a main rope. They were the means by which they captured the people of the world who were not going along with their superior.

27. Heaven's Intent

Mozi said, "The gentlemen of today who want to be humane and righteous must not neglect to investigate the source of rightness." He has said that they must not neglect to investigate the source of rightness; so, what, then, is the source of rightness? Mozi said, "Rightness doesn't come from the ignorant and base. It only comes from the noble and knowledgeable." How do we know that rightness doesn't come from the ignorant and base and that it only comes from the noble and knowledgeable? Mozi said, "Rightness is good governance." How do we know that rightness is good governance? Mozi said, "When there is rightness in the world, it is orderly. When there is no rightness in the world, it is chaotic." This is how we know that the righteous govern well.

Now, the ignorant and base cannot manage to govern the noble and knowledgeable. One the other hand, the noble and knowledgeable can govern the ignorant and base. This is how we know that righteousness does not come from the ignorant and base but only from the noble and knowledgeable. This being the case, who is noble? Who is knowledgeable? In fact, heaven is noble and knowledgeable. And, so, righteousness in the end comes from heaven.

Today the people of the world say, "When it comes to the son of heaven's being nobler and more knowledgeable than the lords, and the lords being nobler and more knowledgeable than the high officials, these things are obvious. But we don't know that heaven is nobler and more knowledgeable than the son of heaven."

Mozi said, "There is a way for us to know that heaven is nobler and more knowledgeable than the son of heaven." He said, "When the son of heaven does what is good, heaven can reward him. When the son of heaven commits brutality, heaven can punish him. When the son of heaven suffers with an illness or injury, he must fast and bathe and offer measures of wines and grains in sacrifice to heaven and the ghosts so that heaven can rid him of it. But we've never known heaven to pray to the son of heaven. This is how we know that heaven is nobler and more knowledgeable than the son of heaven.

"Moreover, this is not the only way for us to know that heaven is nobler and more knowledgeable than the son of heaven. We know it from the fact that the documents of the former kings described the 'glorious and inexhaustible Way' of heaven, saying 'Glorious and bright is heaven, shining down on the lands below.' So, this says that heaven is nobler and more knowledgeable than the son of heaven. And we don't know of anything nobler and more knowledgeable than heaven. I simply say that heaven is noblest and heaven is the most knowledgeable. This being the case, rightness in the end comes from heaven."

Therefore, Mozi said, "Gentlemen of today who truly intend to honor the Way and benefit the people and who first investigate the basis of humanity and rightness cannot but pay heed to the intent of heaven." Given that the one cannot but pay heed to the intent of heaven, what is it that heaven desires? And what does it despise? Mozi said, "The inclination of heaven is such that it doesn't want big states to rule small states or big households to throw small households into chaos. For the strong to bully the weak, the many to do violence to the few, the mendacious to defraud the trusting, and the noble to behave arrogantly toward the lowly - these are what heaven dislikes. But it doesn't stop there. It wants people with power to cooperate with others, people who have the Way to teach others, and people with wealth to share with others. It also wants those above to rule steadfastly with virtue while those below steadfastly pursue their affairs. If those above rule steadfastly with virtue and those below steadfastly pursue their affairs, then the state and households will be orderly. If the state and households are orderly, then the amount of wealth will suffice. If the state and households are orderly and the amount of wealth suffices, then those above will have enough to offer measures of wines and grains in sacrifice to heaven and the ghosts. Externally, he will have jade bracelets and disks, pearls and jade jewels, using them as gifts with which to persuade his neighbors. The various lords will not become indignant and they will not conduct military exercises on the borders. Internally, he will have food for the hungry and rest for the tired, in order to maintain his people. Rulers and ministers will be magnanimous and loyal to one another, respectively, and parents and children, elders and the young, will be kind and filial to one another, respectively. Thus, only when he has become enlightened about following heaven's intention, submitted to it and widely spread it throughout the world will the government create order, the myriad peoples be harmonious, the state and households prosper, the amount of wealth suffice, and the people obtain clothing warm and food ample enough that they may be tranquil and free of worry. This is why Mozi said, "Gentlemen of today who truly intend to honor the Way and benefit the people and who first investigate the basis of humanity and rightness cannot but pay heed to the intent of heaven."

Now, for the son of heaven to possess the world is no different from the rulers of states and the various lords' possessing what lies within their borders. Today, the rulers of states and the various lords possess the territory within their borders. How could they desire their subjects or their people to do what is unbeneficial to one another? Today, those that reside in large states attack small states, and those who reside in large households throw small households into chaos. They desire in this way to seek wealth and glory. But in the end they cannot obtain these, and notoriety and punishment inevitably follow. Heaven's possession of the world is no different from this. Today, those who have large states attack small states. Those who have large cities attack small cities. They desire to seek wealth and fortune but in the end they cannot obtain these and calamity and scourge inevitably follow.

So, whenever what heaven desires is not done and what heaven does not desire is done, heaven does not do what Man wants but does do what Man does not want. What is it that Man does not want? It is said, "Sickness and disease, calamity and scourge." If the one has not done what heaven likes but has done what heaven dislikes, then one will lead the myriad people of the world to pursue their affairs amidst calamity and scourge. Therefore, the sage kings of old were enlightened about what heaven and ghosts would reward with good fortune and avoided what heaven and ghosts despise. In this way they sought what would increase benefit to the world and what would do away with harms to the world. This is why when heaven made cold or hot weather it was temperate, the four seasons were harmonious, yin, yang, rain and dew were timely, the five grains grew to maturity, the six animals were compliant, and disease, disaster, miseries, epidemics, shortages and famines did not occur.

Therefore, Mozi said, "Gentlemen of today who truly intend to honor the Way and benefit the people, and who first investigate the basis of humanity and rightness, cannot but pay heed to the intent of heaven."

However, there are many in the world who are inhumane and ill-fated. Namely, when children who do not serve their parents, younger siblings who do not serve their elder siblings, and ministers who do not serve their rulers, the rulers of the world join together in calling them ill-fated. Now heaven includes everyone the world and loves all. It brings forth the myriad things in order to benefit them. Even the tip of a hair – none of them is not made by heaven. And people obtain them and benefit from them. So, we can call this bountiful. Though this is so, none of them repays heaven, and they don't know that they are inhumane and ill-fated. This is what we call the gentlemen's being aware of the trivial but unaware of the important.

Moreover, there is a reason we know that heaven's love for people is bountiful. Namely, it creates the sun, moon, stars, and planets in order to illuminate the Way. It sets up the four seasons of spring, autumn, winter, and summer in order to provide them regularity and order. It precipitates the snow, frost, dew, and rain in order to nurture the five grains, hemp, and silk and enable people to obtain these and reap the benefits of them.

It distributes the mountains, rivers, ravines, and valleys. It articulated of the hundred offices and created kings, dukes, marquises, and earls in order to oversee the good and bad among the people, causing them to reward the worthy and punish the wicked, to store metals, wood, birds and beasts, and to pursue the tasks pertaining to the five grains, hemp, and silk, for the sake of the commodities that people need. From ancient times until today, it has never been otherwise.

Suppose there were a man who deeply loved his son and exerted his efforts at benefiting him. If the son grew up and did not repay his father, then any gentleman would deem him to be inhumane and ill-fated. But heaven encompasses all under heaven and loves them. It looks after the myriad things in order to benefit them. Even the tip of a hair – there is nothing that isn't made by heaven. So, as people obtain and benefit from them, we may call this bountiful. Yet, only in this case do they not repay heaven and are not aware that they are inhumane and ill-fated. This is why I say that gentlemen are aware of the trivial but unaware of the important.

However, the reasons we know that heaven's love for people is bountiful don't stop there. For also, if one murders an innocent, heaven deals one ill-fate. Who is the innocent? I say he is a human being. Who is it that deals out ill-fate? I say it is heaven. If heaven's love for people were not bountiful, how can we explain that when someone kills an innocent heaven deals him ill-fate? This is a reason we know that heaven's love for people is bountiful.

Yet, the reasons we know that heaven's love for people is bountiful doesn't stop there. There are those who love people, benefit people, obey the intention of heaven, and obtain rewards from heaven. There are also those who despise people, mistreat people, oppose heaven's intent, and receive heaven's punishments.

Now, those who love people, benefit people, obey the intention of heaven, and obtain rewards from heaven – who are they? They were the sage kings of the three dynasties of antiquity: Yao, Shun, Yu, Tang, Wen and Wu. How did Yao,

Shun, Yu, Tang, Wen and Wu pursue their affairs? They pursued their affairs all-encompassingly, and did not pursue their affairs by discriminating. "All-encompassing" means that if you reside in a large state, then you do not attack small states, if you reside in a large household, then you do not throw small households into chaos, the strong do not rob the weak, the many do not assault the few, the clever do not trick the stupid, and nobles do not treat the lowly with arrogance. Examine their affairs. Above, they benefited heaven. In the middle realm they benefited the ghosts. Below, they benefited Man. There was no one who was not benefited by these three benefits. We call this heavenly virtue. The very finest names in the world were applied to them: "This is humanity. This is righteousness. These are ones who love people, benefit people, obey the intention of heaven and obtain the rewards from heaven." But it didn't stop there. This was written on bamboo and silk, engraved in metal and stone, inscribed on bowls and basins, and passed down to descendants in later generations. Why did they do this? In order to make it known that they loved people, benefited people, obeyed the intention of heaven, and obtained rewards from heaven. The *Huangyi*[181] speaks of it:

> God said to King Wen,
> "I am gratified by your bright virtue.
> Not taking your renown as pretext for glory,
> Not taking your rule of the Xia as pretext for change,
> Without thoughts or cogitations,
> You obey the law of God."

God regarded his following the model (*fa*) and laws as good. So, in order to reward him, He gave him the state of Yin, made him esteemed as the Son of Heaven, enriched him with the possession of the world, such that the praise of his name continues even to today. Therefore, those who love people, benefit people, obey the intention of heaven, and obtain rewards from heaven – we do know who they were.

---

[181] A passage from *The Odes*.

Now, those who despise people, mistreat people, oppose heaven's intent, and receive heaven's punishments – who are they? They were the wicked kings of the three dynasties of antiquity: Jie, Zhou, You, and Li. How did Jie, Zhou, You, and Li pursue their affairs? They pursued their affairs by discriminating, and did not pursue their affairs all-encompassingly. "Discriminating" means that if you reside in a large state, then you attack small states, if you reside in a large household, then you throw small households into chaos, the strong rob the weak, the many assault the few, the clever trick the stupid, and nobles treat the lowly with arrogance. Examine their affairs. Above, they did not benefit heaven. In the middle realm they did not benefit the ghosts. Below, they did not benefited Man. There is no one who was benefited by these three benefits. We call this an offense against heaven. The very basest names in the world were applied to them: "This is inhumane. This is unrighteous. These are ones who despise people, mistreat people, oppose heaven's intent, and receive heaven's punishments." But it didn't stop there. This was written on bamboo and silk, engraved in metal and stone, inscribed on bowls and basins, and passed down to descendants in later generations. Why did they do this? In order to make it known that they despised people, mistreated people, opposed heaven's intent, and received heaven's punishments. The *Great Proclamation*[182] speaks of it, saying "Zhou was wanton and depraved[183] and would not serve God on High. He neglected the spirits of his predecessors and did not offer sacrifices. Yet he said, 'I have the mandate,' and shirked his duties to the spirits." Heaven, in turn, abandoned Zhou and did not protect him. If we take a look at the reason heaven abandoned Zhou and did not protect him, it is that he opposed the intent of heaven. Therefore, those who despise people, mistreat people, oppose

---

[182] A now-lost section of the *Documents* (*Shujing*).

[183] I am unsure of the meaning of the text here. I have used "wanton and depraved" as a gloss on it. Knoblock and Riegel have "Zhou kills cruelly," Watson has "Zhou sits with his legs sprawled out" (an outrageous show of disrespect for heaven), and

138

heaven's intent, and receive heaven's punishments – we know who they were.

Therefore, Mozi's having the intent of heaven is no different from a wheelwright's having a compass or a carpenter's having a square. Consider a wheelwright who uses his compass to measure the roundness of things in the world. He says, 'What matches my compass I call round; what doesn't match it I call not round.' Therefore, he can discern and know round and not round. What is his basis? It's that the standard of roundness makes them clear. Take a carpenter who uses his square to measure the squareness of things in the world. He says, 'What matches my square I call square; what doesn't match it I call not square.' Therefore, he can discern and know square and not square. What is his basis? It's that the standard of squareness makes them clear."

Therefore, Mozi, having the intent of heaven, can use it above to measure the governance of the kings, dukes, ministers, officers, and gentlemen of the world. And he can use it below to measure the writings and utterances of the myriad people of the world. He observes their actions. If they follow heaven's intent, then he calls them actions of good intent. If they do not follow heaven's intent, then he calls them bad actions. He observes their utterances. If they follow heaven's intent, then he calls them good utterances. If they do not follow heaven's intent, then he calls them bad utterances. He observes their governance. If it follow heaven's intent, then he calls it good governance. If it does not follow heaven's intent, then he calls it bad governance. Therefore, he establishes this to be used as a model, lets it stand as the standard, and uses it in order to determine the humanity and inhumanity of the kings, dukes, great officers, and ministers of the world. It's like distinguishing between black and white.

Therefore, Mozi said, "Today the kings, dukes, ministers, officers, and gentlemen of the world are really intent upon honoring the Way and benefiting the people, they must first examine the basis of humanity and rightness. The intent of heaven must not be disobeyed. To obey the intent of heaven is the model (*fa*) of rightness."

39. Against Confucianism

Confucians say, "In treating relatives as relatives, there are gradations. In honoring the worthy there are different levels."[184] This refers to the differences between close relatives and distant ones, and between the worthy and the humble. Their rituals call upon them to mourn parents for three years, a wife or eldest son for three years, a paternal uncle, brother, or younger sons for one year, and other family members for five months. If they determine the number of years or months according to the closeness of the relative, the closer should receive more and the more distant fewer. Then, they would treat their wives or eldest sons the same as their fathers. And if they determine the number of years or months according to the degree of honor and humility, then they honor their wives and sons equally to their parents and reduce their uncles and brothers to the same level as their younger sons. How perverse!

When their parents die they lay the corpse out without dressing it for burial and go climbing onto the roof, looking into the well, reaching into rat holes and checking in the wash basins in their search for the person. If they thought he really existed, then this would be idiocy in the extreme. As they take him to have perished but insist on searching for him, the disingenuousness is enormous.

When they take a wife, they call upon her in person, in formal attire and acting as their own driver. They hold the reins and hand her the mounting rope, as though they were attending to their honored parents. The wedding ceremony is dignified and reverent, comparable to a sacrificial prayer. Inferior and superior are reversed. The father and mother are disdainfully neglected, reduced to the level of the wife, while the wife is disruptively elevated. Can treatment of parents such as this be called "filial"?[185]

---

[184] *Doctrine of the Mean*, 20.5

[185] Recall the importance of filiality which we observed in the chapter on Confucius.

Confucians say, "One takes a wife so that she will assist in sacrificial prayers and a son will in the future look after the ancestral temple. This is the reason for taking her so seriously." We reply that this is just bombast. When their uncle or older brother looks after the ancestral temple for decades, then upon his death, they will mourn him for only one year. Their brothers' wives assist in the sacrificial prayers to ancestors, yet they pay them no last respects at all. Hence, their mourning for a wife or son for three years is certainly not because of their having looked after and assisted in the ancestral temple. Such inclinations for a wife or son are highly problematic. But they say, "It's because we place importance on our parents." But it's because they want to favor the one they are more intimate with and treat lightly the one they place more importance on. Isn't this most perverse?

They also firmly believe in the existence of fate and explain the doctrine by saying, "Long life, early death, poverty, wealth, security, danger, order, and chaos, are determined by heaven's fate and cannot be changed. Failure, success, reward and punishment, good luck and bad, are preordained. Human knowledge and effort cannot have any effect." If the many officials believe this, they will be lax at their stations. If the masses believe it, they will be lax in going about their business. Without oversight, there will be disorder, and if agricultural business is neglected, there will be poverty. Avoiding poverty and disorder are the fundamentals of government. But Confucians accept them as the teaching of the Way. They would destroy all the people in the world.

In addition, they make their rituals and music ornate ostentatious in order to debauch people, and they fool their loved ones with long periods of mourning and disingenuous grieving. They uphold fatalism and neglect the poor, while carrying themselves with haughty aloofness. They betray what is fundamental and slough off their duties, content in their laziness and pride. They lust after food and drink but are lackadaisical at work. Though beset by hunger and cold and in danger of freezing or starving, they cannot change. With the air of a pauper, they devour their food like monsters, glowering like goats, and carrying themselves like castrated pigs. When a gentleman laughs at them, they spitefully reply, "Loser! What do you know about how good Confucians are!"

In summer and spring they beg for grain. When the harvests are brought it, they follow large funerals, their children and grandchildren in tow. If they can eat and drink well by managing a few funerals, that's enough for them. They use other people's families as the source of their goods, and they rely on other people's farms for handouts. When rich people have a funeral, they are overjoyed, saying, "There could be some food or clothing in it for us!"

The Confucians say, "A gentleman must wear ancient-style cloths and speak ancient-style words in order to be humane." We reply: What you call ancient-style clothes and ancient style words were all once new. But the people of ancient times wore them and spoke them. So, they weren't gentlemen? Therefore, must we model ourselves on the clothes of people who weren't gentlemen and speak the words of people who weren't gentlemen in order to be humane?"

They also say, "The gentleman takes after others and does not create." We reply: In ancient times, Yi created the bow, Yu created armor, Xizhong created the cart, and Craftsman Qiu created the boat. Therefore, the tanners, smiths, cart makers, and carpenters of today are all gentlemen, while Yi, Yu, Xizhong, and Craftsman Qiu were all small men. In other words, what they "take after" must have been created by someone, and what they take after are all the ways of small men.

They also say, "In victory, the gentleman refrains from pursuing the vanquished. He protects himself with armor but does not shoot. And if they flee, he helps them with their carts." We reply, "If everyone involved is humane, then they won't come into conflict. Humane people tell each other when to give and take and what is right and wrong, and those without a reason follow those with a reason, while those without knowledge follow those with knowledge. Whenever they have no rebuttal, they submit. When they see what is good, they are motivated by it. How could they come into conflict? If two mean sides come into battle and the victors refrain from pursuing the vanquished, wear armor but does not shoot, and help them push their carts when they flee, even exhausting themselves at this they still won't be gentlemen. But suppose there is a mean and oppressive state and a sage endeavors to rid the world of its harm. He musters his soldiers and punish it but in victory uses Confucian techniques to command his troops, saying, "Refrain from pursuing the vanquished, protect yourselves with armor but do not shoot, and if they flee, help them with their carts." The mean and unruly people will live on, and the world will not be rid of their harm. This is to harm mothers and fathers, and do grave damage to the world. Nothing could be more wrong than that.

They also say, "The gentleman is like a bell. If you strike it, it rings. Don't strike it and it doesn't ring." We reply: A humane person serves his ruler with utmost loyalty and serves his parents with consummate filiality. If he works for the good, then he adores them. If they have any faults, he reproves them. This is the Way of being a subject. But 'strike it and it rings, don't strike it and it doesn't ring' is to conceal one's knowledge and spare one's strength, to keep mum and wait to be questioned before speaking. Even having a way to benefit their ruler or parents, not being asked, they doesn't speak. Even if a great rebellion and upheaval is about to occur or robbers and thieves about to make a move, or a trap about to be sprung, and others don't know it, while only they know it, even if their ruler or parents are involved, not being asked they won't speak. This is to inflict the injury of bringing great chaos. We take this as disloyalty in a subject, unfiliality in a child, disrespectfulness in a younger sibling, and miscreancy in social relations. One might wait before speaking at court, but when there is some benefit to be had one should risk speaking up. And if the ruler says something that won't be beneficial, one should clasp one's hand to oneself, look down and in grave and serious tone say, "Things aren't so clear to me. This is a serious matter, but we don't want to go astray."

Now, any Way, technique, study, craft or principle of rightness and humanity is, on the large scale, for governing people, and, on the small scale, for managing an office. It should be applied far and wide and cultivated in oneself near at hand. What isn't right should not be settled for and what isn't according to principles of order should not be done. One should work for what maximizes benefit to the world, whether it is particular or all encompassing: whatever is beneficial and nothing more. This is the Way of a gentleman.

But based on what we've heard of Confucius's actions, they were radically opposed to this. Duke Jing of Qi asked Yanzi,[186] "What sort of person is Confucius?" Yanzi didn't reply. The Duke asked again, but he didn't reply. Duke Jing said, "Many people have described Confucius to me as a worthy man. But now I ask you, and you don't respond. Why not?"

Yanzi replied, "I'm unworthy and unable to recognize a worthy man. However, I've heard that one who is worthy, when entering another's country, always tries to help make relations between its ruler and subject harmonious and to alleviate resentments between its superior and subordinates. When Confucius went to Jing, he knew about the Duke of Po's revolt and put him in touch with Shi Qi. The ruler himself was almost killed, and the Duke of Po was punished.[187] I've heard that a worthy man doesn't waste the favor of a superior or act recklessly with the favor of a subordinate. If the ruler listens to his words, this will always benefit others, and if what he teaches is practiced by subordinates, it will always benefit their superiors. Therefore his words are clear and easy to understand, and his actions simple and easy to follow. His actions and righteousness are enlightening to the people, and his plans and ideas can be made accessible to rulers and subordinates. But Confucius had devious ideas and a system of plans to support a rebel. He feverously schemed and devoted his mind and thoughts to doing

---

[186] Yan Ying (d. 500 B.C.E.).

[187] Yanzi was long dead by the time of the 479 B.C.E. revolt, and there is no independent evidence that Confucius had any part in it. That this is merely a mistake on Mozi's part is doubtful, given that - and I'll not make any further note of this - many other stories about Confucius in this essay are not corroborated by the historical record.

evil. To cause subordinates to throw their superiors into upheaval and to teach ministers to murder their rulers is not the conduct of a worthy man. To enter another's country and meet with its rebels is not the sort of thing that counts as right. Knowing that someone is disloyal and encouraging him to cause chaos does not count as humane or right. To hide oneself and draw up plans, to speak only having withdrawn - this is not conduct and righteousness that are enlightening to the people. These plans and ideas cannot be made accessible to the ruler and subjects. I don't see any difference between Confucius and the Duke of Po. That's why I didn't answer."

Duke Jing said, "Well! You've aided me in many ways. Without you, I would never have known that Confucius was just like the Duke of Po."

Confucius went to Qi to meet with Duke Jing. Duke Jing was pleased and wanted to enfeoff him in Niqi. He told this to Yanzi. Yanzi said, "I wouldn't. Confucians are haughty and bullheaded. They can't be used to guide subordinates. They like music and pervert people. They can't be used in a delicate governmental position. They proclaim fatalism and are lackadaisical in handling affairs. They can't be used to hold a post. They institutionalize funerals and uphold grieving periods. They can't be used to care for the people. They dress strangely and strike poses. They can't be used to lead the masses. Confucius is overbearing in his manner and cultivates the ornamental in order to delude the world. He uses music, singing, drumming, and dancing to attract followers. He uses his etiquette of scurrying and shuffling to show off to the masses. His broad studies can't be used to give counsel to the world. His feverish cogitations can't be used to help the people. Even in several lifetimes you couldn't master his educational program, and at the end of that time you still wouldn't be able to act according to his rituals. A fortune wouldn't enable one to subsidize his music. He uses ornate ornamentation and evil techniques to confuse the rulers the rulers of the world. He makes much of music and song to pervert the ignorant people. His Way can't be used to guide the world. His learning cannot be used to lead the masses. You would now enfeoff him in order to benefit the customs of Qi. But he can't be used to lead that province or guide the masses."

The Duke said, "Very well." With this, in full ritual propriety he set aside the fief, and though he was respectful in meeting with Confucius, he didn't ask about his Way.

Confucius was angry and Duke Jing and Yanzi. He had Chiyi Zipi become a follower of Tian Chang. He told Huizi of Nanguo what he wanted to do and returned to Lu. After some time, he heard that Qi was going to attack Lu. He told Zigang, "Ci, now is when we make our move," whereupon he sent Zigang to Qi. Huizi of Nanguo, by whom Zigang was introduced to Tian Cheng, he urged to attack Wu, and he instructed Gaoguo Baoyan not to do anything to impede Tian Cheng's uprising. And he urged Yue to attack Wu. For three years, Qi and Wu were on the verge of destruction, the numerous corpses layered on upon the other, all by Confucius's design.

When Confucius was Lu's Minister of Justice, he betrayed the ducal house and sided with Ji Sun. When Ji Sun was running from his position as ruler of Lu and was fighting to get away from the men of Lu at the city gate, Confucius lifted the gate bar.

When Confucius was being starved by Cai and Chen he ate vegetable soup with no rice for ten days. Zilu cooked pork for him and Confucius ate it without asking where the meat was from. When he robbed someone's robe to trade it for wine, Confucius drank it without asking where the wine came from. When Confucius met Duke Ai, he would not sit unless his mat was straight and he wouldn't eat food that wasn't sliced correctly. Zilu asked, "Why do you do the opposite of what you did between Chen and Cai?"

Confucius said, "Come, I'll tell you. Then we were trying to maintain our lives. Now we're trying to maintain rightness." So, when he was starving, he didn't scruple to take anything that would keep him alive. When he'd had his fill, he put on airs to give a show of decorum. How could anything be more wicked and deceitful!

146

...These are the Ways Confucius acted and the extremes the workings of his mind reached. His followers and disciples followed his lead....

Suggested Readings

Ahern, Dennis M., "Is Mo Tzu a Utilitarian?" *Journal of Chinese Philosophy* 3(1976): 185-193

Chiu, Wai, "Assessment of *Li* in the Mencius and the Mozi," *Dao: A Journal of Comparative Philosophy* 13(2014): 199-214

Chiu, Wai Wai, "Jian Ai and the Mohist attack of Early Confucianism," *Philosophy Compass* 8(2013): 425-437

Defoort, Carine, "The Modern Formation of Early Mohism: Sun Yirang's Exposing and Correcting the Mozi," *T'oung Pao* 101(2015): 208-238

Duda, Kristopher, "Reconsidering Mo Tzu on the Foundations of Morality," *Asian Philosophy* 11(2001): 23-31

Flanagan, Owen, "Moral Contagion and Logical Persuasion in the Mozi," *Journal of Chinese Philosophy* 35(2008): 473-491

Fraser, Chris, "Mohism and Self-Interest," *Journal of Chinese Philosophy* 35(2008): 437-454.

Fraser, Chris, *The Philosophy of the Mozi: The First Consequentialists* (New York: Columbia University Press, 2016)

Fraser, Chris, trans., *The Essential Mozi*, forthcoming.[188]

Hao, Changchi, "Is Mozi a Utilitarian Philosopher?" *Frontiers of Philosophy in China* 1(2006): 382-400

Ivanhoe, Philip J., "Mohist Philosophy," in *Routledge Encyclopedia of Philosophy*, Edward Craig, ed. (London and New York: Routledge, 1998), 6:451-458

Johnson, Daniel M., "Mozi's Moral Theory: Breaking the Hermeneutical Stalemate," *Philosophy East & West* 61(2011): 347-364

Johnson, Ian, trans., *The Book of Master Mo*, (London: Penguin, 2014)

Knoblock, John and Jeffrey Riegel, trans., *Mozi: A Study and Translation of the Ethical and Political Writings* (Berkeley: Institute of East Asian Studies, 2013)

Lai, Whalen, "The Public Good that Does the Public Good: A New Reading of Mohism," *Asian Philosophy* 3(1993): 125-141

Leong, Wai Chun, "The Semantic Concept of Truth in Pre-Han Chinese Philosophy," *Dao: A Journal of Comparative Philosophy* 14 (2015): 55-74

Li, Yong, "The Divine Command Theory of Mozi," *Asian Philosophy* 16(2006): 237-245

---

[188] Fraser's forthcoming book promises to be the best rendition of the entire book. Knoblock and Riegel's translation of the ethical essays and Watson's short selection are excellent.

Lowe, Scott, *Mo Tzu's Religious Blueprint for a Chinese Utopia: The Will and the Way* (Ontario: Edwin Mellen Press, 1992)

Loy, Hui-chieh, "Argument for Jian'ai," *Dao: A Journal of Comparative Philosophy* 12(2013): 487-504

Loy, Hui-chieh, "On a *Gedankenexperiment* in the Mozi Core Chapters," *Oriens Extremus* 45(2005): 141-158

Lu, Xiufen, "Understanding Mozi's Foundations of Morality: a Comparative Perspective," *Asian Philosophy* 16(2006): 123-134

Maeder, Erik W. "Some Observations on the Composition of the 'Core Chapters' of the Mozi," *Early China* 17 (1992): 27-82

Martinich, A. P. and Wiwing Tsoi, "Mozi's Ideal Political Philosophy," *Asian Philosophy* 25(2015): 253-275

Meyer, Andrew, "What Made Mo Di A Master? Exploring the Construction of a Category in Warring States Sources," *T'oung Pao* 101 (2015): 271-297

Perkins, Franklin, "Mozi and the Daodejing," *Journal of Chinese Philosophy* 41(2014): 18-32

Radice, Thomas, "Manufacturing Mohism in the Mencius," *Asian Philosophy* 21(2011): 139-152

Richey, Jeffrey, L., "Lost and Found Theories of Law in Early China," *Journal of the Economic and Social History of the Orient* 49(2006): 329-343

Soles, David E., "Mo Tzu and the Foundations of Morality," *Journal of Chinese Philosophy* 26(1999): 37-48

Stegeman, Steven A. "Unfolding Mozi's Standard of Sound Doctrine," *Asian Philosophy* 21(2011): 227-239

Taylor, Rodney L., "Religion and Utilitarianism: Mo Tzu on Spirits and Funerals," *Philosophy East & West* 29(1979): 337-346

Thompson, Kirill O., "Mozi's Teaching of Jianai (Impartial Regard): A Lesson for the Twenty-First Century?" *Philosophy East & West* 16(2014): 838-855

Tseu, Augustine, *The Moral Philosophy of Mozi* (Taipei: China Printing Limited, 1965)

Van Norden, Bryan W. "A Response to the Mohist Arguments in 'Impartial Caring'," in Kim-chong Chong, Sor-Hoon, eds., *The Moral Circle and the Self: Chinese and Western Approaches* (New York: Open Court, 2003)

Vorenkamp, Dirck, "Another Look at Utilitarianism in Mo-Tzu's Thought," *Journal of Chinese Philosophy* 19(1992): 423-443

Wang, Keping, "Mozi Versus Xunzi on Music," *Journal of Chinese Philosophy* 36(2009): 653-665

Watson, Burton, trans., *Mo Tzu: Basic Writings* (New York: Columbia University Press, 1963)

Wong, Benjamin, and Hui-chieh Loy, "War and Ghosts in Mozi's Political Philosophy," *Philosophy East & West* 54(2004): 343--363

Wong, David B., "Mohism: The Founder, Mozi (Mo Tzu)," in *Encyclopedia of Chinese Philosophy*, Antonio S. Cua, ed. (London and New York: Routledge, 2003), 453-461

Wong, David B., "Universalism versus Love with Distinctions: An Ancient Debate Revived," *Journal of Chinese Philosophy* 16(1989): 251-272

Yates, Robin D.S. "The Mohists on Warfare: Technology, Technique, and Justification," *Journal of the American Academy of Religion* 47(1979): 549-603

Zong, Desheng, "Studies of Intensional Contexts in Mohist Writings," *Philosophy East & West* 50(2000): 208-229

Interlude

Analytic Philosophy in Ancient China

Let us take a diversion into some "analytic philosophy" of Ancient China. In other chapters, you will see other Chinese philosophers alluding to this stream of thought with mentions of "hard and white" and "white horse." The analytical texts make for interesting reading, particularly for those interested in the history of logic or analytical philosophy. On the other hand, being of far less important than the works in the ten main chapters of this book, they are, I think, optional reading. It will be good to get a taste of what the allusions refer to, and the interlude will give us a short respite with some curious novelty before we proceed on our course.

During the period which we have been studying – The Warring States Period – some philosophers endeavored to understand the nature of language, names, how names refer to things, and the nature of the concepts which names comport. These endeavors often included careful argument intended to be logically rigorous in making distinctions and on the basis of those distinctions, determining where various entailments lay. It was philosophy which strove for clarity, disclosure of ambiguity, rigor of argument and truth in the areas of metaphysics, epistemology, and logic; this is what I mean by "analytic philosophy." On the other hand, I don't mean to beg the question by naming these philosophers. Some of them may simply have been sophists, in the pejorative sense of that term. I'll let you be the judge, in the case of the reading in this chapter.

The analytic philosophers included later members of the Mohist School, who added chapters to the *Mozi*. Those chapters may be of considerable interest, but the material is so difficult that it would take us far afield were we to foray into it with any success. It also included other philosophers, loosely grouped under the heading the School of Names. In this interlude, we will read two essays left by the School of Names. This school included Hui Shi - Huizi - a 4th C. philosopher and statesman who is portrayed in the *Zhuangzi* as a friend and colleague of Zhuangzi. Huizi's work is lost, except for a list of paradoxical statements he is said to have argued for. When you will get to the *Zhuangzi*, you will find him depicted as a foil for Zhuangzi's criticism of analytic philosophy as an endeavor. Another member of the School of names, Gongsun Long, wrote two essays of interest on language and kinds which we will read.

It would be a fine textbook in the history of logic an analytic philosophy which combined all the ancient analytical texts of China into clear and accurate translations and provided sufficient commentary for interpreting them. But we will at least get a flavor of the material here.

The Readings

Here I have included two chapters from the *Gongzun Longzi*: "Whiteness and Horseness" and the "Reference and Object." The former's title – *bai ma* - might also be translated as "White Horse." The latter's title – *zhi wu* - is misleading. It is not an essay about reference and object in general but only about the reference and object of the term "world." Perhaps the essay means to make a general point about reference by taking "world" as a special case. These two essays are the most likely to be genuine. Others in the *Gongsun Longzi* seem to have been added centuries after Gongsun Long lived. "Whiteness and Horseness" is a dialogue, and I have given the names "A" and "B" to its two interlocutors.

Gongsun Longzi

Whiteness and Horseness

A: "Is 'A white horse is not a horse' admissible?"

B: "Yes."

A: "Why?"

B: "Horseness is what determines its bodily form. Whiteness is what determines its color. To determine color and bodily form is not to determine bodily form. That is why I say a white horse is not a horse."

A: "There is a horse. You can't say that it has no horseness. That which you can't say does not have horseness - isn't that a horse? When there is a white horse, how does our taking it to be a white horse make it not a horse?"[189]

B: "When one's intent is 'horse,' then that applies to yellow and black horses. But if one's intent is 'white horse,' that does not apply to yellow and black horses. If 'white horse' were just 'horse,' then what is intended would be one and the same. If what is intended were of one sort, then whiteness wouldn't differ from horseness. If they don't differ in what is intended, then why are the black and yellow ones sometimes acceptable and sometimes unacceptable? The difference between the acceptability and unacceptability is clear. Therefore, yellow and black horses are one and the same in that they may be taken to satisfy 'there is a horse' but mustn't be taken to satisfy 'there is a white horse.' This shows that a white horse is not a horse."[190]

---

[189] Or, if two consecutive Chinese characters in the text were had their places reversed by a copyist's error, then the original text might have read, "Suppose there is a white horse that we take to be a horse. When we take it to be white, how does that make it no longer a horse?"

[190] Gongsun Long could have argued the property of being a white horse is not the property of being a horse. He could have made it clear that that is what he meant by saying "white horse not horse," rather than meaning that a white horse is not a horse. The Chinese sentence is the same and must be

A: "If we take a horse's having a color to make it not a horse, then, as the world has no colorless horses, the world would have no horses. Is that admissible?"

B: "A horses must have a color. Thus, there are white horses. If horses had no colors, there would be 'just plain' horses. How could we pick out the white horses? Therefore, the white ones are not 'horses.' A white horse is a horse and white. It is a horse-and-white horse. That is why I say a white horse is not a horse."[191]

A: "Horseness without whiteness is horseness. Whiteness without horseness is whiteness. When whiteness is combined with horseness, we use the double name 'white horse.' This is mutual compatibility. To make a name out of the mutually incompatible is inadmissible. Therefore, to say 'A white horse is not a horse' is inadmissible."

B: "If we take 'there is a white horse' to mean 'there is a horse', then is it admissible to say 'there is a horse' means 'there is a yellow horse'?"

A: "No."

B: "To take 'there is a horse' as different from 'there is a yellow horse' is to differentiate a yellow horse from horses. To differentiate a yellow horse from horses is to take a yellow horse as not a horse. To take a yellow horse as not a horse while yet taking a white horse to be a horse - this is incoherent

carefully disambiguated. So, Gongsun Long appears to be trading on an ambiguity in Chinese. The fact that the predicate "is a white horse" is not the same as, and is not satisfied by the same set of objects as, the predicate "is a horse" is trivially true. But the claim that a white horse is not a horse is a very strong claim and also obviously false. Is Gongsun Long engaging in mere sophistry or is he trying to get at something important?

[191] Here Gongsun Long is verging on incoherence. He tries to make "is horse-and-white" into a predicate distinct from "is a horse" in order to prove his point. But if this doesn't admit that a white horse is a horse, what does it do, then? If this last sentence means "That is why I say that to be a white horse is not the same as to be a horse," then that would remove the incoherence. However, it would make Gongsun Long's thesis less momentous. The difficulty of philosophy is to avoid saying what is false or incoherent while also establishing an interesting thesis. It isn't clear that Gongsun Long manages to do so here.

nonsense. This is the craziest utterance and most disorderly words in the world."

A: "If there is a horse, the fact that you can't say that 'there is no horse' is a statement which separates off the whiteness. If we couldn't separate it off, then when there is a white horse, you couldn't say that there was a horse. Therefore, what we mean when we say 'there is a horse' is to take just the horse as being a horse and not to take there being a white horse as there being a horse. Hence, when you take there to be a horse, you cannot say that there is not a horse."

B: "As for whiteness, when it isn't determined what is white, overlooking it is okay. But 'white horse' determines what is white in saying 'is white'. What determines what is white is not the whiteness. 'Horse' does not entail any color in particular. That is why it can be applied to both yellow and black horses. But 'white horse' does entail a particular color. Yellow and black horses are both excluded on the basis of their colors. That is why it applies only to white horses. What is not exclusive is not what is exclusive. Hence, I say that a white horse is not a horse."

Reference and Object

When no object is not referred to, then the referrer isn't really a referrer. "World" is without reference. No object can be taken as its object. As for its not being a referrer, if "world" doesn't have an object then can we say that it refers? If it is a referrer, then whatever it refers to is something that does not exist in the world. But an object is something that does exist in the world. To take something that would exist in the world as something that does not exist in the world is inadmissible.

"World" is without a referent. No object can be taken to be its referent. Nothing exists that it doesn't refer to. "Nothing exists that it doesn't refer to" means that among things, there is none that would not be referred to by it. Since there is nothing that would not be referred to by it, the referrer would not be a referrer.[192]

That "world" is without a referent derives from the following. Objects all have their own names and cannot serve as the referent. If we say that they are referred to even though they cannot serve as its referent, this is to make a group of what cannot serve as its referent.[193] But to take what is unable to serve as a referent and make it what is not unable to serve as its referent is inadmissible.[194] And the referent would be what the world contains.[195]

"World" is without a referent. For no object can be taken to be not its referent. That none can't be taken to be not its referent is because nothing exists without being referred to by it. That nothing exists without being referred to by it is because no object is not referred to by it. This referrer is not a referrer, but this referrer's relation to objects is not reference.

If we accept that "world" has no referent, who will maintain that it does not refer? If "world" has no object, who will maintain that it refers? If "world" refers without an object referred to, who will maintain that it does not refer by maintaining that, having no object, it does not refer? Moreover, if the referrer is actually not in itself a referrer, then why is it only in relation to an object that it is a referrer?

---

[192] This seems to be incorrect. Indeed, *every* object is not referred to by "world." Gongsun Long's point might be acceptable, however, if it is just the proposition that if "world" referred to an object, it would have to exclude other objects from reference, which it couldn't do.

[193] I.e., to treat the set of objects in the world as the referent of "world".

[194] Is there a part/whole fallacy here? GSL hasn't shown that "world" cannot refer to the set of objects in the world.

[195] I.e., the idea of a word's object being the things in the object is incoherent. So, the notion of the world as the set of existing objects is untenable since "world" means, in part, "container" of everything else.

Suggested Readings

Dan Robins, "The Later Mohists and Logic," *History and Philosophy of Logic* 31(2010): 247-285

Fraser, Chris, "Truth in Mohist Dialectics," *Journal of Chinese Philosophy*, 39(2012): 351-368

Fraser, Chris, "Distinctions, Judgment, and Reasoning in Classical Chinese Thought," *History and Philosophy of Logic*, 34(2013): 1-24

Fraser, Chris, "School of Names," *Stanford Encyclopedia of Philosophy*, WWW

Hansen, Chad, *Language and Logic in Ancient China* (Ann Arbor: University of Michigan, 1983)

Hansen, Chad, *A Daoist Theory of Chinese Thought* (Oxford: Oxford University Press, 1992)

Hansen, Chad, "Prolegomena to Future Solutions to 'White-Horse Not Horse'," *Journal of Chinese Philosophy*, 34(2007): 473–91

Rosker, Jana S., "Classical Chinese Logic," *Philosophy Compass* 10(2015): 301-309

Schleichert, Hubert, "Gong-Sun Long on the Semantics of 'World'" in Hans Lenk and Gregor Paul, eds., *Epistemological Issues in Classical Chinese Philosophy* (Albany: State University of New York Press, 1993)

4

Mencius

Mencius (Meng Ke, or Mengzi, 371-283 B.C.E.)[196] championed the philosophy of Confucius during a time of rife philosophical dispute: the period of "The 100 Schools" (including Confucianism, Daoism, the Logicians, Mohism, and Yangist egoism.) Although he claimed to be "not fond of disputation," he felt it necessary to defend Confucianism against alternative positions which he thought socially deleterious. He therefore had to develop and argue for the positions to which Confucianism was committed on various questions in moral philosophy. The book, *Mencius* (*Mengzi*), is one of one of the four core works of Confucianism called *The Four Books*, along with the *Analects*, the *Doctrine of the Mean*, and the *Great Learning*. It is a collection of Mencius's dialogues with disciples and opponents as well as with officials whom he met as he traveled the land trying to convince rulers that they should make moral principles their principles of government. The *Mencius* is probably the greatest work of moral philosophy in Chinese history, with the possible exception of the *Xunzi*. Its theory of the nature of morality, the cultivation of virtue, and its rebuttal of utilitarianism are profound. However, while it has many wonderful passages in it and it has long been used as a first reader in Classical Chinese, it is not well-organized on the whole as a book. Although its topical organization is not nearly as fragmented as that of the *Analects*, The book leaves it up to the reader to organize the ideas in his own mind while reading. I've made the job easier for you, as I did in Chapter 1 with the *Analects*,

---

[196] Like "Confucius," "Mencius" is the Latinized version of "Mengzi" name given to him by 16th Century Jesuits in China.

by reorganizing the reading by topic. If you like skip ahead now to the reading. Otherwise, let's first prepare by taking a brief look at the key ideas: human nature, the cultivation of virtue, deliberation in ethics, moral properties, and political theory.

Human Nature and Moral Cultivation

Mencius famously argued that "human nature is good." (We will take up Xunzi's reply – "human nature is wicked" - in Chapter 6.) By "nature" Mencius meant a thing's disposition to show certain qualities in normal circumstances. Also, he took "nature" to refer to the distinguishing feature of a thing, "what makes human beings different from beasts" (4B.19). This distinguishing feature in man is the disposition to feel compassion for others, the potential for moral goodness. This seems plausible. Normally a person who has had a normal upbringing will act morally and feel concern for others. Mencius gives the example of a child about to fall into a well. It is normal for observers to respond with alarm and concern at the sight. And although there are wicked people, Mencius says that this shows only that, like a naturally lush mountain subjected to deforestation, people exposed to abnormal conditions can end up wicked.

As you read Mencius's dialogue with Gaozi, who holds that human nature is neither good nor evil, consider what would count as 'normal circumstances.' Can Mencius specify these in a non-empty and non-question-begging way? If 'normal' circumstances means 'natural' circumstances, in other words, circumstances in which a person's goodness is nurtured, then perhaps he cannot. For example, Mencius says that it is water's nature to flow downwards (thought it can be abnormally splashed up.) However, in the absence of gravity, water does not flow downwards, and it won't do to say that the absence of gravity is unnatural. Why, then, shouldn't the hateful and violent environments in which some children are raised count as normal? It would seem natural for them to grow up to be hateful and violent. On the other hand, it may

160

be possible to define "normal conditions" by reference to the fact that man is a social animal, one whose proper function is social, tribal, or cooperative in some sense. One would not want to say that plants do not by nature grow leaves and spread them in the sun just because when cast into outer space or thrown onto a cement parking lot if they do not do so. To have a nature, a thing needn't always behave in the ways that we take to be typical of that nature.

In any event, Mencius develops a view of moral self-cultivation based on his view of the innate goodness of human beings. Everyone has "a heart[197] which cannot bear the suffering of others." The only thing left is to "deliberate over it." By "deliberate" Mencius means to contemplate one's natural moral inclinations in order to judge consistently with them in all the circumstances in which one finds oneself. In many situations, desires flare up, and we act on them, rather than on our stronger moral inclinations. By "extending" those inclinations to areas in which one fails, one can eventually attain perfect virtue, the state in which one's desires never step outside the bounds of rightness. Mencius lists the four cardinal virtues: benevolence, rightness, ritual (or ritual propriety), and wisdom (*ren, yi, li,* and *zhi*), and he describes them as the complete maturation of "sprouts," which are feelings of compassion, shame, compliance and moral judgment. These sprouts are cultivated through one's deliberation over their consistent application to varied cases, through exposure to exemplars of moral virtue, and through wide learning and experience of adversity. Through this process one gains the skill necessary to judge rightly and act morally, even though there are no rules to guide one.[198]

---

[197] The term is *xin.* It means heart and mind, as well as attitude and mental state. In the reading of the *Mencius,* I have sometimes translated the term as "heart" and sometimes as "mind," depending on the nuance of the text. The semantic capaciousness of this term will come up again in the chapters on Buddhism.

[198] For more on this topic, see my 1998 and 2003 articles, as well as other items listed in this chapter's list of suggested readings.

Deliberation in Ethics

Mencius provides us with a plausible view of ethical deliberation: coherentism. The gist of this position is that the correct moral judgment is the one that is coherent with all of our other moral judgments – or at least with the largest and most coherent group of our other moral judgements.[199] When trying to decide what is the right thing to do, rather than following some universal rule, such as that of utilitarianism (recall the chapter on Mozi), one should check one's judgments in cases analogous to the one in question. For instance, in deliberating over whether abortion is permissible or impermissible, one should consider whether the act is more like either having a cyst removed or killing in self-defense than it is like murdering one's three-year-old child. If so, then the more coherent judgment, and hence the correct one, would be that it is permissible to have an abortion; otherwise the opposite conclusion would seem warranted. In the southern United States in the Nineteenth Century, more and more Americans came to see the inconsistency in their judgment that black people had no right to freedom, given the nation's commitment to the judgment that "all men are created equal," which comprised a host of specific judgments in favor of individual rights to liberty. Selfish desire had obscured their judgment, Mencius might have said.

As you read, consider the relation between moral reasoning and moral virtue according to Mencius. It might seem that he can't mean that any set of coherent judgments is correct, since a set of coherent but evil judgments wouldn't be correct. It would also seem that his emphasis on cultivating desires is necessary, that virtue is required in order for one to perceive what is right. Wisdom, he says, is something that comes at the end of moral cultivation, only its sprouts coming in the beginning. On the other hand, Mencius probably takes it as given that everyone has altruistic sentiments. So, in that

---

[199] See Alan H. Goldman's *Moral Knowledge* (London: Routledge, 1991).

context, perhaps coherence would be enough for having the correct judgment. Wisdom for Mencius may thus be consistent performance in making and adhering to coherent judgments, rather than the development of a faculty of judgment. He says that its substance is "never to leave off benevolence and rightness" (4A.27) and that it is cultivated moral judgment (2A.6). That seems to mean that virtue is simply consistently making the coherent judgment and is not a separate ability to make the correct moral judgment. This is a controversial topic in contemporary philosophy. Philosophers who think that virtuous character is an important prerequisite for moral judgment disagree with philosophers who take virtue as simply the disposition to adhere to correct moral judgment and not to let desires cloud one's judgment. Try to decide which sort of philosopher Mencius is or whether he is of neither sort.

The *Mencius* is full of examples of reasoning for coherence. See how many you can find in the selections as you read them. One well-known example is that of the king who, just before a ceremonial sacrifice, says that he should not sacrifice an ox since it would be too cruel. "Sacrifice a lamb instead," he says. But Mencius points out the analogy between the ox and the lamb, in which there is no morally relevant difference to justify the difference between the king's judgments. What further inconsistency in the king's views does Mencius point out?

According to the coherentist position, there are no moral rules that hold true in all circumstances. Even "do not kill" fails in cases of self-defense, and perhaps in other cases, such as euthanasia or abortion. Can you think of any moral rules that hold true absolutely? For Mencius, the right act is the one that corresponds to our most coherent set of moral judgments, given our "heart which cannot bear the suffering of others," which shows itself in our basic moral judgments, such as "I ought to help the child who is about to fall into the well." This brings us to the topic of moral properties.

Moral Properties

Moral properties are acts' properties of rightness (*yi*)[200] or wrongness. When I steal something, my act has a property of wrongness, and when I return the stolen item, my act has the property of rightness. These properties are not accessible through direct empirical observation in the way that the property 'red' or 'one inch long' is, so there is considerable debate in philosophy over whether they exist and what they are. They seem not to be objective, external properties existing independently of our subjective feelings and desires, because they are values, 'oughts', rather than brute facts. But they seem not to be reducible to mere subjective fantasy, since clearly certain acts really are right, and certain others really are wrong. As David Hume suggested in *An Enquiry into the Principles of Morals*, rightness seems to be "Whatever quality gives to a[n unbiased, informed, coherent] spectator the pleasing sentiment of approbation." The position that moral rightness is subjectively or relationally real (i.e., really existing in acts but only in relation to our subjective desires) seems to be Mencius's position. He says, "Rightness is internal. It is not external."[201] Although the topic comes up in only two small passages (6A.4-5), it is important.

In debate with Gaozi, Mencius provides support for his view. For instance, the deliciousness of roasts, he says, is a property they have only relative to our subjective feelings. It would not make any sense to suppose that something could be delicious even though no one ever likes the way it tastes. Similarly, rightness is a property which acts have in relation to our feelings of compassion.

---

[200] Mencius has one word, *yi*, for both the 'rightness' of an act and 'righteousness,' the virtue which may be defined as the disposition to do right acts. I will usually use "rightness" as a translation, except in cases where Mencius is specifically speaking of the feelings of the heart.

[201] The interpretation I will give here is not the only one. See the books by Shun and Nivison in this chapter's list of suggested readings for alternatives. For more on this topic, see my 1997 article, which is listed there, as well.

This does not make morality purely subjective. Mencius says that everyone has the same natural dispositions, so there is no divergence among people. Rightness is thus not whatever I approve of but a norm by which we may determine whether my approvals and disapprovals are correct. Slavery in the United States was not "right relative to that culture." Rather, there is one true set of universal judgments about the one real set of moral properties. For Mencius this means that unnatural theories, such as Mozi's utilitarianism and Yang Zhu's egoism, cannot be true. Utilitarianism, for example, demands the utterly impartial sacrifice of one's own and one's loved ones' interests for the greater good of all people. That would make it obligatory to feed your own children extremely meagerly, while you divert your resources to starving people. Mencius argues that all coherent deliberation over the heart's inclinations leads to the conclusion that, while we are obligated to help strangers to some degree, we are not obligated to treat them in the same way we treat our own family. The rule of utility, as a rule, is supposed to hold whether or not upon reflection we find it to be abominable. That is why Mencius cannot accept it.

Political Philosophy

Mencius's political theory includes positions on legitimacy, taxation, official promotion, international relations, and the moral duties of government (mainly economic planning and maintenance of infrastructure). We will read only a little of this material in the selections that follow. Section 5A.5 is a remarkable account of political legitimacy. Mencius upheld a moralistic monarchy, in which the people could, as it were, vote with their moral approval. According to tradition, the king had the mandate of heaven to rule the empire. Mencius says that the people's satisfaction with the moral standing of the ruler is tantamount to heaven's mandate. Hence, to have the mandate, the ruler need only do right by the people. This meant not using them as soldiers in wars of aggression but providing for economic stability so that the people could devote some of their energies to the moral life. 5A.5 is a clear rejection of the view that political legitimacy or authority is the same as power. What is not so clear is what Mencius means by equating heaven's bestowal of legitimacy with the people's bestowal of it. It seems to be a humanistic approach to religious tradition in keeping with Confucius's humanism.

The Reading

Below you will find excerpts from the *Mencius*. Each of the seven books of the *Mencius* contains two halves (A and B). I have rearranged the excerpts according to topic and provided topical headings. Some excerpts speak to more than one topic. You have the standard identifiers of each section (for example, 1A.7), so that the standard ordering of the sections is still apparent.

Mencius

Deliberation in Ethics

1A.7 ...[King Xuan of Qi asked], "What sort of virtue must one have in order to be king?"

Mencius said, "By protecting the people, one becomes king. No one can stop it."

"Can someone such as I protect the people?"

"Yes."

"How do you know I can?"

"I heard from Hu He that Your Majesty was sitting in the hall when someone leading an ox crossed below the hall. Your Majesty saw it and said, 'Where is the ox going?' The man replied, 'We are going to use it to consecrate a bell.' Your Majesty said, 'Release it. I cannot bear its trembling with fright, like an innocent man on the way to the execution grounds.' The man said, 'So, shall we cancel the consecration of the bell?'

Your Majesty said, 'How can we cancel it? Use a lamb instead of the ox.' Did that really happen?"

"It did," the king said.

"This heart suffices for kingship. The people saw Your Majesty as niggardly, but I'm sure of Your Majesty's inability to bear [the ox's suffering]."

"Yes, that's really how it was with the people. The country of Qi is small, but how could I begrudge an ox? It was because I could not bear its trembling with fear like an innocent man on the way to the execution grounds that I used a lamb instead."

"Your Majesty shouldn't find it odd that the people saw you as niggardly. You substituted a small thing for a large one. How were they to know the reason? If Your Majesty was pained by its innocently going to the execution grounds, then how could you choose between an ox and a lamb?"

The king smiled. "What was I thinking? I didn't begrudge the cost, but I exchanged it for a lamb. It was fitting for the people to call me niggardly."

"No harm done. Such are the ways of a benevolent person. You saw the ox and hadn't seen the lamb yet. The gentleman's attitude towards animals is that, having seen them alive, he can't bear their death, and having heard their calls, he can't bear to eat their meat. That is why the gentleman stays away from the slaughterhouse and kitchen."[202]

The king was delighted. "The *Book of Odes* says, 'It is someone else's heart, but it is I who fathom it.' This describes you. For I performed the action, but upon reflectively seeking it, I could not find my own heart. When you spoke of it, my

---

[202] Is this reasonable? If it is wrong to slaughter animals, then anyone who buys and eats the meat is acting in collusion with the butcher. That one stays away from the slaughterhouse is irrelevant. On the other hand, Mencius might mean that, though slaughtering animals is permissible, any morally sensitive person will nevertheless feel (misplaced) discomfort upon witnessing the act. Nevertheless, can Mencius coherently maintain that killing animals is permissible, while killing an innocent person is not?

heart was moved. What is it that makes this heart fit for kingship?"

"Suppose someone said to Your Majesty, 'My strength suffices to lift 100 *jun* but does not suffice to lift a feather. My vision suffices to pick out the tip of an autumn hair, but I cannot see a cartload of firewood.' Would Your Majesty accept this?"

"No."

"In this case, your kindness suffices to reach animals, but this laudable attitude hasn't been extended to the people. What is the reason for making an exception? Hence, not lifting a feather is due to no applying one's strength to it. Not seeing a cartload of firewood is due to deciding not to apply one's eyesight to it. The people's not enjoying any protection is due to your not applying your kindness to them. So, Your Majesty's not being kingly is due to not deciding to be so, not due to being unable."

"What is the difference in form between not deciding to do and not being able to do?"[203]

"Taking Mt. Tai under your arm and striding over the North Sea - if you tell people that you can't do that, this is genuine inability. Breaking off a tree branch for a superior - if you tell people you can't do that, this is not deciding to do it. It is not being unable to do it. Hence, striding over the North Sea with Mt. Tai under one's arm - Your Majesty's not being kingly is not of that kind. Breaking off a tree branch - Your Majesty's not being kingly is of that kind.

"Treat your family's elderly," Mencius continued, "as elders, so that it extends to the elderly of other people's families. Treat the young of your family as children, so that it

---

[203] This is the question of whether someone who is beset by selfish desires stronger than his benevolent desires is *unable* to do right. Mencius seems correct in saying that deliberation over analogies enables us to act on values which we recognize upon reflection as stronger than the momentarily overwhelming selfish desires. And yet, when momentarily overwhelmed, how can the benevolent desires prevail? Some answer, "By will power," but that substitutes one mystery for another.

extends to the young of other people's families. You will have the world in the palm of your hand. The *Book of Odes* says, 'He established a principle with his wife, extended it to his siblings, and thereby ruled over family and state.' In other words, one simply takes this heart and applies it to other cases. Therefore, without extending one's kindness, one won't even have a way to protect one's wife and children. The way the ancients far surpassed others is nothing other than this. They simply extended what they did. In your case your kindness suffices to include animals, but your merit does not reach the people. What is the reason for making the exception? After weighing, we know how heavy a thing is. After measuring, we know how long it is. Things are all like that, especially the heart. I ask Your Majesty to measure his heart. Now, when Your Majesty prepares the military, endangers knights and officers, and incurs the anger of the various lords, does it please your heart?"

"No. How could I find pleasure in that? I do them in order to pursue something I strongly desire."

"May I hear about what you strongly desire?"

The king smiled and said nothing.

"Is it that you haven't enough rich and sweet food to satiate your mouth? That you haven't enough light and warm clothing for your body? Or that you haven't enough beautiful colors to look at with your eyes? Or that you haven't enough sounds for your ears to listen to? Or not enough servants to attend to your orders? Your Majesty's subjects are all able to give you these things, so how can it be for them that you act?"

"No, I don't act for those things."

"So, we can tell what Your Majesty strongly desires. You desire to enlarge your territory, to have Qin and Chu bow to your court, to rule the Middle Kingdom, and to subdue the four barbarian tribes. But to do what you're doing in order to seek after what you desire is like climbing a tree to seek fish."

"Is it that bad?"

"Yes, and worse. In climbing a tree to seek fish, although you won't get fish, you won't meet any calamity afterwards. But doing what you do, in order to seek what you desire, you exhaust your heart in doing it and must certainly meet with disaster."

"May I hear about this?"

"If Zou and Chu were at war, who would Your Majesty say would win?"

"Chu would win."

"Since that is the case, the small certainly cannot contend with the large, the few certainly cannot contend with the many, and the weak certainly cannot contend with the strong. The land between the seas are nine areas of 10,000 square *li*. Qi altogether has one of these. For one to try to subdue eight - how can you take this as different from Zou's contending with Chu? Again we must return to the basics. In your case, if Your Majesty sets up a government that shows benevolence, this will cause all officers in the kingdom to desire to have a place in Your Majesty's court, all farmers to desire to farm on Your Majesty's farmland, all merchants to desire to have their stores in Your Majesty's marketplace, all travelers to desire to take Your Majesty's roads, and all in the land who suffer at the hands of their rulers to desire to bring their complaints to you. If that were the way things were, who could stop you?"

The king said, "I am stupid and cannot progress in this area. I ask the master to bolster my intentions and instruct me clearly. Though I am not clever, I will make an attempt to follow you."

Mencius said, "Only a gentleman can have an unvarying heart without having an unvarying livelihood. As for the people, if they have no unvarying livelihood, then they will not have unvarying hearts. Lacking unvarying hearts, they will fall into excesses and depravity without limit. After the people have sunken to crime, for you to pursue and punish them is entrapment. How can there be a benevolent man in charge who allows entrapment of the people? Therefore, a smart ruler regulates the people's livelihood, and insures that, on the one hand, they have enough to serve their parents and, on the other hand, they have enough to support their wives and children. In good years the people will always be full, and in bad years they will evade death. Then, they we be spurred to reach goodness. That is why it will be easy for the people to follow him.

"In your case, in regulating the people's livelihood, you have made it that, on the one hand, they haven't enough to serve their parents, and, on the other, they haven't enough to support their wives and children. In good years, they always face misery, and in bad years they do not evade death. In simply trying to survive, they fear they will fail. What leisure have they for perfecting ritual and rightness?

"If Your Majesty desires to practice this, then you must return to the basics. Plant mulberry trees in every homestead of five *mu*, and fifty-year-olds will be able to wear silk. With the cultivation of chickens, pigs and dogs, if you don't miss the seasons, seventy-year-olds will be able to eat meat. If each 100 *mu* field does not miss its season, then each family of eight will live without hunger. Take care of education in the schools, inculcating in them the rightness of filiality and fraternity, and gray-haired people will not carry loads on the roads. There has never been a case in which the elderly wore silk and ate meat and the masses lived without hunger or cold, while the king did not attain kingliness."

1B.6   Mencius said to King Xuan of Qi, "Suppose one of Your Majesty's ministers left his wife and children with a friend and went to Chu to make his rounds. If upon his return he found that his wife and children had gone cold and hungry, then what should he do?"

The King said, "He should break off the friendship."

"If a chief of officials could not manage the officials, then what should you do?"

The King said, "Fire him."

"If things within your four borders were not well managed, then what should be done about it?"

The King looked to his attendants and changed the subject.

1B.16 Duke Ping of Lu was about to depart, when one of his favorites, Zang Cang, inquired, "On other days, when you are about to leave, you always give instructions to the officers about where you are going. Today the carriage is already hitched, but the officers do not know where you are going. May I ask why?"

The Duke said, "I'm going to see Mencius."

"What?! Sir, do you so demean yourself by extending the first visit to that common man because you take him to be a worthy? Worthies uphold ritual and rightness. But Mencius's later mourning ceremonies outdid his earlier mourning ceremonies.[204] Do not go to see him, sir."

The Duke said, "Very well."[205]

Yuezhengzi went in to see the Duke and said, "Sir, why haven't you gone to see Mencius?"

"Someone told me that Mencius's later mourning ceremonies outdid his earlier ones. That is why I did not go to see him."

"What?! Sir, when you say 'outdid,' do you refer to his using the rites of an officer at the later one and the rites of a gentleman at the earlier one? That is, to his using three tripods at the earlier one and five tripods at the later one?"

"No," said the Duke. "I refer to the quality of the coffin, the coffin shell, the clothing and the shroud."

"That cannot be called 'outdoing.' That was a matter of a difference in his financial situation."

Yuezhengzi saw Mencius and said, "I told the prince [Duke Ping] about you, and he was going to come see you. One of his favorites, a Zang Cang, stopped him. So, he didn't come after all."

---

[204] Mencius mourned his mother with more elaborate ceremonies than the ones he had used for his father.

[205] Apparently the Duke was trying to sneak off to see Mencius because he knew that if any of his advisors heard about it, they would have no trouble in persuading him not to do so. Imagine having so little moral backbone and being so aware of it! And at the same time desiring to improve!

"When one moves forward something causes it," Mencius said. "When one stops something impedes it. Moving forward and stopping are not under others' control.[206] My not meeting the Marquis of Lu [the Duke] was due to heaven.[207] How could the son of the Zang family cause me not to meet him?"

2B.4 Mencius went to Pinglu He said to its governor,[208] "If one of your spearmen failed to report for duty three times in one day, you would get rid of him, wouldn't you?"

"I would not wait until the third time."

"If that is so, then your failures to report for duty are also numerous. In bad years and years of famine, those of your people who were old or feeble and left lying in water ditches and those who were able-bodied but scattered in every direction[209] numbered in the thousands."

"There was nothing that I, Juxin, could do about this."

"Take a case in which someone who has taken another's cattle and sheep into his care to feed them for him. He must seek a place for them to graze. If he seeks a place for them to graze but cannot find one, will he return them to their owner, or will he continue to stand there and watch them die?"

"Given this, it was my fault."

On another day, seeing the King, Mencius said, "Of those who are in charge of Your Majesty's cities, I know five. The only one who knows his faults is Kong Juxin." Mencius repeated the conversation for the king. The King said, "Given this, it was my fault."

---

[206] The text is ambiguous here between "not under others' control" and "not under human control."

[207] Given that the Duke was without the ability to make independent and reasonable moral judgments, it was pre-determined that he was not to meet Mencius. There is nothing Mencius could do about it. It was the fate heaven bestowed upon him.

[208] The governor was Kong Juxin.

[209] I.e., they were not organized or made available by the king.

4A.17 Qunyu Kun said, "When giving or receiving something men and women don't touch. Is that the ritual?"

"That's the ritual," Mencius said.

"If one's sister-in-law were drowning, should one reach out one's hand for her?"

"Anyone who does not reach out his hand for her is a wolf. That men and women don't touch giving or receiving something is the ritual. The case in which one's sister-in-law is drowning, and one reaches out a hand to her is a case of weighing."[210]

"Now the world is drowning, but, Master, you do not reach out your hand.[211] Why not?"

"When the world is drowning, one reaches out to it with the Way. When one's sister-in-law is drowning, one reaches out to her with one's hand. Do you want me to reach out to the world with my hand?"

4A.26 Mencius said, "There are three ways of being unfilial, and not leaving heirs is the worst. Shun's not telling his parents[212] that he had married was in order to leave them heirs. A gentleman takes this to be as good as having told them."

4B.6 Mencius said, "Ritual which isn't ritual, right which isn't right – these a great person does not do."[213]

---

[210] "Weighing" (*quan*) means consistently measuring the competing values at stake in the case at hand. The Chinese term is also translated as "discretion."

[211] Mencius refuses to take up a career in political leadership. The questioner thinks this is because he doesn't want to get his hands dirty by working for morally mediocre political regimes. How do you read Mencius's reply? One might argue that an intellectual who only writes articles criticizing the corruption of a local government should also run for election to the school board or the city council and help clean up the corruption more actively.

[212] They would have forbidden it.

[213] You can probably imagine ceremonies which, while technically correct on one level, are seen to be unseemly, improper, and inappropriately executed when all considerations are taken into account. Also, certain acts may be described as "right" when only a few relevant factors are taken into

174

4B.11 Mencius said, "When a great person speaks he doesn't have necessarily to keep his word. And when acts he doesn't have necessarily to follow through to the end. He aims only at rightness."

4B.15 Mencius said, "Through broad learning and discussion of the details of things, one can return to explain the essentials."

5B.4 Wan Zhang asked, "May I ask about the sort of heart[214] one should have in exchanging gifts?"

Mencius said, "Respect."

"Why is it that to insist upon refusing a gift is taken as disrespectful?"

"If a noble person gives it, to ask, 'Did you obtain it rightly or wrongly?' before accepting it is to be disrespectful. Therefore, one doesn't refuse gifts."

"But if one refuses it without a word, while in one's heart refusing it and saying 'He took it wrongly from the people,' or if one offers some excuse for not accepting it, isn't that okay?"

"If his manners are according to the Way, and he treats one according to ritual, then even Confucius would accept the gift."[215]

Wan Zhang said, "Suppose someone were robbing people outside the city gates. If his manners were according to the Way, and his presentation were according to ritual, could one accept the stolen goods?"

"One could not. The *Kang Gao* says, 'Those who kill people and roll them over for their goods, who are aggressive and do not fear death are despised by all people.' Such people

___

account but certainly not right when all relevant factors are taken into account.

[214] This is *xin*, which we have seen above. Here it might also be translated as "mental state" or "state of mind."

[215] Should a hunger-relief organization accept donations from criminals? The case under consideration is one in which one merely suspects but does not know that the gift was ill-gotten. Confucius said that it is wrong to be distrustful. The next case is different, one in which the giver is known to be 'robbing people outside the city gates.'

one can punish without first instruct them. The Yin Dynasty received this from the Xia, the Zhou from the Yin. It is something they didn't draw into question, and it is obviously so today. How can one accept such a gift?

"Today's feudal lords' taking from the people is also robbery," Wan Zhang said. "Now, if they are skilled in their ritualized dealings, and the superior man accepts their gifts, how can one explain this?"

Mencius said, "Do you think that if a king rose up, he would confront today's feudal lords and punish them? Would he educate them and punish them when they did not change? Now, to say that taking anything which does not belong to one is theft is to fill up a kind and come to the end of rightness...."[216]

6A.10 Mencius said, "Fish is something I desire. Bear's paw is also something I desire. If I cannot have the two together, I will give up the fish and take the bear's paw. Life is also something I desire. Rightness is something I desire. If I cannot have the two together, I will give up life and take rightness. Life is something I desire, but there is something I desire even more than life. Therefore, I would not do

---

[216] The kind here is 'theft.' If you keep placing things in that class until you stretch it beyond its borders, then you've filled it up and come to the end of rightness. Taking someone's food when you can't afford to buy any is still theft, though close to the border. Taking someone's car in order to rush a dying person to the hospital is beyond the border. If you let the person die, rather than take the car, you've come to the end of rightness and have done something wrong. Accepting a gift which is stolen, though you only suspect and do not know this, is beyond the border of theft, though it may be close, in that you might indeed have enough evidence to know that it is stolen. This is Mencius's idea. While this idea may make good sense, Mencius's particular application of it is problematic. One might side with Wan Zhang and hold that kleptocracy is at least as wrong as common robbery. In fact, kleptocracy can destroy more lives than common robbery. But since the kleptocrat doesn't get his hands dirty we don't see it in such a bad light. In any event, that Mencius probably errs here in his moral judgement does not show that his idea of "filling up a kind and coming to the end of rightness" isn't an interesting description of an aspect of moral reasoning.

something illicit to have it. Death is something I dislike, but there is something I dislike more than death. Therefore, there are calamities which I will not avoid.

"If there were nothing people desired more than life, then why wouldn't they use any means that would enable them to have it? If there were nothing people disliked more than death, then why wouldn't they do anything that would enable them to avoid calamity? There are means of survival which some people won't use. There are means of avoiding calamity which some people will not use. This shows that there is something people desire more than life, and there is something people dislike more than death. It is not only worthies who have this heart. All people have it. It's just that worthies can keep from losing it.

"If one basket of rice and one bowl of soup would make the difference between life and death, but they are given with contempt, then even a homeless person won't accept them. And if you step on them and then give them, then even a beggar won't take them. But for 10,000 bushels people will accept it without considering ritual propriety or rightness. But how can 10,000 bushels add to me? Is it for the sake of the beauty of a palatial house, the services of wives and concubines, or the treatment that one will receive from one's destitute acquaintances? In the previous case one wouldn't take something to save one's life. But here people would do it for the sake of the beauty of a palatial house. In the previous case, one wouldn't take something even to avoid death. But here one would do it for the services of wives and concubines. In the previous case one wouldn't take something even to avoid death. But here one would do it for the treatment one would receive from one's destitute acquaintances. Is there no way to stop this? It is called 'losing one's original heart'."[217]

---

[217] There are two things going on here. The first is the moral psychology of maintaining the right moral attitude across cases. The second is Mencius moral reasoning itself: reasoning by analogy for coherence. See my three articles in this chapter's list of suggested readings in order to explore this further.

6B.1 A man of Ren asked Wuluzi, "Which is more important, ritual or food?"

"Ritual is more important."

"Which is more important, sex or ritual?"

"Ritual is more important."

"Suppose that eating only according to ritual would result in starving to death, while eating without regard to ritual would enable one to get food. Would one have to maintain ritual? And if observing the *qinying*[218] would result in one's not obtaining a wife, while not observing the *qinying* would enable to get a wife, would one have to observe the *qinying*?"

Wuluzi could not answer. The next day, he went to Zou and told of this to Mencius. Mencius said, "As for answering this, there is nothing to it. If you do not keep their bottoms even and you put their tips at the same level, then a one-inch stick can be made taller than a large building. Take the point that "gold is heavier than feathers." How can one mean the gold of one clasp and one cartload of feathers?

"[The man of Ren] takes a case in which food is important and a case in which propriety is not important and, comparing them, simply concludes that food is more important. He takes a case in which sex is important and propriety is not important and, comparing them, simply concludes that sex is more important. Go back and reply to him as follows.

"If twisting your older brother's arm and grabbing his food would result in your obtaining food, while by not twisting it you would not get food, would you twist it? If scaling your neighbor's wall and dragging away the daughter of the house would result in obtaining a wife, while by not dragging her away you would not obtain a wife, would you drag her away?"[219]

---

[218] A special ritual way in which the bridegroom was supposed to approach the bride.

[219] There are at least two things going on in this passage. The most important point is that Mencius eschews rule-based moral reasoning. He thinks that competing moral considerations must be weighed in each case

7B.1 Mencius said, "Unbenevolent was king Hui of Liang! A benevolent person extends the class of those he loves to include those he does not love. An unbenevolent person extends the class of those he does not love to include those he loves."

"What do you mean?" asked Gongsun Chou.

"King Hui of Liang, for the sake of territory, let his people be rent and torn in war. Suffering great defeat, he would have sent them back again but feared he could not be victorious. So, he urged the young men whom he loved to die for him. This is called extending the class of those one does not love to include those one does love."

7B.31 Mencius said, "For everyone there is something which he cannot bear. Extending this to the class of things which he can bear is benevolence. Everyone has something which he would not do. Extending this to the class of things which he does is rightness. If a person can fill up with the heart of not desiring to harm others, he will have more benevolence than he can use up. If a person can fill up with the desire not to bore holes or climb walls,[220] then he will have more rightness than he can use up. If a person can fill up with the substance of his refusal to be addressed as 'thou' or 'thee,'[221] then wherever he dwells he will do what is right. To speak to a gentleman who cannot be spoken to is to use words to bait him. If he can be spoken to but you do not speak to him, this is to use your

of their application; no principle trumps any other. Secondly, however, is that Mencius seems to allow certain generalizations, such as that ritual is more important than sex. He doesn't state this outright, but the point about gold being heavier than feathers seems to imply it, as does the famous passage about bear's paw (6A.10). It is not obvious what it means to say that principle A is more important than principle B even though there are cases in which B outweighs A. You can imagine some cases of your own in pondering this. For example, while private property is more important than one's own discomfort, we might think it would be permissible to use someone else's property in order to avoid discomfort when the discomfort is great and the private property is of low importance.

[220] For illicit entry, breaking and entering.

[221] Degrading terms in the ancient Chinese context.

silence to bait him. These are both of the same kind as boring holes and climbing walls."

Moral Properties

6A.4 Gaozi said, "Just as food and sex are matters of human nature, benevolence is internal, not external. But rightness is external, not internal."

Mencius said, "Why do you say benevolence is internal while rightness is external?"

Gaozi said, "If someone is older, and I treat him as an elder, he does not have his oldness relative to me. It is just as when he is white, and I treat him as white. I acknowledge his whiteness, which is external to me. Therefore, I say it is external."

Mencius said, "There is no way to distinguish between the whiteness of a horse and the whiteness of a person. But isn't there a way to distinguish an old horse's oldness from an elderly person's oldness? And which shall we say - that the older person is right or that the person treating him as an elder is right?

Gaozi said, "If someone is my younger brother, then I am concerned for him. If he is the younger brother of someone from Qin, then I am not concerned for him. Here I take my own as what is pleasing. That is why I call it internal. I treat a person from Chu as an elder, and I treat one of my own countrymen as an elder. Here I take the elderliness as what is pleasing. That is why I say it is external."

Mencius said, "Enjoying the roast of a man of Qin is not different from enjoying one of our own roasts. All things are like this. Is the enjoying of a roast external?"

6A.5 Mengjizi asked Gongduzi, "On what basis should we say that rightness is internal?"

"It is acting out of one's reverence. That is why it is called 'internal'," said Gongduzi.

"If someone from one's village were older than one's elder brother by one year, to whom would one show reverence?"

"I would show reverence to my elder brother."

"But in pouring wine, whom would one serve first?"

"First one serves the person from the village."[222]

"What is revered is in the former, and what is [rightly] treated as elder is the latter. Hence, it is an external matter and does not depend on what is internal."[223]

Gongduzi could not reply and told of this to Mencius. Mencius said, "Whom does one respect more, one's uncle or one's younger brother? [Mengjizi] will say, 'One respects one's uncle more.' Ask him, 'If one's younger brother were impersonating a deceased ancestor, then whom would one respect more?' He will say, 'One would respect one's younger brother more.' If you ask, 'What about the respect due to one's uncle?' then he will say, 'It is a matter of the roles they play.' You should also say, 'It is a matter of the roles they play. But ordinarily one shows more respect for one's elder brother, while occasionally one's respect is given to someone from the village.'"

Mengjizi listened to this and said, "When respect is due one's uncle, one should show him respect. When respect is due one's younger brother, one would show him respect. Hence, it is an external matter and does not depend on what is internal."[224]

Gongduzi said, "In winter one drinks hot water, but in summer one drinks cool water. Since that is the case, eating and drinking would be a matter of what is external."[225]

---

[222] The point is that when the person from the village is a guest, one ought to serve him before one's beloved family member.

[223] Rightness is determined by circumstances independent of internal feelings.

[224] Mengjizi counters that Mencius's reply fails to disprove that rightness depends upon external circumstances.

[225] Gongduzi defends the Mencian position by pointing out that though rightness depends on external circumstances, it derives from what we desire (the internal), depending on those circumstances. Here the analogy with

6A.7 Mencius said, "In good years, young men are mostly reliable. In bad years, young men are mostly violent. It is not that heaven has given them natures so different. It is what they have allowed to captivate their hearts that makes it so.

"Consider barley," Mencius continued. "Sow the seeds and cover them up. If the ground is the same, and the time of planting is also the same, then they grow quickly. By the summer solstice all of them are mature. Any difference among them is due to variations in the fertility of the soil or in the nourishment of rain and dew, or to unevenness in the work contributed by people. Therefore, all things of the same kind resemble each other. How can we make an exception and therefore doubt that this holds true for human beings? The sage and I are of the same kind.

"Therefore, Longzi said, 'If you make sandals without knowing anything about the feet they are for, I know you will not make baskets.' Sandals resemble each other, because all the feet in the world are the same. Palates have the same gustatory sensibility in relation to flavors. Yi Ya figured out beforehand what my palate would relish. If we allow that the palates' relation to flavors differs in nature from person to person, just as dogs and horses and I are not of the same kind, then why would the gustatory sensibility of everyone in the world follow Yi Ya in relation to flavors? Regarding flavors, everyone takes after Yi Ya. That is, all the palates in the world resemble each other. The ear is also this way. Regarding sounds, everyone takes after Shiguang. That is, all the ears resemble each other. The eye is also this way. When it comes to Zidu, no one fails to recognize that he is handsome. Anyone who doesn't recognize it is blind. Therefore, I say palates have the same sensibility in relation to flavors. Ears have the same hearing in relation to sounds. Eyes see the same beauty in regard to colors.

"When it comes to hearts, is it uniquely the case that there is nothing upon which they agree? What is that upon

---

food and drink would force Mengjizi to accept that the deliciousness of water is independent of our internal dispositions. That is implausible.

which hearts agree? I say it is order and rightness. The sage figures out beforehand what my heart will agree upon. Therefore, order and rightness please my heart, just as the meat of farm animals pleases my palate."

7B.24 Mencius said, "The disposition of the palate towards flavors, of the eyes towards colors, of the ears towards sounds, of the nose towards smells, and of the four limbs towards comfort, is their nature. There is the mandate in them, and the gentleman does not call them 'nature.' The disposition of the benevolent towards parents and children, of the righteous towards ruler and subject, of the ritually proper towards guest and host, of the wise towards worthies, and of the wage towards the way of heaven is the mandate. There is human nature in them, and the gentleman does not call them 'mandated'."[226]

Moral Psychology

2A.2 ...Gongsun Zhou said, "May I ask what your strengths are?"

"I understand explanations, and I am good at nurturing my flood-like *qi*," Mencius said.

"May I ask what you mean by 'flood-like *qi*'?"

"It is hard to explain. It is the greatest and most resilient that *qi* can be. If sincerely nurtured and not harmed, it can fill

---

[226] Mencius takes a naturalistic view of ethics here. What we ought to do and what is natural for us to do are the same. Yet he implies that speaking of our brute dispositions (of sensation and desire) as natural is misleading. It is better to speak of them as mandated, while speaking of moral action as natural, rather than as mandated. Speaking in the reverse fashion might appear to imply some alienation of our nature from morality, since lesser people might fail to see the sense in which what we ought to do and what we naturally desire to do are the same. Similarly, calling brute sensory dispositions 'natural' might mislead one into identifying oneself with whatever desires one has at the moment, rather than seeing the vagaries of inclination as partly external, as a burden mandated.

up the region between heaven and earth. It is *qi* that attends to rightness and the Way. Without these it starves. It arises from accumulated right acts and one cannot catch it with a single burst of righteousness. If there is anything your heart finds unsatisfactory in your conduct, the *qi* starves. That's why I say that Gaozi never understood rightness because he treated it as external. So, there must be actions in effort to achieve this but one mustn't treat them as correct. The heart must neither forget it nor help it grow. Don't be like the man of Song. The man of Song was frustrated that his corn was not long, so he pulled it up…. The corn withered."

2A.6 Mencius said, "All people have a heart that cannot bear others' suffering. The ancient kings had hearts that could not bear others' suffering and showed it with governments which could not bear others' suffering. By maintaining a government which cannot bear others' suffering by means of a heart which cannot bear others' suffering, in regulating the empire one will have it in the palm of one's hand.

Regarding my point that all people have a heart which cannot bear others' suffering, consider a person who suddenly sees a child about to fall into a well. Anyone would have a heart of concern and compassion. It's not that it is an opportunity to befriend the child's parents. It's not that it is an opportunity to seek the praise of the town or one's friends. It's not that one feels so because one hates the child's cries. Therefore, anyone who sees the child and has no heart of compassion is not a human being. Without the heart of shame and disgust, one isn't a human being. Without a heart of courtesy and compliance one isn't a human being. Without a heart of moral judgment one isn't a human being. The heart of compassion is the sprouting of benevolence. The heart of shame and disgust is the sprouting of righteousness. The heart of courtesy is the sprouting of ritual propriety. The heart of moral judgment is the sprouting of wisdom. Human beings possess these four sprouts as they possess four limbs. To have these sprouts and still to tell oneself, 'I cannot,' is to injure oneself. One who would tell one's ruler, 'I cannot,' would injure one's ruler. Anyone who has these four sprouts in himself knows how to develop and fulfill them. It is like a fire's beginning to burn or a spring's beginning to bubble up. When everyone can develop them, they suffice to protect the whole world. When no one develops them, they don't suffice to serve one's parents."

4B.12 Mencius said, "A great person is one who hasn't lost the heart of his childhood."[227]

6A.1 Gaozi said, "Human nature is like a Qi willow. Rightness is like cups and bowls. To take human nature and make benevolence and rightness out of it is like taking a Qi willow and making cups and bowls."

Mencius said, "Can you make cups and bowls of the Qi willow by following its nature? You must do violence to the Qi willow, in order to make cups and bowls. As for the argument 'you will do violence to the Qi willow in making cups and bowls of it, so, you will do violence to a person in making him benevolent and righteous' - if anything would make everyone in the world take benevolence and rightness as a calamity, these words would."[228]

6A.2 Gaozi said, "Human nature is like roiling water. If you open a way to the east, it will flow east. If you open a way to the west, it will flow west. Human nature's being indifferent with respect to goodness and badness is like water's being indifferent with regards to east and west."

---

[227] This would seem to mean the innocent sweetness that children sometimes feel for others. The passage could also mean "the hearts of his children" and intend to say that a good ruler never loses the hearts of his people.

[228] Mencius would not seem to have a good argument here, if we ask ourselves whether the unsavory consequences of people believing a philosophical theory should count in deciding whether the theory is true. On the other hand, Mencius might mean that no moral theory can be true that construes morality as something abominable to people's natural dispositions. And Mencius makes this point in the sections on Yang Zhu and Mozi. Do you think that it is possible that the true moral principles might turn out to be depressing?

Mencius said, "Water is indeed indifferent as to east or west, but is it indifferent regarding up and down? The goodness of human nature is like the tendency of water to flow downwards. No human beings are not good. No water is not downward-flowing. Now, if you splash water, you can make it leap higher than your forehead, and by forcing it and conducting it, you can make it sit atop a mountain. But would that be the water's nature? It would be the influences on it that made it so. That people can be made evil means only that their nature resembles that case."

6A3.   Gaozi said, "Life is what we mean by 'nature'."

Mencius said, "'Life is what we mean by "nature".' Is that like saying, 'Whiteness is what we mean by "white"'?"

"Yes."

"The whiteness of a feather is like the whiteness of white snow, and the whiteness of white snow is like the whiteness of white jade, right?"

"Yes."

"If that is the case, then is the nature of a dog like the nature of an ox? And is an ox's nature like the nature of human beings?"[229]

6A.6 Gongduzi said, "Gaozi said, 'Human nature is neither good nor evil.' Others say, 'Human nature can be made good and can be made evil. That is why when King Wen and King Wu flourished, the people preferred to be good, but when King You and King Li flourished, the people preferred to be evil.' Others say, 'Some have good natures. Some have evil natures. That is why, with Yao in power, there still could be a Xiang, with the Blind Man as a father, there still could be a Shun, and with Zhou as their nephew and, moreover, their ruler, there still could be Qi, the Viscount of Wei, and Prince

---

[229] Here Mencius means to draw a distinction between a property, such as 'having life' or 'white', and a nature, which is a developmental tendency to manifest certain properties. Gaozi thinks human nature is neutral and malleable, simply life itself. Mencius replies that this is inconsistent with the obvious differences among the species.

Bi Gan.'[230] Now, you say, 'Human nature is good.' Since that is so, are all the other theories off the mark?"

Mencius said, "As far as its natural tendencies are concerned, it can be made good. Thus, I say it is good. But if it becomes evil, it is not the fault of its innate capacities. The heart of compassion all people possess. The heart of shame and disgust all people possess. The heart of respect and reverence all people possess. The heart of moral judgment all people possess. The heart of commiseration is benevolence. The heart of shame and disgust is righteousness. The heart of respect and reverence is ritual propriety. The heart of moral judgment is wisdom. Benevolence, rightness, propriety, and wisdom are not imposed from the outside, but the self already has them. People just don't deliberate over them. Therefore, it is said, 'Seek, and you will find them. Neglect them, and you will lose them.' There are those who differ by twice, five times, or incalculable times in the extent [to which they have developed these virtues]. They cannot all fulfill their capacities.

The *Book of Odes* says, 'Heaven produced the masses. If there are things, there are rules. If these are what the people abide by, then they surely adore virtue.' Confucius said, 'The writer of this ode surely knew the Way.' Therefore, where there are things, there must be rules. These are what the people abide by. So, they surely adore virtue."

6A.8   The trees of Ox Mountain were once beautiful. Since they were adjacent to a large city they were chopped by axes. How could they still be beautiful? Indeed, with the recuperation by night and the nourishment of rain and dew, they were not without buds and grew on the mountain. But cows and sheep also grazed upon them. That is why it is so bald. People see its baldness and assume that it never had trees on it. But is that the nature of the mountain?

"Can it be that in people there is not benevolence or rightness? The reason they lose their innate heart is like the

---

[230] This list shows that people can be virtuous even though they are exposed to the influences of evil people; and they can be evil even though exposed to the influences of good people.

trees and the axes. Can something be beautiful while being chopped day after day? With recuperation by night and the calm energy (*qi*) of each morning, if his inclinations and aversions are yet hardly ever similar to those of other people, then in what he does during the day there is something which inhibits and destroys those feelings. If their inhibition is repeated over and over, then his nightly energy is not enough to store. If his nightly energy is not enough to store, then his difference from beasts is not great. When others observe his beastliness, they assume that he is one who never had any capacity. But how is this the natural tendency of a human being?

"Therefore, nothing will not grow if it receives its nourishment. If it misses its nourishment, nothing will not expire. Confucius said, 'Hold to it and it is stored up. Neglect it and it is lost. Its coming and leaving do not take place at a certain time, and no one knows in which direction.' It is the heart which he speaks of here."

6A.9 Mencius said, "It is no wonder that the King is not wise. Even the easiest things in the world to grow have never survived when they had one day of the sun's warmth and ten days of cold. I see him rarely, and when I withdraw, those who make him cold get to him. What can I do with any sprouts that there are? Consider Yi, one of the lesser arts.[231] If one does not set one's mind to it and exert one's will, then one won't succeed at it. Yi Qiu is the best Yi player in the country. Have Yi Qiu instruct two people in Yi. One of them sets his mind to it, exerts his will, and listens only to Yi Qiu. The other, though he listens to him, has his whole mind on imagining an approaching swan and contemplating bending his bow, putting in the arrow, and shooting it. Although he studies along with the other, he does not become as good. Is this due to his being not as intelligent? No."

---

[231] This is the game now called *weiqi* and known in Japan and the West as "go."

6A.15 Gongduzi asked, "All are equally human, but some are great people, and some are small people. Why?"

Mencius said, "Those who follow their greater substance are great people. Those who follow their lesser substance are small people."

Gongduzi said, "All are equally human, but some follow their greater substance, and some follow their lesser substance. Why?"

Mencius said, "The function[232] of the ear and eye not being to deliberate, they are misled by things. Things come into contact and pull them away. The function of the mind is to deliberate. By deliberating, it gets to it.[233] If it does not deliberate, it does not get to it.

"This is what heaven has given us. If one first stands firm on what is greater in it, then what is lesser in it cannot snatch it away. This is all there is to being a great person."

6A.17 Mencius said, "The desire for what is noble is shared by human beings, and all people have nobility within them. They just have not deliberated over it. Those whom people treat as noble are not genuinely noble. What Zhao Meng[234] can treat as noble Zhao Meng can treat as mean.[235] The *Book of Odes* says, 'Being filled with wine, being satiated with virtue....' This speaks of being satiated with benevolence and rightness. That is why one doesn't long for others' tasty foods. One has a good reputation and praise is widely bestowed upon one. That is why one does not long for others' decorative garments.[236]

---

[232] The word is *guan*, meaning officer and also organ, there being five organs: eye, ear, nose, palate, and mind (or heart, *xin*.)

[233] Here "it" is the greater substance.

[234] A minister of the state of Jin who bestowed rulerships.

[235] This proves that nobility cannot be the same thing as being treated as noble. For the former doesn't come and go by whim, while the latter, by definition, does.

[236] If people seek nobility by trying to be treated as noble, they will try to attain this goal by posing with fine food and clothing. If one rather seeks what is noble, being treated as noble follows inadvertently.

7A.17 Mencius said, "Do not do what you would not do. Do not desire what you would not desire. That is all."[237]

7A.27 Mencius said, "The hungry find food sweet, and the thirsty find drink sweet. They do not get the true taste of food and drink because hunger and thirst impair them. How could only the mouth and stomach be impaired by hunger and thirst? The human heart also has impairments. If a person can keep the impairments of hunger and thirst from becoming impairments of the heart, then people who are better than him will not give him cause to be melancholy."

Mozi, Yang Zhu, and the Nature of Morality

3A.5 The Mohist Yi Zhi sought a meeting with Mencius by asking Xu Bi to recommend him. Mencius said, "I do wish to see him, but I am not well at the moment. When I have recovered, I will go to see Yizi rather than his coming here."

On another day, he came seeking Mencius again. Mencius said, "Now I can see him. If I don't straighten him out, then the Way will not be visible. I will straighten him out. I hear that Yizi is a Mohist. Mo's way of conducting mourning is one of frugality. If Yizi contemplates changing the world's [way of mourning], he must think it wrong and dishonorable. And yet Yizi buried his parents with considerable expense. This means he served his parents in what he would take as a mean way."

Xuzi told this to Yizi. Yizi said, "The Confucian Way says that 'the ancients seemed as though they were caring for

---

[237] This is an interesting aspect of the notion of extending one's desires and reasoning coherently about them. In the end, when one sees that one's desires require an act that one had until now found displeasing (for example, the abolition of slavery or quitting smoking), one must simply act accordingly. Try telling that to people addicted to either the revenue of slavery or tobacco. Mencius would say that if they fail to act accordingly, it is not because they are unable (1A.7).

190

infants.'[238] What do these words mean? I would take them to mean love does not have different degrees, even though it begins with one's parents."

Xuzi told this to Mencius. Mencius said, "Does Yizi honestly take a person's affection for his nephew as equivalent to his affection for a neighbor's infant? He has a particular case in mind: when the infant is innocently about to fall into a well. Moreover, heaven, in creating things, provided them with one root, while Yizi gives them two roots.[239] That is the source [of his error].

"In previous ages, there were those who did not bury their parents. When their parents died, they took them and threw them into a gully. On another day, they would pass by. Foxes and cats would be eating the bodies, and flies and gnats would be sucking at them. Their brows would break into a sweat, and they would be unable to bear the sight. As for this sweat, it was not for others that they sweated. Their inner hearts reached their faces and eyes. They went home and returned with baskets and spades and covered the bodies. If covering them was indeed right, then a filial child or a benevolent person's covering up his parents must also be in accord with the Way."

Xuzi told this to Yizi. Yizi was brought up short. He sat a while and said, "He has instructed me."

3B.9 Gongduzi said, "Outsiders all say that you, Master, are fond of disputation. May I ask why?"

Mencius said, "I am not fond of disputation. I just have no alternative.... The words of Yang Zhu and Mo Di fill the world. The words people speak are those of either Yang or Mo.

[238] Yizi is quoting the *Book of History* (*Shujing* 14.6b), a traditional Confucian text. He is probably implying that even their own classics show that the Confucians should adopt utilitarianism.
[239] The two roots would appear to be one's natural love for one's parents and purely impartial reasoning. A utilitarian would say that a person needs the special nurturing of family in order to become moral, but one also needs purely impartial reasoning according to the rule of utility in order to complete one's moral maturation.

Yang's principle is egoism. This ignores one's ruler. Mo's principle is all-encompassing concern. This ignores one's father. To do without a father or a ruler is to be a beast.... Gongming Yi said, 'In the kitchens there is fat meat. In the stables there are fat horses. The people are pale with hunger and in the countryside die of starvation. This is to lead beasts to eat men.' If the ways of Yang and Mo are not stopped and Confucius's Way is not proclaimed, these perverse teachings will delude people and block the way to morality. When the way to morality is blocked, then we will be leading beasts to eat men, and people will eat each other. I am alarmed by this state of affairs."

4A.11 Mencius said, "The Way lies in what is near, yet people seek it in the distant. Affairs lie in what is easy, yet people seek it in the difficult.[240] If people would show proper affection for their parents and proper reverence for their elders, then the world would be at peace.

4B.26 Mencius said, "Any explanation of human nature must rely on given precedents. These precedents take natural ease as fundamental. What is detestable about the wise men of today is that they bore their way through. If the wise men were like Yu when he conducted the waters,[241] then there would be nothing detestable in their wisdom. Yu's conducting the waters went according to what presented no difficulty for them. If wise men could go along with what presents no difficulty, their wisdom would be great indeed. As high as the heavens are, and as distant as the stars and heavenly bodies are, having sought out their precedents, one may calculate up to the solstice of 1,000 years from now while sitting in one's seat."[242]

7A.26 Mencius said, "Yangzi upholds egoism. If he could benefit the whole world by plucking out one of his hairs,

---

[240] The distant and difficult here would be the austere rules of Yang and Mo.

[241] The ancient King Yu is supposed to have saved the land from great floods by constructing conduits.

[242] The idea is that there is a natural way for people, and a moral theory should not conflict with it.

he would not do it. Mozi upholds all-encompassing concern. If he could benefit the world by shaving his head and showing his heels,[243] he would do it. Zimo clings to a medium. In clinging to a medium, he is closer to the right idea, but clinging to a medium without any weighing is like clinging to one point [as Yang and Mo do]. What is undesirable in clinging to one point is its impairing the Way. Holding up one point, one neglects a hundred others."[244]

Political Philosophy

5A.5   Wan Zhang said, "Is it true that Yao gave the empire to Shun?"

Mencius said, "No. The emperor cannot give the empire to anyone."

"Since that is so, and Shun had the empire, who gave it to him?"

"Heaven gave it to him."

"'Heaven gave it to him.' Does that mean it gave him a detailed mandate?"

"No. Heaven didn't speak. Rather, through his handling of affairs it showed its will."

Wan Zhang said, "'Through his handling of affairs it showed its will.' How is that?"

"The emperor can recommend a person to heaven but cannot make heaven give him the empire. A feudal lord can

---

[243] These were vulgar in ancient China. The phrase could also mean "baring himself from head to heel."

[244] The moral judgments which form a network of values in a society avoid the extremes of egoism, anarchy, or utilitarianism. But they do not avoid them by striking a mathematical midpoint between them. They are much more complicated than that because they fit a set of facts which are of much richer description than "mathematical midpoint." Weighing the many factors involved in moral judgments is not a matter of balancing considerations of equal weight. The considerations have different weights in different circumstances. For instance, the interests of a murderer don't weigh very heavily when we decide his punishment.

recommend a man to the emperor, but he cannot make the emperor enfoeff him. A high officer can recommend a man to a feudal lord, but he cannot make the feudal lord make him a high officer. Among the ancients, Yao recommended Shun to heaven, and heaven accepted him. He presented him to the people, and the people accepted him. Therefore, it is said, 'Heaven didn't speak.' Rather, through his handling of affairs it showed its will."

"May I ask how it is that he was recommended to heaven and accepted by heaven, and that he was presented to the people, and the people accepted him?"

"Yao had him preside over sacrifices and the hundred gods. This is heaven accepting him. Yao put him in charge of affairs, and affairs were well governed, thus making the people confident in him. This is the people's accepting him. Heaven gave him [the throne]. The people gave it to him. Therefore, I say, 'The emperor cannot give the empire to a person.'

"Shun assisted Yao for 28 years," Mencius continued. "This was not what Man could do. It was heaven's doing. After Yao's passing and the three years of mourning, Shun withdrew from Yao's son, going south of South River. But the feudal lords of the empire who sought audience at the court did not go to Yao's son but to Shun. Those who would litigate also went not to Yao's son but to Shun. Singers sang not for Yao's son but for Shun. Therefore, I say, 'It was heaven's doing.' Afterwards Shun went to the Middle Kingdoms and took his place as emperor. Just moving into Yao's palace and putting pressure on Yao's son would have been usurpation. Then it wouldn't have been heaven that gave it to him. The *Taishi*[245] says, 'Heaven sees as my people see.' Heaven hears as my people hear.' This is what I mean."

---

[245] A section of the *Documents of Zhou* (the *Shujing*).

Suggested Readings

Chan, Alan K. L., ed., *Mencius: Contexts and Interpretations* (Honolulu: University of Hawai'i Press, 2002)

Ding, Weixiang, "Mengzi's Inheritance, Criticism, and Overcoming of Moist Thought," *Journal of Chinese Philosophy* 35(2008): 403-419

Geisz, Steven F., "Mengzi, Strategic Language, and the Shaping of Behavior," *Philosophy East & West* 58 (2008): 190-222

Jones, Nicholaos, "Correlative Reasoning About Water in Mengzi 6A2," *Dao: A Journal of Comparative Philosophy* 15(2016): 193-207

Kim, Myeong-Seok, "Is There No Distinction Between Reason and Emotion in Mengzi?" *Philosophy East & West* 64(2014): 49-81

Lau, D. C., trans., *Mencius* (London: Penguin, 2005)

McRae, Emily, "The Cultivation of Moral Feelings and Mengzi's Method of Extension," *Philosophy East & West* 61(2011): 587-608

Mower, Gordon B., "Mengzi and Hume on Extending Virtue," *Philosophy East & West* 66(2016): 475-487

Nivison, David S., *The Ways of Confucianism: Investigations in Chinese Philosophy*, Bryan Van Norden, ed. (New York: Open Court Publishing Company, 1996)

Ryan, James A. "A Defence of Mencius's Ethical Naturalism," *Asian Philosophy*, 7(1997): 23-36

Ryan, James A., "Moral Philosophy and Moral Psychology in Mencius," *Asian Philosophy* 8(1998): 47-64

Ryan, James A., "Moral Reasoning in Mencius," in Keli Fang, ed., *Chinese Philosophy and the Trends of the 21st Century Civilization* (Beijing: Commercial Press, 2003), p. 151-167

Shun, Kwong-loi, *Mencius and Early Chinese Thought* (Stanford: Stanford University Press 2000)

Tanaka, Koji, "Inference in the Mengzi 1a: 7," *Journal of Chinese Philosophy* 38(2011): 444-454

Van Norden, Bryan, trans., *Mengzi: With Selections from Traditional Commentaries* (Indianapolis: Hackett, 2008)

Van Norden, Bryan W., "Mengzi and Xunzi," *International Philosophical Quarterly* 32(1992): 161-184

5

Zhuangzi

We come now to one of the great treasures of world literature: the *Zhuangzi*. The author of much of this eponymous book, Zhuang Zhou, flourished in the Fourth Century B.C.E. The book happens to have what is perhaps the most famous passage in all of Chinese literature, in which Zhuangzi wonders whether he is a butterfly dreaming that he is Zhuangzi. The book's philosophy inspired the formation of Chan Buddhism, the Buddhist school that arose in China about a thousand years after Zhuangzi lived. The text is so funny, coy, weird, and profound that its readers are often enchanted. The issues it raises pertain to how one should understand and feel about one's existence in the most general and yet intimate senses of those terms. And the answers it offers provide the reader with ideas to contemplate for many years.

The book offers the best case there is for a certain anti-conventionalism, according to which human conventions and values are not ultimately satisfactory or meaningful. It recommends a certain Daoist point of view as a better alternative to the ways of thinking to which the reader is likely to be unreflectively committed. Even if, after scrutinizing Zhuangzi's Daoist philosophy, we conclude that it is not sound, the book repays the labor handsomely because it gets something close to right, something of great importance, or at least it articulates ideas that, although not quite on the mark, nevertheless illuminate the terrain surrounding perennial questions about the meaning of life. The book speaks to something important about the human experience, something which few other works are able to describe quite as well.

Zhuangzi seems to have lived after Laozi. He is thus the second of the two great founders of the Daoist school of philosophy. You will notice similarities between the two thinkers - a concern for a natural flow of things and a rejection of scholarship and high civilization, for example. But the *Zhuangzi* is, whereas *The Book of Power and the Way* is not, concerned mainly with the meaning of life for the individual, rather than with discovering the best political system and way of ruling a state. Perhaps Zhuangzi's life made him witness to even more of the horrors of the Warring States Period (403 - 221) than the author(s) of the Laozi text. The shift toward detachment from social conventions which Daoism underwent in Zhuangzi's hands resembles the Stoic shift in Greek philosophy, as the Stoics found themselves in the Hellenistic period of Greek history, which was beset by even more upheaval and uncertainty than the earlier periods. Whereas Laozi advises a well thought-out, *laissez-faire* approach to moral issues and social conflicts, perhaps Zhuangzi has Daoism simply reach the end of its tether, throw up its hands, and walk away from them.

Like *The Book of Power and the Way*, the *Zhuangzi* concerns itself with metaphysics and value and draws connections between these. The book also presents a set of skeptical arguments in epistemology, and these are relevant to his metaphysics and theory of value. However, rather than directly explain the text's presentation of these ideas here, I will let you figure it out on your own. Instead, I will recommend some conceptual tools which you might use in that endeavor. There are several terms and concepts that should prove useful to you.[246]

---

[246] Some might say that these tools are surgical instruments which would murder the text by analysis. I disagree. There is no reason to think that one cannot appreciate the work while also subjecting it to analysis and criticism. It is a very deep and beautiful piece of literature, the appreciation of which doesn't require that the reader use sharp analytic tools. But that doesn't mean that these tools are a distraction. Rather than impoverishing the reader's experience of the work, they might even shed light on some of its

198

Let us begin with some metaphysical terms. The first is "realism," its denial being "irrealism." Realism is the position that there is a way the world is, a way that is independent of how we think or feel about the world. There are things, such as trees and rocks, and facts, such as that trees are alive and that they are real and sometimes have leaves no matter what we think. In many places, the *Zhuangzi* seems to reject realism and embrace irrealism. On the other hand, Zhuangzi also seems to be telling us his theory about the way the world really is. It's just that his theory about the way it is seems to leave out almost all of the facts we normally accept, making him seem like an irrealist. He seems to think that what there really is is a "great clump," out of which all things emerge and into which they return, as if the things of this world are just ephemeral arrangements of the material of this mass.

Zhuangzi's view thus might be labeled "monism." This is the position that there is only one thing, all other things being mere features or epiphenomena of that thing. A similar idea was being developed in India and Greece during Zhuangzi's time (what Karl Jaspers called the "Axial Age" of the writers of the Upanishads, Parmenides, Jewish monotheism, and other philosophical and religious ideas of cosmic unity.) Zhuangzi seems to think that distinctions between things are unreal and that these putative things are one. You should reconstruct any arguments for this position in the text. Is it plausible to suppose that the ephemeral and temporary nature of things and their deriving from the same stuff are reasons to conclude that these things are not real? Or would such a conclusion undercut the very premise intended to support it, namely the premise that there *are* things with an ephemeral and temporary nature? If you make ten clay dolls from a lump of clay and then recombine them into a lump again, have the creation and destruction of the dolls done

---

depths and beauties. Nevertheless, if you'd like to play it safe, read the reading itself before my introduction to it.

anything to show that there were never really any dolls? It would seem that they have not.

If you're not convinced by the monistic argument, you'll be pleased to know that Zhuangzi will also distance himself from it, albeit in apparent inconsistency with the monistic-sounding places in the text. This distancing is what sets the Chinese monist (if he is one) apart from other monists of the "Axial Age." Zhuangzi has a strongly skeptical side. But he is also a mystic, believing that profound knowledge about the nature of reality may be had through a non-conceptualizable and only obliquely communicable experience. It is here that we hit upon one source of the enchantment of his readers. Zhuangzi tries to explain that he is something like an irrealist and a monist (two mutually inconsistent positions). But he emphatically rejects all positions because the truth about reality that he is trying to get at is accessible only by an experience that does not fit into any position.[247] The skeptic tries on positions for size and then casts them aside in an avowedly futile attempt to articulate his actual metaphysical view. Here he crosses the line separating philosophy from religion. As you will see, Zhuangzi is a philosopher who thinks philosophy benighted and misleading. He portrays his friend and opponent, the analytic-style philosopher Huizi as "hunched over his desk" (a decidedly unhealthy position for the human body) and as getting nowhere with his futile logic, reasoning, positions, and standards.

That last term, "standards,"[248] brings us to the issue of value. Zhuangzi argues for a position about the meaning of life, or the nature of the good life. It isn't easy to say what this

---

[247] This is an important idea in the formation of Chan Buddhism. See the chapter on Chan. It also may be found in Indian Buddhism, particularly that of Nagarjuna.

[248] As I note in the text, "standards" is my translation of "*shifei*," a term literally meaning "right/wrong" and "is/is not." English has the same ambiguity as Chinese: "right" and "wrong" can mean factual or metaphysical correctness and incorrectness, but they can also mean satisfaction or failure to satisfy norms or values.

position is. At times it seems to be "nihilism," the position that there is no meaning or value. The denial of nihilism is realism about values. According to nihilism, just as metaphysical irrealism holds that there are no distinctions between things, there are no moral distinctions. And standards are merely subjective projections onto the world and are devoid of any truth. Zhuangzi seems to accept this view because of the many disagreements about what the standards are. He suggests that if there were real standards of value and the meaning of life, then we would discover them, rather than interminably dispute over them. On the other hand, Zhuangzi is no nihilist. He believes that there is something of profound value: the Dao, the Way. Perhaps his view is that the good life, the standard we are to reach, is the life in which one rejects all other standards. Nihilists, if there are any, stare blankly when their spouses die, but, as you will see, Zhuangzi sings with elation when his wife dies. The reader's task is to discern what this Way might be which is so uplifting and valuable.

There are some tangled relationships among the aforementioned terms, some conceptual difficulties which Zhuangzi seems not to have recognized. The first is that nihilism about value and metaphysical irrealism tend to run together in some people's minds, including, apparently, Zhuangzi's. Indeed, nihilism and irrealism are synonyms which I've kept artificially distinct here, reserving the former for the position that there is no such thing as value and the latter for the metaphysical position that there is nothing at all. One can reject irrealism and believe that there are real distinctions among all the various things we normally believe to be distinct, even while one accepts nihilism about value. In other words, one might accept that there are rocks and trees and such, while holding that nothing matters. By the same token, one might accept real distinctions of value but reject real distinctions among things, which would be the odd position that nothing exists, but if it did, moral distinctions would apply. A flaw of the *Zhuangzi* is that it does not distinguish between the two. Because of this, at times it seems that reasons supporting a position on the issue of value are illicitly assumed by the text to be evidence for a position about the nature of reality, and vice versa. Keep in mind the separation between the two issues as you read the text. You might extract from the text's ambiguity a weakness in its argument.

A second confusion is between relativism and nihilism, and between relativism and metaphysical irrealism, two confusions that overlap. Endless disagreements over what is the case can be adduced as evidence either for rejecting that anything is the case - nihilism, irrealism - or for accepting that what is the case depends upon the subject - relativism. Relativism is thus the position that there are indeed real values (or real facts and things), but these values (or facts and things) are real only relative to the subject's beliefs or desires. The concept has some plausibility. After all, the distance of one thing from another is real and relative property, as is, one might argue, the deliciousness of certain foods. It's not that sardines aren't really delicious to anyone, or that nothing is really five miles away; it's just that this deliciousness or distance, when it obtains, is not absolute or independent, but dependent upon some further facts, namely someone's taste or something's location. We should see two distinctions: the distinction between relativism and absolutism (the view that facts and values are independent of beliefs and feelings) and the distinction between realism and nihilism/irrealism. Take some time to ponder these two distinctions; they are too inoften grasped. Unfortunately, Zhuangzi didn't seem to make the distinction between relativism and nihilism/irrealism.

Yet, these shortcomings are by no means crucial. In fact, they paradoxically seem appropriate to Zhuangzi's actual position on value and reality. He thinks that there is true value to be grasped by rejecting all of the various values that people commonly take to be real, or at least by rejecting the view that these values are absolute and not relative. Zhuangzi believes that people tend to be absolutists (or realists) about facts and values, and that this absolutism is the sole reason for their failure to grasp what is of real value: the Way. We strive to fulfill our various values every day and think that doing so is all that matters; we are caught in "the rat race." This ultimate valuational stance shows that we are absolutists, Zhuangzi seems to think. If we thought that values were relative and that there were alternatives to our own values which we might just as well accept, then we wouldn't have such anxiety and stress, feelings that destroy any chance our lives have for meaning and peace of mind. As you can see, however, this analysis makes Zhuangzi seem like a nihilist. Only he and the nihilist would not be devastated by the death of a spouse. On the other hand, the nihilist doesn't even value meaning and peace of mind. What, then, is this supposed space between nihilism and absolutism? How, exactly, can one value one's marriage but not take it too seriously?

Hence, when it comes to Zhuangzi's theory of value, the reader's task is twofold. First, what is this theory of value? What in particular does Zhuangzi think is valuable? Is he a nihilist about ordinary values such as marriage, social harmony, and morality? Does he think that these values are real but that we just shouldn't take them so seriously? Any label you choose to put on his position seems to have difficulties. For example, in "The Human Realm," he seems to care about social harmony when he uses Confucius as a mouthpiece; it's just that he thinks any effort to bring about this harmony is futile.

Second, is his theory of value justifiable? He seems to reject the conventional view that moral life, along with all our various value-laden endeavors, matters greatly, and he seems to offer an alternative. Is it plausible that human beings can accept this alternative? Aren't Confucius and Mencius (and Aristotle, or, for that matter, just about every person who has ever lived) right about human nature, in that human nature is such that moral values, the cultivation of virtue, life, health, security, etc., really matter to it in an ultimate way? Zhuangzi is aware of the difficulty. He writes of Huizi's objection, "Can a human being really have no inherent dispositions?" and asks himself, "What is this? Are you sure you can turn the body into a dried-up tree, and are you sure you can turn the mind into dead ashes?" The second difficulty dovetails with the first. What is this alternative meaning of life that the Daoist espouses? Can we really make sense of such a value for us? What is the difference between the seemingly escapist Daoism of Zhuangzi and the mere failure to have the courage to face the tragedy of life's perennial failure to fulfill our values and to champion those values to the end? Isn't it a kind of coward who says, "Bah! All that conventional stuff isn't worth much anyway!" Doesn't such a coward mistakenly believe that if he doesn't try to fulfill his values then he can avoid failing them? Does Zhuangzi have anything of more philosophical substance to offer than the coward? Clearly there is something important about the phrases, "take time to smell the roses" and "it's all just a rat race." The *Zhuangzi*, mistaken or not, gives the reader the opportunity to address fundamental issues of value and the meaning of life.

Finally, we should notice Zhuangzi's skeptical arguments. The famous passage I mentioned earlier is the argument that, since dreams are indistinguishable from waking experience, we have no grounds for supposing any of our beliefs is true. Zhuangzi also argues that argument itself is hopeless, since any evaluation of competing arguments itself is subject to competing evaluations, such that one can never justifiably claim to know which justification of any position is sound. Of course, one might object that this argument is self-defeating, because if it's sound, we'll never be justified in accepting it. The argument points to the difficulty in evaluating competing arguments, but it doesn't seem to prove the impossibility of evaluating them properly. Zhuangzi is aware of the objection to skepticism that says that skepticism, as a claim to know that we know nothing, is incoherent. He asks himself, "Do you know what you don't know?" and answers, "How would I know that?" At least that's consistent. Or is it? I'm not sure! In any event, clearly Zhuangzi's skepticism is meant to play a role in his attempt to undermine conventional views of reality and value.

There, then, is a set of terms and concepts you might find useful in reading Zhuangzi: monism, nihilism, skepticism, realism, irrealism, and relativism, and the relations among them.

204

However, Zhuangzi himself may not have taken any of these positions. When you see a skeptical or relativistic argument in the text, it would be a mistake to assume that it is an argument for a final position which he holds. It's not that he is sophistically tossing around arguments merely in order to entertain or bemuse the reader and without any seriousness about inquiry at all. This is a book of deep inquiry which employs these arguments and tries on the positions they seem to support in an effort clarify the conceptual map which will lead him to his goal, which, as is clearly stated in "Making Things Equal," to understand why this world and its contents are here, what the point of it all is, and how one should live in the world in view of the answers to these questions. The text also expresses how Zhuangzi feels about the alternative philosophical positions; he is trying them on for size in the most profound way. To make a great effort at developing an interpretation of Zhuangzi as "a monist," say, or "a nihilist," or "a skeptic and a relativist," would probably waste a lot of precious time better spent reading the text a few more times without any such interpretation in mind. Zhuangzi is very serious indeed about getting to the truth of the matters that concern him; he is no sophist. But he may not be so committed to each of the philosophical positions he rehearses and argues for. Those positions and arguments are linguistic and logical tools meant to bring both himself and the reader closer to understanding the answers he craves. But they cannot express those answers.[249]

The reader of Zhuangzi owes him this: to enjoy and read with sympathy his profound text whether it is mistaken or not. One of his points is that we take our familiar values too seriously. We don't take time to smell the roses; if we did, we'd see just how profoundly and mysteriously beautiful their fragrance is. Zhuangzi might recommend that we devote our lives to doing

[249] Zhuangzi's way of using language and deliberation as means of bringing one closer to an urgently needed and inexpressible vision of why this world is here was an influence of Daoism on Chan Buddhism. More than one thousand years after Zhuangzi, the Buddhist school would adopt similar techniques of using concepts to eliminate the mind's habitual employment of concepts to understand the world. We will explore this in Chapter 10.

nothing but smelling the roses, and this may seem implausible. But reading Zhuangzi with sympathy is a prerequisite to giving his view a chance. Still, the reader will always owe the philosophical debt to truth. Profoundly edifying or not, the *Zhuangzi* must withstand scrutiny if it is to count as sound philosophy.

The Reading

The *Zhuangzi*, in English translation, is about 300 pages long.[250] The first seven chapters - the "Inner Chapters" - are probably by Zhuangzi himself, whereas the Outer Chapters (VIII - XXII) and the Miscellany (XXIII - XXXIII) are probably not. I have included almost all of chs. II - VII, along with several of the outer chapters: XVII – XIX and XXII.

Zhuangzi

II: Making Things Equal

Ziqi of South Wall sat leaning in his chair. He looked at the sky and sighed absently, as though he had forgotten about his counterparts. Yancheng Ziyou, who was standing before him in attendance, said, "What is this? Are you sure you can turn the body into a dried-up tree? Are you sure you can turn the mind into dead ashes? The one leaning in his chair now is not the one who was leaning in his chair before."

Ziqi said, "Yan, isn't that a good question you're asking! Just now I forgot about myself. Do you understand? You've heard the pipes of humans, but you haven't heard the pipes of

---

[250] Two complete translations (Watson, Mair) and one other partial translation (Ziporyn) may be found in this chapter's list of suggested readings.

206

earth. Or you've heard the pipes of earth, but you haven't heard the pipes of heaven."[251]

Ziyou said, "May I ask what you mean?"

Ziqi said, "Well, the Great Clump blows out qi[252] and it's called 'wind.' If only it didn't start up! For when it starts up, the myriad holes shriek furiously. Don't you hear the 'Woo! Woo!'? The hollows and thickets of mountain forests, the holes and crevices in great trees of one hundred spans around, like noses, like mouths, like ears, like sockets, like bowls, like mortars, like ditches, like ravines - they crash, whistle, scream, hoot, holler, wail, cry, and moan. Those up front call, 'Eee!' while those in back cry 'Ooo!' In a light breeze, it's a simple harmony, but in a strong wind it's a great orchestration. When the fierce winds subside, then the many holes become empty. Haven't you seen this hullabaloo and carrying on?"

Ziyou said, "By 'piping of earth,' you just mean the many holes. And by 'piping of humans' you just mean flutes. May I ask about the piping of heaven?"

Ziqi said, "Well, it blows myriad differences and causes them to be themselves and each to take its place. The one who drives them - who is that? Does heaven revolve?[253] Does the earth stay still? Do the sun and moon contend for their places? Who controls this? Who ties this together? Who, making nothing of it, pushes this on its way[254]? One idea is that it has a sealed mechanism, which is inexhaustible. One idea is that it spins and can't stop itself. Do the clouds make rain? Does the

---

[251] "Heaven" translates "*tian*," but the concept includes the natural functioning of things. It is not simply equivalent to the Western concept of a supernatural dwelling place of God and the souls of the dead. Indeed, in some cases, it would be appropriate to translate "*tian*" as "nature." We encounter this ambiguity in other chapters.

[252] *Qi*, is the energy or breath which flows through all things.

[253] As the sinologist A. C. Graham pointed out, the passage from this sentence to the end of the paragraph belongs here, though in current editions of the text it is found in a later chapter.

[254] Throughout this translation, the word "way" (lower-case *w*), does not translate "Dao" but entirely different Chinese words unrelated to "Dao." "Dao" is translated "Way" (upper-case *w*).

rain make clouds? Who gives this forth so abundantly? Who, making nothing of it, motivates this with such unrestrained joy? The winds arise in the north, going west and then east, with their gusts and eddies. Who blows them? Who, making nothing of it, fans them out? I would like to know. What is the cause?"

Great understanding is broad and settled; little understanding is unsteady. Great speech flows on and on; little speech keeps harping on something. When we sleep, our spirits meet. When we wake, we take form. In our comportment towards things we get sucked in, daily creating strife with our minds. The petty matters, the important ones, the unnoticed ones - the small fears worry us and the great fears shock us. We shoot off like an arrow from a bow. This is called our 'upholding our standards (shifei).'[255] We stay fast as though we'd sworn an oath. This is called our 'keeping the upper hand.' Our deaths are like fall and winter; in other words, we deteriorate daily. We are drowning, and our actions are not a means of restoring us. We're blocked up, as though sealed off. In other words, we're old and stagnant. The mind that is near death nothing can restore to vigor. Happiness, anger, despair, joy, anticipation and disappointment, revision and determination, elegance and casualness, the outgoing and the reserved - they're music coming from emptiness, mist becoming mushrooms. Day and night alternate in front of us, and no one knows where they sprout from. Enough! Enough! Every dawn and dusk they reach it, and that is what they derive life from. Without it there would be no selves. Without selves it wouldn't have anywhere to take place. It's something like that, but we still don't understand why it is caused to be so. It is as though there is a true master, but you can't get a glimpse of him. That it works is certain, but we don't see its body. It has an inherent disposition but no body.[256]

---

[255] Below you will see how Zhuangzi uses the terms shi (correct, right, accept) and fei (incorrect, wrong, reject), which in their conjunction I've given this interpretive translation.

[256] If you take this paragraph to be a concise statement of the point of the book, you probably won't go far wrong.

The one hundred bones, nine orifices, and six viscera co-exist here. Which do I consider most intimate? All, you say? Is there any favoritism here? So, are they all possessed as subjects and concubines? Can't these subjects and concubines rule each other? Do they take turns as lord and subject? Is there a real ruler among them? Whether or not you find its inherent disposition when you look for it has no bearing on its reality. Once they take their complete bodily form, they don't forget it until it is exhausted. When it encounters other things, they all clash with each other and compress each other. It runs its course like a galloping horse and nothing can stop it. Isn't it sad? With a life of perpetual drudgery, it never sees any goal achieved. Exhausted, it labors without knowing where to repair to. Can you help pitying it? People say, "At least I'm not dead," but does that make it any better? Its body is decaying and its mind is, too. Don't you call that a great sorrow? Do people really live in a fog like this? Or is it only I who am in a fog, while there are those who are not in a fog?

If one follows one's intact mind and makes a teacher of it, then who doesn't have a teacher? Why must it be that only someone who understands how things work when he makes up his mind has one? Even a stupid person has one. To maintain standards before being mature of mind is "Departing from Yue today and arriving yesterday."[257] This is taking what isn't for what is. "What isn't is." Even the godlike Yu[258] couldn't understand that. How am I supposed to understand it?

Speech is not breath. In speech there is something said. But what it says is never quite determinate. So, in the end, is there something said? Or has nothing been said? We take it to be different from the peeps of baby birds, but is there a distinction or is there no distinction? How can the Way be so obscured that there is real and unreal? How can speech be so obscured that there is true and false (*shifei*)? How can the Way leave and not be here? How can speech be here but be unacceptable? The way

---

[257] This is a paradox of one of the logicians, perhaps, as Zhuangzi says in Chapter I, Huizi.
[258] The famous Daoist sage Jie Yu.

is obscured in small achievements. Speech is obscured in splendor and flourish. That's why we have the other standards of the Confucians and the Mohists. One accepts (*shi*) what the other rejects (*fei*) and rejects what the other accepts. If we want to accept what they reject and reject what they accept, then nothing is as good as being clear.

Anything can be made 'that,' and anything can be made 'this.' From the viewpoint of 'that' we cannot see it as such. But from the viewpoint of "this" we can know it as such. Hence it is said, "'That' derives from 'this,' and 'this' is caused by 'that.'" This explains the arising together of "that" and "this." Moreover, what arises together ceases together, and what ceases together arises together. What accepts together rejects together, and what rejects together accepts together. If you bring about acceptability, you bring about unacceptability. If you bring about unacceptability, you bring about acceptability. Therefore, the sage takes a standpoint but illuminates them both with heaven. This also brings about a this, but a this which is also a that, and the that is also a this. 'That' is one set of standards (*shifei*), and 'this' is one set of standards. In the final analysis, is there still a that and a this? Or in the final analysis, is there neither that nor this? Where neither this nor that finds its opposite is the hinge of the Way. As soon as the hinge plugs into its socket it responds without subsiding. Correct (*shi*) is one endless thing, and incorrect (*fei*) is another endless thing. That's why I say, "Nothing is as good as being clear."[259]

Making a point to show that a point is not a point isn't as good as using what is not a point to show that a point is not a point. To refer to something in order to show that the referent

---

[259] "This" and "that" are indexicals which present no real difficulty warranting acceptance of skepticism or relativism. And it is obvious that Zhuangzi is not really interested in using them to achieve such an argument. Nor is he trying to marshal a case against "standards." Rather, his goal is to understand the basis of all things, the hinge and socket; he seeks a certain "clarity." But he can't get to this understanding by these arguments; though only move him closer to it than he would have been had he not considered them.

210

is not a referent isn't as good as not referring to it in order to show that the referent is not a referent. To use a horse to show that a horse isn't a horse isn't as good as using what is not a horse in order to show that a horse is not a horse.[260] The world is one referent, and the myriad things are one horse.[261]

Do you accept it? Then it's acceptable. Do you reject it? Then it's unacceptable. The Way is made when we go along it. A thing is the way it is when we call it so. How is it the way it is? It is the way it is in being treated so. How is it not that way? It is not that way in being treated not so. A thing must have something about it which is treated as so. A thing must have something about it that is treated as acceptable. There aren't any things that are not in some way or other, and there is nothing that is not acceptable. Therefore, when a construction of standards holds up a sprig or a pillar, a monster or a Xi Shi,[262] the bizarre and the strange, the Way takes them all as one. Their distinctions create them. But their creation ruins them. Yet, of all the things, none is created or ruined when they are all again taken as one. Only a person of insight understands how to take them all as one. Have no use for constructions of standards and abide in what is common. The common is the useful. The useful is the pervasive. The pervasive succeeds. Reach success and there isn't much left to do. It is enough just to take your cue from what is. It's enough without knowing the way things are. That is called the Way.[263]

---

[260] This is a famous paradox of the logician Gongsun Long, who argued that, since the class 'white horse' is not the same as the class 'horse,' a white horse is not a horse. See the Interlude on analytical philosophy.

[261] In this paragraph Zhuangzi attempts to draw a distinction between what he intends by the philosophical arguments he makes and what ordinary philosophers intend to do when they make similar arguments. The latter are interested in the philosophical arguments and the positions they support. But Zhuangzi is not really making a point or referring to something when he makes similar arguments. His intention is to use the arguments to reveal something, not to establish their ostensible conclusions.

[262] A legendary beauty.

[263] This paragraph is only on the surface an argument for skepticism or relativism. If you read it a second and third time you see that Zhuangzi is

To create anxiety for your spirit by trying to become enlightened about things' oneness without knowing that they are all the same is called "three in the morning." What does "three in the morning" mean? A monkey keeper was passing out nuts and said, "You get three in the morning and four at night." The monkeys all got angry, so he said, "Okay, four in the morning and three at night." The monkeys were all pleased. There had been no diminution in name or in fact, but he had made use of joy and anger. Thus, he took his cue from what is. Therefore, the sage harmonizes people with standards but rests on heaven's axis. This is called "walking both roads."[264]

The knowledge of the ancients was extensive. How extensive? There were those who saw the world as though there were not yet any things. That's the most extensive. It's exhaustive. You can't add anything to it. Behind them were those who saw things as existing but as they were before there were divisions. Behind them were those who saw them as having divisions among them, but as they were before there were standards. It was because standards showed up that the Way was diminished. The reason the Way was diminished is the reason preferences were created.

---

using skeptical and relativistic points of view in order to push toward a vision of how things are independently of the distinctions and standards which we apply to them. In such a vision, things are not recognized as falling under categories and standards we ordinarily use to describe them. In such a vision, things as we ordinarily think of them are not yet created as such. This is the vision Zhuangzi craves and the categories and standards make it impossible to have that vision; they thus "ruin" the things by creating them. Think of a five-month-old baby's vision of a camera. The baby sees it as it is before it is reduced to the mere aspect of "camera." After the baby grows up and begins to see it as a camera, it is as though the camera is created and the original inchoate thing that only the baby could see no longer exists but is ruined.

[264] The monkeys' preference was wrongheaded. The philosophical monist who desires to use arguments to establish monism is supposedly similarly wrongheaded. It begins with a distinction and tries to overcome it where, *ex hypothesi*, there is no such distinction.

212

But in the final analysis, were there creation and diminution?[265] Or in the final analysis was there no creation or diminution? There being creation and diminution gives us Zhao Wen playing the lute. There being no creation or diminution gives us Zhao Wen not playing the lute. Zhao Wen playing the lute, Shi Guang conducting, and Huizi hunched over his desk - these three masters' understanding was close to the mark. Each had his mastery and maintained it all his life. Only what they liked did they separate from other things. What they liked they took pleasure in illuminating. Other things were not what they intended to illuminate, but they illuminated them. So, they ended up benighted by the logical paradoxes of 'hard and white.'[266] And their disciples also ended up with the threads of their works, being unable to complete them even at the end of their lives. If that is the way it was, can we still say something was fully created? Then even we are fully created. If that was the way it was, can we not say something was created? Then neither things nor we ourselves have been created. Therefore, a torch of indeterminacy is what guides the sage. He has no use for constructing standards but abides in what is common. This is what I mean by "using clarity."

I will now say something here, but I don't know - does it fall into the category of being a standard (shi)? Or does it not fall into the category of being a standard? Whether it is of that category or not, it is similar in that it belongs to a category. So, there is nothing that makes it different from other statements. Nonetheless, allow me to say it.[267]

---

[265] In this paragraph Zhuangzi ruthlessly applies his skeptical dismissals to his own point of view. He never rests with a position because any position makes distinctions, and distinctions are what prevent his achievement of the understanding which he craves. In this case, the immediately previous paragraph is probably pretty close to what Zhuangzi actually believes. But in this paragraph, he is skeptical even of it.
[266] Another of the famous paradoxes developed by the logicians.
[267] Here Zhuangzi is about to attempt to describe accurately the uncanny inexplicability of the fact that this world exists. He thinks that understanding this fact requires dropping the distinctions of language, so he acknowledges here that the attempt, as linguistic, is doomed to fail.

There was a beginning. There was a not yet beginning to be a beginning. There was a not yet beginning to be a not yet beginning to be a beginning. There was being. There was nothingness. There was a not yet beginning to be a nothingness. There was a not yet beginning to be a not yet beginning to be a nothingness. Suddenly: being and nothingness. But I don't know ultimately which of being and nothingness is being and which nothingness. Now I've said something. But I don't know - does what I've said really mean anything? Or does it not mean anything?

Nothing in the world is as large as the tip of an autumn hair,[268] and a great mountain is small. No one lives as long as a child who dies, and Peng Zu died young. Heaven and earth were born with me, and the myriad things and I are one.[269] Given that we are one, can there yet be language? Given that I've called us one, how can there not be language? The one and the language make two. The two and the one make three. If you go on from there, even a clever mathematician couldn't finish it, let alone an ordinary person. So, if in moving from nothingness to being we arrive at three, then what if we go from being to being? Don't do it. Just taking your cue from what is the case is enough.

The Way has never had divisions. Language has never had permanency. When you construct standards, there are boundaries. Let me speak about these boundaries. There is a left, and there is a right. There is a discourse, there are deliberations, there are distinctions, and there are debates. There is competitiveness, and there is contentiousness. These are called the "eight virtues." The sage acknowledges the existence of what lies outside of the six realms but doesn't discourse upon it. He discourses upon what is within the six realms but doesn't deliberate over it. As for histories and records of the deeds of kings of the past, the sage will deliberate over them but will not

---

[268] Animal hair is fine in autumn.
[269] What does Zhuangzi mean by these paradoxical utterances? Consider this. What is most important to Zhuangzi about things is something they all share in common: their uncanny and inexplicable existence in this world. This most important feature unifies them.

debate. So, he is one who makes distinctions, but leaves something indistinct. He is one who debates but leaves something undebated. "What?" you say. The sage embraces things, while others debate them in order to show off to each other. So, I say there is something the debaters haven't seen.[270]

The Great Way is ineffable. The Great Debate is unspoken. Great Benevolence is not benevolent. Great Modesty doesn't hold back. Great Courage doesn't attack. The Way, when illuminated, is not the Way. Speech made debate does not hit the mark. Benevolence that is constant is incomplete. Modesty make pure is not trustworthy. Courage that attacks is not complete. These five are round but almost square. Therefore, knowledge that stops at the unknowable is excellent. Who knows the unspeakable debate, the Way that doesn't form a Way? If there were an ability to know this, it would be called the storehouse of heaven.[271] You pour into it, and yet it doesn't fill up. You draw from it, and it doesn't dry up.[272] But where it comes from is unknown. This is called the "inner light."

Long ago Yao asked Shun, "I want to attack Zong, Kuai, and Xiao. I sit facing south[273] but I can't stop thinking about it. Why?"

Shun said, "Those three still dwell in the midst of weeds and grass. If you can't stop thinking about it, why is that? In ancient times, ten suns came out together, and the myriad things were lit up. How much better is virtue than ten suns?"

---

[270] These last few sentences make it clear that Zhuangzi does not want us to see him as a philosopher who argues for skepticism, monism, relativism, nihilism or any other such position. The arguments only get us to the point where things become indistinct and indeterminate. That point is the goal, and not the philosophical positions.

[271] This sentence and the one previous to it make it clear that Zhuangzi is interested in a kind of understanding which shouldn't even be labeled "Daoist."

[272] References to *The Book of Power and the Way*.

[273] The traditional posture of regal repose, which is supposed to cause all others to submit to the authority of the king.

Tooth Gap asked Extreme Wang, "Do you know what all things affirm?"

"How would I know that?"

"Do you know what you don't know?"

"How would I know that?"

"So, nothing has any knowledge?"

"How would I know that? In any event, if I try to say something, how do I know that what I say I know is not something I don't know? And how do I know that what I say I don't know is not something I know?[274] But I'll try to ask you. When people sleep in dampness, they awaken with sore backs and as stiff as a corpse. But is this so of a loach? If they make their abode up in a tree, then they shiver with fright. But is this so of monkeys? Of the three, who knows the right place to stay? People eat livestock, deer eat brush, centipedes like snakes, and birds of prey enjoy rodents. Of the four, who knows the right flavor? Monkeys take monkeys as companions, deer mix with deer, and loaches go wandering with fish. Maoqiang and Lady Li are whom people consider beautiful, but fish dive deep when they see them, birds fly high when they see them, and deer run away when they see them. Of the four, who knows the actual beauty of the things of this world? From my point of view, the sprouts of benevolence and rightness and the paths of standards are all mixed up.[275] How can I know how to distinguish them?"

Tooth Gap said, "If you don't know profit from harm, then do perfected people know profit from harm?"

Extreme Wang said, "Perfected people are deities. Even in a great grass fire they can't be burned. Even when the He and Han Rivers freeze, they aren't cold. When piercing lightning cracks a mountain or fierce winds churn the sea, they cannot be frightened. People like that ride on the clouds and ethers, straddling the moon and sun, and wander beyond the four seas. Death and life are no changes at all to them, let alone the sprouts of profit and harm."

---

[274] See *Analects* 2.17.

[275] These sprouts were extremely important to early Confucians: the moral capacities that were to be developed through moral education.

Ju Quezi asked Chang Zhuozi, "I heard this from Confucius, 'The sage doesn't make attending to affairs his business, does not seek profit, does not avoid harm, is not pleased by being sought, and does not follow the Way. He takes saying nothing as saying something and saying something as saying nothing. He wanders outside the dust and dirt.' Confucius took this to be crude and impetuous talk, but I took it to go with the subtle Way. What do you think about it?"

Chang Zhuozi said, "Even the Yellow Emperor, upon hearing this, would feel dazed. So, how could Confucius understand it? Moreover, your evaluation of it is too quick. You see an egg and look for a rooster in it. You see a bow and look for roast fowl in it.

"I'm going to speak with abandon; you listen with abandon, okay? Stand next to the sun and moon. Embrace the universe, be its coming together. Let be its murky muddle and exchange salutes with the lowly. Ordinary people are full of strife, while the sage is stupid and doltish. He participates in the myriad ages and unifies himself in simplicity. The myriad things pour themselves into that and in that way they encompass each other.

"How do I know that to live a long life is not an error? How do I know that to hate death is not to be someone who was lost early on and doesn't recognize the way back? Lady Li was the child of the border guard of Ai. When the state of Jin had just taken her, her tears fell until they soaked her collar. But then, when she reached the king's palace, slept with the king, and ate of his table's meats, she regretted her tears. How do I know that those who have died don't regret their first longing for life?

"One who dreams of drinking wine may weep when the sun comes up. One who dreams of weeping may go for a hunt when the sun comes up. In the dream you don't know it's a dream. Inside the dream you even interpret the dreams within it. After you wake up you know it was a dream. Moreover, there is a great awakening after which you will know that this was a big dream. But the stupid take themselves to be enlightened, stridently claiming to know it. This is a ruler and that a herdsman? Are you sure? Confucius and you are both dreaming. My saying that you are dreaming is also dreamt. Words such as these are called 'riddles.' When, after ten thousand generations we finally meet a great sage, someone who knows the solution, it will have taken just one day and night to meet him.

"Suppose you and I have a debate. If you defeat me, and I do not defeat you, are you actually right, while I'm actually wrong? If I defeat you, and you do not defeat me, am I actually right, while you are actually wrong? Is one of us right? Is one of us wrong? Are both of us right? Are both of us wrong? If you and I can't share knowledge together, then another will certainly be even more in the dark. Whom shall we use to judge it? Shall we get someone who agrees with you to judge it? If he already agrees with you, how can he judge it? Shall we get someone who agrees with me to judge it? If he already agrees with me, how can he judge it? Shall we get someone who disagrees with both of us to judge it? If he disagrees with both of us, how can he judge it? Shall we get someone who agrees with both of us to judge it? If he agrees with both of us, how can he judge it?

"Given that, then if you and I and another cannot have knowledge together, should we depend on someone else? Transforming voices' dependence on each other is just the same as their not depending on each other. Harmonize them with heaven's reach. Have them take their cue from the vast effusion, so that they will live out their years. What do I mean by "heaven's reach"? This: correct (*shi*) is not correct. So is not so. If correct were actually correct, then it would so differ from not correct that there would be no debate. If so were actually so, it would so differ from not so that there would be no debate. Forget about the years, forget about rightness. If you jump into the unbounded, you will stay in the unbounded."

Penumbra asked Shadow, "First you go, and then you stop. First you sit and then you get up. Why can't you get a grip?"

Shadow said, "Is there something on which I depend that makes me be a certain way? Does what I depend on depend on something to be a certain way? Do I depend on a snake's scales or a cicada's wings? How should I know what makes me so? How should I know what makes me not so?"

Once upon a time, Zhuang Zhou dreamed he was a butterfly. A butterfly - flitting around, self-content, and doing as he pleased, not knowing it was Zhou. Suddenly he woke up and was starkly Zhou. He didn't know - was that Zhou's dream that he was a butterfly, or was this the butterfly's dream that it was Zhou? There must be a difference between Zhou and a butterfly. This is called "the transformation of things."[276]

III. The Essentials for Taking Care of Life

One's life has a limit, but knowledge has no limit. To use what has a limit to pursue what has no limit is dangerous. Given this, if you are still a knowledge seeker, that's quite dangerous. If you do good, don't go near fame. If you do evil, don't go near punishments. Follow the central line, and take it as the through-route, and you can protect yourself, live your full life, take care of what's dear to you, and live out your years.

A butcher was cutting up an ox for Lord Wenhui. The touch of his hands, the push of his shoulder, the shuffle of his feet, the lung of his knee - *ffft!*, *ssshh!* as he handled the knife with skill - none of this missed a beat. He would have fit in with the *Mulberry Woods Dance* or fit into the middle of the *Symphony for the Leader.*[277]

---

[276] This paragraph is perhaps the most famous passage in all of Chinese literature. It may not be an argument for skepticism. It may be an attempt to express something like the uncanny inexplicability of fact that the world and the things in it exist as they are. The idea that Zhuangzi is real and can dream that he is a butterfly is an ordinary belief which takes it as unquestioned that Zhuangzi exists. This belief needs to be dislodged and moved aside in order to make way for the sort of vision Zhuangzi has in mind. The butterfly passage helps to do that.

[277] The dance and music were to celebrate the sage kings Tang and Yao.

Lord Wenhui said, "Ah, fine! Can skill really reach such excellence?!"

The butcher put away his knife and responded, "What your subject prefers is the Way. It goes beyond skill. The first time I cut up an ox, all I saw was a whole ox. Three years later, I didn't see a whole ox. Nowadays, I encounter it with my spirit and don't look with my eyes. Sensory cognition stops and the desires of the spirit proceed. I rely on heaven's patterns, cutting in at the big gaps, taking the large openings as my guide, and taking my cue from what must be so. I never bump into the tendons or ligament connections, let alone a large node.

"A good butcher changes knives once a year; he cuts. A common butcher changes knives once a month; he hacks. Your subject's knife is now nineteen years old, and the oxen it has cut up number in the thousands. Yet the blade of the knife is as though it has just come from the grindstone. These joints have spaces in them, but the knife blade has no thickness. Take what has no thickness and enter into what has spaces, you can feel free to wander about, for there must be extra room for the blade. That is why the knife blade is as though it has just come from the grindstone even after nineteen years.

"However, when I come to a complicated spot, I observe its difficulties. Timidly, I exercise caution. My gaze is steady and I proceed slowly. I move the blade just a little and abruptly it's cut up. Like a clod of earth it falls to the ground. I stand there holding the knife, looking all around, utterly fulfilled. I clean the knife and put it away."

Lord Wenhui said, "Marvelous! I've heard the words of a butcher and gotten a lesson on how to take care of life from them."

Gongwen Xuan saw the Right Commander and was startled. "What sort of man is this?" he said. "How does he come to be an amputee?[278] Was it heaven? Was it man?"

---

[278] A common form of punishment was amputation of a foot, although perhaps the commander lost his foot some other way.

"It was heaven, not man. In giving me life heaven made me singular. A countenance of the human sort would have a pair. I know it was heaven, not man."

The marsh pheasant has to go ten steps for one peck and a hundred steps for one drink. But it doesn't want to be doted on in a cage. Even were it made king its spirit would not be well.

When Lao Dan[279] died, Qin Shi went to mourn for him. He gave three cries and left. A disciple said, "Weren't you a friend of the master?"

"Yes."

"Then is it okay to mourn for him like that?"

"Of course. In the beginning I took them to be his people, but not anymore. I just went in and mourned. There were elders crying for him, as though crying for a child. The younger ones cried for him as though crying for their mothers. The one for whom they are gathered apparently had those who speak though they are not supposed to speak and who cry though they are not supposed to cry. This is to evade heaven, to add to one's inherent dispositions, and to forget what you've received. The ancients called it 'the punishment of evading heaven.' When it was appropriate to come, the master had his time. When it was appropriate for him to go, the master departed. If you come and go in harmony with time, then sorrow and joy cannot enter into it. The ancients called this 'God-given freedom.'"

The oil in the treated firewood gets used up, but the flame moves on. No one knows where it will end.

IV. The Human Realm

Yan Hui[280] went to see Confucius and asked for leave.

---

[279] Laozi.

[280] Confucius's favorite disciple.

"Where will you go?"

"I'll go to Wei."

"What will you do there?"

"I've heard that the ruler of Wei is young in years and independent in his ways. He makes light of using his country and doesn't notice his transgressions. He makes light of using people to death, and the dead fill the country like grass filling a swamp. The people have nowhere to turn. I have heard you say, Master, 'Leave the orderly states and go to the states in turmoil. A doctor has many sick patients.' I mean to take what I've heard and understand what it implies. I want to make his state well."

"Oo! You're going to get yourself executed. The Way will not accept admixture. With admixture it becomes many. If it is many, it is frazzled, and if frazzled, melancholy - melancholy with nothing to be done for it. The perfected men of old first preserved it in themselves and only afterward stored it in others. When what you've preserved in yourself is not yet secure, how can you have time for a tyrant's deeds?

"Don't you know what erodes virtue and where knowledge comes from? Virtue is eroded by fame and knowledge comes from disputation. Fame is what people step on each other with. Knowledge is the instrument of disputation. Both are wicked instruments and are not to be used to carry out your actions. While your virtue is substantial and your good faith is solid, you haven't grasped human *qi*. You have some acclaim and are not adversarial, but you haven't grasped the human heart. By thus lecturing stridently to the tyrant about humanity and rightness, you're just using another's flaws to have your moment as the fair one. This is called 'harming people.' Someone who harms people must be harmed by people in return. You risk making people harm you! Suppose he likes worthy men and despises those who don't fall in line. Then, why would you want to look for a way to be different? If only you wouldn't speak! Kings and dukes always try to dominate others and get the better of them. Your eyes will be dazzled, you'll lose the color in your face, your mouth will speak in compliance, your comportment will take its proper form, and your mind will even be won over.

222

This is to add fire to fire or to pour water on a flood. It's called 'increasing excess.' Once you start following along, there's no end. And if you risk his not believing your strong statements, you'll definitely die at the tyrant's hands.

"In ancient times, Jie killed Guan Longfeng, and Zhou killed Prince Bi Gan.[281] Both of them had cultivated themselves in order to give solace below to the ruler's people. These were men who opposed their superior from below. Therefore, their rulers responded to their cultivation by getting rid of them. For these were men fond of fame.

"In ancient times, Yao attacked Congzhi and Xu'ao, and Yu attacked Youhu. The countries became empty and unpopulated, and their leaders were executed. Their employment of the military never stopped, and their search for profit had no end. They were all seekers of fame and profit. Haven't you heard of them? People of fame and profit only a sage can outdo, so how can you? But you must have a way, so, come, tell me about it."

Yan Hui said, "'In full decorum but empty, powerful but unified' - will that be okay?"

"What? How could it?! You'll put your energy into sustaining the performance, but your countenance will be unsteady; this is unavoidable for an ordinary person. If controlling what one feels in order to seek peace of mind, which is called 'daily gradual power,' is not enough, how could a great power be? He will cling on and not be changed. He will be externally agreeable but internally dismissive. How can that succeed?"

Yan Hui said, "Therefore, I will be internally upright and externally flexible, I'll compare what I complete to precedents. The internally upright are disciples of heaven. The disciples of heaven know that they and the son of heaven are all children of heaven. So, how could any of them take only his own speech as what others will like to hear spoken or what others will not like

---

[281] Recall that Jie and Zhou were wicked tyrants.

to hear spoken? Someone like this people call 'infantile.' This means 'being a disciple of heaven.'

"The externally flexible are disciples of man. Lifting the ceremonial tablet, kneeling, bending, and bowing are the rituals of ministers. Everyone does them. So, shall I dare not to do them? If I do what others do, they'll have no criticism of it. This is what I mean by 'being disciple of man.' When one completes something, to compare it to precedents is to be a disciple of the ancients. One's words, though instructive and critical in content, are from the ancients, not from oneself. Someone like this, although he corrects others, doesn't injure them. This is what I mean by 'being a disciple of the ancients.' If I do this, will that be okay?"

Confucius said, "What? How could it? You have so many policies and rules that you don't know the facts. Though you will certainly escape blame, that's as far as you'll get. How do you hope to transform him? You're still someone who makes the mind his teacher."

Yan Hui said, "I have nothing else to propose. Would you tell me the right method?"

Confucius said, "You must fast. I'll explain. How easy is it to do something while one has a mind?[282] Bright heaven does not approve of someone who thinks it easy."

Yan Hui said, "My family is poor. We haven't drunk wine or eaten meat for months. So, do I count as having fasted?"

"That's a ceremonial fast for a sacrifice. It's not a fast of the mind."

Yan Hui said, "What is a fast of the mind?"

Confucius said, "Unify your intentions. Don't listen with your ears; listen with your mind. Don't listen with your mind; listen with your *qi*. Listening stops with your ears. The mind stops with getting facts right. But *qi* is something empty that serves things. Only the Way gathers emptiness. Emptiness is the fasting of the mind."

---

[282] Here a better translation than "mind" might be "mental state." The term is *xin*. We will examine this ambiguity in Chapter 10.

Yan Hui said, "When I hadn't yet heard this, I took myself to be Hui. When I heard it, there had never been a Hui. Is this what you mean by 'emptiness'?"

Confucius said, "That's it. I'll explain. You can go walk about in his cage and not be put off by his fame. If you make inroads, then sing. If you don't, then stop. Forget about teachings and cures. If you abide in unity and dwell in the unavoidable, that's close enough.

"It is easy to stop your steps. But to go without walking on the ground is hard. When you work for man it is easy to be inauthentic. When you work for heaven it is hard to be inauthentic. You've been told about flying with wings, but you've never been told about flying without wings. You've been told about knowing with knowledge, but you've never been told about knowing without knowledge.[283] Look to the inner chambers, the empty room that gives off light. Good fortune stops on the stopped. And if you don't stop, this is called 'sitting at a gallop.' Let your ears and eyes come together inside and leave the mind's knowledge outside. Ghosts and spirits will come to stay, so how much more will people! This is the transformation of the world. It is what Yu and Shun were bound by, and what Fu Xi and Ji Qu always practiced, so how much more will common people [gain] from it!"[284]

When Zi Gao, the Duke of She, was about to be sent to Qi, he asked Confucius, "The king is sending me and it's very important. In Qi they treat emissaries with respect but they're not eager about it. One can't even move a common man, let alone a feudal lord! I'm quite afraid of him. You often tell me, 'In all affairs, large or small, few achieve a happy completion but not by means of the Way. If the affair does not reach completion,

[283] "Knowing without knowledge" might be rendered coherent by the translation "knowing without cognition." The term is *zhi*, which means knowledge and cognition. Think of cognitive states as conceptual activities. It might be possible to have knowledge of a sort by keeping the mind still and free from cognitive activities. We will examine this difficulty in Chapter 8.

[284] The figures mentioned are mythical sage kings.

then one will come to harm from others. If affairs do reach completion, then there follows the dysfunction of the yin and yang.[285] To have no dysfunction after reaching or failing to reach completion - only someone with power can manage it.' I'm someone who eats coarsely and not very much, who doesn't need cool drinks when dining. But now I receive my orders this morning and by evening I'm drinking ice water. Is there a fever inside me? I've not yet gotten to the core of the affair and I already have a dysfunction of yin and yang. If affairs do not reach completion, then I'll come to harm from others. There'll be both. I'm not a subject who suffices to be relied upon. Can you give me any advice?"

Confucius said, "A child's loving his parents is fated and cannot be undone in his heart. A minister's serving his ruler is what is right, and there's nowhere he can go without the ruler, nowhere to run between heaven and earth. These are called 'the great constraints'. Therefore, one who serves his parents doesn't choose where he ends up but takes it in stride. This is the perfection of filiality. One who serves his ruler doesn't choose how to serve but takes it in stride. This is the flourishing of loyalty. As for someone who serves his own mind. Suchness and joy do not move or influence him. He knows what he cannot do anything about and takes it in stride as though it were fated. This is the perfection of virtue. A subject or child is bound to have things he cannot avoid. If you go by the inherent dispositions of things and forget about yourself, what time will you have to get to yearn for life or to hate death? This way of going about it will do.

---

[285] This is the view that success has the seed of decline in it. This is represented by the *taiji*, or black and white yin-yang symbol, in which the flourishing of either aspect has the seed of its destruction in it, as represented by a small dot of the opposite color. That success causes dysfunction may sound odd, but it is plausible that only someone of particularly powerful nature can handle the success of changing an entire state's policy for the better. How well would an ordinary person handle suddenly becoming a successful vice president?

"I'd like to pass along what I've been told. For any relationship, if it's close, they will bond to one another in good faith. If it's distant, there must be someone transmitting for them. But to transmit words of two pleased or two angry parties is the hardest thing in the world. With two pleased ones there will be many words exaggerating the good points. With two angry ones there will be many words exaggerating the bad points. Exaggeration of any kind is falsehood. When there is falsehood good faith is absent. Under that absence, the transmitter of words will be endangered. Therefore, the *Legal Sayings*[286] says, 'Transmit his established dispositions; don't transmit his exaggerated words.' In this way, you'll pull through in one piece."

"Those who pit their strength in games of skill begin in a light mood but often end up in a dark one. When it gets bad there is a lot of cheating. Those who drink according to ritual start out orderly but often end up disorderly. When it gets bad there is a lot of perverse pleasure. All affairs are like these. They start out elegant and end up crude. They begin with simplicity and always end up with monstrosity.

"Speech is wind and waves. Action fulfills or comes up short. Speech readily moves people, and fulfillment or coming up short readily endangers them. Thus anger derives from nothing but skillful speech and biased words. When a beast dies it doesn't choose whether to cry out but snarls and hisses, and lets loose a ferociousness in its heart. When pushed to the extreme it is always with an unseemly state of mind that people respond, and this without knowing they're doing it. And if they don't even know they're doing it, then who knows where it will end? Thus the *Legal Sayings* says, 'Do not diverge from your orders. Do not push for completion. Going beyond the mark is excess.' Diverging from orders or pushing for completeness puts the affair in jeopardy. A splendid completion comes in good time. An awful completion cannot be revised. You must be careful!

---

[286] This text is unknown today.

"Just ride on things, so that you let your mind wander. Accept what is unavoidable, so that you take care of the center. That's excellence. What is there to fulfilling commands? Nothing compares to carrying out your mandate. That's what's hard!"

When Yan He was to begin teaching the eldest son of Duke Ling of Wei, he asked Qu Poyu, "There is a man of the following description. He is of naturally perverse power.[287] If one lets him act without constraints, one endangers one's state. If one has him act under constraints, one endangers oneself. He knows enough to recognize others' faults. How should one handle someone like this?"

Qu Poyu said, "Good question! Be on you guard. Be careful, and keep yourself correct. It is best to be appropriate in your comportment and agreeable in your mind. However, there is a risk in these two attitudes. Be appropriate, but you don't want to blend in. Be agreeable, but you don't want to stand out. If your demeanor is appropriate, such that you blend in, you'll be dislodged, destroyed, crushed and trampled. If you're agreeable, such that you stand out, you'll raise voices and be named, blamed, and condemned. If he plays the child, play the child with him. If he acts out of bounds, act out of bounds with him. If he acts recklessly, act recklessly with him. Take him and blend in to the faultless.

"Don't you know about the praying mantis? He waved its arms in front of an oncoming cart, not knowing that he was not up to the task. He was one who showed off his talents. Be on you guard. Be careful. If you bring your achievements together to show them off and thus offend him, you'll be on thin ice.

"Don't you know about the tiger trainer? He wouldn't feed them a living animal, since letting them kill it would put them into a rage. He wouldn't feed them an entire animal, since letting them tear it up would put them into a rage. By marking

---

[287] This eldest son plotted to kill his mother, was banished from Wei, and returned to take the throne away from his own son.

the time when they feed, he understood their angry hearts. Tigers are of a different type from humans, but the one to whom they are gentle follows them, just as the one they kill goes against them.

"The horse lover used a box to catch the dung and a giant clam shell to catch the urine. But if there happens to be a mosquito or a fly bothering it and he slaps it at the wrong moment, it will chomp its bit, smash its head, and ram its chest. There is something excellent about his intentions but something errant about his concern. One must be very careful."

Carpenter Shi went to Qi. When he got to Curved Shaft, he saw an oak shrine tree. Big enough to shade several thousand cows, it was a hundred grasps around and tall enough to mingle with the mountains. Only at eighty feet and above were there branches, ten or more of which could each be used to make a boat. Observers were swarming as they do at a market. The carpenter didn't pay it any attention but kept walking right on by.

His disciple saw his fill of it and went after Carpenter Shi, saying, "Since I first took up an axe to follow you, Master, I've never seen one of such exquisite quality. But you didn't bother to look at it and walked right on by. Why?"

"Enough! Don't talk about it! It's a tree to reject. If you used it to make a boat, it would sink. Make a bowl of it and it will quickly break. Make gates and doors of it and they'll leak tar. Make a post of it and bugs will get it. It's a tree of no capacities. There is no way to use it. That's why it's had such a long life."

After Carpenter Shi had returned, he dreamed of the shrine oak saying, "What were you comparing me to? Were you comparing me to decorative trees? Berry, pear, orange and pomelo, the fruit-bearing foliage - when the fruit is ripe, they are hacked. When hacked, they are damaged. The big branches are broken and the small branches are thinned. Thus to their abilities make their lives bitter. That's why they don't live out their years but pass away midway or let themselves be impaired by the mundane. All things are like this. But I go for what has nothing useful to it and live long. Near death, I understand it only now. It's of great use to me. If I had been useful, would I still have grown so big? Moreover, you and I are both things. How can one judge the other, each being things? And a man to reject who is near death - how can he recognize a tree to reject!"

When Carpenter Shi awoke, he reported of his dream. His disciples said, "If it means to hold to uselessness, then why does it serve as a shrine?"

"Quiet! Don't speak! It's just playing at it. It takes those who don't understand it as a curse to it. If it weren't serving as a shrine, it would always be in danger of being cut down. Moreover, what it conserves is different from that of the rest. So, if you describe it according to the norm, won't you be wide of the mark?"

Ziqi of Nanbo was wandering through by Hill of Shang when he saw a big tree there that was unusual. With a thousand chariots under it, it would shade them all. Ziqi said, "What sort of tree is this? It must have some unusual capacities." When he looked up, he noticed its big trunk, which was knotted and burled, and not usable to make coffins. When he licked a leaf, his mouth was burned and made sore. To smell it could make one so inebriated that it wouldn't stop for three days.

Ziqi said, "It's a tree of no capacities, after all. That's how it grew so big. So, a holy man is thus of no capacities!"

The Jingshi region of Song grows catalpa, cypress, and mulberry trees. Those larger than one grasp around will be cut down by someone needing a post for his monkeys. Those three or four grasps around will be cut down by someone seeking vaulted ceiling posts. One seven or eight grasps around will be cut down by a family of rank and wealth seeking coffin boards. That is why they don't live out their natural years but fall to the axe midway. This is harm due to having capacities. In the Jie sacrifice, a cow with a white forehead, a piglet with upturned snout, and a person with hemorrhoids cannot be offered to the river. All priests know this. So, they take these things as inauspicious. But this is why the holy man takes them as highly auspicious.

Branched Off Shu has his chin stuffed into his navel, his shoulders above his head, back bones pointing up, his five organs too high, and his two thighs acting like ribs. He sews and washes clothes enough to get a bite to eat. When he sifts grain with a winnow, it's enough to feed ten people. When the government calls up the troops, Branched Off wanders among them, waving. When they have a big labor project, Branched Off has his usual illness and is not called upon. When they give out grain to the sick, he receives three bucketsful and ten bundles of firewood. Even with a branched off body, it still suffices for keeping himself well and living out his natural years. How much more would branched off virtue!

When Confucius was in Qu, Jie Yu, the madman of Qu, wandered by his gate, saying, "Phoenix! Phoenix! How your power fades! You can't wait for future generations, and you can't go get past ones. When the world has the Way, the sage becomes complete with it. When the world lacks the Way, the sage lives with it. In times like these, he just escapes punishment in it.

"Good fortune is as light as a feather, but no one knows how to carry it. Bad fortune is as heavy as the earth, but no one knows how to keep away from it. Enough! Enough! Putting people together with virtue - Dangerous! Dangerous! To go along drawing lines on the earth - Idiot! Idiot! Don't impair my gait. I walk with bent steps. Don't injure my feet!"

The mountain trees deplete themselves. A grease fire cooks itself. Cinnamon is edible, so they chop the [cinnamon] trees up. Lacquer is useful, so the [lacquer] tree gets harmed. People all know of the use of usefulness, but no one knows the use of uselessness.

V. The Signs of Complete Virtue

Duke Ai asked, "What do you mean by 'fulfilling one's capacity'?"

Confucius said, "Death, life, having, losing, failure, success, poverty, wealth, worthiness, unworthiness, notoriety, fame, hunger, thirst, cold, heat - these are the vagaries of our affairs and the path fate travels. Day and night they each take their turn, and our cognition cannot discern their beginning. Therefore, they aren't worth allowing your equanimity to be disrupted. They cannot penetrate to the core of your spirit. Bring them to a satisfied repose, but keep them in line and don't be dissipated in pleasure. Make it so that day and night, without fail, you see things as in springtime. This is 'to give whatever you encounter its season in your mind'. This is what I call 'fulfilling your capacity'"....

Huizi said to Zhuangzi, "Can a human being really have no inherent dispositions?"[288]

Zhuangzi said, "Yes."

Huizi said, "Human but without inherent dispositions - what makes him count as human?"

Zhuangzi said, "The Way gave him an appearance. Heaven gave him a form. How could he not count as human?"

Huizi said, "If he counts as human, how can he not have inherent dispositions?"

Zhuangzi said, "Standards (*shifei*) are what I call 'inherent dispositions.' What I mean by 'no inherent dispositions' is someone who doesn't let good and evil cause

---

[288] This is an important criticism of Zhuangzi's philosophy. It seems obvious that there are things that deeply matter to human beings, that there are things that are important for making a life good, and that there are things that are evil in that they are catastrophes for a life. Zhuangzi addresses this sort of objection when he illustrates his point of view with examples of deformities, tumors, and death and portrays in a different way from simply categorizing them as evils. In this passage he defines what he means more generally.

internal injury to his person, but who always takes his cue from the natural without trying to enhance life."[289]

Huizi said, "If he doesn't try to enhance life, how can he survive?"

Zhuangzi said, "The Way gave him an appearance. Heaven gave him a form. He doesn't let good and evil cause internal injury to his person. Now, you shut your spirit out and tax your essential energies, leaning against a tree and muttering or hunched over your desk and falling asleep. Heaven chose your form, but you use it to carp about 'hard and white'."[290]

VI. The Great Ancestral Teacher

To know what heaven[291] does and to know what man does is excellent. One who knows what heaven does lives by heaven.[292] One who knows what man does uses the object of his knowledge to take care of what lies beyond his knowledge, living out the years heaven gave without being cut down along the way. These are the perfection of knowledge.

However, there is a problem. Knowledge depends on something in order to hit the mark, but what it depends on is peculiarly unreliable. How do I know that what I call "of heaven" is not of man, while what I call "of man" is not of heaven? Moreover, real knowledge requires a real human being. What is a real human being? The real human being of ancient times didn't resist destitution, didn't relish accomplishments, and didn't plan affairs. Someone like that errs without regret and hits the mark without dwelling on himself. Someone like that could

[289] This is Zhuangzi's answer to the objection. Is it a psychology for handling catastrophes with equanimity which prescribes not striving mightily to achieve a good life? Is it an unrealistic denial of facts about the reality of evil and the importance of avoiding and opposing it?
[290] "Hard and white" alludes to the logical style of philosophy we saw above in the interlude on analytical philosophy.
[291] Recall that the term *tian* might be translated as "nature," as well as by "heaven."
[292] As "tian" means nature, as well as "heaven," the phrase also means "lives according to nature."

climb high without vertigo, enter water without getting wet, and enter fire without getting burned. Such is one whose knowledge ascends to the Way.

The real human being of ancient times slept without dreaming and woke up without concerns. He ate without savoring and his breaths were deep. The real human being breathes from the heels. The rest breathe from the throat. Broken and subdued, they choke out their words as though retching. They are people whose desires run deep but whose heaven-bestowed functioning runs shallow.

The real human being of ancient times was unacquainted with love of life or hatred of death. He was not glad to emerge or sorry to go back in.[293] His comings and goings were abrupt and without ado. He didn't forget his origin and he didn't seek his end. He enjoyed what he received and forgot about what he gave back. This is called "not using the mind to push the Way along" and "not using the human to help heaven." That's what I call a real human being.

Someone like that has a forgetful mind, a placid face, and a broad forehead. He's cool as autumn and warm as spring. His joy and anger go as the four seasons. He has a way with everything, and no one knows his limits....

The real human being of ancient times was congenial in his manner but not friendly. He seemed to be lacking but accepted nothing. He was given to being alone but not hardened. Expansive in his emptiness, he was not ostentatious. He was cheerful and seemed to enjoy himself. He was hesitant, as though there was no way around something. Any annoyance was palpable in his countenance. He was magnanimous; his virtue brought one up short. Severe, as though jaded. Aloof, as though he could not be pinned down. Pausing, as though he preferred to be closed off. Befuddled, as though he forgot what he was going to say....

---

[293] Probably Zhuangzi refers to birth and death, emerging from and going back into the 'great clump,' which is the earth or something more subtle.

234

Therefore, when he liked something there was a unity, and when he didn't like something, there was a unity. His unity was a unity. And his disunity was a unity. In his unity he was as a companion to heaven. In his disunity he was as a companion to human beings. Neither heaven nor human beings had the upper hand. This is called a real human being.

Life and death are fated. Having the regularity of night and day, they are up to heaven. The only thing people can do nothing about is the inherent dispositions of things. If one especially regards heaven as one's father, loves it as oneself, then how much more something greater than it? If a person especially regards his ruler as superior and would give his life for him, then how much more would something more real than he?

When springs dry up, fish all take their place on land. They blow moisture on each other, keeping each other wet with spit. It's not as good as forgetting about each other in the rivers and lakes. Instead of praising Yao and condemning Jie,[294] it is better to forget about them both and to be transformed by the Way.

The Great Clump burdens me with a body, sets me to the labors of life, sets me at ease with old age, and rests me with death. Therefore, what makes my life count as good also makes my death count as good.

When you hide a boat in a gully or your net in a marsh, you say they are secure. Yet a strong person could carry them off in the middle of the night while you're asleep and don't realize it. Hiding the small in the large makes sense, but you still lose then. But if you hide the world in the world, you never come to lose anything. This is the great inherent disposition of unvarying things.

When we take on a particularly human form, we are delighted. But the one that seems to have a human form goes through a myriad of transformations without even beginning to be limited. Can you add up all their pleasures? Therefore, the sage would wander where things are never lost and all are

[294] Ancient kings, the former good, the latter evil.

preserved. He counts early death or old age as good. He counts the beginning and the end as good. If people take him as a model, how much more should they that which ties together the myriad things and on which each transformation depends!

The Way has an inherent disposition and it has a reliability[295] to it. But it is without action or form. It can be transmitted but cannot be received. It can be gotten but cannot be seen. It is its own basis, its own root; it was solidly in existence from of old, before there was heaven and earth. It inspirited the ghosts and gods, and gave birth to heaven and earth. It existed before the great ultimate[296] but doesn't count as high, and it exists below the six limits[297] but doesn't count as deep. It was born before heaven and earth but doesn't count as aged. It is the elder to the ancients but doesn't count as old....

Nanbo Zikui asked the woman Bent, "You are old in years, but you have the complexion of a child. Why?"

"I've heard the Way."

Nanbo Zikui said, "Can I learn the Way?"

"How? How could you? You're not its type of person. Now Buliang Yi had the capacity of a sage but didn't have the Way of a sage. I have the Way of a sage but not the capacity of a sage. I tried to teach him, to see whether he could become a sage anyway. If not, at least using the Way of a sage to instruct the capacity of a sage should have been easy. So, I instructed him, keeping him for three days, after which he could put the world outside himself. After he had seen the world as outside himself, I kept him for seven days more, after which he could see things as outside himself. After he had seen things as outside himself, I kept him for nine days more, after which he could see life as outside himself. After he saw life as outside himself, he could shine like dawn. After he shone like dawn, he could see solitude.

---

[295] The word is "*xin*," which also means good faith, trust, trustworthiness.
[296] This is the celestial north pole, as well as the source of all things represented by the *taiji* (literally "great ultimate"; yin-yang symbol). It gives its name to the popular Chinese exercises (commonly spelled "*tai-chi*").
[297] These are the six directions: north, south, east, west, up and down.

236

After he saw solitude, he could eliminate past and present. After he eliminated past and present, he could enter the not-dying and not-being-born. The killer of life doesn't die, and the giver of life does not get born. As a thing, there is nothing it doesn't accept, nothing it doesn't send away, nothing it doesn't destroy and nothing it doesn't make. Its name is 'Tumult Tranquility.' This Tumult Tranquility is something that creates only in its tumult."

Nanbo Zikui asked, "Where did you hear this?"

"I heard it from Aid Ink. Aid Ink heard it from the grandson of Try to Recite. The grandson of Try To Recite heard it from See Bright. See Bright heard it from Whispered Agreement. Whispered Agreement heard it from Needs Use. Needs Use heard it from Sigh Ah. Sigh Ah heard it from Profound Darkness. Profound Darkness heard it from Be With Emptiness. Be With Emptiness heard it from I Doubt There's A Beginning."

Master Si, Master Yu, Master Li and Master Lai were all four talking together, saying, "Who can take non-being as his head, take life as his spine, and take death as his buttocks? Whoever knows that life and death, existence and annihilation, are all one substance - I will be his friend." The four of them looked at each other and smiled. None differed in mind, so they became friends.

Soon Master Yu became ill. Master Si went to ask after him. Master Yu said, "How Wonderful is the creator of things to make me all twisted up in this way! My back is hunched out. I have five organs too high and my chin is stuffed into my navel. My shoulders are above my head, and my neck bones point towards heaven." His yin and yang *qi* were out of balance, but there was no problem as far as his mind was concerned. He limped over to a well to see his reflection. "Wow! The creator of things is making me all twisted up!"

Master Si said, "Do you dislike it?"

"No. What would I dislike? If in time my left arm is transformed into a rooster, I'll take the cue and use it to mark the time at night. If in time my right arm is transformed into a crossbow, I'll take the cue and go after owl to roast. If in time my buttocks are transformed into wheels and my spirit into a horse, I'll take the cue and ride them. I'd need no other vehicle! Now, to obtain is due to time, and to lose is a matter of course. If you are at peace with time and make your place in the course, then sorrow and happiness don't enter in. This the ancients called 'untying the binds'. Those who can't untie themselves are constrained by things. But things have never been able to conquer heaven. What do I have to dislike?"...[298]

Confucius said, "They[299] wander outside measured space, but I wander inside measured space. The outside and inside don't meet.... They will be in society with the creator of things and wander in the *qi* that unifies heaven and earth. They see life as a bulging cyst or a burgeoning tumor.... How could they worry about the rituals of worldly convention just to appear well to the eyes and ears of the masses?"

Zigong said, "Then what is the measured space which you are based in?"

Confucius said, "I am a case of heaven punishing man. But that is something you and I have in common...."

Zigong said, "What about your measured space?"

Confucius said, "Fish live off the water, while humans live off the Way. Those who live off the water get their nourishment by passing through a pond. Those who live off the Way secure their lives while making nothing of it. So, it is said

---

[298] Is this philosophical point of view realistic? As Huizi asked above, aren't there inherent dispositions of human beings, according to which getting a terribly deforming and fatal disease is a catastrophe? Philosophical positions which are in conflict with human nature cannot be right. The can also be dangerous because the denial of evil and the failure to face it tend to bring it about. See John Kekes, *Facing Evil* (Princeton: Princeton University Press, 1993) if you would like to explore this issue.

[299] Confucius is referring to characters such as Master Yu.

that fish forget about each other in rivers and lakes, while humans forget each other in the arts of the Way...."[300]

Yan Hui said, "I'm improving."

Confucius said, "What do you mean?"

"I've forgotten about benevolence and rightness."

"Okay. But that's not it yet."

On another day they saw each other again, and Yan Hui said, "I'm improving."

"What do you mean?"

"I've forgotten about rituals and music."

"Okay.[301] But that's not it yet."

On another day they saw each other again, and Yan Hui said, "I'm improving."

"What do you mean?"

"I sit in forgetfulness."

Confucius started and said, "What do you mean by 'sit in forgetfulness'?"

Yan Hui said, "I leave off my limbs, put out my intelligence, do without my body and get rid of cognition. I unite with the Great Connection. This is what I mean by 'sitting in forgetfulness.'"

Confucius said, "If you've united with it, then you have no desires. If you're transforming, then you've nothing permanent. In other words, you're a worthy! I would ask you, please let me follow you."

Master Yu and Master Sang were friends. Once, when it rained for ten days straight, Master Yu said, "Master Sang might not be well." He packed some food and went to feed him. When he reached Master Sang's place, Master Sang was partly singing and partly crying, and playing the lute: "Father? Mother? Heaven? Man?" He could hardly keep his voice and he was hard pressed to get his lyrics out.

---

[300] Probably, Confucius means the various subjects of a conventional gentleman's education. Zhuangzi, we can assume, would not recommend the arts of the Way.

[301] Would Confucius really have approved? Is Zhuangzi intentionally making too much of a Daoist out of him? Probably, but see *Analects* 2.4

Master Yu entered, saying, "The way you're singing the song - why like this?"

"I thought about what brought me to this extreme," Master Sang said. "But I couldn't find it out. How could mother and father want me to be so impoverished? Heaven covers all without bias and earth supports all without bias. How could heaven and earth be biased towards impoverishing me? I sought for the one who did it, but could not find it. So, the one who brought me to this extreme - perhaps it was fate."[302]

VII. For Emperor and Kings

In Cheng there was a shaman named Ji Xian. He could tell all about a person's death, life, conservation, losses, calamities, good fortune, lifespan, and time of death - timing these to the year, month, week, and day. He was like a god. When the people of Cheng saw him they would all drop everything and get away from him. When Liezi[303] saw him, his mind was intoxicated. He went back and told about him to Huzi, saying, "I used to take Master's Way to be unexcelled. But there is someone whose excels it."

Huzi said, "I've covered its adornments with you, but we haven't covered its substance. Do you really think you've attained to the Way? What kind of eggs will you get with a flock of hens but no rooster? You take your Way and parade it around in the world, expecting to be believed, and that's why you enabled that guy to get a hold of you and read you. Next time try bringing him with you and let him have a look at me."

The next day Liezi brought him to see Huzi. When he came out, he told Liezi, "Ay! Your master is dying! He's fading

---

[302] Notice that this example is in tension with the other characters which terrible diseases or deformities, in that the sick man shows anguish and despair, rather than joy.
[303] The third most famous Daoist philosopher, after Laozi and Zhuangzi. The book of his sayings is the *Liezi*.

fast. He doesn't have much more than a week. I saw something strange in him. I saw wet ashes in him."

Liezi went in, his collar soaked with his tears, and told of this to Huzi. Huzi said, "Just now I manifested myself as the earthen adornment - plowed under, motionless, and flat. He probably saw that I had shut down the mechanism of power. Try bringing him back again."

The next day he brought him to see Huzi again. When he came out, he told Liezi, "It is lucky that your master met me. He has recovered and is completely restored to life. I had seen his shut-down system."

Liezi went in and told of this to Huzi. Huzi said, "Just now I manifested myself as heaven's field, where names and substance don't enter, and the mechanism interfaces at one's heels. He probably saw in me the mechanism of the good. Try bringing him back again."

The next day he brought him to see Huzi again. When he came out, he told Liezi, "Your master is unsteady. I could not get a read on him. When he is steady, I'll read him again."

Liezi went in and told of this to Huzi. Huzi said, "I just now manifested myself as the great void where nothing is victor. He probably saw in me the mechanism of balanced *qi*. The depths of a behemoth's wake are an abyss. The depths of still water are an abyss. The depths of moving water are an abyss. There are nine kinds of abyss. This time I showed him three. Try bringing him back again."

The next day he brought him and had him see Huzi again. But before he could even come to a standstill he lost his composure and ran. "Go after him!" Huzi said. Liezi went after him but didn't catch up to him. He came back and reported to Huzi, "He's disappeared. He's lost. I couldn't catch up to him."

Huzi said, "Just now I manifested myself as not yet even begun to emerge from my origins. I met him empty and wiggling like a snake, not knowing who or what, letting myself be bowed and bent, and letting myself surge like a wave. That's why he fled."

Afterwards, Liezi went home, believing himself to have not even begun to learn. He didn't leave home for three years. He cooked for his wife, fed the pigs as one feeds people, and showed no particular inclination in his endeavors. He cut and whittled and returned to the hunk of wood. Like a clump he was alone, standing there with his body. Sealed off against perplexity,[304] he lived the rest of his life in unity like this.

The Emperor of the South Sea was Brief, and the Emperor of the North Sea was Sudden. The Emperor of the Center was Roil.[305] Brief and Sudden met from time to time in Roil's land, and Roil treated them very well. Brief and Sudden discussed repaying Roil's kindness, saying, "Humans all have seven holes with which to see, hear, eat and breathe. He alone has none. Let's try to drill some." Every day they drilled one hole. On the seventh day Roil died.

XVII. Autumn Floods

...The god Ro of the Northern Sea said, "If you view them from the standpoint of the Way, things have no nobility or baseness in them. If you view them from the standpoint of things, they take themselves to be noble and each other to be base. If you view them from the standpoint of ordinary folk, nobility and baseness are not up to oneself to determine. If you take them from the standpoint of measurement, then, going by what makes things big, we will consider them big, and, hence, none of the myriad things will not be big; and going by what makes things small, we will consider them small, and, hence, none of the myriad things will not be small. When you recognize that heaven and earth are as grains, and when you recognize that the tip of a hair is as a hill, then the multiplicity of measurements becomes apparent. If you view things from the standpoint of merit, then, going by what makes them have it, we will consider them to have

---

[304] The text is ambiguous: sealed off *against* perplexity, or *in* perplexity?
[305] "Roil" translates *hundun*, roiling, chaotic, mixed-up.

it, and, hence, none of the myriad things will not have it; and going by what makes them lack it, we will consider them to lack it, and, hence, none of the myriad things will not lack it. If you understand that east and west, in opposing each other, cannot do without each other, then merits will be distinguished and determined. If you view things from the standpoint of preference, then, going by what makes them choiceworthy, we will choose them, such that none of the myriad things will not be chosen; and going by what makes them worthy of rejection, we will reject them, such that none of the myriad things will not be rejected."

XVIII. Perfect Happiness

Is there perfect happiness in the world? Or isn't there? Is there a means of keeping yourself alive? Or isn't there? What should one do? What should one rely on? What should one avoid? What should one abide by? What should one choose? What should one reject? What should one enjoy? What should one detest?

What everyone honors is wealth, nobility, long life and goodness of character. What he enjoys is personal security, rich flavors, pretty clothes, nice things to look at and musical sounds. What he sees as lower are poverty, baseness, early death and badness of character. What he regards as bitter are failure of the person to obtain personal security and ease, the failure of the mouth to obtain rich flavors, the failure of the body to get pretty clothes, the failure of the eyes to obtain nice things to look at, and the failure of the ears to get musical sounds. If you are one of those who fail to obtain these, then you are depressed and afraid.

But isn't this a foolish attitude towards the body? The rich put themselves under stress with overwork. They accumulate a lot of wealth, more than they can use. Isn't that an inhospitable attitude toward the body? The noble are up at night analyzing goodness and badness of character. Isn't that a harsh attitude towards the body? Human beings are born with their dejection, and those who live long grow muddle-minded. A prolonged dejection without death - how bitter! Isn't this an estranged attitude towards the body?

Warriors with a passion for bravery are seen by everyone as good, but it's not enough to keep them alive. I don't know - is their goodness actually goodness? Or is it actually not good? You can take it to be good, but it's not enough to keep them alive. You can take it to be not good, but it suffices to save others. Hence it is said, "When your loyal advice isn't listened to, be restrained and don't fight." Thus, Zixu destroyed his body by fighting.[306] Without fighting, he wouldn't have made a name for himself. Did he actually have goodness? Or did he not?

I also don't know about what ordinary folk do and enjoy - is it really enjoyment after all? Or is it not really enjoyment after all? I look at what ordinary folk enjoy, what they chase after in flocks, in a rush, as though they can't get enough, and at what they all say they enjoy. But I don't enjoy it. Yet, nor do I not enjoy it. Is there such a thing as enjoyment? I take non-action as genuine enjoyment. But ordinary folk take it as a great bitterness. Hence, I say that the ultimate enjoyment is devoid of enjoyment. The ultimate praise is a lack of praise. No one is able to determine standards. However, non-action enables one to determine standards. Ultimate enjoyment is keeping alive. Only non-action brings you close to such preservation. Let me try to explain this.

Heaven is pure through its non-action. Earth is tranquil through its non-action. Therefore, the two non-actions came together to transform the myriad things. Blurry, mysteriously, they came out of nowhere. Mysteriously, blurry, they were without the images[307] of existence. The myriad things in their

---

[306] In 484 B.C.E. Zixu, minister of the state of Wu, was forced to commit suicide after his continuous fretting over the possibility of foreign invasion became too much for the king to bear.
[307] According to traditional cosmogony, the world's creation began with division into basic forms - "images" - of existence: yin, yang, hard, and soft.

244

various capacities all grow out of non-action. So, it is said "They do not act, but there is nothing left undone."[308] Who among human beings can attain non-action?

When Zhuangzi's wife died, Huizi came to mourn her. But Zhuangzi was sitting on the floor, drumming on a tub and singing. Huizi said, "You lived with her, raised your children, and grew old. Now that she has died, not to cry is enough. But drumming on a tub and singing - isn't that going too far?"

Zhuangzi said, "No. When she had died, how could I, of all people, not be grief-stricken? But I examined her beginning and fundamentally she was without a birth. Not only without a birth, she fundamentally was without a body. Not only without a body, she fundamentally was without any *qi*. Mixed up with the place of blurriness and mystery, she changed and had *qi*. The *qi* changed and she had a body. The body changed and she had a birth. Now she has changed again and died. This is like the procession of the four seasons: spring, autumn, winter and summer. She was blissfully taking her rest in roomy quarters while I cried, 'Boo hoo!' for her. I saw that I didn't comprehend fate. So, I stopped."

Uncle Branched Off and Uncle Wobble were looking at the mounds of the Earl of the Dark in the desolation of Kunlun, where the Yellow Emperor rested. Suddenly, a willow[309] was born from Uncle Wobble's left elbow. He seemed to be shocked and to dislike it. Uncle Branched Off said, "Do you dislike it?"

Uncle Wobble said, "No. How could I dislike it? Those given birth to are an embellishment and borrowing. That which is embellished to give birth to the born is a pile of dirt. Life and death are like day and night. You and I were looking at the transformations and the transformations reached me. What is there for me to dislike in them?"

These images are represented in the numerology of the *Yijing* (and on the modern flag of South Korea, as well).
[308] *The Book of Power and the Way* 11(48).
[309] I.e., a tumor.

When Zhuangzi went to Chu he saw an empty skull. It was dry but had its shape. He poked it with his horse baton and then asked it, "Did you come to this because your lust for life led to you lose your reason? Or did you come to this because of a matter of your putting the state in jeopardy, which led you to lay your head under the ax? Or did you come to this because you did something that wasn't good and were ashamed of disgracing your family? Or did you come to this by some calamity of freezing or starving? Or did your springs and autumns just run out at this point?"

When he had finished speaking, he took the skull and, using it as a pillow, went to sleep. In the middle of the night the skull appeared in his dreams. It said, "You sound like one of those philosophers who argue a lot. I see that the things you speak of are indeed the problems of being born human. But when you're dead, then there is none of these. Would you like to hear an explanation of death?"

Zhuangzi said, "Yes."

The skull said, "When you are dead, there is no ruler above and no subject below, and no more of the four seasons' tasks. Rather, our springs and autumns are like those of heaven and earth. Even the happiness of a king facing south is no greater than this."

Zhuangzi didn't believe it and said, "If I had the manager of fate give you birth in a body again, making for you bones, flesh, and muscle, and returning you to your parents, wife, children and acquaintances, would you like that?"

The skull with a frown and a scowl said, "How could I give up the happiness of a king facing south and return to the travails of the humanity?"...

Human beings will go back into the mechanism [of the transformation of things]. The myriad things come out of the mechanism and all go back into the mechanism.

XIX. Reaching Life

...Master Liezi asked Pass Guard Yin, "The excellent man treads underwater without drowning, steps on fire without burning, and goes above the myriad things without being afraid. May I ask how he reaches such excellence?"

Pass Guard Yin replied, "Because he maintains the pure *qi*. Those aren't examples of knowledge, skill, determination, or daring. Sit down and I will explain. Everything that has an appearance, an image, a sound and a color is a thing. How could one thing and another be far apart from one another? And what could make one of them come to the fore? Just the color, that's all. Things are created in formlessness and end in non-transforming. One who attains to this completely cannot be stopped by things. He abides at the level of non-excessiveness, sequesters himself at the limitless degree, and wanders in what begins and ends the myriad things. He unifies his nature, nourishes his *qi*, focuses his power, and interfaces with what creates things. The heavenly in him maintained entire, his spirit without flaw, how could things penetrate to him?

"When a drunk falls from a carriage, even at high speed, he doesn't die. His bones and joints are the same as others', but his injuries are not the same. For his spirit is whole. He doesn't even know that he's riding, or even that he has fallen. Life and death, alarm and fear, do not enter into his breast. That is why he comes up against things without fear. If one can attain wholeness through liquor and fare this well, how much better by attaining wholeness through the heavenly! The sage sequesters himself in the heavenly, so nothing can injure him.

"Someone out for revenge doesn't break his enemy's sword. Even someone with rage in his heart doesn't get angry at a tile that has fallen off. This is how everything is equal. Therefore, one who would eliminate the chaos of fighting and war and eliminate capital punishment should go by this Way.

"Don't go by the human 'heaven'; go by heavenly heaven. One who goes by heaven empowers life. One who goes by the human injures life. Do not show repugnance for their heaven, and don't neglect the human, and your people will come close to getting hold of what's real in them...."

Master Jixing was raising a gamecock for his king. After ten days he was asked, "Is the cock ready?"

"Not yet," he said. "It tends toward empty bravado and making use of its *qi*."

After another ten days he was asked again. "Not yet," he said. "It still responds to echoes and shadows."

After another ten days he was asked again. "Not yet," he said. "It still lets its gaze dart around and overflows with *qi*."

After another ten days he was asked again. "Close enough. The cock won't move even at the sound of another's call. The way he looks resembles a cock made of wood. His power is complete. Other cocks don't dare confront him but turn and run away."

Confucius was having a look at Luliang Falls, a waterfall of thirty fathoms with whitewater extending forty li. Neither tortoise, alligator, fish nor turtle could swim in it. He saw an old master swimming in it, and taking him to be suicidal, he had his disciples stand along the current to pull him out. Coming up several hundred paces downstream, the man was singing and wandering by the bank with his wet hair hanging down.

Confucius went up to him and asked, "I thought you were a ghost, but, upon examination, you're human. May I ask, is there a Way of traveling in the water?"

"No," he said. "I have no Way. I began with what is given, grew according to my nature, and came to completion according to fate. I go in with the flow and come out together with the current. I follow the water's Way and don't act on my own accord in it. That is how I travel in the water."

Confucius asked, "What do you mean by 'I began with what is given, grew according to my nature, and came to completion according to fate'?"

The old master replied, "I was born on land and was comfortable on land. That's what's given. I grew up on the water and am comfortable on the water. That's my nature. Without knowing what makes me so, I let it be so. That's fate."

Woodworker Qing carved a piece of wood to make a bell stand. When the bell stand was complete, those who saw it were amazed that it was not made by a ghost or spirit. The Marquis of Lu saw it and asked him, "What arts did you apply to make it?"

"Your subject is a craftsman," he replied. "What arts would I have? Nevertheless, I do apply one. When I am about to make a bell stand, I refrain from wasting my *qi* about it, and I have to fast so that I quiet my mind. After fasting for three days, I'm restrained from dwelling on congratulations, rewards, ranks or stipends. After fasting for five days, I'm restrained from dwelling on censure, praise, skill or clumsiness. After fasting for seven days, I suddenly forget I have four limbs and a body. At that time, there is no more duke or court, my skill is concentrated, and external distractions disappear. I then enter the mountain woods and examine their heavenly nature. If one is of exquisite form and I then fully see a bell stand, I then add my handiwork to it. Otherwise, I leave it alone. So, I use heaven to bring the heavenly together. That is the reason they suspected the work was made by a spirit...."

XXII. Knowledge Wandered North

Knowledge wandered north to the banks of the Dark Waters. It climbed the hills of Hidden Heights and happened to meet No Acting Or Speaking there. Knowledge said to No Acting Or Speaking (Neither Acting Nor Speaking), "I would like to ask you, how should I think, or contemplate, in order to know the Way?" In which station should I serve, in order to take ease in the Way? What shall I follow, and by which way, in order to obtain the Way?" There were three questions but No Acting Or Speaking didn't answer. It's not that he didn't answer; he didn't know how to answer.

Knowledge, not getting an answer, retreated south of the White Waters. It climbed up Solitary Closed and happened to see Wild Stammer there. Knowledge asked Wild Stammer his questions. Wild Stammer said, "Oh! I know it, I'll tell you." But just when he was about to speak, he forgot what he wanted to say.

Knowledge, not getting an answer, went back to the Imperial Palace. When it saw the Yellow Emperor, it questioned him. The Yellow Emperor said, "It is in no station and without serving that you will begin to take your ease in the Way. It is without following, without a way, that you will begin to obtain the Way."

Knowledge asked the Yellow Emperor, "You and I know, but these two others didn't know. Who among us is correct?"

The Yellow Emperor said, "That 'Without Action or Talk' was really correct. Wild Stammer seemed to have it. You and I never got near it. 'One who knows does not speak. One who speaks does not know'[310]. Therefore, the sage 'practices the unspoken teaching'[311]. The Way cannot be affected and you cannot go get power, though you can be humane, you can determine what's right, or deceive one another with ritual. So, it is said,

If one loses the Way, then one resorts to power. If one loses power, then one resorts to humanity. If one loses humanity, then one resorts to rightness. If one loses rightness, then one resorts to ritual. But ritual, being loyalty and trust worn thin, is a cause of disorder.[312]

"So, it is said, 'Those who hear the Way decrease daily, decrease and decrease, until the point of non-action. They do not act, but there is nothing left undone.'[313]

"Now that we already exist as things, won't it be difficult should we decide to return to the root? The Great Man is the only one who would find it easy.

---

[310] This quotation is from *The Book of Power and the Way* 19(56).
[311] From *The Book of Power and the Way* 46(2).
[312] *The Book of Power and the Way* 1(38).
[313] *The Book of Power and the Way* 11(48).

"Life is the companion of death. Death is the origin of life. Who knows what orders them? Human life is a concentration of *qi*. When it is concentrated, it makes life, and when it is dissipated, it makes death. Since life and death are companions, what do I have to fear?

"Therefore, while the myriad things are one, it is what we count as beautiful in them that we take to be spiritual or rare, and what we count as ugly in them that we take to be foul or rotten. But the foul or rotten return to become the spiritual and rare, and the spiritual and rare return to become the foul and rotten. Hence it is said, 'You have only to see that everything is one *qi*.' The sage certainly values unity."

Knowledge said to the Yellow Emperor, "I asked No Acting Or Speaking but he did not reply to me. It's not that he didn't reply to me; he didn't know how to reply to me. I asked Wild Stammer. Wild Stammer was about to tell me, but he didn't tell me. It's not that he didn't tell me; he was about to tell me but forgot what he wanted to say. But now I'm asking you, and you know it. So, why think you're not near it?"

The Yellow Emperor said, "The one was really correct, since he didn't know. The other seemed to have it since he forgot it. You and I never got near it because we know it."

When Wild Stammer heard of this he took the Yellow Emperor to be someone who knew how to speak.

Heaven and earth have a great beauty which isn't to be spoken of. The four seasons have a clear pattern which isn't to be discussed. The myriad things have an order in which they come to completion which isn't to be explained. The sage goes straight to the beauty of heaven and earth and gets to the order of the myriad things. Therefore, a perfected human, he doesn't act; a great sage, he doesn't do anything. This means that he sees into heaven and earth. Such a one has a spiritual intelligence of refined essence, and in him it has a hundreds of transformations.

Things are already dead or alive, square or round. No one knows their root. But it's everywhere and the myriad things have already existed from of old. The six realms are gigantic but have never left its inside. An autumn hair is small but waits for it to obtain substance. Nothing in the world doesn't coalesce and then disperse, going its whole life without taking a basis. Yin and yang and the four seasons run their courses, each taking its place. Obscure, it seems not to exist but exists. It is amorphous like oil, yet it is spiritual. The myriad things are looked after, but they don't know it. This is called the fundamental root. It can be used to see into heaven.

Gap Tooth asked Leather Coat about the Way. Leather Coat said, "Straighten your body, unify your awareness, and a heavenly harmony will arrive. Gather your knowledge, unify your rate, and spirits will come to abide. Power will be your beauty, the Way will be your dwelling, and your eyes will be those of an unborn calf not looking for the reasons."

But before he had finished speaking, Gap Tooth fell asleep. Leather Coat was greatly pleased and departed, singing as he went, "Body like a skeleton, mind like dead ashes, real, actual knowledge, not using a basis to support himself, dark and murky, having no mind, he cannot be consulted. What sort of human is that?"

Shu asked Cheng, "Can the Way be obtained and possessed?"

"You don't even possess your body. How could you obtain and possess the Way?"

Shun said, "If my body is not my possession, then whose possession is it?"

"It is a form lent to you by heaven and earth. Life is not your possession but a harmony lent to you by heaven and earth. Your nature and mandate weren't your possession but are a norm lent to you by heaven and earth. Your descendants are not your possessions but are shed skins lent to you by heaven and earth. Therefore, walk without knowing where you are going. Stay without knowing what you are holding onto. Eat without knowing what you taste. This is the powerful yang of heaven and earth. How can it be obtained and possessed?"

252

Confucius asked of Lao Dan,[314] "Today you are at leisure, so I would like to ask about reaching the Way."

Lao Dan said, "You must fast and be austere, cleanse your mind, wash and purify your seminal essence and spirit, and destroy your cognitions. The Way is profound and hard to speak about. I'll give you a rough outline of it.

"A glow arises in what is obscure. Orderliness arises in what is formless. Vital essence and spirit arise in the Way. Body originally arises in vital essence, and the myriad things arise codependently with body. Thus, those of nine orifices are born of the womb, and those of eight of the egg. Their comings are without a trace, their goings without an edge. There is no door or chamber. This is the marvels of the wide world. One who hits upon this will have four strong limbs and keen eyesight and hearing. He'll not have to labor in using his mind, and his responses to things will be without bias. Heaven simply must be high, earth simply must be broad, the sun and moon simply must move, and the myriad things simply must flourish - is this not their Way?

"Furthermore, scholarliness doesn't entail knowledge, and arguments don't entail wisdom. The sage therefore leaves them out. But that which neither increases when added to nor decreases when subtracted from is what the sage keeps. Fathomless, it is like the sea. Mountainous, it finishes and then begins again. It propels and makes measured the myriad things without overlooking any. Hence, the Way of the gentleman[315] - is this not external to it? All things go to it for substance and it doesn't overlook any. Is this not their Way?

"The Middle Kingdoms have humans in them. Neither yin nor yang, they abide in the space between heaven and earth. For a while they are humans, and then they may return to their ancestors. Seen from a fundamental standpoint, living things are things made of puffs of breath. Whether they live long or die

---

[314] Laozi.
[315] I.e., the Confucian Way.

young, what's the difference? It can be spoken of as momentary. How can it be sufficient to make Yao and Jie right and wrong?[316]

There are principles for fruit-bearing plants. Human relations, though difficult, have something by which to separate them into kinds. The sage, when he confronts these, does not oppose them. But, though not opposing them, he does not hold onto them. He is harmonious and responsive to them; this is the Way. It is what sustains emperors. It is what raises kings.

Human life in the space between heaven and earth is like a white colt passing a hole in the wall; in one instant it's finished. Gushing forth, none of them doesn't come from it. Dozing, sliding, not one of them doesn't go back into it. When they have been transformed they are born. When they are transformed again they die. Living things grieve over it, and mankind is sorrowful over it: a loosening of your bow sheath and an emptying of your satchel, a reordering, a yielding. Then your spirit and bodily soul depart as though evaporating off, and the body follows after. Thus, the Great Return!

The forming of the formlessness, the making formless of the formed - this is something everyone knows. But it is not what someone who almost has it[317] concerns himself with. It is something everyone discourses upon, but when one gets it, one discourses no more. If one discourses, then one doesn't get it. A clear view won't allow a glimpse of it. Argument isn't as good as silence. The Way cannot be listened to. Listening isn't as good as plugging your ears. This is called the Great Attainment.

The master from the eastern wall asked Zhuangzi, "What you call, 'the Way' - where is it?"

Zhuangzi said, "There is nowhere it isn't."

The master from the eastern wall said, "That's allowable only if you clarify it."

Zhuangzi said, "It is in ants."

"That low?"

---

[316] Yao was a good ruler and Jie and evil one, according to tradition.
[317] I.e., the Way.

"It is in panic grass."

"Even lower still?!"

"It is in tiles and shards."

"More extreme still?!"

"It is in urine and feces."

The master from the eastern wall didn't respond.

Zhuangzi said, "Sir, your questions just don't get at the matter. When the hunting inspector asked the manager of the market how to poke pigs [to test their fatness, he was told,] 'the lower the better'. You, on the other hand, shouldn't need [such a formula]. There is no way to exclude things. The utmost Way is like this, and great speech is, too. 'All around,' 'pervasive,' 'inclusive' - these three are different words with the same substance. Their referent is one.

"Let's wander together to the Palace of Nothing at All. We will come together for discussion that is never exhaustive. Let's be inactive together. Calm and placid, quiet and pure, harmonious and at ease, our wills evacuated, we won't have anywhere to go or know where we've arrived. We'll come and go without knowing when it stops. We'll go and come without knowing how it ends. We'll journey into vastness. Great knowledge enters into it but does not know how to be exhaustive of it.

"One who treats things as things is not limited by things. Things have limits called the 'limits of things': limits that don't limit, non-limits that limit. We talk of filling and emptying, withering and decay, but that which makes full and empty doesn't fill or empty. That which makes withered and decayed doesn't wither or decay. That which makes root and branch doesn't root or branch. That which makes collected or scattered doesn't collect or scatter."

A Hekan and Shen Nong[318] were studying together under Old Long Ji. Shen Nong was hunched over his desk copying texts when A Hekan burst in at midday, saying, "Old Long is dead!"

---

[318] The Divine Farmer, the mythical founder of agriculture.

Shen Nong, hunched over his desk, grabbed his staff and arose. He tossed the staff away with a clatter and laughed, saying, "Heaven knows how vulgar, lowly, arrogant and rude I am. Hence, he left me and died. That's the end. My master died without even a wild word to inspire me."

Yan Gangtiao heard about this and said, "One who embodies the Way will have all the leaders of the world flocking to him. Today, when it comes to the Way, though he hadn't even gotten hold of one ten-thousandth of the tip of an autumn hair, he still knew to keep his wild words to himself when he died. Even more so in the case of the one who embodies the Way! When you look for it, it lies in the body. When you listen for it, it has no sound. Those who discuss it with each other call it 'obscure.' So, the Way they discuss isn't the Way at all."

Then Great Pure asked Without Exhaustion, "Do you know about the Way?"

Without Exhaustion said, "I don't know."

He then asked Without Action. Without Action said, "I know about the Way."

He then asked him, "Does your knowledge of the Way have details?"

"Yes."

"What are the details?"

Without Action said, "I know that the Way is valuable, is odious, can be bound, and can be loosed. These are the details of my knowledge of the Way."

Great Pure asked Without Beginning about these words. "Given that, now, between Without Exhaustion's not knowing and Without Action's knowing, which is right and which is wrong?"

Without Beginning said, "Not to know is deep. To know is shallow. Not to know is on the inside. To know is on the outside."

At this, Great Pure looked up and sighed, "Not to know is to know, and to know is not to know. Who knows about a non-knowing knowledge?"

Without Beginning said, "The Way cannot be heard. If you hear it, that's not it. The Way cannot be seen. If you see it, that's not it. The Way cannot be spoken of. If you speak of it, that's not it. Do you know the formlessness of giving form to form? The Way doesn't fit names."

Without Beginning continued, "One who answers when there is a question about the Way does not know the Way. There is no question about the Way, and any questions have no answers. To ask about what there is no question about is to reach the limit of questions. To answer what has no answer is to be without insight. Someone with a lack of insight who looks to the limit of questions doesn't observe the world outside him and doesn't know the great beginning within. Because of this he doesn't go across the Kun Lun[319] and doesn't wander in the grand void."

Shine Bright asked Not Exist, "Do you exist? Or do you not exist?"

Not getting an answer, Shine Bright stared at his countenance, so vacant and so empty. He stared at him all day but didn't see, listened to him but didn't hear, reached for him but couldn't get at him.

"The Utmost!" Shine Bright said. "Who else can reach it? I can think of nothingness as existence, but I cannot think of nothingness as nothingness. When it comes to treating existence as nothing, how could I ever get that far?"

The Marshal's hook forger was 80 years old but still hadn't lost a bit of his skill. The Marshal said, "Your skill - does it have a Way?"

"Your subject has something he holds to. When I was twenty I liked forging hooks. I didn't look at anything else. If it wasn't a hook, I didn't look into it. This 'using' avails itself of 'not using,' in order to increase its use. And how much more would 'using everything'! Everything would be available for it!"

---

[319] Mythical mountains west of China where immortals live.

Ran Qiu asked Confucius, "Can what was before heaven and earth be known about?"

Confucius said, "Yes. The past is like the present."

Unable to get any more questions answered, Ran Qiu withdrew. The next day he was seen again and said, "Yesterday I asked, 'Can what was before heaven and earth be known about?' You said, 'Yes. The past is like the present.' Yesterday I was clear on the matter, but today I'm unclear about it. Please tell me what you meant."

Confucius said, "Yesterday when you were clear your spirit came forth to grasp it. Now that you're unclear about it, isn't it that you're searching with something other than spirit? There is no 'past' and no 'present'. There is no beginning and no end. Before there are descendants there are descendants. Okay?"

Ran Qiu hadn't replied when Confucius said, "Stop, don't respond! Don't use life to enliven the dead. Don't use death to kill life. Do life and death have something they depend on? Both have what makes them one substance. If there is something born before heaven and earth, is it a thing? What makes things things is not a thing. A thing can't emerge before all things. For there would still be things, and there would still be things, *ad infinitum*. The sage's concern for people never has an end, and it derives from this."

Yan Yuan asked Confucius, "I've heard you say, 'Don't have anything you send, don't have anything you receive.' I'd like to hear about this wandering."

Confucius said, "People of old changed on the outside but not on the inside. The people of today change on the inside but not on the outside. The one who changes with things is identical to the one who doesn't change. Where does he change? Where does he not change? Where is there friction between him and things? He necessarily comports himself toward them without arrogance. But [there was] Master Xi Wei's park, the Yellow Emperor's garden, Shun's palace, and the halls of Tang and Wu. Those who were gentlemen were sometimes teachers of Confucianism or Mohism. They therefore opposed each other with right and wrong. And how much worse are the people of today! The sage abides with things and doesn't impinge upon them. One who doesn't impinge upon things cannot be impinged upon by them. Only those whom nothing impinges upon can send and receive with others.

"Mountains and forests! Hills and dales! They bring us a blissful delight. The delight is not complete when sorrow cuts it off. The arrival of joy and sorrow I cannot prevent. Their departure I cannot stop. How sad that the people of the world are just like inns for things. They know the ones they're entertaining but not the one's they're not entertaining. They know how to do what they can do but not how to do what they can't. A lack of knowledge and know-how will ever be unavoidable to humanity. So, those who labor to avoid what humans can't avoid - how sad, as well! Perfect speech does without speech. Perfect action does without action. To limit what your knowledge knows is shallow."

Suggested Reading

Allinson, Robert Elliott, "Of Fish, Butterflies and Birds: Relativism and Nonrelative Valuation in the Zhuangzi," *Asian Philosophy* 25(2015): 238-252

Bradley, Scott P., *All is Well in the Great Mess: An Adaptation of the Inner Chapters of the Zhuangzi with Reflections* (Booklocker.com, 2015)

Cheng, Kai-Yuan, "Self and the Dream of the Butterfly in the Zhuangzi," *Philosophy East & West* 64(2014): 563-597

Cheung, Leo K. C., "Three Sosaian Responses and a Wittgensteinian Response to the Dream Argument in the Zhuangzi," *Philosophia* 44(2016): 1-23

Chong, Kim-Chong, "The Concept of Zhen in the Zhuangzi," *Philosophy East & West* 61(2011): 324-346

Chong, Kim-Chong, "Zhuangzi and the Nature of Metaphor," *Philosophy East & West* 56 (2006): 370-391

Coutinho, Steve, *Zhuangzi and Early Chinese Philosophy Vagueness, Transformation and Paradox* (New York: Routledge, 2004)

De Reu, Wim, "How to Throw a Pot: The Centrality of the Potter's Wheel in the Zhuangzi," *Asian Philosophy* 20(2010): 43-66

Fraser, Chris, "Wandering the Way: A Eudaimonistic Approach to the Zhuangzi," *Dao: A Journal of Comparative Philosophy* 13(2014): 541-565

Fraser, Chris, "Wu-wei, the Background, and Intentionality," *in Searle's Philosophy and Chinese Philosophy: Constructive Engagement,* Bo Mou, ed. (Leiden: Brill, 2008): 63–92

Machek, David, "Beyond sincerity and pretense: role-playing and unstructured self in the Zhuangzi," *Asian Philosophy* 26(2016): 52-65

Machek, David, "The Doubleness of Craft: Motifs of Technical Action in Life Praxis According to Aristotle and Zhuangzi," *Dao: A Journal of Comparative Philosophy* 10(2011): 507-526

Machek, David, "Emotions That Do Not Move: Zhuangzi and Stoics on Self-Emerging Feelings," *Dao: A Journal of Comparative Philosophy* 14(2015): 521-544

260

Mair, Victor, ed., *Experimental Essays on Zhuangzi*, various editions

Mair, Victor H., trans., *Wandering on the Way: Early Daoist Tales and Parables of Chuang Tzu*, various editions

Sarkissian, Hagop, "The Darker Side of Daoist Primitivism," *Journal of Chinese Philosophy* 37(2010): 312-329

Watson, Burton, trans., *The Complete Works of Chuang Tzu* (New York: Columbia University Press, 1968)

Yearley, Lee H., "Daoist Presentation and Persuasion: Wandering Among Zhuangzi's Kinds of Language." *Journal of Religious Ethics* 33(2005): 503 - 535

Ziporyn, Brook, trans., *Zhuangzi: The Essential Writings: With Selections from Traditional Commentaries* (Indianapolis: Hackett, 2009)

6

Xunzi

Xunzi[320] (c.310-c.215 B.C.E.) was the third of the three great early Confucians. A thinker of great breadth and depth, he left us with dozens of masterful essays, literature unlike the sparse and terse accounts and sayings of Confucius and the records of Mencius. Xunzi was a forceful and independently minded thinker who put forth well-crafted arguments in paragraphs and essays on topics such as virtue, character, civilization, language, government, and poetry. In this chapter, we will read only four of his essays. But the rest of his *oeuvre*, which amounts to about 350 pages in English translation, is well worth reading. They are an ancient literary record of a brilliant mind. In this introduction, I will therefore use passages from these essays to introduce him to you. Whereas Confucius and Mencius perhaps needed some interpretation, in the case of a writer of Xunzi's caliber, one may step aside and let him speak for himself. However, I will emphasize an aspect of Xunzi's thought for which he did not have a name. This is his conservatism.

A Confucian living after the rise of Daoism and many other schools of thought, Xunzi set about defending the Confucian vision in which civilization, ritual, and precision of

---

[320] "Master Xun"; His name was Xun Kuang. Let me help you pronounce the "x" of transliteration. As I write, English speakers are struggling to pronounce the name of the current Chinese president, Xi Jinping. It is close enough to use the "sh" sound of English. If you would like to get even closer, form the sound at the front of your mouth and make it a bit more of a hissing sound. The "u" in "Xun" is, more or less, the same as that in "push." The get even closer, add a bit of umlaut to the sound. Of course, this is the modern pronunciation. The pronunciation of his name was somewhat different in his time.

262

language and thought could act as restraints, molds, and forms in which people's psychological dispositions could be shaped, refined, and elevated. If you will recall Laozi's saying, "Of crimes none is greater than permitting desires" (9(46)) and "the sage desires not to desire and does not value goods that are hard to obtain" (27(64)), then the following quote from one of our readings, "The Rectification of Names," should give you an initial glimpse of Xunzi's thought.

> Those who argue that one brings about good order[321] by eradicating desires are, having no means of guiding desires, troubled by the fact that they exist. Those who argue that one brings about good order by making desires few are, having no means of restraining desires, troubled by the fact that they are so many.

Xunzi develops in Confucianism the idea that the inherent dispositions of human beings produced desires which are disorderly, lascivious, brutish, and therefore, *en masse* and as a whole, wicked. These recalcitrant desires cannot be wished away by the mere creation of a philosophical theory which assumes that they do not exist. The proper response to this is to cultivate civilized control of desires using the traditional forms of character virtue and ritual, rather than fleeing to stoicism, reclusion, or meditative attempts to deaden desires. The very next sentence in Xunzi's essay portrays this as obvious: "Having and lacking desires, as distinct categories, are the living and the dead, not the orderly and the disorderly."[322]

This point of view, realistic about the natural wickedness of man and conservative of the traditions proven over the ages to be the lattice on which man could climb out of his predicament, stems from a certain seriousness and acceptance of

---

[321] I think Xunzi intends "good order" here to include governmental and civil order, as well as individual self-control. But it's possible that he had only one or two of these in mind.

[322] Recall Zhuangzi's seeming to advocate turning the mind into "dead ashes."

human nature. You can find instances of the conservative stance throughout the *Xunzi*. For instance, in "Rectification of Various Theses,"[323] we see an awareness of three justifications of punishment. In response to the proposition that punishments should be all but eliminated, Xunzi replies, "The general grounds for punishing people are to prohibit violence, to treat evil as evil,[324] and to deter it before it happens." This refusal to relinquish the premise that evil should be seriously treated as evil is a mark of the conservative view that there are real facts about human nature which cannot be wished away. Also, in the same essay, Xunzi replies to the philosopher Song Xing, who had maintained the proposition that peace could be had by having people "see it as no disgrace to be insulted." Xunzi says, "If that were so would it not also assume that people would, by inherent disposition, not despise being insulted?" But of course people do naturally despise being insulted. Xunzi argues that Song Xing and his followers are ignoring plain facts about of human nature.

There is a second passage will help to introduce us to the gist of Xunzi's thought. In the essay "Heaven"[325] he says,

> Heaven has its seasons
> Earth has its bounty
> Man has his order

> This is why one can say that he takes his place in a triad with them.

In other words, we have a place in this cosmos, a proper function. Our role is to cultivate morality and good government

---

[323] This essay is not included in our readings.

[324] "To treat evil as evil" could also be translated "to despise evil" or "to despise what is despicable." The sentence in Chinese is *e e* (pronounced in modern Mandarin similarly to "uh uh.") As a verb, *e* can mean "to despise" or "to treat as evil." The noun *e* also can mean wicked, as I suggest below.

[325] This essay is not included in our readings.

264

(order).[326] It elevates us to a place that is on a par with, or at least in the same league as, heaven and earth. It is a project which enables us to build meaningful and noble lives. It is a demanding project fraught with the possibility of failure, as the lengthy disorder of the Warring States Period, which was already two centuries old by the time Xunzi was close to the end of his life, attests.

Xunzi concludes from this point of view that it is important that people not become distracted by projects and philosophical ideas other than the cultivation of good character and good government. There is no time to waste on alternative philosophical ideas. They can seduce one, as the case of Song Xing showed. One can become fixated upon them. In "Undoing Fixation"[327] he says,

> The flaw in common men is that they become fixated upon certain things and oblivious to important patterns. If they control themselves then they return to order. But if they vacillate they will become deluded. In this world there are not two Ways. The sagely man is not of two minds. But the lords of today differ on government and the many households have different ideas, making it inevitable that some will be right, others wrong, and some will bring about order and others disorder. The rulers of the disorderly states and the men of the disorderly households all with sincere

---

[326] One of the main points of "Heaven" is that events we see in nature, although some of them can be quite odd - such as a supernova, an eclipse, or strange sounds coming from a tree - are not omens to be feared but are merely natural processes underlain by mechanisms such as the interactions of yin and yang. The essay also says that it is unwise to endeavor to uncover the underlying mechanisms as they belong to heaven and doing so is not part of our role in the triad. So, the essay encourages a naturalistic and mechanistic stance toward experience and discourages superstitious fear of natural events. But it also discourages scientific endeavors. Daoist and Confucian classic texts have done little to encourage the growth of science in Chinese history. See my "Leibniz' Binary System and Shao Yong's 'Yijing'," *Philosophy East & West* 46(1996): 59-90 for more on this.

[327] This essay is not included in our readings.

hearts seek rectitude and take themselves to be implementing it. They get distracted from the Way by their fancies, and people lead them away from it. They are covetous of their accustomed ways and only fear to hear that they are bad. Clinging to their preferences, when they observe different ways, they only fear to hear that they are fine. This is why they veer away from what would bring order and deem themselves correct without as much as a pause. How is this not a case of being fixated upon a certain point and losing the correct course?

This epistemic vice is endemic to our nature because we by nature have desires and make distinctions. The essay continues,

The causes of fixation? Desires cause fixation, hatreds cause fixation…. The many distinctions among things can all serve as sources of fixation. This is a common pitfall of intellectual pursuits.

Xunzi proceeds to diagnose the wrongheadedness of competitors to Confucianism as due to fixation.

Mozi, being fixated upon utility, was unaware of fine form. Song Xing, being fixated by desire, was unaware of how to fulfill it. Shen Dao, being fixated upon law, had no idea of worthy men. Shen Buhai, being fixated upon techniques, had no comprehension of knowledge. Huizi, being fixated upon words, was unaware of their objects. Zhuangzi, being fixated upon nature, did not understand man. Therefore, to pursue utility and call it the Way is to be absorbed in benefit. To pursue desire and call it the Way is to be absorbed in satisfaction. To pursue words and call them the Way is to be absorbed in discourse. To pursue law and call it the Way is to be absorbed in administration. To pursue power and call it the Way is to be absorbed in expediency. To pursue nature and call it the Way is to be absorbed in taking one's cue from nature.[328]

---

[328] Shen Dao and Shen Buhai were philosophers of the Legalist School, which will be represented by Han Feizi, who was Xunzi's student, in the

Xunzi offers a general description of these epistemic distortions. He continues:

> All of these are particular corners of the Way. But the Way itself is to be constant in substance but absorbed in changes. A particular corner is not worth elevating above the rest. People with peculiar ideas gaze upon a particular corner of the Way without knowing it. Then, they take it to be sufficient and fesis comtoon it for show. Thus, they create disorder inside of themselves and deceive others. If in high position, they use it to cause their subordinates to become fixated. If in low position, they use it to cause their superiors to become fixated. This is the damage done by being trapped by fixation.
>
> Confucius was humane and knowledgeable. Moreover, he was not fixated. This is why his study of various subjects sufficed to make it as if he were one of the former kings. This particular school of thought achieved the Way of the Zhou Dynasty, elevated it above the rest, and made use of it; but he did not become fixated upon what it had achieved. Thus, his virtue equaled that of the Duke of Zhou and his fame paralleled that of the three kings.[329] This is the blessing of not being fixated.
>
> The sage knows the perils of the intellectual pursuits. He sees the damage done by being trapped by fixation.... He lays all things out and hangs a scale in their midst. This is why the many differences are unable to bring disorder to his reason by causing him to become fixated. What do I mean by a "scale." The Way.
>
> ...How can one come to know the way? With the mind. How does the mind come to know the Way? By being empty, unified, and still. The mind never fails to accumulate experiences; yet there is something empty about it. The mind never fails to pursue differences; yet there is something unified about it. The mind never fails to move; yet there is something

---

next chapter. Here "nature" translates *tian*, which has the sense of heaven and nature.

[329] The ancient sage kings Yu, Tang, and Wen.

still about it.... It doesn't let one particular undercut another. This is what I call "unified."

This is a conservative epistemological point of view. The idea is that there are many important factors to consider in making judgements about human affairs, each of which, as valuable, is worth conserving to the degree it is possible for it to be conserved while conserving the other factors. This balance in practical reasoning is the Way for man. It is the opposite of fixation. You might at this point pause to review the passages from the *Mencius* in the section "Deliberation in Ethics" of Chapter Four and compare Mencius's ideas with Xunzi's. If there is a large set of important values which one wants to conserve, then while noticing the importance of any of them the conservative nevertheless conserves the importance of the others at the same time by trying to fulfill as many of them as possible. It is unconservative to choose on value to elevate to the neglect of the others, and doing so inevitably requires going against facts of human nature.

Consider the following illustration of this epistemic component of conservatism. In the United States, political conservatives and libertarians are devoted to liberty. However, whereas conservatives conserve this value while simultaneously conserving other values which sometimes compete with it – such as justice, order, and security – libertarians "elevate it above the rest." Conservatives argue that libertarians are fixated upon liberty and that some libertarians are so completely trapped by it that they accept the anarchist view that government is by its nature illegitimate since it entails encroachment upon individual liberty. On the other hand, American conservatives will oppose competing points of view where they run counter to liberty, for example, political positions which advocate giving American government enormous power to control individuals' lives for the sake of some marginal and unlikely increase in some other value. Thus, the conservative "doesn't let one particular undercut another" but instead strikes a balance by "hanging a scale in the midst" of the various values which, being passed down through the generations by tradition because they have been found to promote good lives, ought to be conserved. There is a sense in which conservatism is simply the epistemic attitude, in moral and political affairs, of not being fixated. This is why Xunzi devoted an entire essay to the attitude.[330]

To one crucial fact of human nature Xunzi devoted an entire essay: "Human Nature is Wicked." Whereas Mencius maintained that human nature was good, Xunzi maintained that our nature was wicked. I translate the term *e* as "wicked," rather than "evil," for the following reasons.[331] Xunzi's idea is that by nature human beings have desires and act to fulfill them, regardless of the social and moral ramifications. Thus, they do evil when they so act. It's not that they are malevolent or intend to do evil as an end in itself; they are not "evil" by nature. It's just that they are disposed to do evil; they are "wicked" by nature. Xunzi sees in man an outflowing of action based upon inchoate, disorganized, and uncouth desires. Moral structures, in particular those laid out in Confucius's philosophy, provide a scaffolding in which these desires can be given form, become organized, and be refined.

Of utmost importance for Xunzi, therefore, is the formative influence of good culture. Good culture is largely made of ritual, and ritual enables us to cultivate character virtue. He describes in "Rectification on Names" how the raw material of our inherent dispositions can be molded into something great.

---

[330] An excellent introduction to conservatism is John Kekes, *A Case for Conservatism* (Ithaca: Cornell University Press, 1998). Notice that Xunzi was a conservative who was not devoted to liberty. Individual liberty was not known to be a value in his time, so he would have been unable to embrace and conserve it. Conservatism is an epistemic structure and devotion to conserving time-honored traditional values. It matters which tradition the conservative wishes to conserve; by historical happenstance, they don't all have the same values.

[331] "Bad" is another possible translation of the term. "Despicable" would be a good translation, as it conveys the connection to the verb form of the word *e*, "to despise" or "to hate."

A particular desire which one receives from heaven may be so thoroughly shaped by what one receives from one's mind that it can be quite hard to tell that it is the kind of thing which one receives from heaven.

The same being that by nature is inclined to be rapacious and nasty over a bit of meat in the wild can also come to take joy in hearing a Beethoven string quartet or speak eloquently and precisely in a jury deliberation. Civilization seems to take us from brutality to civility.

Yet, consider the following. Xunzi begins his essay "Encouraging Learning"[332] as follows.

> The gentleman says, "Learning must never cease." Blue ink dried from the indigo plant is bluer than the indigo plant.... A piece of wood as straight as a plumb line can be steamed into a circular shape such that its curve will match that of a compass. Even after it has been dried in the sun it will not return to being straight, as the bending has made it so.... If a gentleman studies broadly and daily examines himself, then his wisdom will shine and his conduct will be without fault.... There is nothing more divine than to be transformed by the Way.

Now, one might notice that indigo plants are, by their very nature, apt to produce blue ink. It also seems that wood is very well suited, by its very nature, for the products which the wheelwright and carpenter make from it. Stones and many other things are ill-suited for extracting blue ink or wheel rims, nor may they become wise or faultless in action. In the case of the indigo plant, it would seem that the deep blue ink is being brought out from within the plant itself, such that, by analogy, the cultivation of a refined and wise person shows that education is a process of bringing out what is within the person. In prehistoric tribes, one would have observed gentleness and cooperative behaviors, as well as nasty squabbles over bits of meat. One might conclude that human nature is a mixture of

---

[332] This essay is not included in our readings.

goodness and wickedness, and that civilized norms can help to keep a person acting according to his better nature.

In any event, these themes connect most of the four essays which we will read. They are topics you've seen before in Confucius and Mencius, and Xunzi expands on them with his own insights. Finally, I'll note that Xunzi also brings forward a concern for clarity, precision, and stability in language. Living at a time of clever invention in language – recall the interlude in which we read Gongsun Long's proposition that a white horse was not a horse – Xunzi saw much of what he took to be erosion of precision and clarity of thought and resultant confusion about moral categories. In "Rectification of Names" he explains this point of view and argues that to be a virtuous person clarity and correctness in language are required.

The Readings

You have had a taste of Xunzi's essays "Heaven," "Rectification of Various Theses," "Encouraging Learning," and "Undoing Fixation." Below I've included four essays: "Self-Cultivation," "Ritual," "The Rectification of Names," and "The Nature of Man is Wicked." In some places I have left passages out of the translations, in the interest of brevity. There are many other essays in the *Xunzi* which I had to leave out. But we have three good full translations for your future reading. These are the early-Twentieth Century one by Dubs, the deep three-volume study by Knoblock, and the handy recent rendition by Hutton.

Xunzi

Self-Cultivation

When one sees what is good, by cultivating it, one will keep it within oneself. When one sees what is not good, then in shameful regret one will watch out for it within oneself. When good is in one's person, it is a matter of course that one must find it fulfilling. When what is not good is in one's person, then one must abhor oneself with disgust. Therefore, those who confront one with criticisms are one's teachers, and those who bring one approval are one's friends. But those who flatter and butter one up are one's enemies. Thus, the gentleman admires his teachers, is intimate with his friends, and thus despises his enemies. He likes the good without fail. He accepts remonstrations and can heed them. Even if he didn't want to advance, could he help it?

The small man, on the contrary, is in utter disorder and hates for others to criticize him. In his unseemly ways, he still wants others to have esteem for him. With a heart like a tiger or a wolf, and behavior like a beast, he nevertheless despises others enmity. He is intimate with those who flatter and butter him up, and he distances himself from those who would remonstrate with him or oppose him. The cultivated and the correct he laughs at, and the loyalty he treats as enemies. Even if he didn't want to be destroyed, could he help it? The *Odes* say,

> Gathered together they murmur lies
> Filling me with sorrow.
> When a counsel is on the mark,
> They all reject it.
> When a counsel fails to hit the mark,
> They all follow it.

This is what I mean.

Here is the standard of siding with goodness. Use it to regulate your *qi*[333] and nourish your life, and you will live longer than Pengzu.[334] Use it to cultivate yourself and make your name, and you will equal Yao and Yu.[335] It is appropriate in successful times and beneficial when you are impoverished. It is just ritual and good faith.

---

[333] *Qi* is the energy which flows throughout all things.
[334] A Chinese Methuselah, supposed to have lived for 700 years.
[335] King Yao and King Yu were sage kings of ancient times (late 3rd Millennium).

Whenever you use your blood *qi*, your will and intention, and your knowledge and thought from the standpoint of ritual, then good order predominates. If not based on the standpoint of ritual, they will be twisted, disorderly, obnoxious and brutal. →When food and drink, clothing and attire, dwelling place, activity and rest are based on ritual, then they will be harmoniously tied together. Otherwise, they will go awry and you will become ill. If one's demeanor and appearance, one's attitudes, one's entrances and exits, and one's shuffling steps are based on ritual, then they will be refined. Otherwise, they will be arrogant, bull-headed, unrefined, perverse, vulgar, and rustic.

Therefore, without ritual, man cannot live. Affairs, without ritual, will not be brought to completion. A country without ritual will not be settled. The *Odes* says, "Their rituals and ceremonies meet the standard. Their laughter and conversation are entirely appropriate." This is what I mean.

To lead others with the good is called "education." To harmonize others with the good is called "concord." To lead others with what is not good is called "flattery." To harmonize with others with what is not good is called "sycophancy." To affirm what is true and deny what is not is called "knowledge." To deny what is true and affirm what is not is called "stupidity."

To tear down the good is slander, to impugn the good is enmity. To call what is true true and what is not true not true is uprightness. To steal property is theft. To hide your conduct is deceit. To take one's words lightly is prevarication. To have inclinations and aversions that aren't fixed is called inconsistency. To protect one's own interest at the expense of duty is utter malice.

To have learned much is breadth; to have learned little is shallowness. To have seen much is to be experienced. To have seen little is to be uncouth. To have difficulty in advancing is to be incompetent. To forget quickly is to be scattered. To do little but in good order is governance. To do much but with disorder is confusion.

Here are the methods of controlling the *qi* and nourishing the mind. When the blood *qi* is hard and strong, soften it with balance and harmony. If your cognitions are too deep and ponderous, unify them with simple goodness. If your bravery is fierce and rash, regulate it with instruction in the Way. If your responses are quick and overbearing, then order them with alternating movement and rest. If you are narrow and petty, then magnify yourself with the broad and the great. If you are base, lowly and selfish, then lift yourself up with lofty intentions. If you are vulgar and pedestrian, then move forward with teachers and friends. If you are lazy and unmotivated, then take warning from ill omens. If you are stupid but straightforward, then bring harmony to yourself with ritual and music. Of all methods of controlling the *qi* and nourishing the mind, none is more direct than ritual, more important than obtaining a teacher, and more subtle than unifying one's preferences. This is the method of controlling the *qi* and nourishing the mind.

When your will and intentions are cultivated, then you may be proud before the wealthy and eminent. If you are rich in the Way and rightness, then you may take kings and dukes lightly. Inwardly reflective, you will make light of external things. It is traditionally said, "The gentleman employs things; the small man is employed by things." This is what I mean.

If you must labor to purify your mind, do it. If the benefits are few but the rightness great, do it. Serving a disorderly ruler successfully is not as good as serving an impoverished ruler obediently. Thus, just as a good farmer doesn't fail to plow just because of high water or drought, and a good merchant doesn't fail to go to market just because of a shortfall, so, too, does a scholar and gentleman not tire of the Way because of poverty.

With a demeanor of reverence and respect and a mind of loyalty and good faith, with methods of ritual and rightness and a disposition to love others, then whether you are traveling throughout the empire or having to stay with the four barbarian tribes, no one will fail to treat you with esteem. If you contend to be the first to handle laborious and bitter tasks and can defer to others when it comes to delightful tasks, if you are proper, diligent, sincere, and of good faith, if you are responsible and exercise leadership, then whether you are traveling throughout the empire or having to stay with the four barbarian tribes, no one will fail to trust you. But if your demeanor is insolent and inflexible, and your mind is cunning and deceitful, if you follow dark arts and are of incoherent and debased dispositions, then whether you are traveling throughout the empire or even to the farthest corners of the earth, no one will fail to despise you. If you are not up to laborious and bitter tasks, and would avoid them, if you go after the delightful tasks with alacrity and unrestraint, and if you are depraved and lackadaisical, then whether you are traveling throughout the empire or even to the farthest corners of the earth, no one will fail to despise you.

One doesn't walk with arms hanging downwards because the sleeves might fall into the mud. One doesn't walk with bowed head because one might bump into something. When meeting with one's associates, one isn't the first to lower one's eyes due to intimidation. One does these things because one wants to cultivate oneself and not do wrong by the people of one's society.

[The horse] Qiji could travel 1000 *li* per day, but a broken down horse can make it in ten days of riding. Would you attempt to exhaust the inexhaustible and seek out the limitless? You'll break your bones and wear out your flesh, and to the end of your days you will be unable to succeed. But if you undertake what has an end, then even if it is 1000 *li* distant, whether you're at the front or bringing up the rear, how could you fail to make it? Will you be one of those travelers who, without realizing it, would you attempt to exhaust the inexhaustible and seek out the limitless? Or will you intend to undertake that which has an end? It's not that inquiry into "hard and white," "identity and difference," and "dimension and dimensionless" cannot be made.[336] But the gentleman does not argue about these things; he stops at that point. It's not that strange feats are not difficult. But the gentleman does not do these things; he stops at that point. Hence, of studying it is said, "Slowly. Its goal awaits us. We'll go towards achieving it, and with some quickly and others

---

[336] These were topics of concern to the analytic philosophers of Xunzi's time, such as Gongsun Long, the later Mohists, and Huizi.

slowly, some leading the way and others bringing up the rear, how could we fail to reach it together?" Thus, by plodding along without respite, a lame turtle will go 1000 *li*. By piling dirt by the basketful, a mound or hill can be completed. Dam their sources and open their sluices, and the Yangzi and Yellow rivers can be made dry. With one going forward and one retreating, one going left and one right, six steeds will not advance. The distinctions in skill and nature among people are not as great as that between the six steeds and the lame turtle. Yet the lame turtle makes it, while the six horses do not. This is for no other reason than that one acts while the other does not.

Even if the Way is at hand, if you don't go forward, you will not reach it. Thus if the task is small, you won't complete it without acting. If you're a person of the sort who idles the days away, the headway you will make will be very little.

To go forward because you like the models is to be a scholar. To embody them with firm resolve is to be a gentleman. To have keen insight into them without fail is to be a sage. If a man has no models, he runs helter-skelter. If he has models but does not will what they deem right, then he is befuddled. Only after he has relied on models to sound out the kinds of case in which they apply does he achieve human warmth.

Ritual is the means of rectifying oneself. A teacher is the means of rectifying ritual. Without ritual, how will you rectify yourself? Without a teacher, how will you know what makes a ritual correct?

When you allow what the rituals allow, your feelings rest in them. When you say what your teacher says, your knowledge is the same as his. With feelings resting in ritual and the knowledge of your teacher, you will be a sage. Thus, to go against ritual is to do without models. To oppose the teacher is to do without a teacher. If you don't accept your teacher and the models but prefer your own way, I must point out that this is like using the blind to discriminate colors or the deaf to discern sounds; there is no way to avoid chaos and confusion. Thus, what you study is ritual and models. A teacher makes his person the standard and esteems those who rest in it. The *Odes* say,

You didn't understand.
You didn't know.
You followed the Di Ancestor's precedents.

This is my meaning.

If you are correct and diligent, obedient and respectful, you can be called a "good youth." If you also like to learn and are modest and earnest, then you may be considered a gentleman. But if you are withdrawn and evasive of your tasks, if you have no shame and indulge yourself in drinking and eating, then you may be called a "bad youth." If you also are wild, depraved, and disobedient, mean, malicious, and disrespectful, then you are an ill-omened youth. Even the punishments of dismemberment and execution are fitting in such a case.

If you treat the elderly with due respect, then adults will come to you. If you do not aggravate the bitterness of others, then the successful will gather to you. If you go forward in obscurity and are kind without regard for recompense, then both the worthy and those of no account will unite about you. If someone has these three ways, then even if there were a terrible omen, would heaven permit his failure?

The gentleman is perfunctory in his pursuit of profit and efficient in staving off harm. He avoids shame in all seriousness and courageously follows the Way and principles of order. In poverty and lowliness, the gentleman has a breadth of will, and in wealth and high rank he has a respectful demeanor. At leisure and ease, his blood *qi* is not diminished, and when fatigued by labor, his appearance is not disheveled. His anger does not drive him to rapaciousness, and his joy does not drive him to extravagant giving. The gentleman has a breadth of will when poor and lowly because he is in awe of humanity. He has a respectful demeanor when wealthy and of high rank because he eschews undue influence. His blood *qi* is not diminished when he is at leisure and ease because he sides with principles of order. His appearance is not disheveled when he is fatigued because he likes good form. His anger does not drive him to rapaciousness, nor his joy to extravagant giving, because models override self-interest. The *Documents* says,

> Be without what inclinations create,
> Follow the Way of the kings.
> Be without what aversions create,
> Follow the road of the kings.

This speaks of the gentleman's ability to take impartial rightness to override is personal desires.

Ritual

How did rituals arise? Man was born with desires. His desires were not fulfilled, so he had to strive. He strove without standards, measures and divisions, so he could not help but end up fighting. Fighting brought chaos, and chaos poverty. The former kinds abhorred this chaos and therefore instituted ritual and rightness in order to bring distinctions of station to it, to nurture people's desires, and to give them what they strove for. They made it so that desires would never have to do without things, and things would not be used up by the desires. The two supported and grew each other. Thus did rituals arise.

Thus, ritual is nurture. The meat of cattle and farm animals, and the harmony of the five flavors are used to nurture the palate. The aroma of pepper and flowers are used to nurture the nose. Carvings, metalworking, embroidery of white and black, and decorations are used to nurture the eye. Percussion instruments, flutes, chimes, strings, and pipes are used to nurture the ear. Great rooms, chambers, quilted mats, couches, and cushions are used to nurture the body.

Thus, are rituals are nurturing. When a gentleman has received such nurture, he will like their distinctions. What are the distinctions? The gradations of worthy and lowly, elder and youth, poor and rich, and insignificant and important all have their roles. Therefore, the Son of Heaven has a great chariot with quilted mats to nurture his body. On each side are fragrant herbs that nurture his nose. In front there is an inlaid yoke to nurture his eyes. The harmonious sound of the horse and bells nurtures his ears. The pace goes along with the songs, "Martial" and "Symbol." And the hooves go along with "Succession and "Protector," in order to nurture his ears. A nine-fold dragon banner is used to nurture good faith, and images of recumbent rhinoceros, crouching tiger, harnesses of dragon scale pattern, silken carvings and dragon headed yokes are used to nurture a sense of majesty. Therefore, the horses of the great chariot must be fully trained to be obedient before they are harnessed and ridden, in order to nurture a sense of security.

Who understands that to risk one's life at one's post is the way to nurture life?! Who understands that to spend and to use are the way to nurture resources?! Who understands that reverence, respect, courtesy and deference are what nurture security?! Who understands that ritual and rightness, culture, and principles of order are what nurture the dispositions?!

Therefore, if men keep only life in view, they must die. If they keep only benefit in view, they must come to harm. If they are withdrawn and timid in order to be secure, they will certainly come into danger. If they seek enjoyment only in pleasing their dispositions, they will certainly be destroyed. Therefore, if one is devoted to ritual and rightness, then both [ritual and rightness, and desires] will be fulfilled. If one is devoted to one's dispositions and nature, then the two will be thwarted. Hence, Confucianism would cause man to fulfill both. Mohism would cause him to thwart both. This is the difference between Confucianism and Mohism.

Ritual has three bases. Heaven and earth are the basis of life. Ancestors are the basis of family lines. Rulers and teachers are the basis of governance. Without heaven and earth, how would there be life? Without ancestors, how would there be descendants? Without rulers and teachers, how would there be governance? If any of these three were lost, there would be no security for man. Therefore, rituals serve heaven above and earth below, honor ancestors and show respect for rulers and teachers. These are the three bases of ritual.

Therefore, the king treats his ancestor as heaven. The feudal lords don't dare let their ancestral temple decline. High officials and knights have their eternal ancestral sacrifices. This is how they distinguish their eminent origins. Eminent origins are the basis of authority. The Suburban Altar Sacrifice extends only to the son of Heaven. The Soil Altar Sacrifice extends only to the feudal lords. Others include knights and high officials. These are the means of distinguishing between the noble who serve the noble and the base who serve the base. What is appropriate to the great is great, and what is appropriate to the small is small.

Thus, one who possesses the empire serves seven generations of ancestors, one who possesses a state serves five generations, one who possesses a land of five chariots serves three, and one who possesses a land of three chariots serves two. Those who support themselves by manual labor do not get to establish an ancestral temple. This is the way to distinguish between richly amassed accomplishments, with their widely reaching results, and scarcely amassed accomplishments, with their meager results.

At the Great Xiang sacrifice the goblet of dark liquid is offered, raw fish is presented on the table, and the great broth is served first, all to honor the bases of food and drink. At the Xiang sacrifice the goblet of dark liquid is offered and liquor is served. Millet is served first, and rice and sorghum are presented. At ordinary sacrifices, the one sips the great broth and offers delicacies, thus honoring the bases by using what is familiar. Honoring the bases is called "culture" and using what is familiar is called a "principle of order." When the two come together in cultivated form, we have the means to restore a great unity. This is called "great exaltation."...

Ritual is crude at first but completes itself in cultivated form and culminates in joyous rapture. Thus, in its utmost perfection, felt dispositions and cultivated form are fulfilled together. In the next to best, felt dispositions and cultivated form come to the fore in turn. In the lowest form, it reverts to feeling in order to achieve the great unity.

Heaven and earth are thus brought together, the sun and mood made to shine, the four seasons are regulated, the celestial bodies put in motion, the Yangzi and Yellow rivers made to flow, the myriad things made to flourish, and likes and dislikes given measure, and joy and anger given their appropriate objects.

Subordinates are made obedient, superiors made enlightened, the myriad things made to proceed without any disorder. Being untrue to this brings one's own destruction. How perfect is ritual!

Establish and exalt them as the pole star, and nothing in the world can add to or diminish them. Basis and extension will accord with each other, and endings and beginnings correspond to each other. Perfectly cultivated form enables us to have distinctions, and perfect understanding of them enables us to have explanations. A world that follows them is governed, but one that does not is disorderly. One that follows them is secure, but one that does not is endangered. One that follows them is preserved, but one that does not is lost.

The small man cannot comprehend this. The principles of order in ritual are very profound. The investigator of hard and white, identity and difference, upon entering into this matter, is baffled.[337] The principles of order in ritual are very profound. Those who erect systems and those with weird theories, upon entering into the matter, are ruined. This principle of order is so elevated that the cruel, twisted, and uncouth who take themselves to be lofty, upon entering into the matter, are defeated.

Therefore, with a black plumb line set to true, one cannot confuse the twisted and the straight. With a balance set at normal, one cannot confuse the heavy and the light. With a compass and square set aright, one cannot confuse square and round. And if a gentleman is familiar with ritual, he won't be

---

[337] As we've noted before, these are the topics of concert to analytical philosophers of Xunzi's time.

confused by fraudulence. Thus, the plumb line is the utmost in straightness, the balance the utmost in evenness, the compass and square the utmost in squareness and circularity, and ritual the epitome of the human way.

Thus, those who don't make ritual their model or find ritual sufficient are called "people without standards." Those who make ritual their model and find it sufficient are called "scholars with standards." Those who can contemplate the mean set by ritual are called "able to think." Those who can go without deviating from the mean set by ritual are called "steadfast." To be able to think and to go without deviating – if in addition one likes this, then one is a sage.

Hence, heaven is the epitome of the lofty and earth the epitome of the low. The boundless is the epitome of breadth. The sage is the epitome of the Way. Thus, the student studies with the resolve to become a sage, and does not study just to become a person without standards....

Shall we take after stupid rustics and perverse boors? Well, when someone dies in the morning, they forget about it by evening. If we are so permissive, we will not even measure up to the birds and beasts. How can one live with men such as that and not have disorder?

...The point of sacrifice is the feelings of remembrance and longing for the departed. Everyone is at times brought up short by a despondence and shortness of breath. Even when enjoying others' company, a loyal minister or filial son may be affected in this way. When it happens, it is profoundly moving. Left to themselves, the feelings of longing and remembrance will be locked up and unexpressed. One might look upon the measure of ritual as empty or incomplete. Therefore, the former kings enacted the establishment of cultivated forms that allow for the utmost in right expression of honor to the honorable and intimacy to the intimate.

...How mournful! How reverent! To serve the dead as one serves the living, and to serve the deceased as one serves those who survive! It gives shape to what is formless and thus brings cultivated forms to completion.

282

Rectification of Names

As for the later kings' way of rectifying names,[338] they followed the Yin Dynasty in the case of legal names, the Zhou Dynasty in the case of names of official titles, and the *Liji* in the case of names for what is in man. For the various names that are applied to the myriad things of the world, they followed the particularities of the established customs of the Xia states. When it came to villages of differing customs in distant regions, they had them use those terms for the sake of common communication.

As for the various names for what is in man, that which is so because it is congenital is called "nature." That which is produced by the harmonious functioning of this nature, the awareness of objects, being effortlessly just as it is, is called "nature." This nature's affinities, antipathies, delights, resentments, sorrows, and joys are called its "inherent dispositions."[339] Given such inherent dispositions, the minds' choosing among them is called "reasoning." When the mind reasons and can make one act, this is called "manmade." When reasoning has accumulated in one such that one can put it into practice with success, then this is called "manmade." To act having ascertained the benefit is called "work." To act having ascertained what is right is called one's "conduct." That in man by which he knows is called "cognition." When cognition has something to which it connects, this is called "knowledge." That which makes it possible for there to be knowledge in a person is called "ability." When ability has something to which it connects, this is called an "ability." An injury to one's nature is called "sickness." That which one happens to encounter is

[338] The later kings were those of the Zhou Dynasty. See Knoblock, *Xunzi*, vol 2, pp 28-29.

[339] The term is *qing*, meaning one's natural inclinations to feel in certain ways. It can also mean those feelings themselves. The term comes up often throughout the history of Chinese philosophy. There is a great deal of scholarship on this term. You might begin with the book by Holloway listed in the Introduction's list of suggested readings.

called "fate." These are the various names for what is in man. These are names established by the later kings.

Hence, when a king regulated names, the names were fixed and their objects distinguished. His conduct being in accord with the Way and his will being made known, he meticulously led the people into unity. Therefore, since analysis of terms and creation of names on one's own in order to bring disorder to correct names cause the people to become perplexed and confused and increases disputes and litigation among them, this was called a great evil and was a punishable crime, just as the crimes of forging tallies and falsifying measures. Therefore, none of his people dared to create perverse terms on their own in order to bring disorder to correct names. Therefore, his people were honest. Their honesty made them easy to employ. Their being easy to employ led to significant accomplishments in public works. None of his people dared to create perverse strange terms on their own in order to bring disorder to correct names. Therefore, they were single-mindedly devoted to making his laws their Way and conscientious in following orders. In this way, his legacy was made to last. A lasting legacy and successful achievements are the pinnacle of governance. Thus, it was conscientiousness in maintaining names that brought success.

Today, the sage kings are gone and the maintenance of names has decayed. Perverse terms have cropped up, names and their objects have been thrown into disorder, and the senses of "is" and "is not" are no longer clear. Thus, even officials who maintain the laws and the Ru who study the classics are also all in disarray. If a kingly man were to appear, he would certainly proceed to cleave to some of the old names and create some new names. This being so, the purpose of having names, the basis of treating things as the same and treating them as different, and the pivotal considerations in instituting names are all things which we certainly must investigate.

Different forms, separate from one's mind, interact with it, such that different things become objects of names in an indeterminate fashion. Noble and base are left unclear, and same and different are not distinguished. As a result, there will always be the danger that intentions will sometimes be miscommunicated and affairs will certainly beset by frustration and failure. Therefore, one who understands this draws distinctions and institutes names which refer to objects. In lofty matters, he uses them to clarify the noble and the base. In mundane matters, he uses them to differentiate between same and different. The noble and base being clear, and same and different being distinguished, it follows that intentions will be in no danger of being miscommunicated and affairs will not be beset by frustration and failure. This is the purpose of having names.

This being so one what basis do we treat things as the same and treat things as different? I say that the basis is the natural sense faculties. In general, for beings of the same kind and same inherent dispositions, their natural sense faculties' ways of forming representations of things are the same. Therefore, when people compare things side by side to see whether they resemble each other, there is agreement and this is how they cooperate in determining names through mutual expectation. Differences in form, color, and pattern are distinguished by the eye. Tone, treble, bass, key, timbre, and peculiarities of sound are distinguished by the ear. Sweet, bitter, salty, bland, sharp, sour, and peculiarities of taste are distinguished by the palate. Fragrances, odors, perfumes, rotten smells, rancid, putrid, sour, rank stenches, and peculiarities of smell are distinguished by the nose. Pain, itching, cold, hot, smooth, rough, light, and heavy are distinguished by the body. Speech, reasons, joy, anger, sadness, enjoyment, love, hatred, and desire are distinguished by the mind. The mind sometimes cognizes by drawing on the others. Since it cognizes by drawing on the others, it uses the ears as a means of making it possible for it to recognize sounds, and it uses the eyes as a means of making it possible for it to recognize forms. This being so, the cognition which draws on the others must wait for the natural sense faculties to encounter and register their corresponding kinds in order for it to become able to do this. When the five sense faculties register something that one doesn't recognize and the mind draws on them but is not able to say what the thing is, then no one would not therefore say that one doesn't know what it is. This is the basis of telling whether things are the same or different.

After this, one proceeds to name things with the same name if they are the same and with different names if they are different. If a simple name suffices to represent them, then let it be a simple one. If a simple one will not suffice, then use a compound name. If a simple name and a compound name have no points of difference, then use them interchangeably. Although you use them interchangeably, there will be no harm in it. In recognizing that different things are named differently, one sees to it that every different thing has a different name. Do not countenance disorder to the extent that you let different things all have the same name.

Now, although the myriad things are many, sometimes we want to refer to things all together. Then, we call them "things." "Things" is a broad and inclusive name. It has been made inclusive by extending it, making it more and more inclusive until there is nothing it doesn't include and there is an end. Sometimes we want to refer to some things all together and we therefore call them "birds" or "beasts." "Birds" and "beasts" are broad and distinct names. They have been made distinct by extending them, making them more and more distinct until there is no more distinction to be made and there is an end.

Names do not have inherent appropriateness. One stipulates them by fiat, and if the stipulation holds until it becomes a matter of custom, then they come to be called appropriate. With any divergence from the stipulation, they come to be called inapt. Names do not have inherent objects. One stipulates them by decreeing their objects, and if the stipulation holds until it becomes a matter of custom, then they come to be called objective names. Names can be inherently good. Those that are straightforward, easy, and convenient are called good.

There are things that have the same form but exist in different places. There are things which have different forms but exist in the same place. We can make this distinction. Those that have different forms but exist in the same place, although they can be conflated, are said to be two objects. When the form changes while the object remains undivided such that we treat this as a difference, we call this a "transformation." When there is a transformation without any division, we refer to this as one object. This is the business of inquiring into objects and determining their number. This is a crucial consideration in creating names. The later kings' ways of creating names simply must be investigated.

"There is no shame in being insulted." "The sage does not love himself." "To kill a thief is not to kill a man."[340] These are cases of deceptively using names in order to bring disorder to names. By checking these against the reason for having names and noting the extent to which they go along with it, one can do away with them.

"Mountains and ravines are on the same level." "The desires we have by our inherent dispositions are few." "Fine meats do not enhance the savoriness. The great bell does not enhance the music."[341] These are cases of deceptively using objects in order to bring disorder to names. By checking them as to whether they have a basis for distinguishing sameness from difference and noting the extent to which they are suitable for this, one can do away with them.

"Reject and accept a visit." "Pillars have oxen." "A horse is not a horse."[342] These are cases of deceptive use of

---

[340] These were theses of philosophers of Xunzi's time. You have already seen that the first of this was Song Xing's.
[341] These sayings are probably attributable to Hui Shi, Song Xing, and either Song Xing or a Mohist, respectively.
[342] The text we have now may be corrupt in its rendition of these three sentences. Think about that. Xunzi is arguing that they are poorly

names, causing one to bring disorder to objects. If you check them against names as they have been stipulated and use what they accept in order to show contradiction with what they reject, you can do away with them.[343]

All those who, by diverging from the correct way, irresponsibly construct these abnormal propositions can be categorized into three kinds of deceiver. Therefore, an enlightened ruler will recognize these types and will not argue with them.

The people are easy to unify with the way but cannot share in the reasons for it. Therefore, the enlightened ruler rules them with ability, leads them with the Way, moves them forward with commands, regulates them with good reasons, and prohibits their wrongdoing with punishments. Thus, the people are transformed by the Way as if miraculously. What use is argumentative skill to him?

Today, the sage kings are no more and the world is in disorder. Perverse utterances abound. Rulers lack the ability to

---

constructed and go against standard usage. It stands to reason that copyists might make a mistake. It is difficult to copy gibberish accurately.

[343] Xunzi's premise that the prevalence of sophistical nonsense in scholarly debate is a cause of social disorder and poor government might be puzzling. The general idea is that there is one ideology which brings order and prosperity to a society; it comprises the rituals, morals, virtues and literature of traditional Chinese civilization. Meaningless sophistry distracts a people's attention from the vital task of holding to these traditions. There are potential parallels in Western history. First, we have the Athenian court's attitude toward Socrates. It put him to death because it maintained – however honestly or dishonestly – that his argumentation was so perverse and sophistical that it was harming Athenian society. Second, there is the tradition of German philosophy running from Hegel through Heidegger which some people have maintained was sophistical gibberish that provided intellectual conditions for much of the mayhem of the Twentieth Century. Third, there are the recent academic hoaxes, one by Alan Sokal in 1996 and another by Peter Boghossian and James Lindsay in 2017, which demonstrated that there is plenty of meaningless gibberish in contemporary academic journals and that the gibberish is published when and only when it is aimed at eroding traditional values.

rule, lack the punishments to prohibit wrongdoing, and therefore engage in argumentation.

When objects are not clear, they are given names. When names are not clear, stipulations are made. When the stipulations are not clear, explanations are made. When the explanations are not clear, there is argumentation. Therefore, stipulation, naming, argumentation, and explanation are salient characteristics of human functioning and fundamental to the king's occupation. For names to make their objects clear when they are heard is the function of names.

The usage of a name lies in its making its object clear as soon as it is heard. When names are chained together to form sentences, this is the synthetic function of names. When one has mastered its usage and synthetic function, then one can be said to know a name.

Names are what we use to define differences among objects. Statements unite the names of different objects in order to express one idea. Argumentation and explanation are the maintenance of unequivocal names in order to make clear the ways in which one ought, and ought not, to act. The stipulation of names is the function of argumentation and explanation. Argumentation and explanation are how the mind represents the Way. The mind is the chief artisan of the Way. The Way is the pattern and the delineation of order. Keep the mind in line with the Way. Keep explanations in line with the mind. Keep statements in line with explanation. In rectifying names by stipulation, let the substance be brought forth and made clear. When arguing over differences, there will be no mistake. When drawing comparisons between kinds, you won't go astray. What you hear will keep to good form, and argumentation will be meticulous. By using the correct Way, one will refute perverse views as if one were using a plumb line to tell crooked from straight. Thus, outlandish discourses won't be able to cause disorder, and the hundred schools of thought will have nowhere to hide.

He has the intelligence of one who has listened broadly but not a brash or boastful manner. He has the generosity of one who is broadly magnanimous but not the look of one who wears his virtues on his sleeve. When his explanations are put into practice, then the world is rectified. When his explanations are not put into practice, then he makes the Way clear but dwells in obscurity. Such are the argumentation and explanations of a sage. The *Odes* say

> Reverent and dignified
> Like a jade scepter or jade tablet
> Of good name and well regarded
> A gentleman at his ease
> As if a rule for all the four quarters.

This is what I mean.

He hits the mark when it comes to courtesy. He follows the pattern governing elder and younger. He does not speak of subjects which one ought not to speak of. He does not let loose with superstitious utterances. He explains with a humane heart, listens with a studied mind, and debates with an impartial mind. He doesn't act according to popular censure or approval. He doesn't try to bedazzle the eyes and ears of those who look upon him. He doesn't try to curry the favor of men in high positions who have discretionary power. He doesn't show appreciation for the utterances of flatterers. Therefore, he can abide in the Way without being of two minds about it, be spurned but never manipulated, and profit without becoming dissolute. He holds impartiality and correctness in high esteem and has contempt for meanness and nastiness. Such are the argumentation and explanations of a lord or gentleman. The *Odes* say

> The long night passes slowly
> As he dwells on his responsibilities.
> Never irreverent toward great antiquity,
> In ritual and morality without fault,
> How could he be wounded by the words of others?

This is what I mean.

The words of a gentleman are incisive yet fine, suited to his audience yet germane, and varied yet unified. These are men who are correct in the names he uses, choosing his words in effort to make clear the meaning he intends. As for his names and statements, they are to convey his intended meaning. If they suffice to communicate it, then he stops there, for to carry on further is perverse. Therefore, if his names suffice to indicate their objects, and his statement suffice to make his point, then he stops there.

If names and statements going beyond that point are said to be only tedious and are eschewed by the gentleman, then the fool collects them as his prized possessions. Thus, the words of the fool are jarring and course, blurted out and not germane, effusive and glib. He is misleading with his names, and confused in his statements, he lacks depth in his intended meanings. So, he drones on without getting anywhere, laboriously and without success, covetous but of no name.

Therefore, the words of a knowledgeable man, when contemplated, are easy to understand, when practiced, easy to become confident in, and when maintained, easy to take as conclusive. If one follows through with them, one will thus be sure to obtain what one admires and not to be fooled by what one despises. Yet, in the case of the fool it is just the opposite. The *Odes* say

> If you were a ghost or demon
> No one would see you.
> But having a face and eyes,
> You let people observe the extent of your pretentiousness.
> I wrote this nice poem
> In diametric opposition to such vice.

This is what I mean.

Those who argue that one brings about good order by eradicating desires are, having no means of guiding desires, troubled by the fact that they exist. Those who argue that one brings about good order by making desires few are, having no means of restraining desires, troubled by the fact that they are so many. Having and lacking desires, as distinct categories, are the living and the dead, not the orderly and the disorderly. Having many desires and having few are two different categories. This is a matter of number of inherent dispositions, not orderliness and disorderliness.

Desires do not depend on how one thinks they may be satisfied; one seeks to satisfy them however one thinks one may. Desires, since they don't depend on how one thinks they may be satisfied, are what one receives from heaven. As for seeking to satisfy them however one thinks one may, this is something that one receives from one's mind. A particular desire which one receives from heaven may be so thoroughly shaped by what one receives from one's mind that it can be quite hard to tell that it is the kind of thing which one receives from heaven.

Nothing is more desirable to man than life, and nothing is more despised by him than death. Nevertheless, there have been men who, in their pursuit of life, have opted for death, not because they didn't want to live and wanted to die but because they could not deem continuing to live permissible and could deem dying permissible. So, when one's desires overstep the line but one's conduct do not go that far, it is the mind that stops one. When what the mind deems permissible corresponds to principles, then, though the desires are strong, what harm could they do to good order? If desires are insufficient, but one's conduct oversteps the line, then it is the mind that is in control. If desires are insufficient but one's conduct oversteps the line, it is the mind that is in control. When what the mind deems permissible fails to correspond to the principle, then, though the desires are weak, how could they stop one from going all the way to the point where disorder would result? Therefore, order and disorder turn on what the mind deems permissible not on what is desirable to our inherent dispositions. If you don't seek something where it is but seek it where it is not, then though you say, "I got it," you've missed it.

Our nature is given to us by heaven. Inherent dispositions are the substance of this nature. Desires are the corresponding activation of these inherent dispositions. To take what they desire as obtainable and to seek it is what the inherent dispositions must unavoidably do. But to deem it permissible and to take this as the Way requires that the intellect be applied. Even a doorman cannot get rid of his desires. They are supplied to him by nature. And even for a son of heaven, desires cannot be satisfied completely. But although desires cannot be satisfied completely, one can come close to satisfying them. And although one cannot be rid of one's desires, one can limit one's attempt to satisfy them. The Way, in moving one forward, brings one closer to satisfying one's desires and, in holding one back, limits one's attempt to satisfy them. In all the world, there is nothing comparable to it.

In general, there is no one who doesn't pursue what he deems permissible and eschew what he deems impermissible. There is no case in which someone who, knowing that nothing is comparable to the Way, nevertheless does not pursue the Way. Suppose there are a man who wanted to go south very badly and very much despised the prospect of going north. How could he take his inability to go as far south as he liked as cause to leave the south and head north? Similarly, if people long for what they desire and absolutely detest what they despise, how could they take their inability to fulfill their desires completely as cause to depart from the Way, which leads in the direction of their fulfillment, and opt for what they despise instead? Therefore, if they deem the Way permissible and pursue it, how could that be harmful and cause disorder? If they deem the way impermissible and depart from it, how could that be beneficial and create order? Therefore, wise men reason about the Way and nothing else. The prospects for lesser thinkers and their odd theories fade away.

In general, when one obtains something, what one desires is found not to be the only thing that has arrived, and in getting rid of something, what he despises is found not to be the only thing that has gone away. Therefore, people never act without weighing[344] everything involved. If a scale is not correct, then the heavier object being suspended will be higher and people will take it to be the lighter, while the lighter object being suspended will be lower and people will take it to be the heavier. Thus are people deceived about the weights of things. When weighing is not correct, then misfortune will be construed as what one desires and taken to be good fortune, while good fortune will be construed as what they despise and taken to be misfortune. Thus are people deceived about good and bad fortune. The Way, in ancient times and today, is correct weighing. By departing from the Way and making decisions within oneself, one will not know what to construe as good fortune and what to construe as misfortune.

If a trader trades one for one, then people will say there is no gain and no loss. If he trades one for two, people will say there is no loss but only gain. If he trades two for one, then people will say there is no gain but only loss. Measuring is for taking what one deems to be more. Deliberating over what to do is for pursuing what he deems to be permissible. As for trading two for one, no one will do it, being aware of the numbers involved. To go forward with the Way is like trading one for two. How could there be any loss? To depart from the Way and make decisions within oneself is like trading two for one. How could there be any gain? Given the prospect of trading the receipt of all that one desires for one hundred years for a moment's satisfaction, nevertheless to go ahead with it is due to not being aware of the numbers involved.

Let us try to get an even deeper view into what is unclear and difficult to discern here. There has never been a person who meant to treat principles lightly but did not regard things as weighing heavily. There has never been a person who, outside of himself, regarded things as weighing heavily and inside of himself did not feel anxiety. There has never been a person who proceeded after departing from the Way and did not encounter

---

[344] "Weighing" (*quan*) is a word we've seen in Mencius. A good translation might also be "applying discretion to" or "reasoning prudently about."

external danger. There has never been a person who encountered an external danger but did not internally feel fear. When the mind feels anxiety and fear, then though the mouth is full of fine meats one is not aware of its flavor, though the ear hears the bells and drums one is not aware of their sounds, though the eye looks upon fine embroidery one is not aware of the patterns, and though there is light and warm clothing and a nice flat mat, one's body is not aware of their comforts. Thus could one wind up with the luxuries of a myriad of things but be unable to be satisfied. Even were he to obtain a moment's satisfaction from them, he would be unable to be leave behind [his anxiety and fear]. Therefore, even in the midst of the luxuries of a myriad of things he will be beset by anxiety, and even enjoying the benefits of a myriad of things he will be beset by harm.

People like this, who seek to obtain things – have they nurtured their lives? Have they improved their longevity? Thus, desiring to tend to his desires, he gives license to his inherent dispositions. Desiring to tend to his nature, he endangers his form. Desiring to tend to his enjoyments, he impairs his mind. Desiring to tend to his reputation, he brings disorder to his conduct. Such a person, though he be enfeoffed as a marquis or named a lord, would be no different from a thief. Though he ride in a fine carriage and wear a ceremonial cap, he would be no different from a criminal amputee. One would say that he has made himself a servant to things.

If the mind is placid and content, then even when sights are poor, one can tend to one's eyes, even when sounds are poor one can tend to one's ears, with a serving of vegetable and a broth of greens one can tend to one's palate, and with a hempen robe and hempen shoes one can tend to one's body. With a house made of reeds, a reed mat and an old stool and desk, one can tend to one's form.

Thus, even without the luxuries of a myriad of things, one can tend to one's enjoyments, and even without a place among the powerful one can tend to one's reputation. Give someone like that the world and he would do much for the world and little for the sake of his own enjoyments. This is called regarding oneself as weighing heavily and making things one's servants.

Unproven sayings, conduct never seen before, and practical advice that has never been heard of before – the gentleman exercises caution over these.

The Nature of Man is Wicked[345]

The nature of man is wicked. Any goodness in him is artificial.[346] The nature of man is such that he congenitally has a desire for benefit. Because he pursues this, aggression and rapaciousness arise and courtesy and deference are lost to him. He congenitally harbors envy and wickedness. Because he pursues, brutality and meanness arise, and loyalty and good faith are lost to him. He congenitally has desires of the eyes and ears, inclinations toward color and sound. He pursues these and therefore perversion and disorderliness arise, and ritual, rightness, culture and principles of order are lost to him.

This being so, to follow human nature and obey man's inherent dispositions always results in aggression and rapaciousness, along with a rupture of social divisions, a throwing into chaos of principles of order, and a regression into brutality. Therefore, we must be sure to have the influence of

[345] As I mentioned above, I translate the Chinese term *e* as "wicked," despite the fact that it nowadays has somewhat old-fashioned association with witches. Its literal meaning is correct: the disposition to do evil. The term is more commonly translated as "evil," but that term's literal meaning connotes both malevolence, the desire to bring harm to others as an end in itself, as well as natural evils, such as devastating earthquakes and diseases. "Wicked" leaves open whether the person to whom it is applied is malevolent and it does not include natural evils. This is precisely Xunzi's meaning. In fact, I would argue that the wickedness Xunzi has in mind is a selfish disregard for others' interest as one pursues one's natural inclinations. This is functional wickedness, not malevolence. "Dispicable" would be a good translation of *e*, and "bad" would also do.
[346] Here "artificial" does not connote fakery or inauthenticity. It simply means "manmade." It refers to the distinction between a natural object and an artifact. Civilization is an artifact.

teachers and models, the ways of virtue and rightness. Only thus will courtesy and deference result, along with culture and principles of order, and a return to governance. Seen in this light, therefore, the wicked of man's nature is clear. Any goodness in him is artificial.

Thus, warped lumber requires a press frame and steam in order to become straight, and blunt metal requires shaping on the whetstone in order to become sharp. Now, human nature being wicked, it requires a teacher and models in order to become correct, and it must attain to ritual and rightness in order to become well ordered. And when people lack teachers and models, they are biased, dangerous, and incorrect. Without ritual and rightness, they are depraved, chaotic, and disorderly.

The ancient sages took human nature to be wicked, biased, dangerous, and incorrect, to be depraved, chaotic, and disorderly. Therefore, they established for it rituals and rightness and instituted models[347] and standards, in order to shape people's inherent dispositions and nature and to correct them, and in order to train and change people's inherent dispositions and natures and to guide them. They caused them all to be well ordered and to conform to the Way. Today, anyone who is changed by teachers and models, accumulates culture and learning, and makes ritual and rightness his Way is a gentleman. Those who give license to their nature and inherent dispositions, content themselves with lust and crudeness, and diverge from ritual and rightness are small men. Seen in this light, therefore, the wicked of man's nature is clear and any goodness in him is artificial.

Mencius said, "The fact that man can learn means his nature is good." I reply that this is not so. Apparently, Mencius never attained any knowledge of human nature and never noticed the distinction between nature and artifice in man. In general, nature is what is given by heaven.[348] You can't learn it

---

[347] "Models" translates *fa*, which can also mean "law." It is an important term in the thought of Han Feizi, as we will see in the next chapter.
[348] "Heaven" translates *tian*, which also means "nature" or "the natural world," or even something like the sense of "mother nature." *Tian* is

or work towards it. Ritual and rightness are what the sages produced. They are what a person comes to be able to do by studying and what he fulfills by working towards. That which cannot be learned or worked toward yet is in man may be called, "nature." That which can be done after study and can be fulfilled after working towards it, and is in man, may be called, "artificial." This is the distinction between nature and artifice. Human nature is such that eyes can be used to see and ears can be used to hear. The clarity of vision is inseparable from the eyes, and the acuity of hearing is inseparable from the ears. The eyes' clarity and the ears' acuity can't be learned.

Mencius says, "Man's nature is good; it's just that he loses or destroys his nature." But this sort of view is mistaken. Man's nature is such that upon birth he is separated from his original simplicity and basic constitution. He necessarily loses and destroys it. From that point of view, the wicked of human nature is apparent. According to those who consider man's nature to be good, it is fine without departing from its original simplicity, and it is beneficial without departing from its basic constitution. This makes the relation of our basic constitution and original simplicity to their fineness and the relation of mind and intentions to their goodness like the inseparability of eye and clarity of vision, or ear and clarity of hearing. Hence, they say, "It's like the eye's having clarity and the ear's having acuity." But man's nature is such that he wants to eat when hungry, he wants warmth when cold, and he wants to rest when tired. These are man's inherent dispositions and nature. But when a man is hungry and sees an elder before whom he would not eat, he takes there to be someone to defer to. When he is tired but will not seek respite, he takes there to be someone in whose stead he works. Now, a son's deference to a father, a younger brother's deference to an elder, a son's working instead of a father, and a younger brother's working instead of an elder - both of these behaviors go against nature and run contrary to inherent

---

unrelated to the term for the nature of a thing, *xing*, used in terms such as "human nature." English has just the one word for both senses: "nature."

dispositions. Therefore, the way of a filial son is the culture, principles of order, ritual and rightness. Hence, if he follows his inherent dispositions and nature, he will not be courteous or deferential. And if he's courteous and deferential, then he is running contrary to his inherent dispositions and nature. In this light, it is clear that man's nature is wicked and any goodness in him is artificial.

A question: "Since man's nature is wicked, do ritual and rightness arise from wickedness?" I reply to this that, in general, ritual and rightness are created by the artifice of the sages and do not originate in the nature of man. Thus, when a potter shapes clay and makes a vessel, the vessel created is by the artifice of the potter and does not originate in man's nature. By the same token, when a craftsman carves wood and makes a vessel, the vessel is created by the artifice of the craftsman and does not originate in man's nature. The sages accumulated various ideas and suggestions, tried artifice, and thereby created ritual and rightness and give rise to models and standards. Therefore, ritual, rightness, models and standards are created by the artifice of the sages and did not originate in man's nature. Just as the eye likes color, the ear likes sound, the mouth likes flavor and the bones, flesh and skin like pleasant comforts, all this arises from the inherent dispositions and nature of man. They operate spontaneously according to feeling and do not require being worked for in order to come to be. Things that cannot be so but must be worked for in order to be as they are are called "artificial." These are the different characteristics of what arises from nature and what is artificial.

Therefore, the sage changes nature and gives rise to the artificial. Having given rise to the artificial, he creates ritual and rightness. Having created ritual and rightness, he institutes models and standards. Thus, ritual, rightness, models, and standards are creations of the sages. Hence what the sage shares with the masses that wherein he is not different from them, is nature. That wherein he is different and surpasses the masses is artifice.

Now, to like benefit and desire acquisition are man's inherent disposition and nature. Suppose there are some people, an older and younger brother with some wealth to be divided between them, but they obey their inherent dispositions and nature, the fondness for benefit and desire for acquisition. In that case, the older and younger brother will fight and rob each other. But when they are changed by the culture and principles of order of ritual and rightness, they are thus deferential to their countrymen. Therefore, by obeying inherent dispositions and nature, elder and younger brother will be in stasis. But when changed by ritual and rightness, they are deferential to their countrymen.

In general, the fact that people desire to do good is due to the wickedness of their nature. Those without long for plenty, the ugly long to be beautiful, the constricted long for room, the poor long for wealth, and the base long for nobility. In sum, someone who lacks inside seeks for it outside. That is why the rich don't long for wealth, and the noble don't long for high rank. In sum, what one possesses inside, one will not pursue outside. In this light, the fact that people desire to do good is due to the wickedness of their nature. Now, certainly human nature has no ritual or rightness in it. That is why one applies oneself to study in order to acquire them. Our nature does not understand ritual and rightness. That is why one thinks and ponders in effort to understand them. Therefore, at birth people lack ritual and rightness and do not understand ritual and rightness. Without ritual and rightness people are disorderly; without understanding them they are perverse. Hence, at birth they have perversity and unruliness in them. Seen in this light, the wickedness of man's nature is clear. Any goodness in him is artificial.

Mencius says, "Man's nature is good." But it isn't so. In general, throughout history what the world has called "goodness" is correctness, principles of order, peacefulness and orderliness. What is has called "wicked," is bias, dangerousness, perversity and disorder. That is the distinction between good and wicked. Now, do you believe that human nature is supplied with correctness, principles of order, peacefulness and orderliness? If so, what use would the sage kings have been? And what use would ritual and rightness be? And if there were sage kings and ritual and rightness, then what could they add to correctness, principles of order, peacefulness, and orderliness?

As it is not so, man's nature is wicked. That is why the sages took man's nature to be wicked, and considered it biased, dangerous, and incorrect, perverse, disorderly, and unruly. Therefore, they established for him the authority of rulers and superiors in order to oversee him, made rituals and rules clear in order to change him, and set up models and standards to control him, and included punishments and penalties in order to restrain him. They caused the world to come to be governed and to reconcile itself to the good. This is the governance of the sage kings and the influence of ritual and rightness

Now, suppose there were no authority of rulers and superiors, no influence of ritual and rightness, no control of models and correctness, and no restriction of punishment and penalties. Consider the way in which people would treat each other in such a case. In such a case, the strong would harm the weak and rob them, and the many would oppress the few and plunder their possessions. Everyone would fall into perversity and unruliness and destroy each other in no time. Clearly the nature of man is wicked. Any goodness in him is artificial.

Therefore, anyone good at speaking about the ancients should present connections to the present. Anyone good at speaking about nature[349] should present indications of it in the

---

[349] This is *tian*, heaven/nature, i.e., natural world. I have translated it as "heaven" above. Here I wanted to make clear the peculiarly Chinese view that any study of the natural world should pertain to human concerns. Confucian and Daoist philosophy did not support what was once called natural philosophy in the West and is now called science. This explains why this advanced civilization of several thousand years of history did not develop modern science in spite of its native scientific talent. See my article "Leibniz' Binary System and Shao Yong's *Yijing*," *Philosophy East & West*, 46(1996): 59-90, as well as Joseph Neeham, *Science and Civilization in China* (various editions) and Robert Temple, *The Genius of China: 3,000*

human. In general, what matters in a theory is that it have discriminative cogency and evidential basis in fact. Thus, one sits down and articulates it, gets up and is able to apply it, and propounds it and is able to put it into practice.

Now, Mencius says, "Man's nature is good." This has no discriminative cogency or evidential basis in fact. Having sat down and articulated it, one gets up but can't apply it, and one propounds it but can't put it into practice. How can it not be absolutely in error? So, if man's nature is good, then we didn't need sage kings, and could have done without ritual and rightness. As our nature is wicked, we stick to the sage kings and value ritual and rightness.

By the same token, the press frame was created because of bent wood, and the plum line arose because something wasn't straight. The establishment of rulers and superiors and the exhibition of ritual and rightness were done for the wickedness of our nature. Viewed in this light, the nature of man is wicked. Any goodness in him is artificial.

Straight wood doesn't require a press because it's straight by nature. Bent wood requires a press frame and steam in order to shape it and make it straight. For by nature it is not straight. As man's nature is wicked, it need to have the governance of the sage kings and the influence of ritual and rightness in order for everyone to come out in control and in accord with the good. The nature of man is wicked. Any goodness in him is artificial.

Someone will ask, "Ritual, rightness, accumulation [of culture], and artifice are the nature of man. That's why the sage kings could produce them. I reply that this is not so. The potter molds clay and makes a pot, but is the pot or clay part of the potter's nature? A craftsman carves wood and makes a vessel, but are the vessel and wood the nature of the craftsman? The sages' relation to ritual and rightness is comparable to the molding action of the potter as he produces the object. Therefore, how

Years of Science, Discovery and Invention (Rochester, VT: Inner Traditions, 2007).

could ritual, rightness, accumulation [of culture], and artifice be the nature of man?

In general, man's nature is such that Yao and Shun, in comparison to Jie and Zhi are the same in nature, and the gentleman and the small man are the same in nature. Now, how can we take ritual, rightness, accumulation [of culture], and artifice to be man's nature? If this weren't so, why would we esteem Yao and Yu and esteem gentlemen? In general, what we esteem in Yao and Yu and in gentlemen is their ability to change their nature, to give rise to artifice and, having given rise to artifice, to create ritual and rightness. Therefore, the relation of the sage to ritual, rightness, the accumulation [of culture] and artifice also resembles the potter's shaping and producing an object. If you look at it in this way, then how could ritual, rightness, the accumulation [of culture] and artifice be the nature of man? What is base in Jie and Zhi and the small man is that they follow their nature and obey their inherent dispositions, content themselves with lust and crudeness, and therefore end up greedy, combative and rapacious. Thus, it is clear that the nature of man is wicked. Any goodness in him is artificial.

Heaven didn't show special favor for Zeng, Fu, or filial Yi and leave out the masses. So, how were Zeng, Fu, and filial Yi known to be so rich in the fruits of filiality? Because they were superb at ritual and rightness. Heaven didn't show special favor for the people of Qi and Lu and leave out the people of Qin. But when it comes to rightness between father and son and the organization in marriages, Qin doesn't compare to the prevalence of filiality and culture of respect in Qi and Lu. Why? Because the men of Qin follow inherent dispositions and nature and content themselves with lust and crudeness, and are neglectful of ritual and rightness. How could there be any difference in their natures?

"A man in the street can become a Yu." What does that mean? In general, what made Yu a Yu was his attention to humanity, rightness, models, and correctness. Thus there are principles of order that can be known in humanity, rightness, models and correctness. This being so, any man in the street has what it takes to know them, and has what is needed to be able in them. Thus, it is clear how he can become a Yu.

Now if we take humanity, rightness, models and correctness as certainly being devoid of principles of order that one can know and have ability in, then even Yu wouldn't understand or have ability in humanity, rightness, models and correctness. And if we accepted that the man in the street lacked what it takes to know humanity, rightness, models, and correctness, and definitely lacked ability in them, then the man in the street also couldn't know what was right between a father and son when at home and couldn't know what was correct between ruler and subject when at large. But that isn't so. Everyone can know these things. Clearly, therefore, what it takes to know these things and what one needs in order to have ability in them are included within the man on the street. Now, have the man on the street make use of what it takes to know these things and what one needs in order to have ability in them, and let him base himself on the principles of order that can be known in humanity and rightness. Clearly, then he can become a Yu. If you have a man on the street devote himself to these methods, engage in study, focus his mind and unify his will, thing, ponder, reflect, and inquire, make headway every day, and accumulate goodness without respite, then he would be at the level of spiritual intelligence and form a triad with heaven and earth. Hence, sagehood is what a person reaches by accumulation.

Question: "A sage can accumulate and reach it, but not everyone can. Why?" I reply that they can, but you can't induce them to do so. Thus, the small man can become a gentleman, but he is unwilling to do so. A gentleman can become a small man, but he is unwilling to do so. It isn't impossible for the small man and gentleman to become each other, but they don't become each other. For they can but cannot be induced to do so. Hence, while it is so that the man in the street can become a Yu, that he is able to do so is not necessarily the case. That he is unable to become a Yu doesn't negate that he can become a Yu. One can walk across the world, but there isn't anyone who is able to walk across the world. It's not that the carpenter, farmer, and trader can't practice each other's trades. It's just that they are unable to do so. Viewed in this way, that one can doesn't entail that one is able, and even if one is unable, this doesn't negate that one can. Thus there is a great difference between able/unable, and can/cannot. Clearly, one mustn't conflate them....

Suggested Readings

Cheung, Leo K. C., "The Way of the Xunzi," *Journal of Chinese Philosophy* 28(2001): 301–320

Cua, Anthony S., *Ethical Argumentation: A Study in Hsün-tzu's Moral Epistemology* (Honolulu: University of Hawaii Press, 1985)

Cua, Anthony S., *Human Nature, Ritual, and History: Studies in Xunzi and Chinese Philosophy* (Washington: Catholic University of America Press, 2005)

Dubs, Homer H., *The Works of Hsüntze*, (London: Arthur Probsthain, 1928)

Goldin, Paul Rakita, *Rituals of the Way: The Philosophy of Xunzi* (Chicago: Open Court, 1999)

Hagen, Kurtis, *The Philosophy of Xunzi: A Reconstruction* (Chicago: Open Court, 2007)

Hutton, Eric L., *Xunzi: The Complete Text* (Princeton: Princeton University Press, 2014)

Ivanhoe, Philip J., "A Happy Symmetry: Xunzi's Ethical Thought," *Journal of the American Academy of Religion* 59(1991): 309-322

Ivanhoe, Philip J., *Confucian Moral Self Cultivation* (Indianapolis: Hackett, 2000)

Kline, T. C., and Philip J. Ivanhoe, eds., *Virtue, Nature and Moral Agency in the Xunzi* (Indianapolis: Hackett, 2000)

Knoblock, John, *Xunzi: A Translation and Study of the Complete Works*, 3 vols. (Stanford: Stanford University Press, 1988-1994)

Lee, Janghee, *Xunzi and Early Chinese Naturalism* (Albany: SUNY Press, 2005)

Machle, Edward J., *Nature and Heaven in the Xunzi* (Albany: SUNY Press, 1993)

Stalnaker, Aaron, *Overcoming Our Evil: Human Nature and Spiritual Exercises in Xunzi and Augustine* (Washington: Georgetown University Press, 2006)

Watson, Burton, *Hsun-tzu: Basic Writings* (New York: Columbia University Press, 1963)

Yearley, Lee H., "Hsün Tzu on the Mind: His Attempted Synthesis of Confucianism and Daoism," *Journal of Asian Studies* 39(1980): 465-480

7

Han Feizi

Han Feizi[350] (c. 280-233 B.C.E.) lived at a time when war had been a constant for many years (Warring States Period, c. 475-221) and there were several small states which were continually subject to internal disorder and upheaval. We've encountered this bellicose period in earlier chapters. Confucius and Mozi were already tired of the instability, and they lived around the time when the period was just beginning. By Han Fei's time, the instability had continued for hundreds of years. Perhaps he was earnestly driven to an extreme political philosophy as a result. For Han Feizi, as a political philosopher, was a totalitarian, developing a species of totalitarianism, the position that government should have total power without regard to the liberty, property, or other rights of the people it rules. This includes the usual connotations of police state, purges, lack of civil society, and ubiquitous domestic surveillance. The idea of placing the totality of power in a single, central state entices the desperate with the promise of ending war. A similar general description can also be applied to the Seventeenth Century English philosopher Thomas Hobbes, who lived with the insecurity of the English Revolution and the awesome threat of a Spanish invasion. Such could be said of other totalitarian figures in history who were less philosophically serious and more brutal than Han Fei or Hobbes. Fear breeds a love of security. It is a pattern repeated in history whenever a country fails to secure itself and causes its people to become so desperate for security that they will seek the protection of a tyrant.

---

[350] We use both of his names, instead of calling him "Hanzi," in order to distinguish him from the Tang Dynasty thinker called "Hanzi."

Han Feizi's ideas, like those of Hobbes, had an effect on subsequent governments, though this is not usually obvious. I'm sure that before you picked up this book, you had already heard of Confucianism and Daoism. But had you heard of "legalism" or Han Feizi? The totalitarian theory which Han Fei espoused, often called "legalism" in English, has been called the yin of Chinese political philosophy to the Confucian yang; it is the unseen, the dark, equally important but inoften noticed. I don't know how frequently the totalitarianism Plato espouses in the *Republic* or that Hobbes defends in *De Cive* and *Leviathan* evokes disgust in modern, liberty-minded readers. Perhaps legalism's totalitarian ideology might evoke such disgust in you as you read the selections in this chapter. But Han Feizi, like Plato or Hobbes, is a philosopher who deserves a fair reading, at least because it teaches us what sort of political philosophy people might develop at the extremity of protracted war, instability and upheaval. However perverse we may decide that political philosophies of this stripe are, when brilliantly developed and defended, they shed light on an edge of the human mind which we should not allow to remain in the shadows, even if the purpose of making the acquaintance is only to prepare ourselves to refute future instances of its ilk.

The historical records claim that Han Feizi never got to taste the security his ideas promised to create. The state of Qin, which would apply his school of thought in practice when it dominated China from 221 to 207, took to heart Han Fei's advice that the ruler ought to be suspicious of anyone offering him advice and, with exquisite irony, condemned him to death after he offered his counsel. Perhaps Han Fei could have defended himself in writing, but as he would have had to make his defense orally, he preferred to spare himself the futile and humiliating effort and took poison offered to him by his competitor Li Si, who would go on to become prime minister of the Qin Dynasty. For Han Fei was a stutterer, a fact which also accounts for his failure, in spite of his aristocratic birth, to develop a political career in his home state of Han. It may also account for his development of great skill as a writer. He left behind a large collection of fine essays, which have been gathered together in an eponymous volume.

We are about to study Han Fei's "legalism." Before we do so, let us will take the advice of Paul Goldin to heart and notice the mediocrity of this translation.[351] "Legalism" and "legalist" have long been used to translate *fajiao* and *fajia* (literally "law/model/standard" –ism and –ist). The Chinese word for "law" is *fa*; but there are other senses of *fa*. We saw *fa* in Mozi, where it referred to models or standards, rather than statutes; this is its sense in Han Fei's school of thought, too. "Legalism" makes it sound as though the school were focused on statutory law, natural law, common law, or something similar. This is simply not the case. Nor was there any hint of a reverence for the rule of law, litigation, due process or the like. For the ruler could change the standards at will. This is a species of totalitarianism, according to which the state should maintain total control of every aspect of society by enforcing its standards through punishment and reward. This, like any totalitarianism, was rule of man, not of law. Han Fei's school might be called "standardism." Nevertheless, I will continue to call it "legalism" so as not to substitute new confusion for old.

Han Fei's legalism was a synthesis of the ideas of previous legalist philosophers, such as Shen Buhai (fl. c. 400 B.C.E.) and Shen Dao (fl. c. 300 B.C.E.) He developed two of their ideas about how to set up a state in which a single ruler would have (1.) the ultimate authority of *punishment and reward* and would apply these to a system of (2.) *techniques* of defining duties and any subject's divergence from duty known to the ruler. This is the sense of "legalism": strict standards and implementation of enforcement.

The legalists were very serious indeed about the standards. The two ideas refer to a police state, in the sense of a government in which penal authority belongs entirely to the ruling body. The usual connotation of "police state" is entirely appropriate here. Han Fei envisioned a state in which ministers and other subjects would be deeply suspicious of each other. Imagine a society in which everyone you met might have been assigned the duty of spying on you and informing the ruler of any punishable violations of the ruler's standards. The spy would execute this duty assiduously, fearing being spied on himself and being subject to punishment for failure to fulfill his duties as spy.[352] In this network of fear, suspicion, and paranoia, the ruler's people would keep their minds only on the standards. Here is another sense in which legalism is a species of totalitarianism.

Among modern liberty-minded readers the reaction to Han Fei's ideas is likely to be repugnance. He might be seen as having no concern for whether his idea of government was morally justified and as not caring about the welfare of the subjects of the state.[353] One might cynically suppose that totalitarian thinkers developed their theories only in hopes of becoming members of an elite and powerful ruling class that would use them and their rhetorical support for such a class. While this may be so with most totalitarian thinkers, it may not be so of all. Were Plato and Hobbes merely interested in power for themselves or in the truth? It's difficult to know. Plato may have been attracted by the prospect of redesigning society, and the exhilaration may have weakened his determination to hold to the truth. In the case of Han Fei, it isn't obvious, either. While he emphasizes his support for the ruler's tyranny and suppression of dissent, he also makes it clear that the purpose

---

[352] Perhaps this reminds you of much of the history of the Twentieth Century, C.E. If Han Feizi's vision was realized for only a short fourteen years during the Qin Dynasty, it was put into practice, however inadvertently, many times in the various totalitarian regimes of the Twentieth Century, such as the USSR, the DPRK, and, less inadvertently, in the PRC.

[353] Note that if Han Fei's legalism is not meant to be morally justified, then it isn't philosophy but rather political science or a sort of practical advice on how to maintain power.

of these strategies in his view, at least ostensibly,[354] is to protect the innocent from war, starvation, and thieves. And Han Fei doesn't say that the purpose of protecting the innocent is to fulfill the ruler's interests. So, Han Fei's legalism was intended as a morally grounded theory in political philosophy. Even if it was false, it has an element of truth and was thus no more false than the platitude, "Anyone willing to sacrifice liberty for security deserves neither,"[355] which expresses an extreme libertarianism is consistent only with anarchy devoid of police and penal institutions. The truth lies with a political philosophy that aims to conserve both freedom and security, along with many other values, including prosperity, order, justice, and public decency. In fact, anarchy is as untenable as totalitarianism. As Hobbes would point out, a life without freedom of assembly and speech may be uncomfortable, but a life without a police force and an army is solitary, poor, nasty, brutish, and short. But the fact that it is very important to avoid the terrors of anarchy does not show that a totalitarian system is preferable to a moderate system such as the one set up by the American Constitution.

In any event, legalism doesn't hold water. The truth is less extreme and more balanced. Still, studying Han Fei affords insight into the contours of this terrain, and gives one a perspective on the less extreme truth. In addition, it is

---

[354] If a writer argues in favor of totalitarian rule partly on the grounds that it is good for the subjects of that rule, there is no requirement that the reader charitably believe that the writer genuinely has the general welfare at heart. He could be lying in order to garner sympathy and support for the reader. He might harbor nothing but contempt and spite for people.

[355] The saying is a bowdlerized version of Benjamin Franklin's far more sensible one: "They that can give up essential liberty for a little temporary safety deserve neither liberty nor safety" (*Historical Review of Pennsylvania*, 1759). If it's a question of bromides, we may consult one by Franklin's contemporary David Hume: "[A] regard to liberty, though a laudable passion, ought commonly to be subordinate to a reverence for established government" since the latter is "essential to [the former's] very existence" (*History of England*, vol. IX). Hobbes and Han Feizi would argue that Hume has the better use of the word "essential," but of course there is Patrick Henry's famous 1775 "Give me liberty or give me death."

important to understand the thought processes underlying totalitarian thinking of any age or nation. In that way, one can recognize them in one's own society. Whether totalitarian theorists are driven to it by desperate weariness of war and instability or whether they seize upon the idea as a means of taking advantage of the crises of their times, it is important to understand the mechanics of the development of their ideas.

What sort of state, exactly, was Han Fei's legalist state? It was one in which flourishing was sought by the "rectification of names," the checking of each subject's deeds against the description of the duties corresponding to his position. Ruthless punishment and coveted rewards, determined by the ruler, would force everyone to mind his own business carefully and do nothing else. Han Fei would even prohibit going beyond the call of duty because permitting it would open the door to self-promoters and would-be usurpers.[356] Political parties and assemblies would be prohibited, as would be dissent of any kind. The reasoning was as follows. Greed is common to human beings, and greedy and oppressive powers would likely emerge from any political force other than that of the ruler. Moreover, political parties are divisive, division of power is destabilizing, and instability leads to disaster. People are generally stupid and greedy. They need the absolute and authoritative guidance of the ruler's disposition to apply punishment disinterestedly in order to flourish. And flourish they were intended to do. There is not even a hint in Han Fei's writings of the right of the ruler to harm his subjects at whim or to deprive them of happiness or freedom for any purpose other than security and stability of the state. The ruler was to rectify his name as "ruler"; even the ruler was to suppress his desires and simply fulfill his duty of applying an unvarying law.

---

[356] This odd position should stop us short; it may be that a society in which no one puts out more effort than morally required cannot thrive. Also, the perversity of punishing people who perform supererogatory acts on cynical grounds is obvious. It may be that a society can't be morally healthy without holding up such people as paragons of virtue.

312

Perhaps, there is a sense in which legalism envisions a rule of law, rather than a rule of man.

There are problems with Han Fei's theory. First, it may not be true that stability can be had only under totalitarian regimes. In fact, it is now obviously false, though in Han Fei's time it was not obvious yet. Indeed, it is arguable precisely that stability cannot be had under totalitarian regimes. Second, the details of Han Fei's theory of the state may not be clear enough to render it plausible. This is a question which you should keep in mind as you read the essays. The ruler is to keep decisive authority to himself. But how can people under him fulfill their duties without making decisions? It seems impossible. It is probably better to delegate authority and decentralize it, as this brings many more minds to the task of deciding what to do.[357] Also, how can the ruler tell who is lying about having fulfilled his duty, unless he relies on the judgment of others, judgment which he would disallow them from exercising? How would the ruler know whether a spy reporting a political clique's clandestine meetings was not representing a competing clique? No one would have the time or ability to parse the information and misinformation while also ruling a state.

Han Fei intended to make the prospect of a minister's using illicit schemes of self-advancement unlikely due to the threat of punishment. His goal was that ministers would give up any hope of succeeding by illicit means and have nothing left but to fulfill their duties, report facts correctly to the ruler, and thus gain reward. A practical problem with this idea is that one ruler cannot be wise and knowledgeable enough to apply the punishment and reward accurately enough to accomplish this goal. This, combined with the fact that some people will always find the risk of punishment worth taking, brings back in (or even, one might argue, increases) the instability that Han Fei was at pains to eradicate. How could the ruler vouchsafe

---

[357] The classic instance of this in the West is the case of Jethro, Moses's father-in-law, advising Moses to stop trying to decide every legal case in the nation and to delegate this authority down through many levels and all the way to the very small local level. See *Exodus* 18 and *Deuteronomy* 1.

that all punishments had indeed been applied? Han Fei was aware of some of these issues. He said that the ruler would not have enough time or energy to micromanage, to make sure in person that everything was done properly. But whom to trust for this task? His hope was that the threat of severe punishment would make trustworthy ministers of everyone. But if people are as selfish and stupid as Han Fei thought, they will take the risk of punishment often enough to destabilize even the most heavy-handed of regimes.

If you've studied Laozi's *The Book of Power and the Way* in chapter two, you will perhaps be surprised to find that Han Fei meant his totalitarian views to be rooted in that text. Laozi, though no libertarian, seems to be no totalitarian. But the *Han Feizi* includes two essays on the connections between Daoism and legalism, part of one of which is included below, "Explaining Laozi."[358] Han Fei's idea is that the ruler and ministers are to think as little as possible and to let society run on its own, save for those occasions of punishment and reward. Once the certainty of punishment and reward was in place, society would run itself effortlessly. As Daoist as this may seem, consider the following passages from *The Book of Power and the Way* as you read Han Fei.

> 20(57) If legal (*fa*) matters are stirred up, there will be many robbers.[359]
> 41(76) [T]he strong and the great are inferior, the soft and the weak superior.
> 44(81) In the pacification of great resentment, there must be some residual resentment. How can this be taken as good? For this reason the sage holds on to the right hand tally, but does not use it to hold people responsible.

---

[358] Not all scholars believe that Han Fei wrote these essays. Some hold that later legalists forged the Daoism-legalism connection, not Han Fei. If they are right, then at least the Daoistic essays give us insight into legalism, if not into Han Fei.

[359] On the other hand, this sentence seems so pointedly anti-standardist that it may have been inserted into *The Book of Power and the Way* after Han Fei's time, as a Daoist effort to dissociate Daoism from standardism.

314

These passages seem inconsistent with Han Fei's views. He did not address them in his essays. Perhaps he did not have an edition of the book with those passages in it. Or perhaps addressing them would have made it more difficult for him to portray legalism as Daoistic.

Han Fei made his mark on history. Chinese totalitarian regimes found themselves looking to his essays for advice. It is probably a stretch to posit roots of the Tiananmen Square Massacre in Han Fei's brutal strictures against political parties. Yet, he would have whole-heartedly approved of the massacre. I doubt that the motives of the leaders who ordered the massacre had anything to do with the welfare of the people of China. I think that they only wanted to maintain their own power. In Han Fei's case, we can't be sure of his motives for supporting such oppression. The man could scarcely hope to hold power himself,[360] so we have little reason to take his stated reasons regarding the welfare of the people as anything but sincere. On the other hand, perhaps he wanted only the vicarious thrill of being the philosopher of the totalitarian state.

---

[360] On the other hand, could Han Fei have hoped to become prime minister of a state, as his colleague Li Si did? Or, as a stutterer, was he resigned to a scholarly life that would give him no chance of gaining power? The Tiananmen Square Massacre was perpetrated by rulers, people who stood to maintain great power by the action. Yet again, it is not impossible that those rulers sincerely thought the massacre was the best thing to do for China. After all, Han Fei would have agreed. That someone stands to gain great power from an action doesn't by itself prove that he doesn't sincerely believe that the action is the right thing to do. Nevertheless, although during the Warring States Period one might reasonably believe that such suppression of dissent was the best thing, by 1989 the evidence was now so strongly against this belief, that it isn't very plausible to think that the Chinese leaders of 1989 genuinely held it. They were likely servants of their own lust for power and of the cult of the personality of Mao Zedong.

The Readings

Below I've included "The Two Handles," "Wielding Power," and excerpt from other essays found in the *Han Feizi*, numbered as they are in the standard edition of the text, including "Explaining Laozi," "Questioning Mr. Tian," and "Psychology."

Han Feizi

7. The Two Handles

What an enlightened ruler uses to control his ministers is the two handles and nothing more. The two handles are punishment and favor. What do "punishment" and "favor" refer to? Execution and maiming are referred to as "punishment." Honors and rewards are referred to as "favor." Those who act as ministers fear corporal punishment and consider honor and reward beneficial. Therefore, the ruler himself uses his punishment and favor so that the ministers fear his majesty and pursue his beneficence. However, the wicked ministers can cause one to be punished by their ruler. And if one is loved by them, they can have one rewarded by their ruler. Now, if the ruler does not make the terror and benefit of punishment and reward come from himself but listens to his ministers in carrying out rewards and punishments, then everywhere in the country the people will fear the ministers and think nothing of the ruler. They will follow after the ministers and leave the ruler out. This is the calamity of the ruler who loses hold of punishment and favor.

The reason a tiger can subdue a dog is its claws and teeth. If you have the tiger do without its claws and teeth and let the dog use them, then the tables will be turned, and the tiger will be subdued by the dog. As for rulers, they are to use punishment and favor to control ministers. Now, when rulers do without punishment and favor and have ministers use them, then, the tables being turned, the rulers are controlled by the ministers. Thus, Dian Chang requested titles and emoluments [of his ruler Duke Jian] and gave them out to the ministers. He made the grain measures bigger and gave generously to the people. Thus, Duke Jian lost the use of favor and Dian Chang made use of it. That is why Duke Jian saw the day when he was assassinated.[361]

Zihan asked the ruler of Song, "Honors, rewards and gifts are what the people want. The ruler himself should give them out. Execution, maiming and corporal punishment are what the people hate. I request that I handle them." With this the ruler of Song lost punishment and Zihan made use of it. That is why the ruler of Song saw the day when he was coerced.

Dian Chang only used favor, and Duke Jian was assassinated. Zihan only used punishment, and the ruler of Song was coerced. Therefore, when those who act as ministers in this age get to use both punishment and reward, then the danger to the rulers of this age exceeds that of Duke Jian or the ruler of Song. That is why they are coerced, killed, obstructed and suppressed. As for rulers who relinquished both punishment and favor and had ministers use them but didn't face danger or downfall, there have never been any.

If the ruler would like to prohibit wickedness, then he should meticulously match deed and name, word and action. Those who act as ministers make speeches and talk. On the basis of these words the ruler assigns duties and uses strictly these duties as norms for their works. If the works correspond to their duties and their duties correspond to their words, then he rewards them. If their works do not correspond to their duties and their duties do not correspond to their words, then he punishes them. Therefore, those among the ministers of great words but small works are punished. He doesn't punish those of small works but punishes those whose works don't match their names. Those among the ministers of small words and great works are also punished. It's not that he isn't pleased

---

[361] By Dian Chang in 481 B.C.E.

with great works. But he takes the damage from the failure to correspond to name as more important than having done great works. So, he punishes them.

Some time ago, Marquis Zhao of Han got drunk and fell asleep. The crown keeper saw that the ruler was cold and, so, he put an extra coat on top of him. Upon waking up, the Marquis said, "Who put this coat on me?" His attendants replied, "The crown keeper." The ruler therefore condemned both the coat keeper and crown keeper. He condemned the coat keeper because he had failed his duty. He condemned the crown keeper because he had overstepped his post. It's not that he didn't dislike the cold. But he took the harm of official posts being encroached upon to be more important than the cold.

Therefore, when an enlightened ruler oversees his ministers, the ministers will not come to overstep their stations in order to have accomplishments and will not come to utter words without living up to them. If they overstep their stations, they die. If they do not live up to their words, they will be condemned. If they keep to the business of their stations and are true to what they say, then the ministers will not form factions and act on each other's behalf.

There are two calamities facing the ruler. If he employs worthies, then the ministers will exploit their worthiness in order to coerce their ruler. If he promotes randomly, then affairs will be in a muddle and will not come through well. Therefore, if the ruler prefers worthiness, then the ministers will ostentatiously act to satisfy the ruler's desire. Thus, the minister's real motives will not be revealed. If the minister's real motives are not revealed, then the ruler will have no way to differentiate among his ministers. That is why when the ruler of Yue preferred bravery, the people treated death more lightly. When King Ling of Chu preferred slim waists, there were more people starving themselves in the country. Duke Huan of Qi, in his fondness for his inner ladies, showed jealousy towards his outer ministers. So, Shutiao castrated himself in order to be put in charge of the inner ladies. Duke Huan liked delicacies, and Yiya boiled his son's head and offered it to him. Zikuai of Yan liked worthiness. So, Zizhi broadcast that he would not accept the throne.[362]

Therefore, when the ruler displays his antipathies, the ministers will conceal their intentions. When the ruler displays his inclinations, then the ministers will lie about their abilities. If the ruler's desires are seen, then the ministers' attitudes will have their basis. Hence, Zizhi, by pretending to be worthy, made a grab for the rule. Shutiao and Yiya, by making the ruler's desires their aim, encroached upon their ruler. In the end, Zikuai died in the chaos, and Duke Huan had maggots pouring out of his door before he was buried. What is the reason for these things? They are the calamities of a ruler displaying his real feelings to his ministers. As for a minister's real feelings, he needn't be able to love his ruler. Substantial benefit is his motive. Nowadays the ruler doesn't hide his real feelings and doesn't conceal his motives, and so he provides the ministers with the conditions by which to encroach upon his authority. Then for the ministers to act as Zizhi and Dian Chang did is not difficult. Therefore, it is said, "Get rid of inclinations and antipathies,[363] and the ministers will display genuineness. When the ministers display genuineness, then a great ruler will not be misled."

8. Wielding Power

Heaven has an overarching mandate. Man has an overarching mandate. Now, fragrant and delicious delicacies, strong wine, and fat meat, please the palate but sicken the body. Delicate lines and gleaming teeth titillate the feelings but waste the vital essence. Therefore, be rid of extremes and be rid of excessiveness, and your body will be without harm. Do not show your power. Be simple and actionless. Affairs occupy

---

[362] He knew that a worthy would show such humility.
[363] "Get rid of" here might mean "keep concealed." The literal interpretation is favored by other passages in *Han Feizi*, as we will see below.

the four directions, while the drive is in the center. The sage holds on to the drive, and the four directions come into its service. All within the four seas have been taken care of. Empty, he waits for them, and they go at it on their own. From the darkness he sees the bright ones. When his men are in place, he opens the gate and faces them. Without changing, without alteration, he carries on with the two [i.e., punishment and reward], carries on and doesn't stop. This is called "going forth according to principle."

For things there is that which suits them. For talents, there is that which makes them manifest. They each abide in what suits them, and, therefore, superior and subordinate are both without intention to act. Have the rooster keep watch at night, and make cats catch rats, each using its abilities. The superior thus has nothing to do. If the superior has a place where he can make improvements, then business will not be taken care of. If he proclaims that he admires ability, then he will be subjected to the lies of his inferiors. If he urges mercy and is fond of life, then his subordinates will make an occasion of this tendency. Superior and subordinate will exchange functions, and the state will thus not be ordered.

Use the way of unity, and take names as its heads. When names are rectified, then things will be stable.[364] If names are relative, then things will be unstable. Therefore, the sage holds to unity with quiescence, has names command themselves, and makes things stabilize themselves. He doesn't show his true colors, and his subordinates are therefore plain and correct. He assigns them appropriately, and he causes them to busy themselves of their own accord. He gives to them appropriately, and they will get promotions in rank of their own accord. He is correct in placing them, and he has them all stabilize themselves. He relies on names in promoting them. If

---

[364] The idea of rectifying names (*zhengming*) is to see to it that people act according to the duties of their posts, and that the posts are clearly defined. Confucians also included family relations, making, for example, the positions of parent and child posts to be checked as to whether one is living up to one's name as "father" or "child."

he is unsure about the name, then he repairs to their forms.[365]
He checks the form and name for correspondence and uses the
upshot of this. When the two are genuine and reliable, then
subordinates will offer up their true motivations.

If one carefully attends to affairs, awaits the mandate of
heaven and does not lose one's drive, then one counts as a sage.
The way of the sage is to get rid of wisdom and skills.[366] If
wisdom and skills are not discarded, it is difficult to be
constant. When the people use them, their bodies are greatly
imperiled. When the ruler uses them, his country is in danger
of destruction. Make the way of heaven your motive, revert to
the principles of forms, observe, examine, and make inquiry
into them. At the end, begin again. Be empty, quiet and
withdrawn, never using yourself. All calamities to the ruler are
the fruition of his need to be merged [with the ministers and
people]. Rely on them, but do not merge with them, and the
myriad people will follow you as one.

As for the Way, it is vast and formless. As for power, it
illuminates principles and reaches everywhere. It reaches all
creatures and they partake in using it. The myriad things all
flourish, but it doesn't rest with them. As for the Way, it is
present in all inferior things.

Inquire into heaven's mandate and make it your motive.
Live and die in time. Scrutinize names and distinguish deeds.
Pervade, unify and merge with your natures. Thus, it is said,
"The Way does not merge with the myriad things. Power does
not merge with yin and yang. A scale does not merge with the
light and the heavy. A plumbline does not merge with the
hollows and bumps. A reed organ does not merge with dryness
or humidity.[367] A ruler does not merge with the ministers." All
these six are what emerge from the Way. The Way is not two.

---

[365] "Form" is the actual facts about a minister's recent deeds.
[366] Han Fei seems to refer to esoteric wisdom and new-fangled skills offered
up by subjects. On this reading, the passage does not mean that he would
eschew common sense "inquiry" or competence in carrying out duties.
[367] It thus stays in tune, no matter what the weather, and is able to provide
the standard pitch for other instruments to be tuned.

So, it is said to be "one." Therefore, the enlightened ruler values solitariness, the content of the way. The ruler and ministers do not merge their ways. Subordinates make entreaties with names, and the ruler holds them to the names. Ministers put forth their forms. If, upon examination, form and name correspond, then ruler and subordinates harmonize.

The way of all auditing is to take what is coming out of them and compare it to the charges that have been given them. Therefore, examine names in order to set ranks. Clarify duties in order to discriminate among difficult kinds. The way of listening to speech is to be motionless, as if drunk. Lips! Teeth! I will not be the first [to speak]. Teeth! Lips! Be as though in a stupor! Others will betray themselves, and I will thereby know them.

Affirmations and denials converge upon him, but the ruler does not get tangled up in them. Emptiness, quiescence and non-action are the essence of the Way. What is reached by investigating, checking, and comparing with reality is the form of deeds. Investigate them by comparing with reality. Check them by checking them against the empty [i.e., the names].

If root and stem are unshakable, then whether moving or still, there will be no loss. Whether you move your subjects or you keep them still, through non-action you will transform them. If you like them, then you will be making more work. If you dislike them, then you will create anger. So, be rid of inclinations and be rid of antipathies. Empty your mind, in order to be an abode for the Way.

The ruler is not together with them, and the people thus have esteem for him. The ruler does not give them counsel, but has them do things on their own. The ruler tightly locks his inner door and views the court from his room. With the yardstick already supplied, everything falls into place. He has those to be rewarded rewarded and those to be punished punished. Each person determines this himself by doing what he does. When these goods and evils are certain to be met with, who will dare doubt it? When the compass and square have set the pattern [i.e., one corner of a square], then the other three angles will follow the example.

If the ruler above is not like a god, then those below will have opportunities. If his deeds are not appropriate, those below will surmise of their regularities. Be like heaven and be like earth. This is called "the undoing of tangles." Be like earth, be like heaven, and who will be distant? Who will be close? Being able to resemble heaven and earth is called "being a sage."

If you desire to keep order inside the government, then make appointments without favoritism. If you desire to keep order outside, then for each post appoint one person. If you do not let him give himself any leeway, how will he be able to shift and annex a second post? As for the gates of the high ministers, fear only that there will be many people there. The pinnacle of all governing lies in subordinates' being unable to empower themselves. Gather and compare forms and names, and the people will hold to their posts. Discarding this and searching elsewhere is to be considered a great delusion. Treacherous people will come in hoards, and villainy will swarm at your sides. Thus, it is said, "Do not enrich a person to the extent that you must borrow from him. Do not ennoble a man to the extent that he coerces you. Do not put all your trust in one person and thereby end up losing the country."

If the calf is larger than the thigh, it is hard to run. If the ruler loses his godliness, tigers will stalk his back. If the ruler above doesn't realize this, the tigers will have dogs to hound him. If the ruler doesn't stop this in time, the dogs will multiply without limit. The tigers will form a band in order to kill their mother. By being a ruler without ministers, how can one keep the state? If the ruler presents his laws, the big tigers will shrink back. If the ruler presents the punishments, the big tigers will submit. If the law and punishments are reliable, then the tigers will transform into people and revert to their actual selves.

If you want to act on behalf of the state, you must chop down its assemblies. If you don't chop down its assemblies, they will assemble in hoards. If you want to act on behalf of the land, you must grant favors appropriately. If you don't grant favors appropriately, then disorderly people will seek the benefits. If you give what they seek, then you will be lending an enemy an axe. You must not lend it, for they will use it to chop you down.

The Yellow Emperor had a saying: "Superior and subordinates have one hundred fights a day." Subordinates conceal their self-interest, and thereby test their superior. The superior holds the measures in order to keep his subordinates in check. Therefore, the establishment of the measures is the treasure of the ruler. The maintenance of parties and meetings is the treasure of the ministers. The reason ministers don't assassinate their ruler is that the parties and meetings are not maintained. Therefore, if the ruler gives an inch, the subordinates will gain a yard.

A ruler who possesses a state doesn't make the cities large. A minister who has the Way does not ennoble those in his ministry. A ruler who has the Way does not ennoble his ministers. Ennoble them and enrich them, and they will eclipse you. Prepare for danger and suspect peril. Designate your heir right away. Misfortune will then have no place from which to arise.

In internal inquiries and external crackdowns, you yourself must hold fast to your rulers and measures. Decrease the thick and increase the thin. The decrease and the increase have a measure. Don't let the people get together and collude to deceive their ruler. Reduce them like the moon, and increase them like the heat.[368] Simplify regulations and be careful in applying corporal punishment. But you must go through with the punishments.

Don't unstring your bow, or it will be "two males on one perch." With two males on one perch, the fighting will be fierce. With a jackal and a wolf in the pen, the sheep will not multiply. With two heads of one household, things will not go

---

[368] Perhaps this means "gradually."

well. If both husband and wife hold command, the children will have no one to follow.

One who would rule people frequently prunes his trees.[369] He doesn't let the trees' branches grow luxuriant. If the trees' branches grow luxuriant, they will block the ruler's gate. Private gates will be rich [with crowds], but the ruler's court will be empty, and the ruler will be surrounded. Frequently pruning his trees, the ruler will not let the tree branches block him in from outside. If the tree branches block him in from outside, then they will squeeze the ruler's position. If he frequently prunes his trees, he will not let the branches get big while the trunk remains small. If the tree branches get big while the trunk remains small, then they will not survive a spring wind. If they do not survive a spring wind, then the branches will damage the heart of the tree. When the royal cadets become numerous, the family will have anxiety and sorrow. The way to stop this is frequently to prune the trees, not letting the branches get thick. With the trees frequently pruned, parties and cliques will be dispersed. Dig up their roots, and the trees will then not be so awe-inspiring. Fill in the ponds and do not let the water become clear.[370] Try to discern the inner thoughts of others. Take their authority away from them. The ruler uses it like lightening, like thunder.

20. Explaining Laozi[371]

Dedaojing: 21(58) If the government is muddled and addled, the people will be genuine. If the government is meticulously discriminating, the country will be divided. Calamity is something good fortune requires. Good fortune is something that calamity covers. Who knows its limits? It

---

[369] In Western languages there is a similar euphemism to "prune the trees": "purge."

[370] I.e., to stay long enough for it to become clear.

[371] Han Fei quotes most of the passages from the sections he cites, but you might want to review the sections fully by turning to chapter 2. I have provided here the numbering scheme of the *Dedaojing* passages which I used in chapter 2.

has no correct state. The correct returns to deviation. The good returns to weirdness. Man's perplexity has lasted a long time. Therefore, be square but do not cut. Be pointed but do not pierce. Be straight but not inflexible. Shine but do not be bright.

Commentary: When a person has a calamity, his mind is fearful and apprehensive. When the mind is fearful and apprehensive, conduct becomes strict and straight. When conduct is strict and straight, thought and reflection are thoroughgoing. When thought and reflection are thoroughgoing, they get to the principles of order underlying affairs. When conduct is strict and straight, there will be no calamity or harm. When there is no opportunity for calamity or disaster, one will live out one's natural lifespan. When one gets to the principles of order underlying affairs, one is certain to accomplish meritorious works. If one lives out one's natural lifespan, one will keep oneself intact and live to an old age. If one is certain to accomplish meritorious works, one will have wealth and noble rank. One who keeps himself intact, lives to old age, and is wealthy is called "fortunate." But this good fortune derives from having a calamity. Thus, it says, "Calamity is something good fortune requires." This is the means of accomplishing one's meritorious works.

If a person has good fortune, wealth and noble rank will come. If wealth and noble rank come, his clothing and food will be fine. If his clothing and food are fine, this will bring about an arrogant mind. An arrogant mind having arisen, his conduct will become wicked and devious, and his actions will abandon principles of order. If his conduct becomes wicked and devious, the man will die young. If his actions abandon principles of order, he will not carry out works of merit. Internally to face the hardship of a dying young, and externally to have no reputation for carrying out meritorious works are the greatest of calamities. But they are calamities that arise on the basis of having good fortune. Thus, it says, "Good fortune is something that calamity covers."

Of those who take the Way and principles of order as their basis in pursuing affairs, none are unable to complete them. None being unable to complete them, the greatest are able to achieve the authority and honor of the Son of Heaven, and lesser ones easily obtain the rich emolument of high office or military general. As for those who abandon the Way and principles of order and are foolish in deciding how to act, even if they have, on the one hand, the authority and honorable position of the Son of Heaven or a feudal lord, and, on the other, the wealth of a Yi Dun, Tao Zhu, or Bu Si, they will still lose their subjects and destroy their wealth. Ordinary men who make light of abandoning the Way and principles of order and who are foolish in deciding how to act do not understand that this is how profound and great the cycle of calamity and good fortune is and how the broad and far reaching the Way is. Thus, it says, "Who knows its limits?"

No man does not desire wealth, noble rank, staying intact, and old age, but none can avoid the calamities of poverty, abasement, and premature death. In the mind to desire wealth, and noble rank, staying intact, and old age, but in fact to be poor and lowly and to face premature death, is to be unable to achieve what one wants to achieve. Anyone who loses the path to what he desires and carries on foolishly is said to be "perplexed." Those who are perplexed are unable to achieve they want to achieve. Today common people are unable to achieve what they want to achieve. Thus, it says that they are "perplexed." That the common people are unable to achieve what they want to achieve has been true from the separation of heaven and earth until today. Thus, it says, "Man's perplexity has lasted a long time."

The meaning of "be square" is the correspondence between internal and external, the agreement of word and deed. The meaning of "be pointed" is to treat the fate of life and death as necessary and to treat matters of property and wealth as trivial. The meaning of "be straight" is righteously to be strictly impartial and correct, to have an impartial mind that isn't partial or partisan. The meaning of "shine" is to have an office and title, nobility and honor, and to have clothing and furs that are hardy and attractive.

The scholars of today who possess the Way, though within and without of good faith and obedient, do not therefore slander the defamed or humiliate the fallen. Though they die when the occasion demands it and they treat wealth lightly, they do not insult the weak or shame the greedy. Though righteous, even-handed, and not partisan, they do not therefore eschew the wicked or vilify the selfish. Though holding positions of honor and wearing beautiful clothing, they do not therefore show off before the lowly or abuse the poor. What is the reason for this? If you are one who has lost the path and would listen to those who are well versed in it and to learn from those who know, you would not be so perplexed.

The fact that nowadays ordinary people want to accomplish meritorious works but on the contrary produce only failure is due to their not knowing the Way and principles of natural order and to their unwillingness to learn from the knowledgeable and listen to the able. Ordinary people are unwilling to learn from the knowledgeable or listen to the able, but if a sage insists on using their calamities and failures to reprimand them, they resent it. Ordinary people are numerous and sages are few. That the few do not control the masses is a matter of the numbers. To take action and make an enemy of the world is not a Way to keep oneself intact and lengthen life. Therefore, go with the ruts and acts on the appropriate occasion. Thus, the text says, "Be square but do not cut. Be pointed but do not pierce. Be straight but not inflexible. Shine but do not be bright."

> *Dedaojing*: 22(59) In regulating human affairs and serving heaven, nothing compares to being sparing. Simply being sparing is a means of early repair. Early repair is called "accumulating layers of power." If one repeatedly accumulates power, then there is nothing it does not overcome. If there is nothing it does not overcome, then no one knows its limits. If no one knows its limits, then one may possess the country. Possessing the mother of the country,

one can last long. This is called making deep the roots and securing the trunk. It is the Way of prolonging life and prolonging one's everlasting gaze [of the ruler facing south].

Commentary: Keenness of hearing, clarity of vision, cleverness, and intelligence are matters of nature. Activity, repose, thought, and contemplation are matters of man. Man's place is to go by our natural clarity in order to see, to rely on our natural keenness in order to hear, and to hold to our natural intelligence in order to think and cogitate. Thus, if we look stressfully, our eyes will not see clearly. If we listen too hard, our ears will not be keen. If we think and cogitate beyond measure, our intelligence and consciousness will be confused. If our vision is not clear, we will be unable to tell the difference between black and white. If our hearing is not keen, we will be unable to distinguish sharp and dull sounds. If our intelligence and consciousness are confused, we will be incapable of judging levels of success and failure. We say that an eye that is unable to tell the difference between black and white is "blind," that an ear that is unable to distinguish sharp and dull sounds is "deaf," and that a mind that cannot judge levels of success and failure is "insane." If blind, one is unable to avoid dangers in broad daylight. If deaf, one is unable to recognize the warning of thunder. If one is insane, one is unable to avoid calamity at the hands of human laws and regulations. When the text means by "regulating human affairs" is making suitable the occasions of action and quiescence and not spending too much on thought and cogitation. What means by "serving heaven" is not going beyond the limits of the power of hearing and seeing and not exhausting the ability of wisdom and consciousness to meet their responsibilities. Whenever one goes beyond those limits and exhausts those abilities, the spirit is utterly spent. When the spirit is utterly spent, the calamity of blindness, deafness, or insanity arrives. On account of this, one should "be sparing" with it. One is sparing of it by treating one's seminal essence and spirit as dear and by being sparing with one's wisdom and consciousness. Thus, the text says: "In regulating human affairs and serving heaven, nothing compares to being sparing."

The common people's employment of the spirit is stressful. Under stress, it expends much of itself. This great expenditure is called "wastefulness." The sage's employment of the spirit is quiescent. Being quiescent, it expends little of itself. This slight expenditure is called "being sparing." Being sparing is called a "method" and grows out of the Way and principles of order. Now, to be able to be sparing is to follow the Way and to repair to principles of order. When common men meet with disaster or are fall into calamity, they still do not know that they must retreat, and so they do not submit to the Way and principles of order. The sage, although he does not yet perceive the form disasters and misfortunes will take, being empty and lacking, submits to the Way and principles of order. We call it, "early repair." Therefore it says, "It is called 'being sparing' and it is a means of early repair."[372]

The thoughts and cogitations of those who know how to govern the people are quiescent. The cavities and openings of those who know how to serve heaven are empty. When thoughts and cogitations are quiescent, the old power doesn't leave. When the cavities and openings are kept empty, harmonious *qi* comes in every day. Thus, it says, "accumulating layers of power." This ability to command the old power not to leave and the new harmonious *qi* to arrive every day is early repair. Thus, it says, "Early repair is called 'accumulating layers of power.'"

Only after accumulating power will the spirit become quiescent. Only after making the spirit quiescent will there be plenty of harmony. Only after there is plenty of harmony does one plan what to achieve. Only after planning what to achieve can one harness the myriad things. If one can harness the myriad things, then in battle one will easily conquer the opponent. If in battle one will easily conquer the opponent,

---

[372] As you can see, the version of the text Han Fei was using to write his commentary was slightly different in syntax from the one we have, as this exact line is not found in our version.

then one's proclamations are certain to hold for an entire generation. Thus, it says, "[T]here is nothing it does not overcome." There being nothing it does not overcome derives from accumulating layers of power. Thus, it says, "If one accumulates layers of power, then there is nothing it does not overcome."

If in battle one will easily conquer the opponent, then everywhere the world will be in one's possession. When one's proclamations are certain to hold for an entire generation, the people will follow. One will advance into the entire world and retreat with the people following. His techniques will be so far-reaching that none of the common people will see where [his power] begins or ends. No one will see where it begins or ends, and therefore no one will know its limits. Thus, it says, "If there is nothing it does not overcome, then no one knows its limits."

In general, those who first possess a country and then lose it or who first possess their own bodies and ruin them cannot be said to be capable of possessing their own country or capable of keeping their own body. To be capable of possessing one's state one must be able to keep its altars of soil and grain in peace. To be capable of keeping one's body one must live to the end one's heaven-given years. Only then can one be said to be capable of possessing one's own country or capable of keeping one's own body. One who is capable of possessing his country or keeping his body must also embody the Way. If he embodies the Way, his wisdom is profound. If his wisdom is profound, his calculations will be far-reaching. If his calculations are far-reaching, then none of the common people will be capable of seeing what limits him. Only a person who embodies the Way is capable of making the people not see the limits of his affairs. One who can make others not see the limits of his affairs does keep his own body and possess his country. Thus, the text says: "No one knows its limits," and, "If no one knows its limits, then one may possess the country."

When it says, "possessing the mother of the country," 'mother' is the Way. To be of the Way arises from the techniques by which the state is possessed. They are techniques by which the state is possessed, so it calls them "possessing the mother of the country." As the Way is something that runs throughout a generation, the lives it creates are long and the prosperity it supports lasts. Thus, it says, "Possessing the mother of the country, one can last long."

Trees have winding roots and upright roots. An upright root is what the text calls a "trunk." The "trunk" is what the tree uses to create its life; the winding roots are what the tree uses to support its life. Power is what people use to create their lives. Prosperity is what people use to support their lives. The person who creates by principles of order will support his prosperity in a lasting way. Thus, it speaks of "making deep the roots." The person who embodies the Way lengthens his life every day. Thus, the text speaks of "securing the trunk." If the trunk is secure, life is long, and if the roots are deeper, the fixed stare lasts. Thus, it says, "This is called making deep the roots and securing the trunk. It is the Way of prolonging life and prolonging one's everlasting gaze."

> *Dedaojing*: 23(60). Governing a large country is like cooking a small fish. If you manage everything in accordance with the Way, spirits will not become ghosts. If it is not the case that spirits do not become ghosts, then the ghosts will not harm people. If it is not the case that the ghosts will not harm people, the sage still does not harm them. For if the two do not harm each other, then powers are exchanged and returned between them.

Commentary: If an artisan makes numerous changes in his craft, he will lose what he has achieved. If a workman makes numerous shifts of abode, he will ruin his achievements. If the work of one man is half ruined every day, in ten days the achievements of five men will be ruined. If the work of ten thousand men is half ruined every day, in ten days the achievements of fifty thousand men will be ruined. So, the more numerous the changes in craft, the more people involved and the greater the loss involved.

In general, when laws and regulations are altered, what counts as beneficial and harmful changes. When what counts beneficial and harmful changes, the people's occupations change. The change of occupation is what is meant by "change of craft." Therefore, looking at it from the point of view of principles of order, [one sees that] as tasks become large and manifold, and are often modified, meritorious achievement becomes more rare. If you store a large vessel but move it too often, you frequently will damage it. If you cook a small fish but stir it too much, it will destroy the flavor. If you govern a large country but frequently change the laws, the people will be embittered by it. This is why a ruler who possesses the Way values quiescence and does not repeatedly change the laws. Thus, it says, "Governing a large country is like cooking a small fish."

When people are sick, they value physicians. When they suffer a calamity, they are in awe of ghosts. When a sage is in power, the people have few desires. If the people have few desires, their blood *qi* is well regulated. When their blood *qi* is well regulated, the activities they undertake are in accord with principles of order. When the activities they undertake in accord with principles of order, there are fewer calamities and injuries. When within there are no harms arising from ulcers and cancers or from exhaustion and without there are no calamities arising from punishments, penalties, or legal executions, people think nothing at all of ghosts. Thus, it says, "If you manage everything in accordance with the Way, spirits will not become ghosts." The people of orderly generations do not become involved with harming and being harmed by ghost and spirits. Thus, it says, "If it is not the case that spirits do not become ghosts, then the ghosts will not harm people."

For ghosts to cast a spell of sickness on people is called "ghosts harming people." People exorcising and driving out ghosts is called "people harming ghosts." The people violating laws and regulations is called "the people harming superiors." Superiors penalizing and executing the people is called "superiors harming subjects." If the people do not violate the law, then superiors will also not apply punishments. Superiors not applying punishments is called "superiors not harming the people." Thus, it says, "The sage still does not harm people." Superiors and subjects do not harm each other and people and ghosts do not injure each other. Thus, it says, "The two of them do not harm each other."

If the people do not dare violate the law, the superior will not use punishments and penalties and will not endeavor to benefit from their business and crafts. If the superior does not use punishments and penalties and will not endeavor to benefit from their business and crafts, the people will flourish. When the people flourish, stores and supplies will grow. The condition of subjects flourishing and stores and supplies expanding is called "possessing power."

In general, "casting a spell" refers to the condition where the *hun* and *po* souls have left and the seminal essence and the spirit are in disorder. With the seminal essence and the spirit in disorder, one lacks power. If ghosts do not cast spells on people, the *hun* and *po* souls will not leave and the seminal essence and spirit are not disordered. When the seminal essence and spirit are not disordered it is called "possessing power." If the superior expands stores and supplies and ghosts do not disorder the seminal essence and spirit, power will be everywhere among the people. Thus, the text says: "For if the two do not harm each other, then powers are exchanged and returned between them."

> 45(1) The Way that can be spoken of is not the unvarying Way. The name that can be named is not the unvarying name. Nameless, it is that which started the myriad things. Named, it is the mother of the myriad things. Therefore, be unvaryingly devoid of desires so that you perceive its subtlety. One unvaryingly possessed of desires thereby sees only what he pines for. These two were merged when they came out. Of different names, both are called "more profound than the profound" and "the doorways to all subtleties."

Commentary: In general, principles of order are distinctions between the square and round, short and long, coarse and fine, hard and brittle. Thus, only when principles of order have been determined can the Way be attained. Thus, determinate principles of order include existence and perishing, life and death, and rise and fall. Indeed, anything that exists and perishes, that lives and dies, and that first rises and then falls cannot be called "unvarying." Only that which came to life with the partition of Heaven and Earth and which will not die or decline until heaven and earth wane and fade can be called "unvarying." Yet what is unvarying is without the remotest change and has no determinate principles of order. Since it has no determinate principles of order, it is not located in an unvarying place and therefore cannot be the Way. The sages observed its mysterious emptiness and employed its pervasive workings, forced the name "Way" on it, so that they could discuss it. Therefore, the text says, "The way that can be spoken of is not the unvarying Way."

14. Ministers who Betray, Encroach upon, or Kill the Ruler [Excerpts]

The lord of men will genuinely exhibit the techniques of the sage and will not follow mundane sayings. He will judge right and wrong according to name and fact, and check what is said by endeavoring to verify it.

In this way, attendants and ministers of the court will understand that deception and lies will afford them no safety. They will certainly say, "If we do not stop our mean and selfish ways and exhaust our efforts and devote our wisdom to serving the ruler, but instead gather together to hatch schemes and make specious assertions of blame and praise, it will be like bearing 10,000 pounds and falling into a bottomless pit and expecting to survive."....

If the ways to safety and danger and so clear, how can the attendants fool the ruler with empty talk? And how will the 100 officials dare to exploit those below them?....

So, the men of the world who pursue mindless studies are to masters of technique what an anthill is to a large mound; they are far apart. And the sage is one who enquires into the facts about right and wrong by examining the conditions of government and disorder. Thus, in governing the state, he sets clear laws and establishes severe punishments, in order to save all living things from chaos, to stop all the calamities of the world, to make the strong stop oppressing the weak and the many stop imposing upon the few, to bring relief to the aged, to enable the young and orphaned to grow up, to stop the borders from being invaded, to endear master and servant to one another, to have father and child take care of one another, and to eliminate the threat of death or being taken prisoner. This is the richest of meritorious achievements.

Stupid people don't understand and see this as cruel. Stupid people certainly want government but hate the means to government. They all hate danger but take pleasure in what brings danger. How do I know? Well, severe punishment and heavy sentences are what people hate but are what brings government to the state. Pity and mercy for the people and light punishments and sentences are what the people like but are the means of endangering the state.

The sage's establishment of law in the state cannot but go against the world and follow the Way and its power. Those who understand this favor rightness and go against the common ways.[373] Those who don't understand this go against

---

[373] One must be very careful when considering whether to accept this statement of radicalism. In the 20th Century, its acceptance caused many millions of innocents to have been unjustly murdered in China (approximately 12 million), the Soviet Union (approximately 15 million), Germany (approximately 18 million, not counting Germany's approximately 25 million foreign victims), Cambodia (approximately 1.5 million), and elsewhere, not to mention the millions upon millions brutally injured, imprisoned, and otherwise deprived of liberty and the chance of leading good lives. Consider the conservative alternative formula: maintain common ways and values unless one of them proves faulty, based on error, or inconsistent with the others; then change only that faulty way and no

rightness and favor the common ways. Those who understand it are few in this world, which is why rightness is rejected.

42. Questioning Mr. Tian [Excerpts]

The reason why I have given up the teachings of the former kings and gone with the teachings I uphold is that I take the establishment of law and technique and the enactment of standards and codes as the way to benefit the masses. Thus, not to fear the threats of calamity at the hands of a disorderly ruler or benighted superior and to persist in thinking of how to spread profit and advantage over the people are the practice of humanity and wisdom.

54. Psychology [Excerpts]

The sage governs the people by taking stock of fundamentals, not by following their desires. He seeks only to benefit the people and nothing more. Therefore, his administering punishments to them is not because he hates them but because he loves them. When punishment prevails, the people are tranquil. When rewards are plentiful, scoundrels arise. Therefore, in governing the people, the prevalence of punishment is the foundation of government, while the abundance of rewards is the condition for disorder.... If you want to institute law but have a problem with changing traditions, then there will be no way to bring government to the disorder of the people.

---

other, and do so with the minimal upset and harm to the other ways and values.

Suggested Readings

Barcenas, Alejandro, "Han Fei's Enlightened Ruler," *Asian Philosophy* 23(2013): 236-259

Carreiro, Daniel Rodríguez, "The Dao Against the Tyrant: The Limitation of Power in the Political Thought of Ancient China," *Libertarian Papers* 5(2013): 111-152

Flanagan, Owen and Jing Hu, "Han Fei Zi's Philosophical Psychology: Human Nature, Scarcity, and the Neo-Darwinian Consensus," *Journal of Chinese Philosophy* 38(2011): 293-316

Fu, Zhengyuan, *China's Legalists: The Early Totalitarians* (London: Routledge, 1996)

Goldin, Paul R., "Persistent Misconceptions about Chinese 'Legalism,'" *Journal of Chinese Philosophy* 38(2011): 88-104

Goldin, Paul R., "Han Fei's Doctrine of Self-Interest," *Asian Philosophy* 11(2001): 151 – 159

Harris, Eirik Lang, "Constraining the Ruler: On Escaping Han Fei's Criticism of Confucian Virtue Politics," *Asian Philosophy* 23(2013): 43-61

Harris, Eirik Lang, "Aspects of Shen Dao's Political Philosophy," *History of Philosophy Quarterly* 32(2016): 217-234

Harris, Eirik Lang, "Legalism: Introducing a Concept and Analyzing Aspects of Han Fei's Political Philosophy," *Philosophy Compass* 9(2014): 155-164

338

Hutton, Eric, "Han Feizi's Criticism of Confucianism and its Implications for Virtue Ethics," *Journal of Moral Philosophy* 5(2008): 423-453

Ivanhoe, Philip J., "Hanfeizi and Moral Self-Cultivation," *Journal of Chinese Philosophy* 38(2011): 31-45

Liao, W. K., trans., *The Complete Works of Han Fei Tzu* (London: Probsthain, 1939)

Moody, Peter R., "The Legalism of Han Fei-tzu and Its Affinties with Modern Political Thought," *International Philosophical Quarterly* 19(1979): 317-330

Moody, Peter R., "Rational Choice Analysis in Classical Chinese Political Thought: *The Han Feizi*," *Polity* 40(2008): 95-119

Moody, Peter R., "Han Fei in His Context: Legalism on the Eve of the Qin Conquest," *Journal of Chinese Philosophy* 32(2001): 14-30

Wang, Hsiao-po and Leo S. Chang, *The Philosophical Foundations of Han Fei's Political Theory* (Honolulu: University of Hawaii Press, 1986)

Interlude

Buddhism

We now turn our attention to Buddhism. This is a significant change from the classical Chinese philosophy with which we have been occupied. This is analogous to a change China itself made in the first few centuries C.E. as it absorbed Buddhism from a very different society. Let us orient ourselves before we proceed to read any Chinese Buddhist texts.

One of China's first contacts with any developed civilization other than its own was the slow trickling of Buddhism into China beginning in about 100 C.E. and proceeding for the next few hundred years. As anyone who has visited a museum exhibition of Chinese art of the First Millennium C.E. might already have surmised, many Chinese converted to the Indian religion during this period. During the first couple of centuries of the encounter, many Chinese were fascinated by the existence of a sage in a country other than China: Siddhartha Gautama, Shakyamuni Buddha, who lived in the Fifth or Sixth Century B.C.E. Indeed, some Chinese, having trouble coming to grips with the existence of an advanced civilization other than their own, one with its own sages, thought that Shakyamuni was so wise that it must have been the case that the sage Laozi had not died in China but had moved to India and become the Buddha. Over the course of the First Millennium C.E., Buddhism flourished in China as the Chinese developed it in their own ways. Some of these ways included peculiarly Chinese sects of Buddhism, such as Tiantai, Pure Land, and Chan ("Zen"[374] in Japanese and English), which were adopted in Korea or Japan.

---

[374] "Zen" is now an English word derived from Japanese. In its nontechnical sense, it refers to the particular school of Buddhism which was transmitted

This development of Chinese Buddhism is a very long and rich story which we cannot explore here.[375] In this book we will instead examine a few exemplary Chinese Buddhist texts. It would be good if you were already well acquainted with Buddhism in its original Indian form. But I can't assume that. Nor would it be a good idea for me to provide a thorough introduction to Indian Buddhism here. But we can let the following thumbnail sketch of it suffice. It will also give you a smattering of basic Sanskrit Buddhist terms which should come in handy in your reading.

The Basics of Buddhism

The gist of the teaching of the Buddha, passed down in scriptures purporting to be his words (skt.: *sutras*), is that everything is deeply disappointing[376] and that one can escape the disappointment through morally upright living and by coming to see that many or perhaps all of the things in the world which we take to be real and independently existing things with natures of their own, simply are not real or existent, or at least not in any strong senses of those terms. The reason things do not have the ontological status we suppose they do is that they do not exist independently of their causes.

Ordinary people – those who have not achieved enlightenment about the negligible degree of reality that things of the world have - are under the impression that things really exist, having selves or natures independently of any other things. Ordinary people might acknowledge that things have material, component, or constituent causes, that they come to

---

from China to Japan and which is called "Chan" in Chinese. In this book, I will use the term "Chan" in order to be precise.

[375] The book by Kenneth Ch'en found in the suggested readings listed at the end of this interlude is a good place to investigate this story further. After that, if you want more, proceed to the book by Erik Zürcher listed there.

[376] "Deeply disappointing" is how I translate the Sanskrit term *duhkha*. You will commonly see it translated as "suffering."

be in dependence on other things, and that they cease to be as a result of other things. But they don't recognize that this acknowledgement is inconsistent with their belief that things have real being, and they don't see that they hold these two inconsistent beliefs. They crave satisfaction of their desires for some of the things which they suppose are independently real. But the objects of these desires are always ultimately disappointing precisely because of their ephemerality, their lack of the real being or essence which they seemed to have when they were longed for.

To this diagnosis of the human predicament the Buddhists also attached a mythology of reincarnation, according to which each person lives many consecutive lives. But instead of a real soul persisting through the succession of lives, there was a stream of desires, impressions, and good and bad deeds resulting, by the law of *karma*, in the consequence of reward and retribution, respectively, in the subsequent stream of experience. This reincarnation and retribution was based on desire and the illusion that there is a self, all of this coming to an end, called *nirvana*, when the desire is subdued and the illusion eradicated.

For this reason, the Buddha taught that it is especially important to see that even one's own person is not real, or at least not real in any strong sense.[377] The human being is just a composite of body (physical matter and form), consciousness, sense perception, feeling, and volitions. These the Buddha called the five *skandhas*, which means "aggregates," implying that each of us is nothing more than an aggregation of primitive components or materials. Aside from the five *skandhas* there is

---

[377] If it isn't clear to you that "real" and "exists" can have a strong or weak sense, I share your misgivings. But in order to understand Buddhism, suppose for the moment that they do. Also, consider the following object. Its components are the three largest objects on your desk, for example the pen, the coffee cup and your arm. We don't have a name for such an odd object, yet that's what it is. This object's components are exchanged for others over time, of course; they might even come and go from moment to moment. We might like to say that such an object is "real" in some weak sense, but certainly not in the strong sense that the coffee cup is real.

no self. And yet any human being thinks of himself as having a real self that is neither the same as any of these component parts nor the same as just their aggregate. This is an illusion causing striving and, sooner or later, deep disappointment. This point is the Buddha's teaching of *anatman*, literally "no-self." It is based on the idea of "dependent origination," according to which the putative self, as well as most or perhaps all other ordinary objects, comes about and ceases to exist in dependence on other things.

Buddhism takes a middle way between nihilism (the view that nothing exists[378]) and the view that things have real existence. You might wonder whether there is any semantic space between "existing" and "not existing." Does the Buddhist view accept that things exist albeit not independently of other things? It is not easy to pin down exactly what is meant by this middle path. Buddhists themselves have argued and deliberated over the point for thousands of years. Possibly, the Buddha meant that the truth is inexpressible. It may be that he wasn't particularly concerned with the clarity of any metaphysical view he may have espoused but rather was using his arguments about reality only in order to help people to break through their illusions about reality. Having obtained the wisdom (skt.: *prajña*) of this disillusionment, they would be able to avoid the deep disappointment that would otherwise have awaited them – an escape known as *nirvana* – regardless of what the best positive theory about the nature of reality should be. But this wisdom would only be negative, in the sense of knowledge of what is not the case. It would not embody any well-defined metaphysical positions. It would be the disillusionment that counts.

The metaphysical views of Buddhism were married to practical teachings in addition to the aforementioned upright living. Central to Buddhism is meditation. In meditation the practitioner is able to relinquish the mental habit of attributing

---

[378] "Nihilism" in another perhaps more common sense means that nothing is of value.

reality to things and clinging to them. These habits are so deeply ingrained in us that we cannot simply relinquish them by following philosophical arguments any more than a person experiencing a hallucination can easily relinquish his belief about what he perceives by listening to arguments proving that he is having a hallucination. The philosophical arguments are part of the process of attaining wisdom, but the meditation is also necessary. There is a neurocognitive lower level at which the false beliefs persist and where they must be eradicated by practical and noncognitive techniques. Indeed, it may be that the noncognitive element of Buddhist wisdom (*prajña*) dovetails with the possibility that the metaphysical view the Buddha espoused about the ontological status of things was, as noncognitive, inexpressible.

There is one more point to clarify. Does Buddhism not attribute reality to the fundamental components of selves and other non-real objects? Are the five *skandhas* real according to the Buddha? Or, if my coffee cup is not real according to Buddhism, then are the component parts (skt.: *dharma*[379]) to which Buddhism reduces it? This question is up for grabs and there were several schools of thought devoted to analyzing it: Abhidharma schools.[380] Some Abhidharma schools held that these ultimate constituents are real and not themselves ephemeral or unreal in some sense.[381] Indian Abhidharma scholasticism devoted enormous quantities of intellectual energy over several centuries to listing and explaining the roughly one hundred *dharmas* which some of its members held to be real.

On the other hand, the Mahayana School of Buddhism answers the question by denying that these *dharmas* are real. Mahayana ("Greater Vehicle") Buddhism unequivocally

---

[379] N.B., the Sanskrit term *dharma* has two meanings in Buddhist texts: 1. The "teaching" of the Buddha. 2. These fundamental constituents of all things.

[380] *Abhidharma* means "higher-order analysis of the Buddhist teaching."

[381] See the chapters on Abhidharma in the Liu and Sidirits books in the list of suggested readings at the end of this interlude.

maintained that everything was empty, where "empty" (skt.: *sunya*) was a technical term denoting a middle path between realism and nihilism which we have just discussed. In China, while many early students of Buddhism became quite well versed in Abhidharma, Mahayana flourished. Two important philosophical schools of Mahayana, which we will study in their Chinese forms, were developed in the First Millennium C.E. in India. The first is Madhyamaka, the school devoted to arguing for emptiness. The second is Yogacara, the school associated with the position that objects are empty and also "just mind" or "mind only" in some sense, rather than existing independently of mind. Both of those Mahayana schools flourished in China.

That is our thumbnail sketch of Indian Buddhism. If you have time to get a deeper understanding of the topic, please explore the suggested readings listed below. For the moment, I would suggest the following considerations before we turn back to China. Buddhism rests upon the premise that life is deeply disappointing. One might object that this premise is false if it is possible that there are people who lead good lives. It may be that life is very difficult and that many lives turn out poorly. But if it is reasonable to make an attempt to create a good life for oneself, and if it sometimes turns out that people succeed in making good lives for themselves, then Buddhism has taken a wrong turn from the very beginning, and its teaching would discourage and divert people from making efforts to make good lives for themselves. As for the metaphysical claims Buddhism makes about the unreality of things, we will consider those in the next chapter.

Buddhism in China

Before we move to our readings in Chinese Buddhism, let us get a bird's-eye view of it. Chinese Buddhism, like Indian Buddhism, is a vast field of study. In this introductory reader we will examine texts from four representative streams of

Mahayana Buddhism in China: Chinese Madhyamaka, Chinese Yogacara, Huayan (literally "flower garland"), and Chan. The Huayan and Chan schools were not found in Indian Buddhism but were inspired by Indian Buddhist texts. The Huayan School concerned itself with explaining the interdependence of things as an entailment of each thing in the world of all other things in the world. Chan concerned itself primarily with attaining enlightenment through simple meditative techniques. All four schools shared concerns; for instance emptiness and meditation were important to all four. The readings in the three chapters that follow will acquaint you with this field.

As I suggested above, the change in China comprising its embrace of Buddhism was remarkable. Think of ancient China suddenly seeing monasteries, monks, and Buddhist scholars assiduously studying the Buddhist *sutras* with no modern transportation or communication and with a deep linguistic divide between Chinese and Sanskrit. One might wonder what sort of a thing Chinese Buddhism turned out to be. Whereas Indian Buddhism had to do with cessation of desires, *karma*, and extinction in *nirvana*, you will read, in the chapters below, key texts in Chinese Buddhism which seem to echo ideas and linguistic structures of non-Buddhist classical Chinese texts which you have read in previous chapters. For instance, in Chapter 8, you will read an essay by the Chinese monk Sengzhao which says,

> [W]isdom has a mirror which penetrates the profound, but there are no cognitions in it. The spirit has a function of responding to occasions but it has no intentions. That the spirit has no intentions is why it can rule its domain. That wisdom has no cognitions is why it can mysteriously illuminate what is behind mundane events.

The rhythm and sense here remind one of the *Dedaojing*, even though Sengzhao's essays were noted precisely for marking a point at which Chinese Buddhist scholars, having spent over one hundred years becoming aware of places in which they had forced Buddhism into a Daoist mold, had finally turned a corner and begun to understood Buddhism on its own terms. Yet, can't one understand a thing on its own terms and explain it in one's own? Indeed, it would seem that if one can explain a thing only in its own vocabulary, translation being impossible, then one might suspect that that thing is a private self-referential language game with no genuine meaning outside of itself. However, the cases will grow more extreme as you read on. In Chapter 10 the Chinese monk Huangbo, living some four centuries after Sengzhao, responds to a question about Indian Buddhist doctrine as follows.

> What's the point of explaining such creeping weeds! How can we discuss what is fundamentally pure with bogus words? Just being without any mental states is what we mean by 'undefiled wisdom.' Every day whether walking or standing, sitting or lying, and in every word you utter, in your comportment toward things just do without clinging to their existence.... Most of you students of Chan are attached to all the sounds and forms. Why don't you be like me and let each mental state be empty and be gone, gone as if it were a rotten log or a rock, gone as if it were cold ashes or a dead fire?

Having read much of the *Zhuangzi*, you should hear echoes of that text in this passage. Even more at a distance from Buddhism's Indian roots is the record of Huangbo's student, Linji, which, from which we will read in Chapter 10 passages such as the following.

> Dayu grabbed [Lingji] and said, "What a bed-wetting little devil! Coming here asking whether you're at fault or not! And now even saying that there's not much to Huangbo's Buddha Dharma! What sense did you make of it? Speak! Speak!"
> [Linji] punched Dayu three times in the ribs.

Over the course of the last few decades, there has been some debate among academics about what Chinese Buddhism is. Is it a misunderstanding or misshapen form of Indian Buddhism? Or was it a direct and undistorted transmission of the pure meaning of Buddhism, from the intention of the Buddha himself through to the Tang and Song dynasties across 1,500 years and generations of faithful master-disciple relations, with no embellishment at all? I would propose that Chinese Buddhism is neither of these things.

If the Buddha had something very profound to say about human beings and the nature of reality, and if what he had to say were at least in part interestingly true, then it might be that the Chinese would develop this idea by saying new things about it, things of their own, other than exactly what the Buddha said. And if that were so, then it might be that they neither simply copied it literally nor misrepresented it. Would we want to say that recent studies of atomic nuclei were unfaithful to insights made by Mendeleev in the Nineteenth Century or by physicists of the early Twentieth Century? They would be very different, after all. Would we want to say that the *Sermons* of Bishop Joseph Butler were either a misunderstanding of the Bible or an unadulterated, unembellished restatement of the Bible? Probably not. As you read through the texts in the pages that follow, ideas that seem either Daoist, somehow Chinese, or unrelated to Buddhism might upon further consideration turn out to be developments of original Buddhist ideas in ways that anyone with any esteem for those ideas would deem to be loyal extensions of them. To split hairs in determining which traditionally esteemed Chinese Buddhist thinker fell short of accurately understanding original Buddhist doctrine when the Buddha himself may have held that the ultimate core of his teaching was not conveyable in words is probably not likely to be a viable academic exercise. Of course, it does not make sense to suppose that anything at all is Buddhism, including points of view that are clearly inconsistent with what the Buddha taught; not everything is Buddhism. But it is not the case that Buddhist ideas cannot be

varied and widely scattered across a vast field of intellectual endeavors intended to explain a very few core teachings, especially if those teachings really hit on deep truths. It is precisely because Buddhism in India hit upon some profound truths that Buddhism was able to develop and change in Chinese hands; it is because Buddhism has an essence that it can develop in various ways. On the other hand, if what the Buddha taught was not even in part true, then neither Chinese Buddhism nor Indian Buddhism is moored to any truths. In that case, there is no fact of the matter about whether a peculiarly Chinese school of Buddhism is authentically Buddhist or not, and the question isn't even interesting to begin with.[382]

Suggested Readings

Carpenter, Amber, *Indian Buddhist Philosophy* (London: Rutledge, 2014)

Ch'en, Kenneth, *Buddhism in China: A Historical Survey* (Princeton: Princeton University Press, 1964)

Conze, Edward, *Buddhist Scriptures* (London: Penguin, 1959)

Conze, Edward, *Buddhist Thought in India: Three Phases of Buddhist Philosophy* (London: George Allen & Unwin, 1962)

---

[382] If you're interested in pursuing these matters, then you might consider reading Robert H. Sharf, *Coming to Terms with Chinese Buddhism* (Honolulu: University of Hawaii Press, 2005), Bernard Faure, *Unmasking Buddhism* (New York: Wiley-Blackwell, 2000)), Ray Grigg, *The Tao of Zen* (New York: Tuttle, 1994), and James D. Sellmann, "A Belated Response to Hu Shih and D.T. Suzuki," *Philosophy East and West* 45(1995): 97-104, as well as the books by McRae, Grigg, Welter, and Heine found below in the list of suggested readings at the end of the chapter on Chan.

Gethin, Rupert, *The Foundations of Buddhism* (Oxford: Oxford University Press, 1998)

Hagen, Steve, *Buddhism Plain and Simple* (Boston, Tokyo: Tuttle, 1997)

Garfield, Jay, *Engaging Buddhism: Why It Matters to Philosophy* (Oxford: Oxford University Press, 2015)

Liu, Ming-wood, "Early Buddhism as a Religious Teaching Centering on Praxis," "The Abhidarmika Schools and the Emergence of Scholastic Buddhism," and "The Advent of Mahayana Buddhism and the Teaching of the *Prajñaparamita-sutras*" in *Madhyamaka Thought in China* (Leiden, New York, Köln: E.J. Brill, 1994), pp. 1- 26.

Rahula, Walpola, *What the Buddha Taught* (New York: Grove Press, 1974)

Schumann, H. W., *The Historical Buddha: The Times, Life and Teaching of the Founder of Buddhism* (New York: Penguin, 1990)

Sidirits, Mark, *Buddhism as Philosophy* (Indianapolis: Hackett, 2007)

Warren, Henry Clarke, *Buddhism in Translations*, 1906 (various editions)

Williams, Paul, Anthony Tribe, and Alexander Wynne, *Buddhist Thought: A Complete Introduction to the Indian Tradition* (London: Routledge, 2013)

Williams, Paul, *Mahayana Buddhism: The Doctrinal Foundations* (London: Rutledge, 1989/2008)

Zürcher, Erik, *The Buddhist Conquest of China* (Leiden: Brill, 2007)

8

Chinese Madhyamaka

Obviously it's Chinese Madhyamaka. What other kind of Madhyamaka would there be in a Chinese philosophy reader? Yet, I wanted to emphasize the distinction from the Indian original. The story of the absorption of Buddhism by the Chinese in the First Millennium C.E. is fascinating, and the Chinese acceptance of Madhyamaka Buddhism is an interesting part of the story. The Chinese had to bridge the linguistic gap between Chinese and Sanskrit and to grasp this abstruse philosophical doctrine from the vantage point of one steeped in Daoist philosophy. In this chapter we will witness the achievement of a breakthrough in understanding by a noted early Fifth Century writer, one who stood at the point where the Chinese, after about two centuries of effort, were beginning to get a good grasp of Buddhism, and Madhyamaka in particular, albeit in their own terms.

As we saw in the interlude on Buddhism, Madhyamaka Buddhism is the school of Buddhist thought devoted to arguing that all things are empty. Emptiness here means lack of intrinsic nature, an ontological status somehow lying between intrinsic reality and nothingness. This is the sense of the name "*madhyamaka*", which means "middle way." The Chinese procured Indian Madhyamaka philosophical texts beginning in the Third Century C.E., finally adopting three of these as most important: two works by Nagarjuna (fl. c. 200 C.E.) and one by Aryadeva (fl. c. 250 C.E.)[383] The *Sanlun* ("Three-Treatise")

---

[383] These included Nagarjuna's *Mulamadhyamakakarika*, or *Fundamental Verses on the Middle Way*, which, when combined in a Chinese version with commentary by an unidentified author whose name translates as "Blue Eyes," was called the *Zhonglun* or *Middle Treatise*. The other two texts

School of Chinese Buddhism was therefore the principle representation of the Madhyamaka School in China, especially as later expounded by the Tang Dynasty monk, Jizang (549-623 C.E.) These treatises were translated in the late Fourth Century by one of the great transmitters of Buddhism to China, Kumarajiva (334-413 C.E.), with the assistance of his students. In this chapter, we will read of the attempt by one of the disciples of Kumarajiva to explain Madhyamaka ideas. This is the writer I alluded to in the preceding paragraph, Sengzhao (384-414 C.E.)

In order to have a complete picture of Chinese Madhyamaka, one would have to come to a reasonably good understanding of both Indian Madhyamaka and Daoism, and then take the time to discern the extent to which Chinese madhyamikas[384] came to understand and explain the former and made creative use of the latter in doing so. Here we don't have the time to discuss Indian Madhyamaka deeply and must introduce ourselves almost directly to the Chinese Madhyamaka texts. But let us at least scratch the surface of the Indian origins. As for the Daoist flavor imbuing Chinese interpretations of Madhyamaka, if you have read the preceding chapters on Daoism you will notice this flavor as you move through the readings.[385] Meanwhile, let us take a brief look at Indian Madhyamaka.

Indian Madhyamaka

Consider this section a crash-course introduction to Madhyamaka. The Madhyamaka school of Buddhist philosophy began in India in about 200 C.E. It thrived in the Tibetan Buddhist tradition, and it is alive today even in

---

were Nagarnuna's *Treatise on the Twelve Gates*, along with Aryadeva's *Hundred-Verse Treatise*. See this chapter's list of suggested readings for more on these texts, including several translations.

[384] A Buddhist who subscribes to Madhyamaka is called a "madhyamika."

[385] If you haven't read the two chapters on Daoism recently, you might consider doing so now before proceeding with this chapter.

America and Europe in many European-language books and articles. Madhyamaka history includes the fascinating and abstruse philosophical treatises of the aforementioned Nagarjuna and Aryadeva and also later thinkers such as Candrakirti (600-650 C.E.) The idea of the school is to refute the widely held belief that there are real things, including the real things embraced by earlier schools of Buddhism which reduced ordinary objects to mere aggregates of real component parts. Nagarjuna put forth many arguments for this, and I recommend that you investigate them by reading a translation of his *Fundamental Verses on the Middle Way* listed at the end of this chapter in the suggested readings. We don't have time to delve deeply into them here, but we can briefly get the gist.

Whereas earlier Buddhist thinkers had eliminated most ordinary objects by reducing them to their material causes, Nagarjuna found this to be insufficient, believing that it perpetuated an illusion that the material causes were real and therefore represented an obstacle to the full wisdom (*skt.*: *prajña*) of a buddha about the nature of reality. The gist of his arguments was that the belief that *dharmas* (the components of things) were real or had intrinsically real natures of their own was inconsistent with the belief that they were brought into existence at one time and later ceased to exist. Hence he offered *reductio ad absurdum* arguments to both ordinary people's beliefs and the beliefs of contemporary and earlier Buddhist philosophers. Even the belief that things arise and cease was untenable because it assumed that there was something real that could be created and destroyed. In short, according to Madhyamaka, the belief that all things depend for their existence on various causes and that the belief that they were inherently real were mutually inconsistent and also untenable.[386] Things are, instead, empty (*sunya*).

---

[386] Consider the following, however. If the argument moves from the premise that things arise and cease to the conclusion that they do not really exist, and from there on to the additional conclusion that things do not really arise and cease, then it would seem to undercut its own premise.

Madhyamaka is thus the school of emptiness, providing arguments for this basic Mahayana concept. The concepts "empty" and "middle" try to avoid both positing that anything exists and also the nihilistic stance that nothing exists. Instead, no stance about the ultimate nature of reality is tenable and the ultimate truth is inexpressible, and the Madhyamaka arguments were intended to help Buddhists move toward a vision of the ultimate truth. In sum, madhyamikas offered a variety of arguments of the general aforementioned form in order to support a middling stance toward the ontological status of all things or at least to refute nihilistic and realistic stances. What exactly that middle is has been a matter of some dispute among adherents of the school for over 1500 years. In fact, I'm sure many scholars of Madhyamaka would take issue with some of the sketch which I have just given. But in any case, you have the general gist of it.[387] The point is that following these arguments was supposed to help one move toward *prajña*.

Sengzhao himself can help explain this. Sometime between 404 and 408 C.E. - two centuries after Nagarjuna set forth Madhyamaka - Sengzhao wrote an essay which (we will read) entitled "In Prajña There Are No Cognitions." In a letter to the scholar Liu Yimin, who had asked questions about the essay, Sengzhao explained the Madhyamaka stance as follows.

> ...the *sutra*[388] says, "True *prajña* doesn't attribute existence and doesn't attribute nonexistence. Nothing arises and nothing ceases. It cannot be explained to people. Why? To say it doesn't attribute existence is to say that it doesn't posit that something exists. It is not to say that it posits that something doesn't exist. To say that it doesn't attribute nonexistence is to say that it doesn't posit that something does not exist. It is not to say that it posits that something is not nonexistent. It doesn't attribute existence and doesn't

---

[387] If you have time, read one of the books on Madhyamaka listed in this chapter's suggested readings.

[388] Probably a paraphrase of a passage in the *Prajñaparamita Sutra*.

deny existence. It doesn't attribute nonexistence and doesn't deny nonexistence. This is why Subhuti[389] always explained *prajña* by saying that there was nothing to be explained. This is the Way that does away with language.

So, Madhyamaka intends to move from the relatively uncontroversial premise that everything is subject to causation to the conclusion that all things are devoid of intrinsic natures and are not real in the sense that almost everyone – except for a buddha - believes them to be real. The religious soteriology at play here is the Buddhist view that this tendency to believe in the intrinsic reality of things is the root of deep disappointment (skt.: *duhkha*) in life, whereas the wisdom of the insight into the emptiness of things is the key to salvation. And it may be that the soteriology is more important to Madhyamaka philosophy than any metaphysical claim that it uses in service to that soteriology.[390]

The metaphysical claim might be subject to criticism, however. First, is it really the case that things' being subject to causation entails that they do not have natures? This seems to be an invalid inference which you should scrutinize when you have an opportunity to read Nagarjuna's *Fundamental Verses on the Middle Way* and to see whether he shows it to be valid. Second, suppose the argument is for the weaker conclusion that things' being subject to causation entails that they do not have *intrinsic* natures, natures that they have independently of other things. If that is the core Madhyamaka argument, then it doesn't seem to take issue with anything that we non-buddhas believe. Do we believe that things have *intrinsic* reality in some sense of reality independent of all causes? If not, then the argument of Madhyamaka for emptiness may be sound, but its conclusion is trivial and lacking in the momentous force it pretends to have. In other words, Madhyamaka might trade on an ambiguity between things' having natures and really

---

[389] A figure in the *sutra*, a monk closely associated to the Buddha.

[390] Possibly, Madhyamaka makes no positive metaphysical claims but only negative ones, such as "nihilism is false" and "realism is false."

existing, on the one hand, and things' having natures and really existing *independently of anything else*, on the other.

We can parse still further. Notice that "existing independently" is ambiguous. It could mean a thing's existing independently of its causes - either its material causes or the things that created it. It could also mean a thing's existing independently of any mind's perception of it. The latter meaning will come up again in the next chapter, when we read Yogacara texts that take the position that nothing exists externally from mind or minds. It is the former meaning that is relevant in this chapter. But notice that it, too, contains a further ambiguity between logical independence and causal independence. The logical independence of a thing A from another thing B means that it is no contradiction - it is coherent to propose - either that A exists even while B does not or that B exists even while A does not. Now, if Madhyamaka arguments move from the probably tautological premise which we all accept – that nothing exists in causal independence from its causes – to the conclusion that nothing has independent existence or any intrinsic nature of its own, then we might object as follows.

"Intrinsic nature" could easily be construed to refer to a thing's existing and being the sort of thing it is with logical independence, rather than causal independence, from others. For example, it is no contradiction to posit that a thing A (be it oneself, a fish, a rock, or a basketball) exists even though the things which create it do not, or that A exists even though *nothing else in the universe exists*. It may be a false supposition, but it is not self-contradictory. Indeed, it is no contradiction to design, as a thought experiment, a universe in which some object X - for example, a basketball - is the only thing that exists. This thought experiment may show that X has an intrinsically real nature of its own in the sense of logical independence. X might not even be logically dependent on its parts and materials. Although X must have some parts and be composed of some materials in order to exist, it might have existed and it might continue to exist were it made of different parts and materials. This point might recall the ship of Theseus in the reader's mind. But surely we in some cases attribute continuing existence to a thing across a substitution of one of its parts, and there might not be a good reason in Madhyamaka arguments why we should not do so.

You would have to take some time studying Madhyamaka in order to decide these matters. But if you are persuaded that Madhyamaka is indeed trading on an ambiguity and pretending to prove something interesting (that nothing really exists or has a nature) when in fact it has only proved something trivial (that nothing exists or has a nature causally independent of other things), then consider that perhaps there is a psychological claim underlying the Buddhist view, namely that we non-buddhas, deep in our subconscious minds, really do cling to the view that things have reality and nature causally independent of other things. The Buddha taught that we believe we have selves, while in fact each of us has only a body, some sensations and perceptions, some activities, and some consciousness (five *skandhas*), none of which is worthy of being called a "self," due to their impermanence, plurality, and inability to control themselves as a self should. We all believe we have selves but it is very difficult to say satisfactorily what counts as a self or to show that one has a self. We may admit at a certain superficial level of thought that we know we and the things of this world are merely causally dependent, evanescent, and not fully real, but perhaps at a deeper psychological level we don't believe it.

Consider that we coolly acknowledge that people will die. But when a loved one dies we are shocked and overcome by grief, belying this coolness. Melancholy reflections on earlier stages in one's own life, now gone forever and destroyed by change and the passage of time, can evoke a certain despair, disappointment, or even outrage, as if the Buddha were right about the unavoidable pervasiveness of deep disappointment. For, though we deny it, we really do believe at a subconscious level that we are immortal and unchanging. Even the destruction of objects other than people can bring on profound melancholy, as for example when one finds that a charming city or natural area one knew years ago has ceased to exist. All things decay, and that we despise this fact is demonstrated from time to time. The Japanese poet Kobayashi Issa (1763-1828) wrote, "A world of dew is a world of dew. And yet...." In other words, contemplation of the ephemerality of everything can be extremely disquieting and belie one's previous assurances that one has acknowledged it, having laid the proposition to rest as if it were but a trivial tautology lacking any moment whatsoever. Perhaps we are horrified by the confrontation between the ephemerality of things in the world and a deeply seated and cherished belief we have that they are not ephemeral but permanent, independent, and reliable.

In addition to trying to decide whether the aforementioned ambiguity in Madhyamaka undermines its philosophical position, we might also wonder whether, in its ambiguity, Madhyamaka emptiness still manages to skate the thin line of the middle way between nihilism and metaphysical views that posit the reality of things. This tension is another issue on which madhyamikas have spent enormous amounts of intellectual energy over the centuries; it is another issue for you to pursue later if you like.

Sengzhao's Madhyamaka

The foregoing sketch scratches the surface of Madhyamaka. Meanwhile, we must press on to its Chinese interpretation. In any event, we will spend our time with the leaves of Madhyamaka at the tips of the branches that it extended to China. We will not concentrate on the classical period of Chinese Madhyamaka by focusing on Jizang and the Sanlun School but will instead read the earlier roots of it in Sengzhao.[391] He gives us a glimpse into the Chinese

[391] While Jizang's writings would perhaps be the more quintessential example of Chinese Madhyamaka, in comparison to Sengzhao's more archetypical essays, the latter are clearer and more accessible to a beginning reader such as this.

appropriation of Buddhism of the first three centuries of Chinese contact with Buddhism.

Sengzhao enjoyed the *Dedaojing* and the *Zhuangzi* before, upon encountering the *Vimalakirti Sutra*, he converted to Buddhism.[392] A Buddhist well versed in Daoism, he strove to convey the ideas of Buddhism in his essays and yet did so with the aid of many Daoist ideas and turns of phrase.

Rather than focus his essays on Nagarjuna's arguments, Sengzhao takes on the task of describing the wisdom that those arguments are supposed to produce. This difficult task involves explaining the type of wisdom, knowledge, or cognition that has no real object but instead strikes a middle way between a cognition of objects and a nihilistic stance toward objects and does this without violating the principle of noncontradiction. In "Emptiness as Unreality," which we will read below, he shows that he is aware of the peril of violating this principle when he says, "[H]ow can one reconcile oneself to the space between 'exists' and 'does not exist?'" As you can see from the very title of our other reading, "In *Prajña* There Are No Cognitions," the wisdom he describes is a mental state in which there are no cognitions. "Cognitions" are conceptual activities in the mind which are supposed to be able to refer to real objects and which may be expressed in language. This concept of wisdom as a mental state devoid of conceptual activity occupied Chinese Buddhist thinkers for many centuries. It led them to embrace apparent contradictions, such as "noncognitive cognition" or patently false or unintelligible statements, such as that a conscious Buddha "has no mind." As you will see, Sengzhao does not shy away from the problems. He makes a reasonable attempt at resolving them by showing

---

[392] A translation of the *sutra* is listed in the suggested readings at the end of this chapter. Please consult the suggested readings at the end of this chapter in studying the influence of Daoism on Sengzhao's understanding of Buddhism. In particular, consult Ming-wood Liu's chapter on Sengzhao and the article by Mingran Tan. See also Kenneth Ch'en's book mentioned in the previous chapter's list of suggested readings.

360

the idea of Buddhist wisdom not to be contradictory or patently false.

In this chapter I would like to suggest that there is a fairly straightforward way of rendering the notion of Buddhist wisdom coherent and cogent. I will expand upon this way of understanding it again in the chapter on Chan Buddhism, but for now, consider the following. Buddhist wisdom involves meditation in which one makes one's mind still and conceptual activity ceases even though one remains conscious. In this state, one is able to comprehend or become aware of the world without subjecting it to any concepts, and therefore without positing that anything in it exists or does not exist. This might be described as a "mental state without mental states" if we take the term "mental state" to have two senses: conscious awareness, on the one hand, and conceptual activity, on the other.

Consider an analogy. Suppose it were true that we called the waves which we see on lakes and other bodies of water "waters." We might say when a lake had become perfectly calm that the water was without any waters; and we could render this infelicitous formulation coherent by parsing "water" into two senses. Similarly, the conceptual activity of one's mind can subside as waves do, while one remains entirely conscious. Imagine that we were to observe a representation of the mental states of someone who was hooked up to a machine that could represent brainwaves graphically for us on a display screen. Suppose the subject had various sorts of thoughts and these came across as waves in the graphic representation. With each new mental state of the subject, we might ask ourselves, "What mental state is he in now?" We might reply by naming each wave pattern on the graphical display. Then, when the subject went into a meditative state and made his mind very still and devoid of cognitive activity while he remained fully conscious, we might ask ourselves, in view of a flat and wave-free graphical display of his brainwave activity, "What mental state is he in now?" Our reply at first might be, "Well, no mental state at all. Or a mental state without mental states." As before, we could render this utterance coherent by parsing "mental state" into two senses.

Sengzhao himself tries to help resolve the confusion when he says in "In *Prajña* There Are No Cognitions," "It isn't that he has no mental state but that his is the mental state of not having mental states." We can resolve the apparent contradiction by parsing the term "mental state" into two meanings. It can mean "cognitive mental state" and it can mean "consciousness." Given that Buddhist meditation involves consciousness without any of the disruptions of cognitive activity, we could resolve our confusion. Keeping this in mind will help you as you read Sengzhao; it will be even more important in the chapter on Chan where we will discuss it further.

I have only broached these issues with you. Let us take a look at how Sengzhao understands Madhyamaka.

The Readings

Below you will find Sengzhao's essay on Buddhist wisdom, "In Prajña There Are No Cognitions," the appearance of which in about 405 C.E. was a significant event in the history of Chinese Buddhism. The essay was widely read and well received. Kumarajiva himself said that it had hit the mark. There are three other short essays written subsequently by Sengzhao, and I have included one of these here: "Emptiness as Unreality." The other two, "Things Do Not Change" and "Nirvana is Nameless," may be found by consulting the suggesting readings.[393]

---

[393] In reading the following two essays by Sengzhao, the reader will find the chapter on Sengzhao in Ming-wood Liu's book to be helpful. The four essays, together with the correspondence with Liu Yimin, are called the *Zhaolun*, the *Treatises of Zhao*. Readers fond of Zeno-type paradoxes may want to read "Things Do Not Change," in particular, in Robinson's book and in Wing-tsit Chan and Liebenthal's books, as well. Robinson provides a list of Sengzhao's writings on p. 125. The Chinese text of the *Zhaolun* is

Treatises of Sengzhao

In Prajña[394] There Are No Cognitions

Prajña's emptiness and obscurity is due to its being the origin of the Three Vehicles.[395] It is actually one truth without distinctions. Yet, there are numerous theories of it have been prevalent for a long time.

There was a time when the Indian ascetic Kumarajiva, in his youth, entered the great field,[396] tried to get to the nub of it, alone grasped what is outside of words and symbols, and attained the subtle recognition of the level beyond the range of the senses. He reconciled the differing teachings of the land of the Buddha and raised a fresh breeze which he fanned toward the east. He would have carried his light to different lands but he was confined in the land of Liang.[397] In this the Way did not function meaninglessly. When it functions it must have a reason. In 401 C.E. the ruler of Qin invaded that state in order

---

number 1858 in Junjiro Takakusu and Kaigyoku Watanabe, eds., *Taisho Shinshu Daizokyo* (Tokyo: Taisho Issaikyo Kankokai, 1924-35)

[394] I use the Sanskrit word that Sengzhao uses, because there is no good English equivalent; it is a standard technical term which you will encounter in Buddhist scholarship. "Buddhist wisdom" is the meaning of the term. It is the wisdom a person obtains in becoming enlightened to the Buddhist teaching.

[395] The Three Vehicles are the Hinayana, or early Buddhist teachings, as represented by the *sravaka* and *pratyekabuddha* – two "vehicles" or modes of Buddhist practice in which, respectively, the practitioner listens to the sermons of others or analyzes Buddhist philosophy on his own. The third vehicle is the Mahayana teachings as represented by the *bodhisattva*, the "enlightened being" who understands emptiness and has compassion for every being still subject to delusion.

[396] Possibly a euphemism for "Mahayana Buddhism."

[397] Kumarajiva was captured by the Chinese in 383 C.E. in his native Kucha (what is now in Xinjiang), brought to Liang and held captive for eighteen years. During that time he was unable to continue his teaching.

to bring Kumarajiva to Qin.[398] This fate of the North was in accord with prophecy.

The divine King of the Great Qin, whose Way is equal to any of the one hundred kings of old and whose virtuous deeds will affect one-thousand generations after him, perspicaciously executes his affairs and spreads the Way every day. In the final periods, he will be like what people regard as heaven and what the teaching of Shakyamuni will rely upon.

Hence, the King gathered more than five hundred scholar-monks in the Xiaoyao Garden Hall. Interested in the Chinese versions, he helped with the *Vaipulya Sutras*.[399] What he helped set forth is not only a benefit to the current time but also will be a ford and a bridge in future epochs.

Although I hadn't much to offer, I was given a place in this illustrious assembly. I then heard something different, important, and new.

The wisdom of a sage is obscure and fine, deeply hidden and hard to understand, lacking in characteristics or names, and unreachable by language and symbols. Shall I try to festoon what I have in mind by entrusting it to wild language? How can I describe the mind of a sage?[400] But I will try to explain it.

The *Prajñaparamita Sutra* says, "*Prajña* has no characteristics at all.[401] It lacks the characteristics of arising and

---

[398] In 401 C.E. Kumarajiva was brought to Changan, the capital of the Qin Dynasty, and was encouraged to continue his teaching.

[399] These *sutras* include the *Avatamsaka* (*Huayan*) *Sutra*, the *Heart Sutra*, the *Lankavatara Sutra*, the *Lotus Sutra*, and others.

[400] During Sengzhao's time, the generic term "sage," with all its Confucian and Daoist connotations, was used to refer to a buddha. Later Chinese Buddhist texts would use the special term *fo* (Buddha).

[401] The lack of characteristics is a key Buddhist concept. It refers to a things' having no intrinsic nature of its own. According to Madhyamaka, nothing has any intrinsic nature; nothing has any characteristics. The *Prajñaparamita Sutra* is the Mahayana *sutra* stating that all things, including the rudimentary components or *dharmas* to which earlier Buddhist scriptures had reduced all other things, are empty, a proposition for which Madhyamaka was devoted to providing arguments. The sutra is available in translation in Edward Conze, trans., *The Large Sutra on Perfect Wisdom* (Berkeley: University of California Press, 1975).

cessation." The *Daoxing*[402] says, "There is nothing that it cognizes, nothing that it perceives." This describes wisdom's function of illumination. How is it that it has no characteristics and no cognitions? There is simply a cognition which has no characteristics, an illuminating brilliance which is not cognitive. But what is it?

Now, if there is an object of cognition, then there are objects that are not cognized. Since the sagely mental state[403] has no object of cognition, there is nothing that it doesn't cognize.[404] It is a noncognitive cognition, and so we can say that it is cognition of everything. Thus, a *sutra* says, "The mental state of wisdom has no object of cognition, and there is nothing that it doesn't cognize."[405] We may rely on this.

Therefore, the sage empties his mind, makes his illumination full, and always cognizes without really cognizing. Thus he dims his brilliance and covers his light. He has an empty mind that is a mysterious mirror. Hiding his wisdom and suppressing his cleverness, he alone perceives what is most profound.[406]

This being so, wisdom has a mirror which penetrates the profound, but there are no cognitions in it. The spirit has a function of responding to occasions[407] but it has no

---

[402] The *Dasasahasrika Prajñaparamita Sutra*, an early, small version of the *Prajñaparamita Sutra*.

[403] Here I translate the term *xin*, commonly translated as "mind" rather idiosyncratically as "mental state." I do so because, as I have suggested above, it enables us to parse the meanings of the text and resolve what might otherwise be construed as contradictory passages. When we come to the chapter on Chan, I will explain this choice of translation more fully.

[404] A patently invalid inference.

[405] Probably a paraphrase of a passage in the *Visesacinta Brahmapariprccha Sutra*. We see here that Sengzhao, like other Buddhist thinkers, attributes great powers of insight and sound judgement, perhaps even omniscience, to Buddhist wisdom.

[406] See *Dedaojing* 48(3) and 51(7).

[407] "Occasions" (*hui*) refers to states of affairs in which one has the opportunity to act. To respond to these occasions appropriately was by Sengzhao's time already a perennial concern of Chinese philosophy.

intentions. That the spirit has no intentions is why it can rule its domain. That wisdom has no cognitions is why it can mysteriously illuminate what is behind mundane events. Although wisdom penetrates to what is behind mundane events, it never treats those mundane events as nothing. Although spirit has the entire world, it is always in its domain. Therefore, whether looking up or looking down, they are in accord with changes. In receiving them, there is nothing they leave unexamined in their penetration into the profound. And this is without any effort in illuminating them.

These things are what is cognized by a lack of cognition. They are what the spirit of the sage can do. But what sort of thing is it? It is full but does not exist. It is empty but is not nothing. It is something that subsists but cannot be explained.

What makes it a sagely wisdom? When you would speak of its existence, there are no representations or names. When you would speak of its not existing, a sage would with it shine. A sage would with it shine, so although he treats it as empty he nevertheless illuminates it. There are no representations or names, so though he illuminates it he nevertheless treats it as empty. This is why he leads the blind when he moves.

This is the reason that the function of sagely wisdom is unceasing. If you try to find its form and characteristics, it has no delimitation you can get at. This is why Ratnakuta said, "It is with no mental states or intentions that he appears and acts."[408] And the *Prajñaparamita Sutra* says, "Motionless in deep meditation, the Buddha establishes the various *dharmas*."[409] Therefore, the traces of a sage are manifold, but their end is one and the same.

Political power and virtue were of course of particular concern in this regard, as we have seen in the chapters on Confucius, Laozi and Han Feizi.
[408] From the *Vimalakirti Sutra*.
[409] I leave the term "*dharma*" (chn.: *fa*) untranslated here. It is ambiguous. It is a technical term referring to the ultimate components of the universe (which earlier Buddhism had construed as real whereas Madhyamaka Buddhism argued that they were not real.) The term might have been translated as "thing" but this would have lost the technical sense of

366

Hence, prajña can treat things as empty and illuminate them. The ultimate truth can do away with them and cognize them. The myriad movements can go on while being still. And the sage's responses can treat things as nothing and yet act. This is not cognizing and yet spontaneously cognizing, not acting and yet spontaneously acting. What cognition could there be beyond that? What action could there be beyond that?

An objection: The actual mental state of a sage has a special clarity. It illuminates things. He responds and leads without limiting himself to any of them. He moves in accord with the occasion. He illuminates things and therefore his cognition leaves nothing out. He moves in accord with the occasion and therefore on no occasion does he miss any opportunity. Since on no occasion does he miss an opportunity, there must be real occasions. Since his cognition leaves nothing out, there must be real cognitions corresponding to what he cognizes. Since there must be cognitions corresponding to what he cognizes, sagehood doesn't treat cognitions as empty. Since there must be occasions which he treats as occasions, sagehood doesn't treat occasions as empty. There being cognitions and occasions, what does it mean to say that there are no cognitions and there are no occasions? If it is just that he forgets the cognitions and ignores the occasions, then this is just a matter of the sage having no self-interest in his regard for cognitions and occasions and therefore fulfilling his self-interest.[410] This can be described as his not treating his cognitions as his own. How does it mean that he has no cognitions?

Reply: The sage's great deeds are as lofty as heaven and earth, yet he is not benevolent.[411] He is brighter than the sun and moon and still he is dim. How could I say that in not having cognitions he is as blind as wood or stone inside? It's

---

"ultimate component." As noted earlier, the word "*dharma*" also has another meaning: the Buddhist teaching.
[410] See *Dedaojing* 51(7).
[411] See *Dedaojing* 49(5).

just that he differs from people in his spiritual intelligence. This is why you can't define this using ordinary characteristics.

Your idea is to portray the sage as not treating his cognitions as his own and that it was never the case that the sage doesn't have cognitions. Doesn't this misconstrue the sagely mental state and miss the point of the scriptures? Here is why.

The *sutra* says, "Real *prajñā* is as pure as an empty void. It has no cognitions, no vision, no effect and no objective condition."[412] Given this, the cognition is in itself noncognitive. Why does the illumination have to be turned off in order for it to be noncognitive? If it has cognitions which are said to be pure because devoid of any nature, then this doesn't distinguish it from deluded wisdom. The three poisons and four errors would be as pure.[413] Why would we have any special regard for *prajñā*? If it would be for what *prajñā* cognizes that we particularly fancy it, then since what it cognizes is not *prajñā*, it is what it cognizes that was in itself pure while *prajñā* was never pure. There would be no cause to treat *prajñā* as pure and desirable.

So, when the sutra says that *prajñā* is as pure as an empty void, we should take this to mean that its intrinsic nature is truly pure. It is fundamentally devoid of deludedly grasping cognitions. Since it is fundamentally devoid of deludedly grasping cognitions, we can't apply the name "cognitive" to it. Why call only a lack of cognitions by the name "noncognitive"?[414] This cognition is in itself devoid of cognitions. Thus, the sage, by means of prajña, which is devoid of cognitions, illuminates the ultimate truth which is devoid of

---

[412] From the *Prajñāparamita Sutra.*

[413] There is a tacit premise here, commonly accepted by Buddhists, that all things are devoid of any nature. The three poisons are lust, wrath, and foolishness. The four errors are the delusions that our selves and lives are permanent, satisfactory, real, and substantial, rather than ephemeral, disappointing, devoid of selfhood, and empty.

[414] In other words, Sengzhao asks why the term should apply only to things which are not conscious at all when it may be that some people are capable of maintaining conscious awareness without any cognitive activity.

characteristics. In the ultimate truth there is no leaving anything out as the hare and the horse did.[415] There is nothing that prajña does not completely reflect. Therefore, on every occasion it doesn't fall short. In meeting them it posits nothing. It is devoid of cognition but there is nothing it doesn't cognize.

An objection: Because things have no means of getting themselves across,[416] we establish names in order to get across to things. Although things are not names, ultimately there are things which can be named and which correspond to these names. This is why having its name, we look for a thing and the thing cannot hide. Yet, you have stated that the sagely mental state is devoid of cognitions.

You also said, "There is nothing it does not cognize." But a principle states that the noncognitive is not cognitive, and the cognitive is not noncognitive. This is common in the teaching of names.[417] It is a fundamental principle of formulating statements. But what you have stated would make them one and the same in the sagely mental state, differing only in the written meanings. When I look for this truth in the scriptures, I do not find such a coincidence. How so? If "cognitive" applies to the sagely mental state, then "noncognitive" doesn't describe it. And if "noncognitive" applies to the sagely mental state, then "cognitive" doesn't describe it. If neither of the two apply to it, then there is nothing to say about it.

---

[415] In previous Buddhist texts, the hare and the horse were unable to plumb the depths, whereas the elephant with its long trunk was able. See p. 72 of the volume by Liebenthal listed in the suggested readings.

[416] I have preferred "to get across" here, where "communicate" would have been clearer, because I wanted to preserve some of the connotation of the Chinese term *tong*.

[417] The teaching of names or "School of Names" refers to the various efforts of Chinese philosophers beginning in the Third Century B.C.E. to clarify concepts in logic and language. Here we see something like the principle of noncontradiction being raised in the objection. See the interlude on Analytic Philosophy in Ancient China and "The Rectification of Names" in the readings by Xunzi.

Reply: The sutra says, "The meaning of prajña is unnamable, inexplicable, not existing and not being nonexistent, not substantial, and not empty."[418] Being empty, there is nothing it fails to illuminate, but in illuminating it doesn't fail to be empty. This is a nameless teaching. It is not something that can be expressed in language. Although language cannot express it, nevertheless, without language there is no way to get it across. Therefore, the sage spends all of his time speaking of it but does not express it. Here I will try to describe it to you in wild language.[419]

The sagely mental state is very subtle and wonderful. It has no characteristics. You can't treat it as existing. Yet, its functioning being nevertheless active, you cannot treat it as nonexistent. Since you can't treat it as nonexistent, sagely wisdom subsists in it. Since you can't treat it as existent, the teaching of names reaches its limit here. Therefore, in saying "cognitive" I don't mean it to be cognitive. I only want to let its reflectivity come across. "Not cognitive" is not not cognitive. I only want to use this to describe its characteristics. I describe the characteristics but do not mean it to be nonexistent. I let the reflectivity come across but do not mean it to be existent. It does not treat things as existing. Therefore, it is cognitive and yet noncognitive. It does not treat them as nonexistent. Therefore, it is noncognitive and yet cognitive. Hence, in being cognitive, it is noncognitive; in being noncognitive, it is cognitive. Do not let the linguistic difference imply any difference in the sagely mental state.

An objection: The ultimate truth is very abstruse. Without wisdom you can't fathom it. Sagely wisdom's prowess is thus obvious. This is why a sutra says, "Unless you obtain *prajña*, you can't see the absolute truth." The ultimate truth is thus the object of *prajña*. It is of this object that one seeks wisdom. So, wisdom is cognitive.

---

[418] Likely a paraphrase of a passage in the *Prajñaparamita Sutra*.
[419] An allusion to Zhuangzi. See p. 255 above.

Reply: You seek wisdom by means of an objective condition, but wisdom is noncognitive. How so? The *Prajñaparamita Sutra* says, "Consciousness unconditioned by an object is called 'not perceiving." It also says, "The five *skandhas*[420] are clean and pure. *Prajña* is clean and pure." *Prajña* cognizes and the five *skandhas* are what is cognized. What is cognized is the objective condition. Now, the cognizing and what is cognized exist in dependence on one another, and being in dependence on one another, do not exist. These being in dependence on one another and hence not existing, it is not the case that as things they exist. As things exist in dependence on one another, it is not the case that as things they do not exist. Because it is not the case that as things they do not exist, they come to act as objects. But because it is not the case that as things they exist, they cannot really amount to objects. It is because they cannot really amount to objects that there is a reflection of the objects that is noncognitive. They come to act as objects, which is why the cognizing and the object come to be in dependence on one another. This is why the cognitive and the noncognitive arise from what is cognized. Here is why.

As wisdom cognizes what is cognized, it groups certain characteristics and so we call it "cognitive." But since the ultimate truth has no characteristics in itself, how can real wisdom be cognitive? The reason that this is so is that what is cognized is not cognized; what is cognized comes about due to cognition. As what is cognized gives rise to cognition, so, too, does cognition give rise to what is cognized. What is cognized is dependently arisen and, as such, is a conditioned *dharma*. Since it is a conditioned *dharma*, it is not ultimately real. Since it is not ultimately real, it is not the ultimate truth. This is why

---

[420] Recall that these are the fundamental components which in aggregate cause there to seem to be a human self, according to Buddhism: body, sensation, perception, activity, and consciousness.

the *Zhongguan* says, "Things exist due to causes and conditions. Hence they are not actually real."[421]

What is not due to causes and conditions is ultimately real. Now, the "ultimately real" in "ultimately real truth," since it is ultimately real, is not a conditioned object. Since the ultimately real is not a conditioned object, there is nothing in it that comes about due to an objective condition. This is why the *sutra* says, "I do not see existing *dharmas* that come about without any conditions."[422] Therefore, real wisdom perceives the ultimately real truth without ever grasping for what is cognized. Since this wisdom doesn't grasp for what is cognized, how can wisdom be cognitive? Even so, wisdom is not altogether without cognitions. It's just that the ultimate truth is not what they cognize. So, ultimate wisdom is also noncognitive. Yet, you would seek wisdom by means of an objective condition. And that's why you take wisdom to be cognitive. But the object is not really an object, so how can you find any cognitions?

An objection: You speak of not grasping.[423] We can take this to mean not having cognitions and hence not grasping. Or we can take it to mean to have a cognition and afterwards not to grasp. If it is not having cognitions and hence not grasping, then the sage is as blind as someone a traveling at night and unable to tell black from white. If it is to have cognition and afterwards not to grasp, then cognition is different from not grasping.

Reply: Neither is it a matter of not having cognitions and hence not grasping, nor is it a matter of having cognitions

---

[421] Possibly a quotation from the *Fundamental Verses on the Middle Way* or the *Zhonglun* ("Middle Treatise"), a Chinese Madhyamaka commentary on the former which appeared in 409 C.E. (see footnote 383 above) and which has been translated in the book by Brian Bocking found in the suggested readings.

[422] Possibly a paraphrase of the *Prajñaparamita Sutra.*

[423] Here "to grasp" probably means the cognitive activity of discerning that an object is there and recognizing or believing that it exists.

and afterwards not grasping. In cognition he does not grasp. So, he can have cognition without grasping.

Objection: You speak of not grasping, meaning that the sagely mental state doesn't treat things as things and therefore doesn't grasp them incorrectly. But if he doesn't grasp them, then he doesn't posit anything. And if he doesn't posit anything, then he doesn't correctly correspond to anything. Then, what correctly corresponds to the sagely mental state such that we can say that there is nothing that it doesn't cognize?

Reply: It is as you describe it; this not positing and not correctly corresponding. But since it doesn't correctly correspond, among things there is none to which it doesn't correctly correspond. And as it doesn't posit, among things there is none which it doesn't posit. Among things there is none which it doesn't posit. Hence, it posits without positing. Among things there is none to which it doesn't correctly correspond. Hence, it correctly corresponds without correctly corresponding. This is why the *sutra* says, "He perceives all *dharmas*, yet there is nothing which he perceives."[424]

An objection: It isn't that the sagely mental state cannot posit. It's just that it takes the lack of positing to be what is posited. Hence, in not positing, it corresponds and posits. Therefore, the sutra says, "The ultimate truth is without characteristics and thus *prajña* is noncognitive." This just means that *prajña* doesn't have cognition of anything that has characteristics. If it takes what has no characteristics as not having characteristics, how is this different from the ultimate truth?

Reply: The sage treats what has no characteristics as not existing. How so? If he were to treat what has no characteristics as not having characteristics, then not having characteristics would become a characteristic. Eschewing being in favor of non-being is like avoiding the mountains and cleaving to the river gullies. In neither way will you avoid

---

[424] From the *Prajñaparamita Sutra*.

danger. This is why the man of excellence stays with what exists without treating it as existing and abides with nonexistence without treating it as nonexistence. Although he doesn't grasp at existence and nonexistence, he nevertheless doesn't do away with existence and nonexistence. This is how he harmonizes his radiance with the dust and travail, mingling with the five stations.[425] At rest and repose, he yet comes and goes. Placid and calm, he does nothing, yet there is nothing he leaves undone.[426]

An objection: The sagely mental state, although noncognitive, nevertheless has a way of responding to occasions. This is why that which may be responded to he responds to, and that which may not be responded to he lets be. Therefore, the sagely state of mind at times arises and at times ceases. Would this meet with your agreement?

Reply: Arising and ceasing here pertain to arising and ceasing mental states. But the sage has no mental states. How can arising and ceasing come about in him? Yet, it isn't that he has no mental state but that his is the mental state of not having mental states. And it's not that he doesn't respond. It's that his responding is without any responding.[427] This is how the sage's way of responding to occasions is as true as the course of the four seasons. He simply takes emptiness as the basic substance. There is nothing that counts as arising and nothing that counts as ceasing.

An objection: Sagely wisdom's treating something as not existing and deluded wisdom's treating something as not existing both attribute lack of arising and cessation. So, what is the difference?

---

[425] The five stations are the forms of life one might take during transmigration, according to Buddhism: humans, animals, gods, demons, and hungry ghosts.
[426] An allusion to the *Dedaojing* 48(4).
[427] You could take this to mean something like what Laozi would advise, namely literally doing nothing. Or you could construe it to mean responding without any cognitions, planning, or intentions.

Reply: Sagely wisdom's treating things as nonexistent is noncognitive. Deluded wisdom's treating things as nonexistent includes cognitions about not existing. Although the nonexistence is the same, the reasons they treat things as nonexistent differ. Here is why.

The sagely mental state is empty and still. It has no cognitions that attribute nonexistence. So, we may say that it is noncognitive. We wouldn't speak of it has having cognitions of nonexistence. Deluded wisdom has cognitions. So, it has cognitions which attribute nonexistence. We can speak of them as cognitions of nonexistence. We don't say they are noncognitive.

The nonexistence of cognitions is prajñā's treating things as nonexistent. Cognition of nonexistence is the nonexistence attained in the ultimate truth. Therefore, when we compare prajñā and the ultimate truth, in speaking of their activities, then they are the same and yet different. When we speak of their stillness, we would say they were different and yet the same. They are the same, and so there are no mental states dividing one from the other. They differ and so they do not err in their illuminative activity. So, these two similar things are the same in differing, and these two things are different in being the same. Here is why.

Inside there is a uniquely shining brilliance. Outside there is the substance of the myriad things. The myriad things, although having substance, nevertheless cannot be reached without illumination. It is this relation between inner and outer that constitutes their illuminative activity. This being the case, what isn't construed to be all the same in sagehood is the activities. Inside, although it illuminates, it has no cognitions. Outside, although there is substance, there are no characteristics. The inner and the outer are quiescent. In their relation they are both nonexistent. This being the case, what can't be differentiated in sagehood is the quiescence.

Therefore, when the sutra says, "The various things do not differ,"[428] how can this mean that we must stretch the duck's legs and shorten the crane's, reduce the mountains and fill up the valleys and only then have there be no difference? Actually they differ in not differing. Thus, although they differ, they do not differ. Thus, the sutra says "How strange, World-Honored One, amidst the various non-differing things to explain that the various things differ." It also says, "*Prajña* does not attribute the characteristic of unity to the various things, nor attribute the characteristic of difference to them." This is so.

An objection: You have said, "When we speak of its activity, we construe these as different. When we speak of its stillness, we construe them as the same." But how can you tell that in *prajña* there is a difference between activity and stillness?

Reply: The activity is the stillness; the stillness is the activity.[429] Activity and stillness are in substance one. They come from the same place but differ in name.[430] There is no inactive stillness which is superior to the activity. Therefore, the darker the wisdom, the brighter the illumination. The clearer the spirit, the more active the response. Why would you speak of a difference between dark and bright or calm and active? Thus the *Established Sayings* says, He does not act but

---

[428] From the *Prajñaparamita Sutra.*
[429] In *Language, Truth and Logic*, A. J. Ayer, having picked a passage at random from F. H. Bradley's *Appearance and Reality*, wrote,

> [S]uch a metaphysical pseudo-proposition as "The Absolute enters into, but is itself incapable of, evolution and progress," is not even in principle verifiable. For one cannot conceive of an observation which would enable one to determine whether the Absolute did, or did not, enter into evolution and progress.... [The utterance] has no literal significance.

It is appropriate to view the various metaphysical claims made in the texts presented in this reader with skepticism especially if they appear to be abstruse.
[430] See *Dedaojing* 45(1).

goes beyond acting." Ratnakuta says, "He has no mental states or conceptual activity, but there is nothing he doesn't intuitively know."[431] These passages speak of the perfect spirit and the ultimate wisdom, of what is beyond the reach of symbols. With these explanations of what I have written, you can understand the sagely mental state.

Emptiness as Unreality[432]

Now to treat of the void in which nothing arises. It is, one might say, the subtle abode of the mysterious mirror of nirvana. It is the origin and end of all existing things. Without a sagely brilliance and a penetrating grasp, how can one reconcile oneself to the space between "exists" and "does not exist"? This is why the perfect man merges his spiritual mind with the limitless. Limits being unable to constrain him, his aural and visual faculties reach their utmost in seeing and hearing. Sound and form cannot control him. How could we not take this to mean that due to things' being empty in themselves, things cannot reduce the brilliance of his spirit? This is why the sage goes with the true mental state and follows the natural principles,[433] so that there is no constraint which he cannot move beyond. He keeps to the one energy[434] in observing events. Thus, he fits right in with whatever he encounters. Because there is no constraint which he cannot move beyond, he can make the murky and confused become clear. Because he fits right in with whatever he encounters, he attends to particular things in a unifying way.

---

[431] From the *Vimalakirti Sutra*.

[432] The title (chn.: *Buzhen Kong*) means that the term "emptiness" has a technical sense in Buddhism, referring to the idea that things are "empty" of real existence. Sengzhao explains the title toward the end of the essay. He is introducing his audience to a technical Buddhist usage of a word of which they already know non-technical meanings.

[433] "Natural principles" translates *li*, which we have seen before as "pattern."

[434] This is *qi* (energy, breath).

This being so, the myriad phenomena, although distinguished, cannot be differentiated in themselves. Since they cannot be differentiated in themselves, we know that phenomena are not real phenomena. Since phenomena are not real phenomena, although they are phenomena they are not phenomena. Therefore, both things and one's self have the same root. "Is" and "is not" are of one energy.

This is abstruse, subtle, obscure and hidden - certainly unfathomable to the ordinary sensibility. This is why when current discussions come to the school of emptiness, everyone disagrees. But if everyone tries to reach agreement through the disagreements, is there anything for them to agree upon? In the end, the various theories compete and are in fundamental disagreement. Some examples:[435]

Those who maintain the "emptiness of mind." They do away with mental states in confronting the myriad things. But they have not yet done away with the myriad things. They get the idea of spiritual stillness right, but they overlook the emptiness of things.

Those who maintain "It is just form."[436] They make it clear that form is not in itself form. So, although it is form it also is not form. So, to say "form," while this indicates the form which "is just form," why reserve this term for an occasion when we treat form as form?[437] They are correct in saying that form is not in itself form. But they do not grasp what it is for form not to be form.

Those who maintain "fundamental nonexistence."[438] They are partial to nonexistence. Each and every thing they say

---

[435] In what follows Sengzhao discusses competing Chinese interpretations of Madhyamaka. You will find the details of these in Appendix I of the book by Liebenthal listed in this chapter's suggested readings.

[436] From the *Heart Sutra*: "Emptiness is just form." Form (chn.: *se*, skt.: *rupa*) means physicality, materiality, substantiality.

[437] In other words, why make the distinction between emptiness and substance to begin with?

[438] This Daoist term (*benwu*) was matched to the Buddhist concept of emptiness during the early stages of the introduction of Buddhism in which attempts were made to "match concepts" (*geyi*). It took Chinese Buddhists

serves nonexistence. Thus, to say "does not exist" means that existence is just nonexistence, while "is not nonexistent" means that nonexistence is nonexistent. However, in the fundamental meanings of these phrases, they just indicate that to say "does not exist" means "does not really exist" and "is not nonexistent" means "is not really nonexistent." Why suppose that a nonexistence doesn't exist when there is something here? Or that a nonexistence is not nonexistent when there is nothing there? This way of speaking on the part of those who like nonexistence[439] – how can we say that it coheres with the facts or with the essence of things?

Now, if you treat something which is a thing as a thing, then what you treat as a thing may be treated as a thing. But if you treat something which is not a thing as a thing, then although you treat it as a thing, it is not a thing. Therefore, things do not, merely by being named, have substance, and names do not, merely by positing things, get to reality. Therefore, the ultimate truth is separately quiescent and beyond the teaching of names.

Yet, someone will ask, "Can language discuss it?" So, I mustn't be closed off and reflective. I must put forth a position and defend it.

The *Mahayana Treatise*[440] says, "Dharmas do not have the characteristic of existing, and they do not have the

quite a while to tease apart the differences between Daoist and Buddhist terms, and Sengzhao represents a point where they are understanding Buddhism but still able to use Daoist terms to discuss it. Some might say that if you are using Daoist terms to discuss it, then you don't understand it. Others might argue that if both Daoism and Buddhism are converging on important truths, then it might be appropriate to merge the vocabularies somewhat as Sengzhao does.

[439] Here one madhyamika is criticizing another for erring on the side of nihilism. This criticism may be found in many Madhyamaka texts of India and Tibet. It is not easy for madhyamikas to pin down their own doctrine, and they criticize each other for going astray. You can find many books and articles in English on this topic.

[440] This is the *Treatise on the Perfection of Wisdom*, presented in Chinese by Kumarajiva as a translation from the original Sanskrit of Nagarjuna. It is not clear who the author was. It would be *Maha-Prajnaparamita Sastra* in

characteristic of not existing." The *Middle Treatise* says, "Things do not exist but are not nothing." This is the principal, ultimate truth.

All this about "not existing" and "not being nothing" - does it mean to obliterate everything, to block out sight and sound and be vacuous and still like a gap in a mountain range, only then being the ultimate truth? It's rather that, given that things comply with our communications, things will not obstruct them. Whether you treat them as fake or real, none of their natures changes. Since none of their natures changes, it follows that although they are nothing, they exist. They don't obstruct us, so although they exist, they don't exist. Although they exist, they don't exist; this is what "not existing" means. Although they don't exist, they exist; this is what "not being nothing" means. This is the point. Hence, it's not that there are no things but that things are not real things.

Things are not real things. So, on what basis can we treat them as things? The *sutra* says, "The nature of form is emptiness; form is not made empty by being destroyed."[441] This sheds light on the sage's view of things. As they are empty in themselves, why must he first destroy them in seeking to communicate about them? This is why Vimalakirti's illness was spoken of as unreal. It is the meaning of the assertion of emptiness in *Sutra of the Samadhi Brighter than Sunshine*.[442] So, the Tripitaka scriptures have various ways of speaking but the general trend is the same. Therefore, the *Prajñaparamita Sutra* says, "In the ultimate truth there is no coming to be or attainment; such things are only of the worldly truth." Thus, "to have attained" is an artificial designation of non-attainment, and "non-attainment" is the true designation of attainment. It's the true name, so although it's true, the attainment doesn't exist. As for the artificial designation, however artificial it is, it isn't nothing. This is why to speak

Sanskrit. See the book by Ramanan in the suggested readings for more on this text.
[441] *Vimalakirti sutra.*
[442] Contained in the *Mahayana Treatise.*

truly by no means implies nothingness. The two ways of speaking are not at all the same, but the two principles are not at all different.

Therefore, the *sutra* says, "'The ultimate truth and the conventional truth – do you say they are different?' The Buddha replied, 'There is no difference.'"[443] The *sutra* straightforwardly describes the ultimate truth in order to explain "not treating things as existent" and the conventional truth in order to explain "not treating things as nonexistent." Why take the fact that the truths are two to mean that they split things into two?

This being so, everything has that which warrants treating it as not existent and also has that which warrants treating it as not nonexistent. It has what warrants treating it as not existent. So, although we treat it as existent, we also treat it as nonexistent. It has that which warrants treating it as not nonexistent. So, although we treat it as nonexistent, we also treat it as not nonexistent. The "treating as nonexistent" in "Although we treat it as nonexistent, we also treat it as not nonexistent" does not mean treating it as absolutely void. The "treating as existing" in "Although we treat it as existing, we also treat it as not existing" does not mean treating it as genuinely existing. Since the existence is not entirely real and the nothingness isn't annihilation, therefore "existence" and "nothing" have different meanings but the same referents.

This is why the young man sighed and said, "You explain how things do not exist yet are not nothing, and that due to cause and effect the many things arise."[444] The *Bodhisattva-keyura Sutra* says, "As for the one who turns the wheel of the Dharma, there is no turning and there is no

[443] *Prajñaparamita Sutra.* The doctrine of the two truths is that the many normal beliefs which people have about things are true on one level but refer to things which do not have quite the independent reality which people suppose them to have. Hence, there are conventional truths and an ultimate truth.
[444] From the *Vimalakirti Sutra.*

absence of turning." This means that in turning there is nothing being turned. These are the profound utterances of the *sutras*.

What does this mean? That things are nonexistent? Then, nihilism wouldn't be heretical. That things exist? Then, eternalism[445] wouldn't be untenable. Because things are not nothing, nihilism is a heresy. Because things do not exist, eternalism isn't tenable. This "not being and not nothing" is the accurate way to speak of the ultimate truth.

This is why the *Daoxing* says, "The mind on the one hand does not exist but on the other hand is not nonexistent." The *Middle Treatise* says, "Things depend upon causes and conditions. Therefore, they do not exist. They come about from conditions. So, they are not nonexistent." This is what the aforementioned principles mean.

Here is the reason for this. If existence were real existence, then to exist would be to exist eternally. For why would a thing depend on conditions in order to exist? This applies to real nonexistence. Not to exist would entail eternal nonexistence. For why would a thing depend on conditions in order for it not to exist? For a thing to exist is not for it to exist in itself but for it to depend on conditions in order to exist. We therefore know that existence is not real existence.

Existence is not real existence. Even though a thing exists, we should not call this "existing." As for its not being nonexistent, nonexistence is still and unmoving; we may call it nonexistence. If the myriad things were nonexistent, then they couldn't cause one another to arise. But they do arise. So, they are not nothing. This explains the line, "Things come about from conditions; so they are not nothing."

The *Mahayana Treatise* says,

All the myriad things, due to their causes and conditions, must be treated as existing. All the myriad things, due to causes and conditions need not be treated as nonexistent. As for all nonexistent things, all their causes and conditions are

---

[445] Eternalism is the view that there are independently real objects. As such, they have eternal existence.

a reason we must take them to exist. As for all existing things, all their causes and conditions are a reason we must take them not to exist.

These sayings about existence and nonexistence – are they really just contradictions? When we must take something to exist, then we treat it as existing and we ought not to say it is nonexistent. When we must take something not to exist, then we treat it as nonexistent and we ought not to say it exists. The utterance "exists" is a provisional treatment of something as existing in order to make clear that it is not nonexistent. And we borrow "nonexistent" in order to describe a thing as not existing. There is one principle with two explanations. The sentences have the appearance of being different. If one can just grasp how they are the same, then there is no difference, though they aren't the same.

Given all this, the myriad things actually have that which warrants treating them as not existing; you can't find a reason to treat them as existing. But they have what warrants treating them as not nonexistent. You can't find a reason to treat them as nonexistent. What follows from this? We want to speak of things as existing, but their existence does not really arise. We want to speak of their being nonexistence, but objects and images have appearances and these phenomena are thus not nothing. They are not real and do not have substantial being. This clarifies the meaning of "emptiness" as "unreality."

Thus, the *Prajñaparamita Sutra* says, "All things are conventional determinations and not real, like a person produced by magic."[446] The person isn't nonexistent; he's a person produced by magic. But he's a person produced by magic; he isn't real.

If you try to find things for names, there are no things which correspond to the purport of the names. If you take things and try to get names for them, there are no names which match the things' characteristics. Things which do not

---

[446] A noted passage in which the *sutra* tries to explain the concept of emptiness by analogy to a magician's trick.

correspond to the purport of names are not things. Names which do not match things' characteristics are not names. Therefore, names do not correspond to reality, and reality doesn't correspond to names. But if names and reality have no correspondence, how can the myriad things count as existing?

Therefore, the *Middle Treatise* says, "Among things there is none which is this or that." But someone takes this as this and that as that, while someone else takes this to be that and that to be this. Neither this nor that is determined by a single name. But people who are deluded cling to a definite reference. This being so, this and that are from the outset to be treated as not existing. But the deluded from the outset treat them as not being nonexistent. When they become enlightened to the nonexistence of this and that, what things are there to be regarded as having existence?

Therefore we know that the myriad things are not real but were all along conventional designations. This is why the *Established Sayings* speaks of stipulative names. And Zhuangzi used the illustrations of the indicator and the horse.[447] Such profound and far-reaching utterances can be found everywhere.

The sage is one who rides the myriad changes without changing and abides the myriad delusions while passing right through them. For, having come to regard this and that as void in themselves, he does not make a convention of "void" by which to render all things void. Therefore, the *sutra* says, "How marvelous, World Honored One! The unmoving realm where things take place!" They do not take place separately from reality. Taking place, they are real. So, can the Way be far away? Come into contact with ordinary matters, and there is reality. Can sagehood be far away? Embody it and there is your spirit.

---

[447] You can find this passage in the selection from Zhuangzi on p 209-210 above.

384

Suggested Readings

Bocking, Brian, *Nagarjuna in China: A Translation of the Middle Treatise* (Lewiston, Queenston, Lampeter: Edwin Mellen Press, 1994)

Chan, Alan K. L., ed., *Philosophy and Religion in Early Medieval China* (Albany: State University of New York Press, 2011)

Ho, Chien-hsing, "Emptiness as Subject-Object Unity: Sengzhao on the Way Things Truly Are," in Jeeloo Liu and Douglas L. Berger, ed., *Nothingness is Asian Philosophy* (London: Routledge, 2014), p. 104-118.

Ho, Chien-hsing, "Ontic Indeterminacy and Paradoxical Language: A Philosophical Analysis of Sengzhao's Linguistic Thought," *Dao: A Journal of Comparative Philosophy*, 12(2013): 505-522

Ichimura, Shohei, "A Determining Factor that Differentiated Indian and Chinese Madhyamika Methods of Dialectic as *Reductio-ad-absurdum* and Paradoxical Language Respectively," *Journal of Indian and Buddhist Studies* 33(1985): 834-841

Ichimura, Shohei, "On the Paradoxical Method of the Chinese Madhyamika: Seng Chao and the *Chao-lun* Treatise," *Journal of Chinese Philosophy* 19(1992): 51-72

Lai, Whalen, "Early Prajña Schools, Especially *Hsin-Wu*, Reconsidered," *Philosophy East & West* 33(1983): 61-77

Liebenthal, Walter, *Chao Lun: The Treatise of Seng-Chao*, 2nd Ed. (Hong Kong: Hong Kong University Press, 1968)

Liu, Ming-wood, *Madhyamaka Thought in China* (Leiden, New York, Köln: E.J. Brill, 1994)

Nagarjuna, *Nagarjuna's Middle Way: Mulamadhyamakakarika*, Mark Sidirits and Shoryu Katsura, trans. (Somerville, MA: Wisdom Publications, 2013)

Nagarjuna, *The Fundamental Wisdom of the Middle Way: Nagarjuna's Mulamadhyamakakarika*, Jay Garfield, trans. (Oxford: Oxford University Press, 1995)

Ramanan, K. Venkata, *Nagarjuna's Philosophy as Presented in the Maha-Prajñaparamita-Sastra* (New Delhi: Motilal Banarsidas, 2016)[448]

Robinson, Richard H., *Early Madhyamika in India and China* (Madison, Milwaukee and London: The University of Wisconsin Press, 1967)

Tan, Mingran, "Emptiness, Being and Non-being: Sengzhao's Reinterpretation of the Laozi and Zhuangzi in a Buddhist Context," *Dao: A Journal of Comparative Philosophy* 7(2008): 195-209

Thompson, John M., *Understanding Prajña: Sengzhao's "Wild Words" and the Search for Wisdom* (London: Peter Lang, 2008)

Vorenkamp, Dirck, *Fa-tsang on Madhyamaka: Nagarjuna's Treatise on the Twelve Gates and Fa-tsang's Commentary*, available on WWW.

Watson, Burton, trans., *The Vimalakirti Sutra* (New York: Columbia University Press, 2000)

---

[448] An analysis of the *Mahayana Treatise.*

9

Huayan and Chinese Yogacara

During the Tang Dynasty (618-907 C.E.) Chinese Buddhism flourished socio-politically and matured doctrinally. Zhiyan (600-668), Fazang (643-712), and Zongmi (780-841)[449] developed the philosophy of what came to be known as the "Huayan School," and Fazang had the ear of the first Buddhist ruler of China, Empress Wu (625-705).[450] Xuanzang[451] (596-664) traveled to India, returning to China to translate many Buddhist texts into Chinese and to organize the theories of the Faxiang School of Yogacara Buddhism, eventually becoming an inspiration for the character Sanzang (skt.: Tripitaka, meaning the three divisions of Buddhist scripture) in the famous Sixteenth Century novel *Journey to the West* (*Xiyouji*, a.k.a. *Monkey*).

Here we will study works from both the Huayan School and Chinese Yogacara which espoused "mind-only" (chn.: *weishi*, skt.: *vijñaptimatra*). But we will not examine the works of the Faxiang School of Xuanzang or his pupil Kuiji (632-682).[452] Although the Faxiang School was better known

---

[449] Around Zongmi's time, these philosophers began to be considered the second, third, and fifth patriarchs, respectively, in the Huayan school's line of succession. The first was Dushun (557-640) and the Fourth Chengguan (738-839). (There were other important Huayan thinkers at the time, too.) The school faded away in China in the 9th C. but was transmitted to Korea and Japan. The important Japanese temple Todaiji is a Huayan (jpn.: Kegon) temple.

[450] See Jinhua Chen, *Philosopher, Practitioner, Politician: The Many Lives of Fazang (643-712)* (Leiden: Brill, 2007)

[451] You may recognize his name in the transliteration "Hsüan-tsang."

[452] Xuanzang, in addition to being a prolific and important translator, produced the *Treatise on Establishing Mind-only* (*Chengweishi lun*), which included Dharmapala's (530-561 C.E.) *Vijñaptimatratasiddhi-sastra*, Vasubandhu's *Thirty Verses* and various Indian commentaries. Several of

than the Dilun and Shelun schools of Yogacara Buddhism,[453] a certain text that probably emanated from the Shelun and Dilun schools is more important than any Faxiang text: *The Awakening of Faith*.[454] Since the works of Xuanzang and Kuiji would be appropriate only for advanced readers, and since the *Awakening of Faith* is an important text which is understandable to readers new to Chinese Buddhism, the latter is the one we will examine as a sample of Chinese Yogacara. This text, written perhaps in the Sixth Century by a member of the Dilun or Shelun schools, was a favorite text of Buddhist philosophers in East Asia for centuries afterwards. It summarizes clearly and neatly, and without the cumbersome detail of scholarly citations, the mind-only theory of idealism. The most important commentary on *The Awakening of Faith* is the one written by Fazang, and the translation of the text which I have provided below includes many excerpts from Fazang's commentary as footnotes.

The Yogacara School of Indian Buddhism was transmitted to China. The Huayan School, however, had no

---

this chapter's suggested readings, including a translation of *Treatise on Establishing Mind-only* itself, can help you learn more about this book. One point that set Faxiang apart from other idealists was its view that the seeds of Buddhahood could not be created since they were not mundane things subject to causation. That meant that some people were doomed never to become buddhas. A popular idea in Chinese Buddhism is that everyone has the potential to become a buddha eventually. The Faxiang view was thus not popular.

[453] These were schools surrounding the works of Asanga and Vasubandhu: the former's *Mahayanasamgraha-sastra* (*Embracing the Mahayana*; chn.: *Shedasheng lun*, or *Shelun* for short) and the latter's *Dasabhumikasutra-sastra* (*Commentary on the Sutra on the Ten Stages*; chn.: *Shidijing lun* or *Dilun* for short). The fact that the *Sutra on the Ten Stages* was a chapter in the *Huayan Sutra* testifies to the vagueness of the distinction between Huayan and Chinese Yogacara.

[454] *Dasheng qixin lun* (*The Mahayana Treatise on Awakening Faith*). The word "faith" in the title is misleading, since it is taken in the West as contrasting more sharply to knowledge and understanding than the text would imply. The text aims to awaken the reader's faith that he can become enlightened precisely by giving him knowledge and understanding.

predecessor in India. It derived its inspiration and name from
The Avatamsaka Sutra (chn.: *Huayan jing*; *Flower Garland
Sutra*), a massive tome translated into Chinese in the Fifth
Century and again in the Seventh.[455] It is a grandiose epic of
the travels of a man called Sudhana as he goes from teacher to
teacher (all *bodhisattvas*, enlightened beings on the verge of
full buddhahood), seeking enlightenment. Eventually, Sudhana
has a vision of the interpenetration of all things. This is the
addition which Huayan philosophers say is lacking in other
Mahayana philosophy. It is the view that each thing, in being
dependent on all other things for its nature, entails or contains
all other things within itself. Sudhana comes to see all things in
a grain of dust and all time in a single pore on a *bodhisattva's*
skin. The salient image is Indra's net, a net in which a jewel has
been placed at every juncture in the webbing, such that a
reflection of all of the jewels can be found in each, and in each
reflection further reflections, ad infinitum. This imagery is a
gloss on emptiness. When one asks of anything, "What is really
there?" the answer is that it is empty of inherent reality or
nature. If the question is repeated, as it may rightly be, then the
answer is ineffable and best captured with images such as those
abundant in the *sutra*.

On the other hand, Huayan philosophers provide
philosophical reasoning for this view. They used the idea of
'emptiness' of the Madhyamaka school of Buddhism. They also
employed Yogacara ideas. Although they go to great lengths in
many tomes to demonstrate the superiority of Huayan to those
two schools, they mean by this that Huayan is complete and
not that the other two schools are wrong. Huayan embraces
both Madhyamaka and Yogacara and tries to say the important
things that it thinks they leave out.

The other texts by Fazang which we will read, in
addition to his notes on *The Awakening of Faith*, are *Treatise
on the Golden Lion* and a small part of *Treatise on Delimiting*

---

[455] It was translated in full into English by Thomas Cleary as *The Flower
Ornament Scripture*. See the suggested readings at the end of the chapter.

the Meaning of the Unified Vehicle of Huayan. These show how Fazang supposes Huayan philosophy to be complete in that it argues for the metaphysics of interpenetration.

The "ten subtleties" listed in *Treatise on the Golden Lion* explain the interpenetration of a statue of a golden lion and the gold out of which it is made – its material cause. If we consider that the lump of gold exists before the lion does, as well as afterwards when the lion has been melted back into a lump, then we can understand what Fazang means when he says that the lion is "not existent." For if it exists, then it is the same as the lump of gold, but the latter exists even when the lion does not. So, the two are not the same, and the lion does not exist. The gold represents suchness (skt.: *tathata*; chn.: *zhenru*) and emptiness. Fazang says that it is a symbol for that which has no properties in itself. However, it is not different from the lion (albeit not the same as it!) and it therefore has properties in some sense. In his notes on *The Awakening of Faith*, Fazang agrees with that treatise's view that suchness is replete with innumerable meritorious qualities. Huayan, as the perfect teaching, wants to have its cake and eat it too. Whether the position is coherent is something for you to figure out. In any event, it is here that the self-ascribed "completeness" and "perfection" of Huayan metaphysics lies. Fazang says, "The power [gold] and its activity [the lion] embrace each other, unfolding and contracting at ease. This is called 'The Perfect Teaching of the Unified Vehicle.'"

If the lion is not different from the gold, which seems difficult to deny, then it is not different from the gold that makes up the lion's eye. Fazang's argument seems to be that since the gold is a symbol for suchness - amorphous, inchoate, devoid of distinctions - there is no distinction between the entire lump of gold and the part out of which the eye is formed. There is nothing about the eye gold that can't be said of the entire lump. Gold is gold, it would seem. Therefore, since the lion is no different from the eye's gold, the eye contains the whole lion. This line of reasoning will lead us to identify the eye with the ear. Thus, to borrow two important slogans from the Huayan School, not only is there "no obstruction between the principle and the phenomena" - between the gold and the lion - but also there is "no obstruction among the phenomena" - between the eye and the ear. All things contain and interpenetrate each other. Fazang says, "In the lion's eyes, ears, limbs and joints, in each and every hair, there is a golden lion... This is called 'the concept of the realm of Indra's net.'" To mold the gold in one of the lion's hairs into a tiny lion statue adds nothing to that bit of gold. Therefore, there is nothing standing between it and lionhood.

We shouldn't let any of these games - the delightful imagery of Indra's net or the trivial fact that a bit of the lump of gold could be molded into a small lion - distract us from Fazang's metaphysical thesis. As you read the selections, try to figure out just exactly what this thesis is (and, of course, whether it is trivial and, if it is not trivial, whether it is true.) Perhaps Fazang is telling us that everything is everything else and that ultimate reality is one and many in the sense that, while one, it is contained fully in many microcosms, each of which, since identical with it, are mutually identical, so that the ultimate reality never suffers any real division. One might object that this is merely the trivial claim that there is a sense in which all the matter in the world is one and a sense in which it is many. It is one big lump of matter, and yet we can recognize different regions, of differing shapes, into which it is divided: a rock here, an airplane there. This doesn't seem to be an interesting claim. Try to discover whether Fazang's thesis is something different from this. Be careful to scrutinize whichever of his claims you consider. For if the claim is that the ear is the eye (or that the lion is the ear), this seems patently false. Or has Fazang proven it true?

The excerpts from *Treatise on Delimiting the Meaning of the Unified Vehicle of Huayan* contains vigorous arguments for the Huayan view. In one passage, Fazang asserts that a rafter of a building contains the building. He explains this idea by examining six properties which everything has: wholeness, division of a thing's qualities, sameness of its parts, difference of its parts, formation of the thing by its parts, and the dissolution of the thing into its parts (in that all that is really there is the thing's parts). Fazang provides arguments for his assertion that everything has each of these properties, and the assertion seems interesting.

Still, you should scrutinize the arguments to see whether they are sound. It seems obviously false that a rafter is a building. For example, what is the basis for the claim that the rafter contains the building? According to Fazang, without the rafter, there would be no bonafide building. And if the rafter is there then the building is there. For, it wouldn't be a bonafide rafter if it weren't actually part of a building. Thus, the rafter is a necessary and sufficient condition of the building. Hence, it contains the building. Fazang says, "A rafter itself is the building."

One might object at this point that perhaps Fazang has not proven anything interesting. If we define the word "rafter" to mean "a beam, helping to hold up the roof and *being presently part of a building*," then it follows trivially by definition that the existence of a rafter is sufficient for the existence of the building. And if we define "contains" as "sufficient for the existence of," then, trivially, the rafter contains the building. And vice versa, if we define "building" to include "not missing any parts," then the argument running in that direction would also seem to prove only something trivial.

Perhaps Fazang has not redefined words to play a semantic game but rather shown us that our own concepts of physical objects entail the startling thesis that everything contains everything else. Otherwise what he has shown us is trivial. It may be that the ordinary concept of "rafter" does not entail being presently part of a building, but rather "an object of physical properties that render it able to help to hold up a roof (as a beam could.)" Thus, it would not seem to contain the building since it could exist even when no building existed. Fazang's argument would then be undercut. However, there might be reason to believe that this is not our ordinary concept of "rafter." For if it were, then it would be correct to say of a lumberyard full of beams, "There is a yard full of rafters" and of a tree limb, "There is a rafter." But it would sound strange to say that of a lumberyard. And a tree limb is not a rafter. (Or is it?) On the other hand, if all of a building were destroyed except the rafter, Fazang would seem to be wrong to deny that "all that is left is a rafter." Our concepts and the terms in our language may be too vague and amorphous to press them this hard for clear delimitations. But that may be a point in Fazang's favor. He seems to mean that what a thing is is a matter of vague conventional construction. The terms in a language may be vague but things cannot be vague. Therefore, no objects correspond to our terms and concepts. If we point at a so-called rafter and say, "What is that?", then Fazang's thesis would be: "It contains all things. It is suchness." As you read through Fazang's discussion of each of the 'six properties', consider what exactly this thesis means and evaluate his arguments for it.

Fazang's notes on *The Awakening of Faith* may hold some clues to unraveling Fazang's own metaphysics. An interpretive concern is whether Fazang illegitimately reads his own views into the text. However, you should also consider the text in its own right as a Yogacara (and also a *tathagatagarba*[456]) text. Purporting to have been translated into Chinese from Sanskrit, *The Awakening of Faith* bears the name "Maming," the Chinese translation of "Asvaghosa," as its author. Some scholars believe that it was written in Chinese and falsely attributed. It might have been written by Paramartha (499-569), its purported translator. In any event, there is no record of it in India, and it is immensely important

---

[456] This Sanskrit term means "womb, embryo, seed (*garba*) of Buddhahood (*tathagata*)," the inherent potential a person has within to become a buddha. *Tathagatagarbha* texts are texts that espouse such a potential in all beings. The term *tathagata* (chn.: *rulai*) is composes of *tatha* – "thus" – and *gata* – "come" probably indicating that the Buddha's coming into this world is not describable in ordinary terms because he was not subject to ordinary intentions and desires.

in East Asian Buddhism.[457] So, I have chosen to include it in this reader of Chinese Philosophy. It is appropriate to put it together with Huayan, since Fazang held it in high esteem, and since Zongmi held that *The Awakening of Faith* was the most profound statement of Buddhist philosophy.

The Awakening of Faith tries to elaborate on the Yogacara view that all things are "mind only."[458] There are many terms in the text that seem to refer to the same thing: "mind," "suchness," "the dharma body," and "*tathagatagarba*." As the Huayan school would agree, all things are the one thing to which those terms refer. To Buddhists, monism is quite incorrect. In a note to *The Awakening of Faith*, Fazang says that the "one" in question here is not the "one" of arithmetic but rather refers to the non-duality and emptiness of suchness. As you read the text, try to determine whether it is putting forth a monistic view, monism being the view that there is only one thing.

True to Mahayana form, *The Awakening of Faith* argues that even the distinction between enlightenment and ignorance is unreal. Where Fazang uses the golden lion, the author of *The Awakening of Faith*, Asvaghosa, uses water and waves. Asvaghosa argues that, since the disturbed water in

---

[457] Along with the even more influential *Lotus Sutra*, *The Awakening of Faith*, especially its idea of original enlightenment, had a profound effect on the development of Buddhism in East Asia. The notion that any person was already an enlightened Buddha was intriguing there, leading to many remarkable ways of uniting the sacred and the profane in the ordinary person's life. Schools that represent these various remarkably different ways include the Pure Land School, and the Nichiren and Soka Gakkai schools of Japan.

[458] Even the interpretation of what this Yogacara position means is not straightforward. "Mind only" could mean any of the following. (1.) Any supposed object that a particular mind perceives is merely internal to that mind – a sort of solipsistic view. (2.) All things in the world, including individual minds, are merely features of a single, universal mind. (3.) The things we know of from experience exist independently and externally to our minds but not in the way that our experience portrays them. The Lusthaus and Schmithausen books listed in this chapter's suggested readings are a good place to start examining this issue.

waves exists before and after the waves when the surface is calm, it isn't disturbed in itself. Similarly for the mind; it isn't ignorant or full of the perturbations of defilements in itself. And similarly for suchness, it isn't really in itself divided into the many things. Conventional language can stipulate that these distinctions are to be counted as real. And if ignorant, we have thoughts that cling to these conventional distinctions as real. But none of that makes them real. Hence, all things exist only relative to the mind's conceptual schemes.

There is little argument in the text that all things are mind only. Rather, Asvaghosa devotes the essay to developing and explaining the mind only position itself. Asvaghosa was probably assuming as common knowledge the arguments of the Indian Yogacarins, Vasubandhu and Asanga, since he was immersed in these arguments in the Dilun and Shelun schools.

A puzzling feature of the text derives from its admirable consistency in denying the reality of all distinctions. Even suchness is neither pure nor real nor enlightened. The categories of pure and impure, enlightened and ignorant, simply don't correspond to reality. "Enlightenment," for example, is a conventional mark for an event that ends ignorance. But ignorance isn't real. Things become puzzling when Asvaghosa gives the reason for this. He says that ignorance isn't real, since it is reducible to an enlightened mind's being mistaken about its own mental states! As enlightenment depends on ignorance, ignorance depends on enlightenment. A calming depends on waves, which depends on a body of water. The text says the same about impurity and defilement and about reality and emptiness. Asvaghosa is aware of the apparent contradiction. He raises the question as to how suchness, devoid of properties, can be pure, real, and enlightened. Is his answer plausible? In addition to evaluating the reasons for the position, you should also scrutinize the position for consistency.

One objection to consider is that the temporary formation of things doesn't seem to entail that they are "mind only." Even if we allow that all things are unreal in some sense, due to their wavelike ephemerality, it still doesn't seem to follow that their pseudo-existence depends on the mind. If no sentient beings or minds existed, there would still be the pseudo-sun, pseudo-moon, pseudo-planets, etc. The text might have responses to this worry. Determine what they are and evaluate them.

Another concern is about just what is supposed to be interesting about suchness as the ultimate reality of things. It seems little different from matter as the ultimate reality of things. (Compare the two.) We already knew that matter was this ultimate reality. Then again, Asvaghosa would remind us that he has said that we are already enlightened. So, perhaps there is no inconsistency here. But what, then is the text doing? If it is not informing us philosophically, then perhaps it is providing affective therapy, therapy that reduces our worrying about and clinging to things. Indeed, the Buddha sometimes denounced metaphysics in favor of psychotherapy. But the text does seem to be philosophical. What is the philosophy it presents?

The Readings

Below are three texts. First, Fazang's *The Treatise on the Golden Lion*. Second, a selection from his *Treatise on Delimiting the Meaning of the Unified Vehicle of Huayan* Chapter 10, Sections 3 and 4, which includes Fazang's analogy of the ten coins and his analogy of the building and the rafter. Finally, a selection from *The Awakening of Faith*, including more than half of the treatise. I have included footnotes containing lengthy excerpts from Fazang's book-length *Notes on the Meaning of* The Awakening of Faith.[459]

---

[459] The Chinese texts are, respectively, *Jinshizi zhang* (number 1880), *Huayan yisheng jiaoyi fenqi zhang* (number 1866; excerpts from p. 503-508; this text is also known as the *Treatise on the Five Teachings* or *Wujiao zhang*), *Dasheng qixin lun* (number 1666), and *Dasheng qixinlun yiji* (number 1846) in Junjiro Takakusu and Kaigyoku Watanabe, eds., Taisho Shinshu Daizokyo (Tokyo: Taisho Issaikyo Kankokai, 1924-35).

Treatise on the Golden Lion
Fazang

1. *Explanation of Conditioned Arising.* This means that the gold has no self-nature. Only following upon the skillful workman's conditioning is there the arising of the property of being a lion. It arises only if there are conditions. Hence, the name "conditioned arising."

2. *Discriminating between Thinghood and Emptiness.* We say the property of being a lion is hollow, and only the gold is real. The lion is not existent, and the gold is not nonexistent. Hence, the names "thinghood" and "emptiness." Now, emptiness has no properties of its own. Its only appearance is through things. It does not obstruct illusory existence. We call it the "emptiness of thinghood."[460]

3. *The Three Natures, in Brief.* The lion exists in our sensations. We call it "widely fathomed." The lion seems to exist. This is called "other-dependent." The gold does not change. So, it is designated "perfect."[461]

4. *Showing the Lack of Properties.* This is to say that the gold takes on lionhood completely. Besides the gold there are no properties of a lion that we can get at. Hence, the words "lacking properties."

5. *Explaining the Lack of Arising.* This is to say that at the moment we see the lion arise, it is only gold that arises. Besides the gold there is not one thing. Although the lion has an arising and an extinction, the substance of the gold fundamentally lacks any increase or reduction. That is why we say "lack of arising."

---

[460] The lion analogy makes Fazang's view seem to be Vedantic, with the gold representing *brahman* the monistic absolute being. But here Fazang labels the gold empty and devoid of properties in itself. This would seem rather Buddhist than Vedantic.

[461] For more on the three natures, see Ming-wood Liu, "The Three-Nature Doctrine and its Interpretation in Hua-Yen Buddhism," *T'oung Pao* 68(1982): 1981-220.

6. *Describing the Five Teachings.*[462]

6.1 Although the lion is a thing conditioned by causes and from moment to moment arises and ceases, actually there are no properties of a lion that we can get at. This is called "The Lesser Vehicle Teaching of the *Sravakas*"

6.2 Accordingly, these conditionally arisen things are called "lacking in self-nature" and "thoroughly and only empty." This is called "The Beginning Teaching of the Greater Vehicle."[463]

6.3 Although, again, they are thoroughly and strictly empty without obstruction, they conditionally arise and exist by convention. These two properties co-exist. This is called "The Final Teaching of the Greater Vehicle."[464]

6.4 Accordingly these two properties consume each other, and both vanish. The constructs of the sense faculties do not remain, and they no longer have any power. Emptiness and being together are destroyed. The road of names and language is cut off. The mind is settled, having no attachments. This is called "The Sudden Teaching of the Greater Vehicle" [i.e., Zen].

6.5 Then these things, rid of their sensible qualities and with their substance revealed, mix and become of a piece. The great activity, in its resplendent abundance, arises utterly in complete truth. The myriad phenomena, in wide variety, mingle but without confusion. All is one, since all alike lack a nature. One is all, since causes and effects fall in line. The power and its activity embrace each other, unfolding and

---

[462] Philosophers of the Huayan School and the Tiantai School were obsessed with the ranking of (the Buddha's) teachings (*panjiao*) from the shallowest to the most profound. Here we have a small sample from the hundreds of pages they wrote on this topic. See Ming-wood Liu, "The P'an-chiao of the Hua-Yen School in Chinese Buddhism," *T'oung Pao* 67(1981): 10-47.

[463] Lesser Mahayana included Madhyamaka and Yogacara, according to Fazang.

[464] This Final Mahayana included the doctrines which upheld more positive views: *tathagatagarba* and suchness. *The Awakening of Faith* represents this level.

contracting at ease. This is called "The Perfect Teaching of the Unified Vehicle" [i.e., Huayan Buddhism].

7. *Mastering the Ten Subtleties.*

7.1. The gold and the lion are established at the same time, completely included. This is called "the concept of simultaneous inclusion."

7.2. If the lion's eye takes in the lion completely, then all of it is purely the eye. If the ear takes in the lion completely, then all of it is purely the ear. The various sense organs take each other in, and everything is included. Thus, each one is mixed in, and each one is pure. This constitutes a perfectly complete storehouse. This is called, "the concept of the storehouse of variety, in purity and admixture, and inclusive of qualities."[465]

7.3. The gold and lion contain each other, establishing one and many without obstruction. Between them principle and particular are each distinct. Whether taken as one or many, each stands on its own. This is the concept of the one and many containing each other without being the same.

7.4. Each of the lion's various sense organs, and each and every hair, completely takes in the lion by means of the gold. Each one thoroughly penetrates the eye of the lion. The eye is the ear. The ear is the nose. The nose is the tongue. The tongue is its body. They are self-possessed[466] and established without hindrance and without obstruction. This is called "the concept of the various things being mutually identified and self-possessed."

7.5. If we see the lion and only a lion without the gold, then the lion is revealed and the gold is hidden. If we see the

---

[465] This is the storehouse consciousness. It was posited by Buddhists in order to provide a substrate for continuing development of karma, or the deeds and their effects which make up a being's transmigration from life to life. It is an enormous topic in itself. See William Waldron's book in this chapter's suggested readings.

[466] "Self-possession" (chn.: *zizai*) is freedom from the torments of the passions. It means complete, unconstrained, unimpeded, and masterful. We will encounter this term again in *The Awakening of Faith* and in the readings in the chapter on Chan Buddhism.

gold as only gold without the lion, then the gold is revealed and the lion is hidden. If we see the two aspects, then both are hidden and both are revealed. This is called "the concept of the secret, the hidden and the manifest each being established."

7.6. The gold and the lion, whether hidden or revealed, whether one or many, whether definitely pure or definitely mixed, with or without power, being this or that - each one and its counterpart illuminate each other. Principle and particular alike are apparent. Each contains the other. Without obstruction they are easily established, and the minute details are accomplished. This is called "the concept of the minute details containing each other and being easily established."

7.7. In the lion's eyes, ears, limbs and joints, in each and every hair, there is a golden lion. All the lions in the hairs at the same time immediately enter into every single hair. In each and every hair there is an unlimited number of lions. Also, each and every hair in turn contains these unlimited lions and still enters into each hair. In this way the repetition is never exhausted, like the jewels of the lord's net. This is called "the concept of the realm of Indra's net."

7.8. We speak of the lion in order to represent ignorance. We speak of its gold body in order to manifest the real nature. When principle and phenomena are spoken of together to describe the storehouse consciousness, this brings about the correct understanding. This is called "the concept of relying on phenomena to reveal things and bring about understanding."

7.9. The lion is a conditioned thing. Every moment it arises and ceases. These moments are divided into three periods, namely past, present and future. Each of these three periods has a past, present and future. Altogether there are three times three places, which constitute the nine worlds. They together form the teaching's concept of a single length of time. Although there are thus nine time periods, each has separate features. Since they are established as fused and merged without obstacles, they are alike the same moment.

400

This is called "the concept of the ten periods' individual formations as distinct things."

7.10. The gold and the lion, whether hidden or manifest, whether one or many, each is devoid of self-nature. They revolve due to the mind. Whether we are speaking of phenomena or principle, each has its formation and establishment. This is called "the concept of excellent formation by the revolutions of mind only."

8. *Bringing Together the Six Properties.* The lion is the property of wholeness. The distinctions among the five sense organs are the property of division. Their arising from a single condition is the property of sameness. That the eyes, ears, etc. do not overflow into each other is the property of difference. That the several organs come together and cause the lion to exist is the property of formation. That each of the several organs stands on its own is the property of dissolution.

9. *Attaining Bodhi [Enlightenment].* "Bodhi" means "the Way." It is enlightenment. This is to say that to see the lion is to see that all the conditioned things, prior to the dissolution, are fundamentally quiescent and extinct. Escaping the various attachments and renunciations is to flow along this path into the sea of knowledge. That is why it is named "the Way." It is to understand that all along, the whole time, whatever misconceptions there were originally lacked any reality. This is named "enlightenment." The thorough wisdom of all kinds is called "Bodhi."

10. *Entering Nirvana.* In seeing the lion and the gold, both properties together exhausted, one's afflictions won't arise. When beauty and ugliness appear before one, one's mind is as calm as the sea. Ignorant ideas come to an end, and there are no longer any oppressions. Free of bondage and liberated from obstacles, one shakes off forever the source of suffering. This is called "entering nirvana."

From *Treatise on Delimiting the Meaning of the Unified Vehicle of Huayan*
Fazang

"The Ten Coins"[467] - Chapter 10, Section 3. The Meanings of Ten Concepts in the Teaching of Subtle Dependent Origination and Nonobstruction

The dependent origination of the *dharmadhatu*[468] is self-possessed and unlimited. Here I will divide the essential concepts into two summary parts. First, I make clear the correct concept of the ultimate effect, which is the ten buddhas' own realm. The second is the teaching on determination by causes in accordance with conditions, which is the realm of Samantabhadra.[469]

I. The first concept is being perfectly interfused and self-possessed, the one which is identical with all and all are identical with the one. One simply cannot describe its form or characteristics. It is the concept of the oceans of lands and the ten buddhas' own bodies being fused and so forth, which we find in the *Huayan Sutra*. That's what it concerns. The inexplicability of Indra and the miniscule pertain to this indescribable concept.[470] Why is this so? Because they have no correspondence to a teaching. The *Dilun* says, "The causes can be explained. The effect cannot be explained."[471] That's what this means....

II. As for the second concept, we have two parts. The first uses a comparison to describe it succinctly. The second is a lengthy description of it in relation to the teaching.

---

[467] I have inserted this title. It is not in the original text.

[468] This is the basic nature of reality. It literally means "the realm of things."

[469] Samantabhadra is the most important *bodhisattva* in the *Huayan Sutra*.

[470] This reference to Indra concerns Indra's net, with its infinite interconnections that defy summary explanation.

[471] The causes which bring about enlightenment can be explained, but enlightenment itself is indescribable.

402

II.1 First, the comparative description. It is a model in which we count ten coins. The reason we say ten is that we want to accord with perfect numbers in order to manifest inexhaustibility. In this there are two topics. First, difference in substance. Second, sameness in substance. The reason we have these two is that the various teachings of conditioned arising have two concepts in them. The first is mutual independence. This means having qualities within themselves and therefore not requiring the conditioning of their causes and the like in order to be so. The second is mutual dependence and thus requires conditioning of their causes and the like in order to be so. That former is sameness in substance. The latter is difference in substance.

II.1.1 When we turn to difference in substance, there are two teachings. The first is mutual identity. The second is mutual penetration.

II.1.1.1 The reason there are two teachings is that all conditioned things have two aspects. One is the aspect of emptiness and existence, which are viewed from the standpoint of their having substance in themselves. The second is their having efficacy or not, which are viewed from the standpoint of their functioning efficaciously or not. It is due to the former aspect that there is mutual identity. It is due to the latter aspect that there is mutual penetration.

II.1.1.1.1 As for the former aspect, this is a case in which when something, X, exists, certain other things, Ys, necessarily do not. Here it follows that the Ys are just X. Why is this? Because the Ys have no nature, owing to the fact that X creates them.[472] Next, when X is empty, the Ys must certainly exist. Why is this? Because X has no nature, owing to the fact

---

[472] Consider the example of a bowling ball. Notice that it comprises two halves of a bowling ball. In fact, it comprises an infinite set of pairs of halves delimited by any number of planes bisecting the ball at its center. Fazang's idea seems to be that there is a sense in which the ball is real but its two halves are not, being just the ball itself.

that the Ys create it.[473] Because neither the pair of emptinesses nor the pair of existences occur simultaneously, there is nothing distinct which fails to be mutually identical. Whether one exists while the others do not or the one does not exist while the others do, they are not two and in both cases they are mutually identical. If this weren't so, conditioned arising wouldn't be the case and there would be the errors of [believing in] self-nature and the like. If you think about it, you will see that.[474]

II.1.1.1.2 Regarding the second aspect, efficacious functioning, the fact that X has all the efficacy is the reason it can include the Ys. The fact that the Ys are completely without efficacy is the reason it can penetrate X. We can recognize this by supposing that the Ys had efficacy and X did not. It wouldn't rely on X's substance, and therefore they wouldn't be identical. Because efficacious functioning infuses them, a mutual penetration comes about. Because neither the pair of efficacies nor the pair of lacks of efficacy occur simultaneously, there is nothing distinct which fails to be mutually identical. Whether one has efficacy while the other does not or the one does not have efficacy while the other does, they are not two and in both cases they are mutually penetrate one another. So, with functioning including substance and without a separate substance, it's just mutual penetration. With substance including functioning and without a separate functioning, it's

---

[473] Consider the example of the strange object I mentioned in footnote 377. It comprises three objects on your desk: a wristwatch, a bit of chewing gum (already chewed), and a scrap of paper with a doodle drawn on it. There is a sense in which only these three objects are real and the object which is their aggregate is not.

[474] Perhaps this passage refers to the idea that a thing is nothing more than its parts. When the parts exist in proper formation, the thing exists and is really nothing else than the parts. But Fazang probably has in mind the idea that everything in the world is empty and does not exist while also reflecting and containing everything else in the world. In this sense, for each thing in the world or part of the world there is a standpoint from which it seems that it is the only thing and everything else in the world, which it reflects and contains, is unreal.

404

just mutual identity. This represents the content of the six meanings of "depending on a cause."

II.1.1.2 [Of the two teachings on difference in substance] we first explain mutual penetration. We begin by counting up to ten. The first, number 1, is the basic number. How so? Because of coming to be due to conditions. When we arrive at a group of ten, the ten are within number 1. How so? Because without number 1, the ten would not come to be. Since number 1 has all the efficacy, it includes the ten. Yet, the ten are not number 1. The rest of the other nine follow suit. Each one possesses the ten. You can understand this by comparing the cases.

Counting downwards, there are also ten counts. The first one, the ten, includes number 1. How so? Because of coming to be due to conditions. We say that if it weren't for the ten, the first would not come to be. As the first is completely without efficacy, it devolves into the ten. Yet, number 1 is not the ten. The same pattern holds for the rest.[475] In this way, within both the starting and the ending points, ten points are embodied. Each one of the other coins can be considered in the same way. This summarizes the teaching on difference, which can be thought of and explained similarly.

Q: Having said it was "the first," how can you conclude that number 1 has the ten within it?

A: Because of the great teaching of containment due to dependent origination. Because without number 1 the lot would not come to be. This is how it must be understood. What does this mean? What I called "the first" is not by its self-nature number 1, because it comes to be due to conditions. This is why number 1 has the ten within it; it comes to be number 1 due to conditions. If this were not the case, its self-nature would not be conditionally arisen and it would not come to be

---

[475] Thus, next would be the group of nine containing coins number 1 through number 9. 'We say that if it weren't for the nine, the first would not come to be. As the first is completely without efficacy, it devolves into the nine. Yet, number 1 is not the nine.' Next the group of eight containing coins number 1 through number 8....

named "number 1." All the way to the tenth, all ten are without self-nature. Due to this conditioned coming to be, we speak of the ten as having the first within them. This group of ten is conditionally arisen and has no nature. If this were not the case, its self-nature would not be conditionally arisen and it would not come to be named "the ten." Therefore, all are conditionally arisen and without self-nature. How so? If we did away with any of the conditions, the lot would fail to come to be. This is why "within the one there are many" is a gloss on the one being dependently arisen.

Q: If we did away with any of the conditions, the lot would fail to come to be. This implies that they have no natures. How can things without natures come, one and all, to be dependently arisen?

A: It is precisely because they lack natures that they can come, one and all, to be dependently arisen. How so? Because this dependent arising is the real power of the *dharmadhatu* class. Because the realm of Samantabhadra is supplied with this power, self-possessed and boundaryless. The *Huayan Sutra* says, "A *bodhisattva* is good at observing dependently arisen things. Within one thing he recognizes the plethora of things. In the plethora of things he discerns the one." Therefore, one must know that the ten in the one and the one in the ten occupy one another without obstruction but without being one another.

Since the first concept is replete with the ten, we can see that the first concept has an infinity within it. The same holds true for the other concepts.

Q: Does the first concept contain the ten completely?

A: Completely and yet not completely. How so? The ten are in the first, so this is completely. But the first is in the ten, so it's not completely. The four alternatives guard against errors, do away with nihilism, and reveal the virtues.[476] If you

---

[476] The four alternatives are a component of Buddhist philosophy, in particular Madhyamaka. They are the position that a thing exists (independently), that it does not exist, that it both exists and does not exist, and that it neither exists nor does not exist. In the case Fazang has

406

compare this to them, you will understand it. Each permutation can be understood like this. The subtle principle of dependent arising should be understood in this way.

This concludes the first teaching [i.e., mutual penetration].

II.1.1.3 In this first teaching, the difference in substance, the second aspect was the concept of identity. In it there are two teachings, the first being increasing order and the second being decreasing order. The former teaching has ten points. The first is number 1. How so? Because of coming to be due to conditions, number 1 is identical to the ten. How so? Because if there were no number 1, there would be no ten. Assuming that number 1 has substance and the others are empty, we can conclude that number 1 is identical to the ten. In this way, as we move upwards in increasing order to ten, each one can be understood likewise to those before it.

When we speak of decreasing order, there are also ten points. The first is the tenth. How so? Because it is conditionally arisen, the ten are identical to number 1. How so? Because if there were no ten, there would be no number 1. Assuming that number 1 has no substance and the others all exist, we can conclude that this tenth is identical to the one. In this way as we move downwards in decreasing order to number 1, each one can be understood likewise to those before it. One should recognize that every single coin is identical to many coins.

Q: What is the error in supposing that number 1 is not identical to the ten?

A: If we say that number 1 is not identical to the ten, there are two problems. The first is the problem that the ten coins would not come to be. How so? If number 1 were not identical to the ten, then adding one more to it wouldn't make the ten come to be. How so? Because each single one would

in mind, the four alternatives would be that the first and tenth coins are the same, are different, are both the same and different, and are neither the same nor different. Buddhist wisdom (prajña) is to see that, for any given thing, none of these alternatives is correct.

not be ten. Yet, there are ten. So, number 1 is identical to the ten. The second problem is that number 1 would not cause the ten to come to be. How so? If the one were not identical to the ten, the ten would not come to be. Since it would not cause the ten to come to be, the meaning of "number 1" would also not come to be. How so? Because without the ten, whose number 1 would it be?

So, since we have ascertained that there is a one, we clearly recognize that the one is identical with the ten. Moreover, if they were not mutually identical, then emptiness and existence, the two meanings of the teaching of dependent arising, wouldn't be made obvious, which would lead to great mistakes, such as treating things as having self-nature and the like. Think about it and you will understand. The following topic of sameness in substance can be understood by comparison to this. And the rest of the topics can be understood by analogy.

Q: If the number 1 were identical to the ten, it would certainly not be number 1. If the ten were identical to number 1, they would certainly not be the ten.

A: It is precisely because number 1 is identical to the ten that it is named "number 1." How so? What you've called "number 1" is not what I mean by "number 1." It is a number 1 that derives from conditions and has no self-nature. It is this one which is identical to many that is named "one." If it weren't such a thing, it wouldn't be named "number 1." How so? Because it has no self-nature, without conditions it would not come to be.

The fact that ten are identical to one may be grasped by analogy with the preceding. Do not misunderstand. You must understand the rest by comparison.

Q: The aforementioned one and many – are they simultaneously the same but over time not the same?

A: They are both the same and varying over time. How so? They are like this because of the dependent arising of the nature of things, because they have a substance which is the same through admixture and uniformity without

408

inconsistency, and because in efficacy and function they are self-possessed and without obstruction. This is how to understand all of this.

Q: What are the characteristics of going "forward" and coming "backward" which you explained above?[477]

A: Their places do not move but they are always going forward and coming backward. How so? Because going forward and coming backward and not moving are one and the same thing. It's just that in order to bring about wisdom and present these principles, we explain them terms of going forward and coming backward and the like. When you achieve wisdom, they will all be inexplicable. This is the same as the idea of result which we spoke of above.

Q: If it is due to wisdom, then it doesn't exist beforehand. How can you say that it was always so?

A: When wisdom comes about one no longer discusses dependent origination. It is because it is tied to wisdom that we say it was always so. How so? Because not coming to be is identical with already having come to be, which is identical to being independent from having a beginning or ending. Wisdom and things have always been.

Q: Is it due to wisdom? Or are things like this?

A: It is due to wisdom. And things are like this. How so? Because both are simultaneously given.

You can understand the remaining concepts by analogy with the preceding. This concludes the major section and first topic, difference in substance....

---

[477] This refers to direction of count, which was mentioned earlier in the text as counting the coins in "upward" or "downward" order.

"The Rafter and the Building"[478] - Chapter 10, Section 4. The Meaning of the Six Properties' being Perfectly Fused Together

The conditioned arising of the six properties I divide into three parts. First, I will give a brief explanation of their names. Second, I will explain the prominent concepts of the teaching. Third, I will make the interpretation understood through questions and answers.

1. *Presentation of the Names.* They are the "property of wholeness," the "property of division," the "property of sameness," the "property of difference," the "property of formation," and the "property of dissolution."

"The property of wholeness" refers to a single thing's comprising many qualities.

"The property of division" refers to the many qualities' not being one. For the divisions must be associated with the whole in order for that whole to be fulfilled.

"The property of sameness" refers to the many parts' not opposing each other. For they all alike form one whole.

"The property of difference" refers to the many parts' each being different with respect to each other.

"The property of formation" refers to the formation by conditioned arising through these several parts.

"The property of dissolution" refers to the several parts' each standing as a thing in itself without being disturbed.

2. *The Prominent Concepts of the Teaching.* This teaching is supposed to show the perfect teaching of the unified vehicle: the property of self-possession and infinite and perfect fusing of ultimate reality and conditioned arising, from the unobstructed interpenetration and fusing to the inexhaustible principle and particular of Indra's net, and the like. With these ideas present before all the obstacles, when one obstacle is cut

---

[478] I have inserted this title. It is not in the original text.

410

down all are cut down. One is able to extinguish the attachments of the nine (or ten) temporal points of view.[479] In practicing the virtues, when one is attained, all are attained. As for the natures of things, when one is revealed, all are revealed. Both commonality and division are fully available. Beginning and end are both present. When one for the first time has an inkling of enlightenment one also attains perfect enlightenment. This is due to the interpenetration and fusing of the six properties of ultimate reality and dependent arising. The simultaneity of cause and effect is self-possessed and comes along in full supply.[480] The goal is the practice and understanding of the Bodhisattva Samantrabhadra, as well as his enlightenment. The effect is the infinity revealed in the realm of the ten Buddhas. This is explained the *Huayan Sutra.*

3. *Making the interpretation understood through questions and answers.* While the law of dependent arising is common to all things, here, however, I will rely on the example of the conditioned formation of a building to discuss it.

3.1. The property of wholeness.
Q[481]: What is the property of wholeness?
A: It is the building.

Q: That is nothing but the rafters and the rest of the conditions. What, then, is the building?

A: A rafter itself is the building. Why? Because a rafter completely and by itself makes a building. Without the rafter, the building is not created. When you get the rafter, you get the building.

---

[479] These are the past of the past, the present of the past, the future of the past, the past of the present, the present of the present, the future of the present, the past of the future, the present of the future, the future of the future, and all ten seen together in one moment.
[480] I.e., cause and effect entail a relation of simultaneity between them, and this holds true for the case at hand, in which the cause - the first inkling of enlightenment - contains the effect: full enlightenment.
[481] Here and below, I will use "Q" and "A" to denote "Question" and "Answer."

Q: As for a rafter completely and by itself making the building, when there are no roof tiles, etc., can it still make a building?

A: When there are no tiles, etc., it's not a rafter. That is why it doesn't make one. We don't say "It is a rafter, but it can't make one." These words "can make" only refer to a rafter being able to make one. Why? Because a rafter is a condition, and when the building hasn't been made, there are no conditions. It isn't a rafter, but if it were, it would completely make a building. If it didn't completely make one, it wouldn't be called a rafter.

Q: What is the error in saying that the rafter and the rest of the conditions each contributes some power that, together with the rest, can make a building but cannot itself completely make one?

A: There would be the errors of nihilism and eternalism.[482] As for those that cannot completely make a building but just have some power, each of the various conditions has some power, and this is only many individuals of some power, which wouldn't make a building. Hence, it is nihilism. As for the various conditions each having some power but none making the building completely, while we persist in attributing existence to the building, the building would exist without a cause. Therefore, this is eternalism. As for each not making it, when we leave out a rafter, the building should continue to exist. But the building is not completely made. Therefore, we know that each doesn't have partial power but completely makes it.

Q: Why is there no building when it lacks a single rafter?

A: It is only a broken building, not a complete building. So, we know that a complete building completely inheres in a

---

[482] Nihilism is the view that nothing exists. This strange view seems clearly false. Eternalism is the more ordinary view that things (or, in the case of monism, one thing) exist independently of anything else. This is false, because it would mean that things exist eternally.

single rafter. Since it inheres in a single rafter, we know a rafter itself is the building.

Q: Since the building is a rafter, the other wallboards, tiles, etc. must themselves be the rafter.

A: As a whole they are all the rafter. Why? Since taking away the rafter means that there is no building. The reason is that if the rafter is gone, then the building dissolves. Since the building is dissolved, we don't name them "wallboards," "tiles," etc. Therefore, the wallboards, tiles, etc. are themselves the rafter. If they weren't themselves the rafter, the building wouldn't be made. The rafters, tiles, etc. together would not make it. Now, since together they make it, we therefore know that they are each other. Since this is so for one rafter, it is similarly so for the rest. Therefore, for all conditionally arisen things, if they are not formed, then they end. They are formed, so they are each other. They interpenetrate and fuse in unobstructed, self-possessed perfection. This is difficult to comprehend and goes beyond the ordinary grasp of things. The natures of things are dependently arisen in all places, as we know from the example.

3.2. The property of division is based on the rafter and the rest of the conditions' being divisible from the whole. If the whole weren't divisible, then it would not be formed. For when there are no divisions, there is no whole. What does this mean? Fundamentally the divisions are used to make the whole. If there were no divisions, the whole wouldn't be made. Therefore, the divisions themselves are divisions by means of the whole.

Q: If the whole is just the divisions, why wouldn't it not be formed as the whole?

A: Because the whole itself is the parts. That is why they come to make the whole. Just as the rafter itself is the building and is therefore named "property of wholeness," since it is a rafter, it is therefore named "property of division." If it weren't itself the building it would not be a rafter. If it weren't itself the rafter, it would not be the building. This is how we should think of the properties of wholeness and division.

Q: If they are the same as one another, how can you say "division"?

A: Since they are one another, they can make the divisions. If they were not the same as one another, the whole would be external to the divisions and would therefore not be the whole. The divisions would be external to the whole and would therefore not be the divisions. Think about it, and you can understand it.

Q: What is the error in saying that there aren't any divisions?

A: There would be the errors of nihilism and eternalism. If there were no divisions, there would be no division between rafter and roof tile. And without any divisions between rafter and roof tile, the whole building would not be formed. Hence, this is nihilism. If there were no divisions of rafters and tiles, etc., and yet there were the whole building, then it would exist without a cause. This is the error of eternalism.

3.3. The property of sameness is based on the rafter and the rest of the conditions all alike come together to make the building. They do not differ from one another, so they are all called "conditions of the building." They don't make something else. Hence the name "property of sameness."

Q: What is the difference between this and the property of wholeness?

A: The property of wholeness is spoken of only in view of the unified building. Here the property of sameness holds for the rafters and the rest of the conditions. Although in substance they are each divided, in the aspect of their power to create, they are alike. Hence, the name "property of sameness."

Q: If we say they are not the same, what is the error?

A: In saying that they are not the same, there would be the errors of nihilism and eternalism. Why? If they are not the same, then the rafters and the rest of the conditions mutually oppose each other and cannot all alike make a building. The

414

building is unable to exist, so this is nihilism. If they are mutually opposed and don't make a building, but we maintain that there is a building, then there exists a building without a cause. So, this is eternalism.

3.4. The property of difference is based on the rafter and the rest of the conditions' in their forms and kinds being mutually distinct.

Q: If they are different, then they can't be identical.

A: It is because they are different that they are the same. If they were not different, then since the rafter is 10'2" long[483], the roof tile must be so, as well. Since this would ruin the things as original conditions, we would lose the previous sense in which they all alike and the same form the building. Now, since the building has been formed, their being all alike conditions must be known as different.

Q: How is this different from the property of division?

A: As for the aforementioned property of division, we speak of the property of division with respect to the rafters and the rest of the conditions being divisible from the unified building. Here the property of difference is the rafter and the rest of the conditions, in their respective mutual relations, being each different from the others.

Q: If we say that there is no property of difference, what error would there be?

A: There would be the errors of nihilism and eternalism. Why? If there were no difference, then the tiles would be the same as the rafter: 10'2". Being ruined, these conditioning things wouldn't together make a building. So, this is nihilism. As for saying that the ruined conditions don't make a building while clinging to an existing building, in this case there would be a building without a cause. So, this is eternalism.

3.5. The property of formation is based on the building being formed from the conditions. Since they form a building

---

[483] I have converted to English units.

the rafters and the rest are conditions. If it were not so, neither would be formed. Now actually there is a building, so we know of the property of formation.

Q: We actually see the rafter and the rest of the conditions. Each as a thing in itself fundamentally does not become a building. On what basis do they come to cause there to be the formation of a building?

A: Precisely because the rafter and the rest of the conditions do not become it, the building comes to be formed. The reason for this is that if the rafter became a building, we would then lose the original conditioning thing. The building would not be formed. Now since they do not become it, the rafter and the rest of the conditions appear before us. Since they thus appear before us, the building comes to be formed. And were they not to make a building, the rafter and the rest of the conditions would not be called "conditions." Now, since they get the name "conditions," it is clearly known that they do indeed make a building.

Q: If we say they don't form one, what is the error?

A: There would be the errors of nihilism and eternalism. Why? The building fundamentally relies on the rafters and the rest of the conditions in order to be formed. Here, since they don't make one, the building does not come to be. This is nihilism. Originally, since they formed a building, they were called "rafters." Now, since they don't make a building, there are no rafters. This is nihilism. If they don't form one, the building exists without a cause. So, this is eternalism. And since the rafters don't make a building but get the name "rafters," this, too, is eternalism.

3.6. The property of dissolution is based on the rafter and the rest of the conditions each as things in themselves fundamentally.

Q: We see before us the rafter and the rest of the conditions making a building, forming it and completing it. Why say that they fundamentally don't become anything?

416

A: Just because they don't become anything, the building is formed. If they became a building, they would not be the things in themselves, and the building wouldn't be formed. It is clearly known that they don't become it.

Q: If we say that they become the building, what would be the error?

A: There would be the two errors of nihilism and eternalism. If we say the rafter becomes a building, then we lose the thing that is a rafter. Since we have lost the thing that is a rafter, the building, lacking a rafter, cannot come to be. This is nihilism. If we lose the rafter but there still is a building, then there would be a building without conditions. This is eternalism.

The whole is a unified building. The divisions are the various conditions. Sameness is their mutually not opposing each other. Difference is the conditions' each being divided. Formation is the conditions' making the result. Dissolution is each being a thing in itself. We put it in a verse:

The one being in the many is called the "property of wholeness."

The many not being one is the property of division.

The many kinds are in themselves the same in the whole.

The division and difference of each in substance appears in their sameness.

The principle of the one and the many being conditionally arisen is subtle formation.

Dissolution is based on each thing in itself continuing not to become anything.

The only wisdom of the world is not mundane consciousness.

With this skillful means one can master the unified vehicle.

From *The Awakening of Faith*
(The Mahayana Treatise on Awakening Faith)
By The Bodhisattva Asvaghosa
Translated by Paramartha (the Indian Buddhist
master)[484]

...1.0 *Exhibiting the correct meaning*

Based on the teaching of one mind, there are two kinds of sphere. What are the two? First, the sphere of the mind's suchness.[485] Second, the sphere of the mind's arising and cessation. Each of these two spheres encompasses all things. What does that mean? It means that the two spheres are not mutually exclusive.[486]

---

[484] The author's identity is unknown. It may be that Paramartha himself wrote it in Chinese, rather than translating it from the Sanskrit of an Indian writer into Chinese as he purports. I have used standard ways of dividing the text into sections and providing section headings and numbers of the standard sorts.

[485] Suchness (skt.: *tathata*; chn.: *zhenru*) is the nature of things independent of the concepts and analyses which we commonly bring to them. It is thus inexpressible.

[486] Fazang (hereafter "FZ"): "It is like fine clay being the ubiquitous property of pieces of pottery. Outside of this ubiquitous property, there are no separate pieces of pottery. Each piece of pottery is encompassed by the fine clay. The sphere of suchness, one should know, is like this.... The sphere of arising and cessation is the distinct properties of impurity and purity. Things of these distinct properties are encompassed by arising and cessation. And if we take this as being suchness united with conditions and transformed to make things, then things do not have a substance different from it. They still include the sphere of suchness. It is the same as the pieces of pottery including the fine clay. Since these two spheres are equal in what they encompass, they are non-dual. That is why it is able to speak of them as one mind."

418

1.1 *The mind's suchness*

1.11   This is the substance of the teaching's concept of the universal property of the one[487] realm of things.[488] That which is called "the mind's nature" is not created or destroyed. All things are distinct only in dependence upon deluded thoughts. If we separate them from the mind's thoughts, then they do not have the characteristics that objects have.[489] Therefore,[490] all things are originally separate from verbal properties, separate from the properties of names and written words, and separate from the properties of mental conditions. Ultimately even and pervasive,[491] they are without any changes or differences and are unable to be damaged. They are only one mind. Therefore, they are called "suchness."[492] Since all language and artificial names lack truth, follow deluded thoughts, and cannot refer to anything, the word "suchness" also has no properties [to which it refers]. Let us say that it is

---

[487] FZ: "This is not the 'one' of arithmetic. It means that as the principle is void, evenly pervasive, and non-dual, it is referred to as 'one.'"

[488] The "realm of things" (skt.: *dharmadhatu,* chn.: *fajie)* is an ultimate reality of everything, or the totality of everything as it is independently of our delusions. Buddhists are always at pains to deny that it is a monistic substance, such as the one embraces by much of Hindu philosophy.

[489] FZ: "Someone who doubts this will say, 'How do you know that they are created on the basis of deluded thought?' I would explain by saying that, since sages are separated from deluded thoughts, their having no objects of experience verifies that these objects are certainly created from delusions." Notice that Fazang appeals to testimony about private meditative experience as a basis for his argument.

[490] FZ: "'Therefore' is to be taken to mean 'since things are fundamentally empty' and 'since the true mind does not move.' From this is to be inferred that all things are just suchness."

[491] FZ: "Although it permeates through impurity and purity, its nature is unvaryingly non-dual."

[492] FZ: "[The name 'suchness' refers to] separation from falsehood, delusion...and difference.... Since [suchness] is never altered during exposure to conditions, it is said to be 'without any changes.' The reason it is able to be unchanged and undifferentiated among conditioned things is that it is not the same as the conditioned, the destructible and that which can be ruined. From that we see that in impurity it is not destroyed. In regulating, it is not ruined."

the limit of language. This is to use a word to drive away words.[493] The substance of this suchness has nothing in it to drive away, since all things, one just as much as the next, are *such*. It also has nothing in it that can be established, since all things all alike are such. One should know that all things are ineffable and unthinkable. That is why we refer to them as "suchness."[494]

Question: If that is the meaning [of Mahayana Buddhism], then what shall we say that sentient beings can follow in order to gain entry into it? Answer[495]: If they know that among all things, although there is speech, there is nothing that speaks or is spoken of, and that although there is thinking, there is nothing that thinks or is thought of, then this is called

---

[493] FZ: "An ordinary person hearing the above term 'suchness' will say that the author has contradicted himself. The text thus says that it is separate from the properties of names and words.... Here he explains that it drives away artificial names that are not true. He doesn't contradict himself.... It is like an utterance that brings about silence. Without this utterance one wouldn't stop the other voices."

[494] FZ: "Non-Buddhists will see the previous two 'driving away' properties of the term 'suchness' and say that the basic substance of suchness is also a thing that can be driven away.... [This] passage explains that although it drives away the properties corresponding to vacant and deluded terms, it does not drive away the real thing that is suchness. For it is the object contemplated by subtle wisdom. Why not drive it away? The next passage explains, saying 'since all things are such.' So, there is nothing that can be driven away. Non-Buddhists, hearing that the real principle is not driven away will say that there is a thing that can be established, which must be an attachment conditioned by passions. Hence, it says, 'It also has nothing in it that can be established,' since it is separate from deluded passions....

"[Others] will say, 'That which cannot be driven away - is it not to be taken as a real substance that drives away things that are created and destroyed.' Why does it not drive them away? It explains, 'Since all things all alike are such.' Since all impure and pure things of the sphere of arising and cessation have no self-nature and do not differ from suchness, they are not subject to being driven away."

Fazang reads the text as making an effort to distance itself from monism, the position that there is only one thing.

[495] Hereafter I will abbreviate "Question" and "Answer" as "Q" and "A."

"following it." If they separate themselves from speech and thoughts, this is called "gaining entry."[496]

1.12 *This "suchness."* In dependence upon language, it is divided into two kinds of meaning. What are the two? The first is "actually empty." With it one can ultimately reveal reality. The second is "actually non-empty," for it has an inherent substance replete with an untainted nature and meritorious qualities.[497]

1.121 It is called "empty" because from its beginning defiled things do not correspond to it. It is said to be separate from all the properties of things as distinct from one another, since it is devoid of the defiled mind's thoughts.

One should know that the nature in itself of suchness neither has properties nor has no properties; neither is without properties nor is not without properties. Nor is it both with and without properties.[498] It does not have the property of

---

[496] FZ: "This makes clear that thought is no-thought and that [the meaning of the Mahayana, i.e., suchness] is not destroyed in thoughts. That it isn't destroyed in thoughts is the reason for the words 'although there is thought.' This separates [the Mahayana] from nihilistic views. Since it is not thinkable, nothing is a subject or an object. This separates [the Mahayana] from eternalistic views. In one moment, one separates oneself from these two views and sees this thing that is non-dual. This can be referred to as 'following the middle way and following in accordance with the nature of things.' Or if it is such that although one seeks [suchness] through these very words, thoughts, etc., if one can look upon these thoughts, etc., as always devoid of any subject or objects, then although one cannot yet separate oneself from thoughts, one still follows no-thought. Hence, it is named, 'following no-thought.' This we explain as the viewpoint of skillful means. It will not have been a long time using this viewpoint when one can separate oneself from deluded thoughts and accord with the true principle of no-thought.... Although [suchness] is not the realm of objects of deluded thoughts, it will not appear in the notion that it is cut off and divided from them."

[497] FZ: "As for the words, 'actually empty,' this is because emptiness in actuality is devoid of impurity and defilement. To say 'actually empty' is not to say that the actual itself is empty." Fazang means that ultimate reality is empty of impurities but not of meritorious qualities.

[498] FZ: "A doubter will say, '... Here the double negative is negated, so the existence and lack [of properties] I spoke of are again posited.' I would

unity and does not have the property of difference. Nor has it both the properties of unity and difference. By way of summary, I would say that since the defiled minds of all sentient beings from moment to moment make discriminations all of which fail to correspond [to suchness], it is said to be empty. But as separate from the defiled mind, in truth there is nothing in it which may be taken as empty.[499]

1.122 It is called "non-empty" because we have shown the emptiness and lack of defilement of the substance of things. It is the real mind, always unchanging, perfectly full of pure things.[500] Hence, it is named "non-empty." Yet it has no properties that can be grasped,[501] for it is separate from the world of thoughts and only corresponds to certain enlightenment.[502]

---

explain that the 'not' I'm speaking of is not your double negative. Hence, to say 'not not' doesn't allow a double positive. Since there is no way to have any more attachments, it says 'nor is it both with and without.'"

[499] FZ: "In referring to a lack of defilement we say that suchness is empty. It is not because there is nothing such that it is like in its substance that we take it to be empty." Fazang means that suchness isn't just blank nothingness and that that isn't the reason it is said to be empty.

[500] FZ: "[These pure things are pure] because they are separated from doubts and defilements."

[501] FZ: "Doubters will hear that pure things are not empty and say that they are the same as the existence grasped by the passions. That is why the text comments that 'it has no properties that can be grasped.' As that is the case, not being empty does not differ from being empty."

[502] FZ: "'For it is separate from the world of thoughts' explains the reason why it has no properties. If it were something conditioned by deluded thoughts, then it would have properties. As it is only the object of true wisdom, clearly we know that it lacks the properties of deluded attachments."

1.2 *The mind's arising and cessation*[503]

Due to the *tathagatagarba*,[504] there is the arising and cessation of the mind.[505] That which is said to be the harmony of non-arising and non-ceasing with arising and ceasing, neither unified nor differentiated,[506] is named "the storehouse consciousness."[507] This consciousness has two aspects which

---

[503] "Arising and cessation" (also translated "creation and destruction") also means "samsara," the wheel of rebirth.

[504] The seed/womb of enlightenment. This is embryonic buddhahood within anyone who will ultimately become a buddha.

[505] FZ: "The mind that does not arise or cease causes the wind of ignorance to move and make arising and cessation. Hence, we may explain that the mind that arises and ceases depends on the mind that does not arise or cease. So, these two minds are ultimately not two different substances. But we present the two meanings in order to explain this mutual dependence. It is like motionless water making moving water by being blown by the wind. Although motion and quiescence are distinct, the substance of the water is one, and we can say that due to the quiescent water there is the moving water.... The mind that is clean and pure in its self-nature is called the '*tathagatagarba.*'"

[506] FZ: "If they were one, then when the properties of the arising and ceasing consciousness were destroyed, the mind of suchness would have to be destroyed. Hence, we would be falling into the error of nihilism. If they were different, then when the winds of ignorance perfumed and moved it, the substance of the quiescent mind would have to be not in accord with conditions. Hence, we would be falling into the error of eternalism. We separate ourselves from these two biases. So, the mind and its properties are neither one nor different."

[507] FZ: "Sentient beings take this as a self. The reason is that, though the mind of suchness does not contain a self-nature, it unites with [arising and cessation] according to perfuming and seems to be one and seems to be eternal. Thus the benighted take what seems to be suchness and cling to it as an inner self. Embodying these views of selfhood, it is called the 'storehouse.' For that reason, at the level at which the views of selfhood permanently no longer arise it loses the name 'store.'"

The storehouse consciousness (*alayavijnana*) is the eighth in the scheme of consciousnesses (levels of the mind) presented by the Yogacara school and by the *Awakening of Faith* below. It stores the perfuming influences (pure and impure) from one's deeds and these bear fruit (good or bad) later when their seeds mature in the ground of the storehouse consciousness. Also, physical objects are merely the products of seeds stored in the storehouse consciousness.

can encompass all things and give rise to all things.[508] What are they? The aspect of enlightenment and the aspect of non-enlightenment.

1.21 *What we call "the enlightened aspect"*

This refers to the mind's substance as separate from thoughts. The property of being separate from thoughts is like the realm of empty space. There is nowhere it does not reach. The property of unity of the realm of things is the same as the Tathagata's pervasive dharma body.[509] Referring to this enlightenment body we speak of it using the name "original enlightenment."[510] Why? Because the aspect of original enlightenment is spoken of in contrast to the aspect of beginning enlightenment. But we take beginning enlightenment to be the same as original enlightenment. As for the aspect of beginning enlightenment, it is on the basis of original enlightenment that there is non-enlightenment.[511] On the basis of non-enlightenment we say there is beginning enlightenment. In referring to becoming enlightened about the

---

[508] FZ: "In this consciousness, since nonenlightenment perfumes original enlightenment, it gives rise to defiled things and causes the flow and revolution of samsara. Since original enlightenment perfumes nonenlightenment, it gives rise to pure things, opposes the flow, casts off the bonds, and accomplishes beginning enlightenment."

[509] The *dharmakaya*, which Fazang equates with perfect wisdom, is one of the three bodies of the Buddha. The other two bodies in the Three Body doctrine are the transformation body (*nirmanakaya*) and enjoyment body (*sambhogakaya*) which are bodies of the Buddha that enable him to lead sentient beings toward enlightenment, his absolute *dharma* body being too subtle for them to comprehend.

[510] Original enlightenment (*benjue*) is an important concept in the history of East Asian Buddhism. See for example, Jacqueline I. Stone, *Original Enlightenment and the Transformation of Medieval Japanese Buddhism* (Honolulu: University of Hawaii Press, 1999). The term "original" (*ben*) also means basic, such that at the base of oneself one is enlightened, however much confusion has been allowed to obscure and overlay this foundation. No precedent for *benjue* has been found in Indian Buddhist texts, lending credence to the idea that *The Awakening of Faith* is an originally Chinese text.

[511] FZ: "This means that the substance of this mind is a condition for motions and makes deluded thoughts in accordance with ignorance."

424

mind as the source, we name it "ultimate enlightenment." If one hasn't become enlightened to the mind as source, then it can only be non-ultimate enlightenment.[512]

What does this mean?   Since ordinary people's enlightenment recognizes that previous thoughts aroused evil, they can stop subsequent thoughts and cause them not to arise. Although this is still named "enlightenment," actually it is not enlightenment. As for the views and wisdom of those such as the secondary vehicle and *bodhisattvas* who have just hatched the intention [to attain enlightenment], they become enlightened about the variations of thought, and their thoughts no longer have the property of variation. Due to its property of having gotten rid of attachment to coarse discriminations, this is named "the appearance of enlightenment." Those such as *dharma*-body *bodhisattvas*[513] are enlightened to the abiding of thoughts, and their thoughts no longer have the property of abiding. Due to its property of being separated from discriminations and apparent thoughts, this is called "partial enlightenment." As the stages of the *bodhisattva* are exhausted, and the skillful means fulfilled, a single thought corresponds [to suchness], one is enlightened about the mind's incipient arousals, and the mind lacks the property of incipient [arousals]. Since one has distanced oneself from subtle thoughts, one gets to see the nature of the mind, and the mind abides unwaveringly. This is named "ultimate enlightenment." That is why the *sutras* say, "If there is a sentient being who has insight into no-thought,[514] then it is because he is advancing toward the wisdom of a Buddha."

---

[512] Beginning enlightenment is the occasion of first insight into the nature of suchness. Original enlightenment is the innate nature of the mind as suchness. The *Awakening of Faith* identifies the two, perhaps because beginning enlightenment is a tapping into or breaching original enlightenment. Zen Buddhists made great use of this paradoxical idea that people are at once enlightened and not enlightened.
[513] A *bodhisattva* of advanced insight.
[514] "No-thought" means the cessation of thoughts (discriminations, categorizations, etc.) while still conscious (though early Indian Buddhist

As for the arisings of the mind, they have no initial properties that can be known. So, when we say that one knows of the initial properties, this is just to say that there are no thoughts.[515] That is why sentient beings are not given the name "enlightened." For, since the beginning their thoughts continue from one to the next, and they have never been free from thoughts. Hence, we speak of this as beginningless ignorance.

If one is without thoughts, then one understands the arising, abiding, changing and subsiding of the properties of the mind. For they are the same as no-thought.[516] And in reality they are not different from beginning enlightenment. For the four properties exist simultaneously, and none is self-established. And they are fundamentally the same and one with enlightenment.[517]

1.211 Now, original enlightenment, in accordance with defiled discriminations, gives rise to properties of two sorts (from which original enlightenment never separates itself.) What are the two? The first is the property of wisdom and purity. The second is the property of inconceivable action.[518]

1.2111 The property of wisdom and purity. It is based on the power of the teaching to perfume,[519] on genuine

---

meditative traditions may have thought of this goal as entailing the loss of consciousness).

[515] The initial properties would be the properties of the mind as suchness, in its quiescent state before the arising of thoughts. The idea here is that to say that one knows these properties is only a figure of speech, since it does not have properties.

[516] FZ: "They are originally the same."

[517] FZ: "Because these four properties are constructed by the one mind, as hooks and chains flowing in succession but not having a before or an after. Separately from the pure mind, they have no external and separate substance themselves. Not having a substance in themselves, they are originally the same and the same as the single original enlightenment."

[518] "Action" refers to karma.

[519] "Perfuming" is the effect one's actions have on the subconscious elements of one's character, the seeds that will have effect on one's future, including one's future lives. Good actions, hearing the teaching, meditation, and the like make these seeds bear good fruit, while selfish actions make them bear bad fruit.

practice, and on fulfilling the skillful means. For one breaks through the properties of the compound consciousness,[520] causes the perpetually continuing properties of the mind to subside, reveals the dharma body, and has wisdom clean and pure. What does this mean? It means that all the properties of the mind and consciousness are each ignorant. But the property of ignorance is not separate from the nature of enlightenment, cannot be destroyed, and is not indestructible.[521]

Like the water of a large sea, in which waves are caused to move by the wind, the property of the water and the property of the wind are not mutually separable. But water does not move by nature. For if the mind stops and subsides, the property of motion will subside, while its wet nature is not destroyed. In this way, the mind of sentient beings, pure in its nature in itself, is moved by the wind of ignorance. The mind and ignorance are both without the properties of form and cannot be mutually separated. But the mind does not move by nature. For if ignorance subsides, the perpetuation [of thoughts] subsides, while the wise nature is not destroyed.

1.2112 The property of inconceivable action. Since it is based on the purity of wisdom, it can make all the supremely sublime worlds. It is called the property of having innumerable meritorious qualities which are unvarying and never cut off. For, following sentient being's capacities and naturally corresponding to them, it manifests [the teaching] in a variety of ways, and they obtain benefit and profit.

1.212 The substance and properties of enlightenment are of four sorts of general aspects, which are the same as

---

[520] I.e., the mind's seven layers: the five sense faculties, the center consciousness (the mental faculty which takes in information and imagines), and the discriminating intellect. These are all contained in the eighth level: the storehouse consciousness. *The Awakening of Faith* discusses these levels below.

[521] FZ: "This property of ignorance is neither identical with nor different from original enlightenment. Since it is not different, it cannot be destroyed. Since it is not identical, it is not indestructible." Consider that letting a wave on a body of water subside is neither to destroy it nor not to destroy it. Perhaps this is what Asvaghosa and Fazang have in mind.

empty space and like a clear mirror. What are the four? 1. An actually empty mirror. It is separate from the properties of mental objects. There are no things that can appear.[522] For it is the aspect of not being aware of images. 2. A mirror that causes perfuming. This is to say that it is actually not empty. All mundane objects appear in it, neither leaving nor entering, neither being lost nor being destroyed. They abide permanently in the one mind, since all things are of the real nature of suchness. And it cannot be defiled by any of the impure things. The substance of wisdom does not move but is supplied with untainted things that perfume sentient beings.[523] 3. The mirror of things that are separated off. This refers to things that are not empty yet are taken away from the obstacles of defilements and wisdom and separated from the properties of the compound consciousness.[524] [The mirror] is unadulterated, pure and clear. 4. The mirror that is the condition of perfuming. This is to say that, having separated itself off from things, it widely illuminates the minds of sentient beings, making them cultivate good capacities. For in appearing, it accords with their thoughts.

1.22 *What is spoken of as "the aspect of non-enlightenment"*

This is not actually to know of the unity of things and suchness. The non-enlightened mental states arise and there are

---

[522] FZ: "Here 'things' refers to real things that are widely fathomed and attached to. That is why they cannot appear. Q: The seeming things that do appear [elsewhere than this mirror] - why can't they exist as a result of our clinging to the real? A: Although they appear due to attachments to reality, they are pseudo-permanent and not real. They are like shadows. This is in contrast to the third sort below."

[523] FZ: "'Not entering' means that separately from the mind, nothing can perfume it, so nothing enters from outside. 'Not lost' means that, although it is true that they don't go out from inside or enter from outside, dependently arisen things still appear and aren't nothing.... 'Not destroyed' means that things arise from a host of conditions and aren't from anywhere. They are not different from suchness and, so, cannot be destroyed."

[524] FZ: "[These things] have no substance in themselves and, hence, are not different from suchness."

thoughts. The thoughts have no properties in themselves and are not separate from original enlightenment. It is like a person who has gone astray. It is relative to his direction that he goes astray. Independently of direction, there is no going astray. Sentient beings are thus. Based on enlightenment, they go astray, but independently of their enlightened nature, there is no non-enlightenment. Since there is an unenlightened mind with deluded notions, we can understand the meaning of the terms in order to speak of true enlightenment. Independently of the unenlightened mind there is no property of enlightenment in itself that can be spoken of.

1.221 Next, based on non-enlightenment, properties of three kinds are created to which non-enlightenment corresponds without being separate. What are the three? 1. The property of ignorant action. It is due to its being based on non-enlightenment that the mind moves. We speak of it with the name "action." If it were enlightened, it would not move. Since it moves, this includes suffering, for the effect is not separable from the cause. 2. The property of being a perceiver. It is due to being based on movement that it can perceive. If it didn't move, then it would have no perception. 3. The property of being an object. It is due to being based on the perceiver that the objects falsely appear. Independently of perception, there are no objects.[525]

1.222 Since there are the objects as conditions, there also arise properties of six sorts. What are the six? 1. The property of discernment. Due to the world of objects, the mind gives rise to discriminations, likes, and dislikes. 2. The property of perpetuation. Due to discernment, it creates its experiences of suffering and pleasure. The mind gives rise to thoughts which perpetuate one another without end. 3. The property of attachment. Due to the perpetuation, one makes the world of objects an object of thought. With an abiding grasp on suffering and pleasure, the mind gives rise to attachments. 4.

[525] This is the central thesis of idealism, the doctrine of Yogacara Buddhism. See the book by Thomas Kochumuttom in this chapter's suggested readings for issues in the interpretation of this claim.

The property of fathoming names and words. Due to false attachments, one distinguishes among the properties of conventional names and speech. 5. The property of giving rise to action. Due to names and words, one pursues names and attachments and creates various actions. 6. The property of the bondage of action. Due to actions, one receives the effects and is not at ease with oneself. One should know that ignorance can produce all defiled things, since all defiled things are the properties of non-enlightenment.

1.223 Next, the relation between enlightenment and non-enlightenment has properties of two types. What are the two? The first is the property of sameness.[526] The second is the property of difference.

1.2231 The term "the property of sameness." This is like pottery of various kinds all alike having the property of having the nature of fine dirt. Thus, non-defilement and the illusions of ignorant actions of various sorts all alike have the property of the nature of suchness. Therefore, the *sutras* say that based on this aspect of suchness, we say that all sentient beings originally are always abiding and have entered into nirvana. The thing that is enlightenment is not a property that can be cultivated or a property that can be made. Ultimately there is no attainment of it. It also has no physical properties that can be perceived. So, any perceived physical properties are only constructs that follow the illusions of impure action. They aren't a non-empty physical nature of wisdom. For the properties of wisdom cannot be perceived.

1.2232 The term "property of difference." This is like various sorts of pottery each being different from the others. In this way, non-defilement and the illusions of ignorance that accord with impurity are distinguished. Nature and the illusions of impurity are distinguished.

---

[526] FZ: "Both impure and pure things alike take suchness as their substance. Suchness takes the two as its properties."

1.3   The causes and conditions of arising and cessation[527]

What are referred to as "the discriminating intellect" and "the center consciousness"[528] evolve due to the minds of sentient beings. What does this mean? On the basis of the storehouse consciousness, we explain the existence of ignorance. Not being enlightened, it gives rise to the perceiver, the revealer and the grasper of the world of objects.

1.31 *It gives rise to the perpetuation of thoughts.* So, we speak of it as "the discriminating intellect." This discriminating intellect is of five sorts.[529] What are the five? The first one is named "active consciousness," which refers to the unenlightened mind moving by the power of ignorance.[530] The second is named the "revolving consciousness," which refers to the moving mind's property of being a perceiver.[531] The third

---

[527] FZ: "That the storehouse consciousness does not have a nature in itself is the cause of arising and cessation. That fundamental ignorance perfumes and moves the substance of the mind is the condition of arising and cessation."

[528] The discriminating intellect (Sanskrit *manas*, Chinese *yi*) and center consciousness (Sanskrit *mano-vijnana,* Chinese *yishi*) are two (numbers seven and six, respectively) of the eight levels of the mind according to Yogacara (number eight being the storehouse consciousness, and numbers one to five being the five sense faculties). The discriminating intellect makes value distinctions and forms preferences. The center consciousness is the conscious state in which the five senses come together in unified conscious experience and in which the mind contemplates and imagines.

[529] These five sorts correspond to mind in its first becoming ignorant, mind as the sense faculties, mind as the center consciousness, as the discriminating intellect itself, and as the storehouse consciousness. The text seems to be showing the connection or unity between the discriminating intellect and all the other levels of consciousness. Thus this Yogacara text contains a bit of Huayan "interpenetration," in which the discriminating intellect contains aspects of all the other levels of mind.

[530] This is the mind as suchness at the point of being moved by ignorance to let evolve the eight layers of mind.

[531] "Revolving" refers to the flux of mental states, the motions in the mind. Experience and perception being such a flux, they are the revolving of the mind. Due to ignorance, the mind starts to perceive objects: the sense faculties.

is named it "appearing consciousness." It is what we speak of as able to make all the objective realms appear. It is like a clear mirror causing the images of physical things to appear. The appearing consciousness is also thus. In pursuing its five sense objects, when it confronts them, they appear, without any temporal sequence [simultaneously]. For at all times it arises as a matter of course and is always there beforehand.[532] The fourth is named "the consciousness of discernment," since it discriminates between tainted and pure things.[533] The fifth is named "perpetuating consciousness,"[534] for the thoughts respond to one another and are not cut off. It has an abiding hold on the good and bad actions of innumerable past lifetimes, making it so that they are not lost. And it can bring to fruition their bitter and happy repercussions in the present and future without fail. It can make past and present events suddenly come to mind. In its non-enlightenment, it has fantasies about future events. That is why the triple world[535] is empty and false. It is merely the doing of the mind. Separate from the mind, there are no objects of the six sensory object fields.[536]

What does this mean? It means that all things arise from the mind's bringing up false thoughts.[537] All distinctions are just distinctions in the mind itself. The mind does not perceive the mind. It has no properties that can be gotten at. One should know that all mundane objective realms come to subsist in

---

[532] This is the center consciousness, which is similar to the Cartesian arena in which one's perceptions can come together and appear on a pre-existing "stage" or place in the mind.

[533] This is the discriminating intellect.

[534] This is the storehouse consciousness.

[535] The world of desire, the physical world, and the non-physical world.

[536] The objects of the five senses, plus the center consciousness (see below): color, sound, texture, odor, flavor, and metal image or concept.

[537] FZ: "Q: There appear to be objects of perception. How are they mind only? A: Since all things are brought about by the mind in accordance with perfuming, they do not have a different substance.... Q: If things are mind only, why don't I see it? So, what I see is different from mind. A: To say 'different from mind' is a distinction made from your ignorant thoughts."

dependence on sentient beings' ignorant and deluded minds. Therefore, all things are like images in a mirror, without any substance that can be gotten at. They are only mind, vacant and false. When the mental states arise, then the various things arise, and when the mental states cease, then the various things cease.[538]

1.32 *The term "center consciousness."* It is the perpetuating consciousness. Due to ordinary beings' clinging revolving deeply, they posit a subject and an object and various false graspings. Directing itself to each phenomenon, it mulls it over, distinguishing the six sensory objects fields. We name it "center consciousness," but it is also named "the consciousness that makes discriminations." And it is also named "the consciousness that distinguishes among phenomena." For this consciousness, due to the defilements of views and passions, increases and extends itself....

1.4 *The properties of the substance in itself of suchness* Suchness does not increase or decrease in ordinary beings, *sravakas, pratyekabuddhas,*[539] *bodhisattvas,* or

---

[538] FZ: "A doubter will ask, 'If they don't have any substance, how can they yet appear?' I would explain that they are appearances superimposed on the mind of suchness. Where can they have a substance that one can get at? ... A doubter will say, 'How do you know they are appearances superimposed on the mind?' I would explain that we know this because [the text says], 'When the mind arises, then the various things arise, and when the mind ceases, the various things cease.'"

This is an example of private meditative insight being used as evidence for a metaphysical claim. Here "mental states" is a translation of *xin*. "The mind arises" doesn't make sense, whereas mental states arising, like waves in water, does make sense. In all three of the chapters on Buddhism in this book, I suggest that the Chinese term xin has both senses: mind and mental state(s). Please turn to the discussions of water and waves above in this chapter and in the introduction to the chapter on Madhyamaka. Here the Asvaghosa's seems to be that the existence of objects depends on the mental states which correspond to them.

[539] *Sravakas* and *pratyekabuddhas* are practitioners of early non-Mahayana Buddhism. They listened to sermons or privately analyzed the Buddha's philosophy, respectively.

buddhas. It did not arise at a previous time, and it will not cease at a later time. It is perfectly eternal. From its origin forward, its nature in itself is replete with all meritorious qualities. What we speak of as the substance itself has an aspect of great wisdom and radiant clarity, an aspect of pervasively illuminating the realm of things, an aspect of true consciousness and knowledge, an aspect of clear and pure mind in its nature in itself, aspects of permanence, pleasure, self, and purity, and aspect of clean and cool unchanging self-possession. It has these in supply as plentifully as the sands of the Ganges. It is not separate from, cut off from, or different from the inconceivable teaching of the Buddha. And it even has an aspect of being replete without any deficiency. It is called the "*tathagatagarba.*" It is also called the dharma body of the Tathagata.

Q: The above-mentioned suchness, being even in its substance, is separate from any properties. How can you yet say that its substance has so many kinds of meritorious qualities?

A: Although it actually has these aspects of meritorious qualities, it has no differentiated properties.[540] All alike of one flavor, it is only one: suchness. What does this mean? Since it has no divisions and is separate from the property of division, it is therefore non-dual. So, in what sense can one speak of it as differentiated? Due to the active consciousness, the properties of arising and cessation appear. How do they appear? Since all things are fundamentally only mind, there actually are none as thoughts construe them. But there is the deluded mind. Unenlightened, it gives rise to thoughts and perceives objects. Hence, we speak of its ignorance. The nature of mind does not give rise to them, and so it is the aspect of the brilliant clarity of great wisdom. If the mind gives rise to perceptions, then there are aspects that are not perceived. The

---

[540] This is how Huayan defends its positive-sounding metaphysics against the charge that it is inconsistent with the Madhyamaka theory of emptiness. Is it plausible?

nature of the mind is separate from views, and so it is the aspect of widely illuminating the realm of things.

If the mind has movements in it, it is not true consciousness or knowledge. They have no nature in themselves. They aren't eternal, aren't bliss, aren't a self, and aren't pure. They are torment, deformity, and lack of self-possession to the point of containing aspects of delusion and defilement more numerous than the sands of the Ganges. In contrast to these aspects, the nature of the mind does not move and has pure meritorious qualities and properties more numerous than the sands of the Ganges appearing in it. If the mind has arisings in it and sees the things before it as thinkable, then there will be something that it lacks. Pure things and innumerable meritorious qualities such as these are just one mind and none can be thought. That is why, being replete, it is called "the dharma body" and "the tathagatagarbha"....

1.5 *Showing how to go from arising and cessation into suchness*

It is what is called "examining the five aggregates and the relations of the physical to the mental." The objects of the six sense-objects are ultimately devoid of thought. Since the mind has no characteristic of form, even by seeking them in the ten directions, in the end they cannot be found. It is like a person getting lost.[541] We say that he takes east for west, while the directions actually do not change. Sentient beings are like that. Being ignorant, they are lost. We say that they take the mind to be thoughts. But the mind actually doesn't move. If they can investigate and understand that the mind is devoid of thoughts, then they come into accord with and enter into suchness.

---

[541] The ten directions are up, down, north, south, east, west, northwest, southwest, northeast, and southeast.

2.0 *Correcting heretical attachments*

All heretical attachments are based on the view that there is a self. Separate from the view that there is a self, there are no heretical attachments. The view that there is a self is of two sorts. What are the two? First, the view that there is a personal self. Second, the view that there is a self of things.

2.1 *The view that there is a personal self*

It is pertains to ordinary beings. I explain it as of five types. What are the five? First, they hear *sutras* say that the Tathagata's dharma body is ultimately quiescent and like empty space. Since they don't understand this as an attachment breaker,[542] they say that empty space is the nature of the Tathagata. How do you correct this? You clarify that the property of being empty space is an illusory thing, devoid of substance and unreal. Since it opposes the physical, it has perceivable properties that make the mind arise and cease. But since all physical things are originally mind, actually there is no external physicality. If there is no external physicality, then there are no properties of empty space. What we call "all objects" are only the mind and exist in dependence upon the arising of delusion. When the mind is separated from all delusory movements, then all objects cease, and there is only one real mind which pervades everywhere. This is to say that the ultimate aspect of the wisdom of the vast nature of the Tathagata is not like the property of empty space.[543]

Second, [ordinary beings] hear the *sutras* say that mundane things are ultimately empty in substance, and even the things that are nirvana and suchness are also ultimately empty. From the beginning they have been empty in themselves and separate from all properties. Since ordinary beings don't understand this as an attachment breaker, they say that the nature of suchness and nirvana is just their emptiness.

---

[542] In other words, it is language intended to stop attachments and delusions but not to be taken as true.

[543] FZ: "Since [the nature of the Tathagata] pervades everywhere, like space, the text uses empty space as a metaphor."

How do you correct this? You clarify that the substance itself of suchness and the dharma body is not empty. For it is replete with the meritorious qualities of innumerable natures.

Third, they hear the *sutras* say that the womb of the Tathagata has no increase or decrease, and its substance is supplied with all things of merit. Since they don't comprehend this, they say that the tathagatagarbha includes the distinctions between the properties in themselves of mental and physical things. How do you correct this? [You make it clear that] the *sutras* are explaining only the aspect of suchness. To cause the aspects of arising, cessation, and defilement to be manifest, they speak of distinctions.[544]

Fourth, they hear the *sutras* say that all mundane and defiled things of samsara exist in dependence upon the *tathagatagarba*. Nothing is separate from suchness. Since they don't comprehend this, they say that the *tathagatagarba* contains all mundane things of samsara. How do you correct this? [You make it clear that], since the *tathagatagarba* from the first has only purities and meritorious qualities more numerous than the sands of the Ganges and is neither separate, cut off, nor different from suchness; and since defiled and tainted things more numerous than the sands of the Ganges are only of illusory existence, their nature in itself is fundamentally nonexistent. From beginningless generations past they have not been linked to the *tathagatagarba*. If the substance of the *tathagatagarba* contained illusory things, then bringing about realization and forever laying delusions to rest would never occur.

Fifth, they hear the *sutras* say that on the basis of the *tathagatagarba* there is samsara, and on the basis of the *tathagatagarba* one obtains nirvana. Since they don't comprehend, they say that sentient beings have a beginning. Since they perceive a beginning, they also say that the nirvana attained by Tathagatas has an end, and they become sentient

---

[544] The idea is that while suchness has things of merit and the innumerable merits and qualities mentioned in the previous paragraph, there are no real distinctions among these things. Is that a tenable position?

beings again.[545] How do you correct this? [You clarify that] since the *tathagatagarba* has no initial boundary, the property of ignorance also has no beginning. If one says that external to the triple world there is a beginning and coming about of sentient beings, then that is the theory of heretical scriptures. The nirvana attained by the buddhas corresponds to [the *tathagatagarba*] and thus has no final boundary.

2.2 *The view that there is a self of things*[546]

Because of the dull faculties of those of the secondary vehicle, the Tathagata intended to explain that a person has no self. Since the explanation is not ultimate, they took the view that there were five *skandhas*.[547] They had anxiety about samsara and deludedly grasped for nirvana. How do you correct this? [You clarify that] the natures themselves of the things that are the Tathagata and the five *skandhas* do not arise, thus have no cessation, and are fundamentally nirvana.

Next: ultimately being separated from deluded graspings. One must know that tainted things and pure things all mutually inform each other and have no natures in themselves that can be expressed. Therefore, all things from their origin forth are not physical, not mental, not wisdom, not consciousness, not being, not non-being, but ultimately of inexpressible properties. So, if there are words that express them, one should know that the good and wondrous skillful means of the Tathagata employ words by convention to guide sentient beings. Their aim is to have all intend to separate themselves from thoughts and return to suchness. For thinking about all things makes the mind arise and cease and not enter true wisdom....

3.0 *The nature of wisdom*

...Q: Since empty space has no limit, the world has no limit. Since the world has no limit, sentient beings have no

---

[545] This scheme reflects Hindu and ancient Chinese mythology.
[546] A "self" of a thing is an inherent nature or substance in itself of a thing.
[547] The five *skandhas* are the constituents of the person. See footnote 420.

438

limit. Since sentient beings have no limit, the distinctions in mental acts also have no limit. Thus, objects cannot have distinctions drawn among them, and they are hard to know and hard to comprehend. If ignorance were cut off, there would be no notions at all in the mind. How should we understand the term "all types of wisdom"?

A: All objects fundamentally are one mind and separate from thoughts and cognitions.[548] Since sentient beings falsely perceive objects, in the mind there is the drawing of distinctions between them. Since they falsely give rise to notions and thoughts that do not match the natures of things, they cannot understand with certainty. But buddhas and tathagatas have separated themselves from the properties of perceptions. There is nowhere they do not penetrate. Since their mind is true and real, it is of the nature of things. Its substance in itself sheds light on all false things. They have the function of great wisdom, and its immeasurable skillful means. And they follow what sentient beings need in order to comprehend. All of them can lay bare the various meanings of the teaching. That is why this gets the name "all types of wisdom."

Suggested Readings

Asvaghosa, *The Awakening of Faith,* Haketa, Yoshito S., trans. (New York: Columbia University Press, 1967)

Asvaghosa, *The Awakening of Faith,* D. T. Suzuki, trans., various editions.

---

[548] This would seem to conflict with the earlier passage that indicated that objects arise and cease in dependence on the arising and cessation of mental states. However, the idealism is two-layered. Objects as we know them are dependent on our mental states – our concepts and points of view. Objects as they are in themselves exist independently of these mental states but not independent of mind itself.

Brown, Brian Edward, *The Buddha Nature: A Study of the Tathagatagarbha and Alayavijnana* (Delhi: Motilal Banarsidass, 2010)

Cleary, Thomas F. *Entry Into the Inconceivable: An Introduction to Hua-Yen Buddhism* (Honolulu: University of Hawaii Press, 1995)

Cleary, Thomas, *The Flower Ornament Scripture* (Boston: Shambala, 1987)

Fa-tsang,[549] *An English Translation of Fa-Tsang's Commentary on the Awakening of Faith*, Dirck Vorenkamp, trans. (Lewiston, Queenston, Lampeter: Edwin Mellen Press, 2004)

Gold, Jonathan, *Paving the Great Way: Vasubandhu's Unifying Buddhist Philosophy* (New York: Columbia University Press, 2014)

Jones, Nicholaos, "Buddhist Reductionism and Emptiness in Huayan Perspective," in K. Tanaka, Y. Deguchi, J. Garfield, and G. Priest, eds., *The Moon Points Back* (New York: Oxford University Press, 2015)

Jones, Nicholaos, "Huayan Metaphysics in Fazang's *Huayan Wujiao Zhang*: The Inexhaustible Freedom of Dependent Origination," in Sandra A. Wawrytko and Youru Wang, eds., *Dharma and Dao: Chinese Buddhist Philosophy* (New York: Springer, 2017)

Jones, Nicholaos, "Huayan Numismatics as Metaphysics: Explicating Fazang's Coin-Counting Metaphor," *Philosophy East & West* 67(2017):

---

[549] Fazang.

Kochumuttom, Thomas, *A Buddhist Doctrine of Experience: A New Translation and Interpretation of the Works of Vasubandhu the Yogacarin* (Delhi: Motilal Banarsidass, 1982)

Liu, Ming-Wood, "The Mind-Only Teaching of Ching-Ying Hui-Yüan: An Early Interpretation of Yogacara Thought in China," *Philosophy East & West* 35(1985): 351-376

Lusthaus, Dan, *Buddhist Phenomenology: A Philosophical Investigation of Yogacara Buddhism and the Ch'eng Wei-shih Lun* (London: Rutledge, 2003)

Schmithausen, Lambert, *On the Problem of the External World in the Ch'eng wei shih lun* (Tokyo: International Institute for Buddhist Studies, 2005)

Waldron, William, *The Buddhist Unconscious: The Alaya-vijñana in the Context of Indian Buddhist Thought* (London: Routledge, 2003)

Xuanzang, *Treatise on Establishing Mind-Only*, in Francis H. Cook, trans., *Three Texts on Consciousness Only* (Moraga, CA: Numata Center for Buddhist Translation and Research, 1999)[550]

---

[550] Cook translates the title as "Demonstration of Consciousness Only." His book also includes translations of two texts by Vasubhandu.

10

Chan

Chan[551] is a school of Buddhism that places great emphasis on achieving an enlightened mental state in meditation. This mental state is somehow a blissful and wise one which offers release from the inherently disappointing nature of existence. Because the meditation requires the cessation of conceptual activity in the mind, the resultant mental state is said to be indescribable, and the content of its wisdom and significance of its bliss cannot be easily conveyed in words. It's not clear what to say about a non-conceptual mental state. For example, the visual sensation of red is difficult to describe. Chan's wisdom, however, is not as rudimentary as a raw sensation. It purports to include wisdom that resolves deep questions about reality and the meaning of life. Unlike the sensation of a color, therefore, Chan's wisdom should be describable because it has content. Yet, according to Chan texts yet it is indescribable.

This is the difficulty of Chan; it is by its own definition of itself indescribable. And yet the last 1500 years of its history have seen many thousands of pages of attempts to describe it by its own adherents. Why would they spill so much ink over something they hold to be indescribable? The reason might be that there are ways of using language that, while not describing

---

[551] "Zen" is now an English word, recently derived from the Japanese and referring to the school of Buddhism, called "Chan" (pronounced with a long "a") in China, which was transmitted to Japan. "Zen" is the Japanese adaptation of the Chinese word which in turn was derived by the Chinese as a transliteration of a Sanskrit term for "meditation" *dhyana* (chn.: *channa*.) I might have simply used the colloquial term "Zen" in this chapter, but I have decided to be more precise and use "Chan" because the chapter pertains only to the Chinese segment of the school.

the wisdom achieved by Chan Buddhists, nevertheless somehow move the reader or listener closer to understanding it. The text to which this chapter is devoted serves as a good example of such language. It is the recorded utterances of the Chan master Huangbo (fl. c 835 C.E.) We will also read a passage from the record of Huangbo's student Linji (d.866 C.E.), in which certain uses of language bring Linji to understand Chan fully. Perhaps in this way we will get a glimmer of it.

Chan History

A detailed account of the rich history of Chan may be found elsewhere and is not needed here.[552] Yet we should have some historical context before we turn to the readings. This is because Chan takes itself to be essentially a transmission of its indescribable wisdom from master to disciple over many generations and centuries, from India to China, and it insists that this transmission may be traced back to the Buddha himself. The enlightenment achieved in Chan Buddhism is supposed to be passed from master to disciple, because the master is needed in order to guide the disciple toward enlightenment and to verify his enlightenment experience if it ever occurs. It cannot be verified in the ways that mastery of other subjects can, including the doctrines of other forms of Buddhism, for example by written examination. No test of linguistic mastery can verify that the disciple understands Chan, because the insight is ineffable. Therefore, in order to be counted as genuine, one's understanding of it must be observed in the entirety of one's countenance and behavior by someone who recognizes it. Eventually, the Chan master whose student understands will share with him a moment of mutual recognition of enlightenment, a "tacit reconciliation,"

---

[552] The book by Dumoulin mentioned in the list of suggested readings found at the end of this chapter is the best place to begin studying of Chan history.

leaving the disciple qualified to pass the wisdom on to others. Huangbo said,

> How could this teaching be the sort of thing you could comprehend by means of language? You can't come to see it through subject and object. The idea is obtained by a tacit reconciliation. This gate is called the Gate of the Teaching of Non-Action. If you would obtain it, you need only know how to have no mental states and you will suddenly become enlightened and obtain it.[553]

Perhaps an analogy may be found in sports. In order to master a sport, reading a book about it isn't sufficient, and no conceptual mastery of it will prove that the student has mastered the sport. Only a non-conceptual demonstration of his ability will do. So, Chan is by nature passed along from one generation to the next as a way of understanding the world and the human mind and is not encapsulated in texts. In Chan, however, what is passed down is not a skill but a mental discipline and insight into the nature of the world. It sometimes borrows the Daoist term, "Way," in order to express this. It is not a theory or doctrine but a certain way of experiencing. Experiencing what, exactly? We'll return to that question later.

First, a caveat: Chan history is a rich field, and the story is more complicated than I will make it here. Its history is more than that of an experience transmitted from the Buddha directly through an unbroken line of disciples over the centuries, and, indeed, it may even be less than that, as well.[554]

---

[553] *Wan Ling Record*, text number 2013, in Junjiro Takakusu and Kaigyoku Watanabe, eds., *Taisho Shinshu Daizokyo* (Tokyo: Taisho Issaikyo Kankokai, 1924-35), p. 527. The *Wan Ling Record* is a Huangbo text that is not included in our readings. "Gate" (chn.: *men*) is a term used for lesson or unit of a teaching. Notice the usage of the Daoist term "non-action."

[554] It is curious that Chan Buddhists have treasured the Buddhist scriptures and written thousands of pages on Chan, given that the wisdom is only privately and nonlinguistically shared between master and disciple. The last thirty years in academic Chan historiography have shown that Chan history isn't simply a transmission of enlightenment through a certain authoritative

Various movements in Chinese Buddhism of the Fourth and Fifth Centuries C.E., such as developments in meditation and of the Chinese form of Madhyamaka, had a role in the development of Chan. Some of the stories of transmission are probably only inaccurate myths developed long after their purported subjects' times, and Daoism, with its iconoclasm and disdain for rigorous protocols and ponderous institutions, contributed to Chan. So, the story I present here is a mere introduction to the subject of Chan history. It assumes that some sort of putative enlightenment experience exists and is something like what is described in the notable texts. This is not to beg any questions about the status of this experience as putative wisdom. It may be wisdom and it may be delusion. But I assume that it exists.

The transmission of the experience of enlightenment began when the Buddha silently triggered and acknowledged enlightenment in a disciple named Kasyapa. After about nine hundred years of subsequent and continuous transmissions, the legendary figure and Persian monk, Bodhidharma, extended the transmission to China by going there himself in the Fifth Century C.E. The transmission would continue and reach Huangbo in the Ninth Century, the subject of this chapter's primary reading. A few generations after Huangbo, his teachings were acclaimed as superb and his words were recorded. The transmission continued to Japan, Korea, and elsewhere. Even today, unbroken chains of transmission are supposed to obtain between masters of old and contemporary Chan/Zen masters. Even in the small town in Virginia where I now sit, there are Americans intending to uphold this

---

line of adherents. It was subject to the foibles and vices of human nature, such that some of the stories you will find as you read about Chan were written for reasons of ambition and fancy instead of truth. The books by McRae, Heine, and Welter, as well as McRae's essay in the book by Dumoulin, in this chapter's suggested readings will introduce you to these issues. Of course, when a cherished institution is shown to have members who were subject to the standard human vices and ambitions, this does nothing to diminish the value of the institution.

transmission by traditional verificatory interviews between master and disciple. Bodhidharma, then, is considered to be the first Chinese patriarch[555] of Chan. He is credited with saying that Chan Buddhism is a "special transmission outside the *sutras*" which points directly to the nature of the human mind, letting one see one's true nature and attain enlightenment.

It is difficult for even the most cursory history of Chan to leave out the case of the Sixth Patriarch, Huineng (638–713), a prominent traditional example of transmission from master to disciple. *The Platform Sutra of the Sixth Patriarch*, the Eighth Century record of his life and sayings, is the only Chinese text called in the Chinese Buddhist tradition a "*sutra*," meaning "words of a buddha." The text tells of the transmission from the Fifth Patriarch, Hongren (601 – 674), to the humble and illiterate Huineng, in preference to the more obvious candidate of Shenxiu (d. 706), the accomplished monk at Hongren's monastery. When it was time for Hongren to choose his heir, the monk who understood Chan better than all the other monks and would therefore become the next patriarch, he asked that anyone in his assembly believing himself to be a suitable candidate write a poem expressing the meaning of Chan. Shenxiu wrote the following poem.

> The body is a tree of enlightenment.
> The mind like a clear mirror's stand.
> Always strive to keep it polished.
> Don't allow dust to land.

The poem was admired by the other monks, who thought Shenxiu would be chosen to be the Sixth Patriarch. However, Huineng, who had not even attained the status of monk at the monastery, composed this poem in response to Shenxiu.

---

[555] The term "patriarch" is commonly used to translate the Chinese word *zu*, which literally means "ancestor."

Enlightenment fundamentally has no tree.
And the clear mirror has no stand.
Buddha nature is always clean and pure.
Where could dust land?

Hongren favored this poem and gave the patriarchal robe to Huineng.[556] Huineng's poem expresses the nature of Chan Buddhism from the standpoint of one who has attained Buddhist enlightenment, not that of one who is striving to attain it. It is one of many examples of attempts by Chan Buddhists to express the experience of enlightenment in words or deeds, an experience which they say is ineffable. The readings in this chapter contain many other examples of such attempts. One trope seen in Huineng's poem is to aver that enlightenment is always already present in the mind but also covered over by the manifold and busy cogitations of our intellect's analyses, plans, and imagination.

The tradition surrounding Huineng's poem is rich. There is also a version of it in which line three is "Fundamentally there is not a single thing." When Huangbo was asked about this line, he said, "We don't posit anything" (*Wan Ling Record* 11). In other words, there is a kind of experience, impossible to describe, to which the mind may be directed by certain linguistic and behavioral indications. An excellent example of this is the story of the enlightenment of Linji,[557] Huangbo's student, which we will read below. If you like, please skip forward to the selection from the *Record of Linji* now and read it before continuing.

---

[556] Of course, Shenxiu's poem also expresses Chan cultivation, as well, and the so-called Northern School of Chan, as opposed to Huineng's Southern School, also flourished. See John McRae's book on *The Northern School* in this chapter's suggested readings. Notice the irony of a transmission of a supposedly ineffable understanding being verified by the *words* of Huineng's poem.

[557] Linji's name in Japanese pronunciation, "Rinzai," is the name of the large sect of Japanese Buddhism existing today.

Chan Philosophy

Let us take a look at what is of philosophical import in Chan. One doesn't want to call Chan philosophical.[558] It proclaims nothing on the matters of philosophy that one would assume to be of concern to a meditative Buddhist tradition interested in what is ultimately real. There is no tradition of Chan philosophical literature in metaphysics, epistemology or ethics, even though such may be found in other streams of Buddhism.

Yet there is more to the story. The roots of Chan lie in Yogacara and Madhyamaka Buddhism, represented by other chapters in this volume, as well as in the eccentric Daoism of Zhuangzi. In the Chan texts, we find many statements akin to the idealism of Yogacara, according to which all phenomena are just mind. Chan also accepts the Madhyamaka notion that everything is empty of inherent existence. We can find a typical example of this rapport with Madhyamaka in the *Huangbo*, in a passage from which we just read a snippet. The passage in full runs as follows.

> A questioner said, "'Fundamentally there is not a single thing.' To deny the existence of a thing involves position and negation."
> Huangbo said, "We deny existence but we don't posit anything. Enlightenment is at every point without position and has no conception of not existing either." (*Wan Ling Record* 11)

If you've read the chapter on Madhyamaka, you can see its philosophy in this passage.

Chan also places great emphasis on the value of refraining from making distinctions of any kind, especially between good and bad, deluded and enlightened. In this it

---

[558] The number of books and articles on Chan *philosophy* is not large. The books by Izutsu, Hagen, Wright, and Davis in this chapter's list of suggested readings are examples, as are the articles by me and by Wienpahl.

draws near to the views of Zhuangzi and also shares his fondness for the eccentric behavior that someone who has ceased making distinctions might make. The Chan literature is full of tales of bizarre antics by its adherents. Like Zhuangzi and perhaps unlike Indian Buddhism, Chan embodies a deeply joyous satisfaction at the fact that this world exists. Chan is certainly a conglomeration of Indian Buddhism and Daoism of the Zhuangzi spirit.

Nevertheless, the idea that Chan has no philosophical content is a reasonable one, given that Chan texts commonly proclaim that Chan has no such content. But I would like to suggest a way in which Chan enlightenment has a philosophical content which is consistent with this denial. Chan's pretense to vacuity may be a psychological tool rather than a thesis. That Chan texts say that Chan enlightenment is vacuous does not entail that it in fact is vacuous.

Chan has a philosophical soteriology, a theory of the meaning and methods of spiritual salvation. It is an implied theory, rooted in Madhyamaka and Yogacara philosophy and never fully articulated in the Chan literature, but I think we can tease it out in the following way. Consider this a naturalistic account of Chan enlightenment, one which reduces the indescribable mystery associated with Chan to understandable terms.

Let us begin with three observations about Chan. First, Chan advocates simple meditation in which one allows higher-order conceptual thinking and cognitive activity to subside and cease while one remains lucidly conscious. Second, when doing this, one should be able to recognize one's mind's participation in an enlightened state. Chan masters say that this enlightened state is ineffable, having no content that may be subsumed under any concepts, because in order to have the experience, one must refrain from conceptual mental activity. However, the third observation is that Chan texts seem to say that in the enlightened state, one's concerns about the value, purpose, or importance of the world (by which I mean totality of everything there is) are laid to rest. What is it that lays these concerns to rest? How is it that meditation brings one access to it? It would seem that there must be some content of Chan's enlightenment after all, if this enlightenment lays these concerns to rest. It may be that this content is there but not readily available to description because it is so tightly coupled to the nonconceptual meditative state. It may be that this content is very difficult to put into words even though it is possible to say something about it if we analyze it carefully.

Consider the following inference from the three observations. Since something of immense value is apprehended in Chan meditation, a value so profound that all mundane concerns are dwarfed into obscurity and joy ensues, and since in meditation there is no longer any conceptual activity in the mind in this state, we may infer that what is of immense value is not a particular thing. This is because all particular things are subject to conceptual description. Now, I think we can assume that nothing else is real except particular things, the world, and facts about particular things and the world; at least, I know of nothing else. Hence, the object of enlightenment, since it is not a particular thing, must therefore be the world itself or a fact about the world. By "world" I mean something like the container of all particular things or their totality. The concept doesn't have much more content than that, and if it were the object of enlightenment, this would help explain why it is difficult for enlightened Chan masters to say much about it; there isn't much content in the concept of the world. I propose the following conclusion, therefore. It is the world, or the fact that it exists rather than nothing, which has immense value. It is the world and the fact that it exists having enormous value that must be the objects of enlightenment. As the prerequisite to all other values, this value dwarfs them in degree.

The proposition that states the content of enlightenment, then, is "this world, or the fact that it exists rather than nothing, has immense value." Call this proposition "P." Chan enlightenment has content P but it is nevertheless viewed as ineffable. This is because P cannot convey the experience of the magnitude of value it refers to. P is not very significant to the mind as long as the mind is employing its usual battery of concepts. If you were to utter P someone selected at random, he would probably shrug and reply, "I suppose so." He would not attain any sort of profound enlightenment by hearing and understanding your utterance. He would have yet to experience the immense value. The value is comprehended not by reading or hearing that the world has immense value, but only by the experience of dropping conceptual activity in meditation in order to have direct experience of this value. This is analogous to the difference between being told that a certain painting is very beautiful and seeing the painting for the first time. When one hears that it is beautiful, one shrugs and says, "I suppose so." Then, when one sees the painting, one apprehends its beauty with a sense of awe.

This interpretation of Chan explains why the value recognized in Chan enlightenment not only dwarfs all other values but is invisible to the mind when it is engaging in conceptual activity. While concepts of particular things are being shuffled about in the mind, the mind can apprehend only the particular things that are the objects of those concepts. The special value of the world is recognizable only by remaining conscious without allowing any cognitive activity to take place in one's mind. It is similar to the impossibility of apprehending a body of water as an undifferentiated unity while there are waves on the water. Only when the waves subside and the surface is flat may one peer into the depths and apprehend the unified body of water experientially. Similarly, it is only in meditation in which conceptual activity stops that one may fully experience the world and the value of the fact that it exists rather than nothing.

We can also explain why the meditative state in which conceptual activity has ceased while one remains lucidly conscious is necessary for enlightenment but not sufficient. Obviously, the state is not sufficient, because achieving it does not immediately result in enlightenment. The records show practitioners of Chan meditation achieving this state without any enlightening result. Additional tools are used to supplement the state, for example *gongan* cases, which you might have heard of by their Japanese name "*koan*," or little puzzling anecdotes thought to help push the meditating mind over the threshold into enlightenment. This is because the mind needs to adjust itself to its object before it can grasp it. Consider the water analogy again. The waves abate and the surface is calm. But the observer doesn't yet see the cavernous vista of the body of water. It will pop into view when his visual faculties adjust to it, as, for example, they do in the case of a drawing of an old woman which also is a drawing of a young woman.[559] It takes a while for the mind to parse what it is perceiving properly. When it does for the meditator, suddenly he experiences what E refers to. With this he is enlightened and saved.

Even to get to the meditative state in the first place is difficult. Try to remain conscious but without thinking for a few moments. You will notice how difficult it is. Our minds engage in conceptual activity nearly all the time. So, according to Chan Buddhism, one will be dissatisfied with life as long as one doesn't engage in the special technique of meditation. One will observe only the values of particular things, their impermanence, and the competing evils which diminish them. Right before us lies a world the ineffably profound value of which is concealed by conceptual activity. We can recognize this world's value only by the cessation of this conceptual activity, but from the beginnings of our lives until their ends, we never manage to let it cease while we are conscious. The presence of this activity makes it so that only particular things are available to our minds. We will die never recognizing that the world in which we dwelled for our entire lives had a depth of value which would have brought us joyous salvation as a relief from mundane cares. This immense value, dwarfing all

[559] There is a famous example of this in a German drawing of 1888 which you will be able to find on the World Wide Web.

other values, is enough to make their narrowness, fragility and impermanence, their unsatisfactoriness, turn out to be not of grave concern. Think of Zhuangzi's celebration of disease, of tumors, and of returning to the great clump. One cannot recognize this immense value if one is given to high-order conceptual thinking, as almost all human beings are. We distinguish, cogitate, plan and analyze. This is why Buddhist enlightenment requires a special but very simple meditative practice. This is a philosophical stance peculiar to Chan.

The Readings

The main reading in this chapter is *Huangbo Xiyun's Essential Teachings of the Transmission of the Mental State (Huangbo Xiyun Chuanxin fayao)* of Huangbo,[560] except that I have omitted the preface by Pei Xiu. I have also included a short excerpt from *The Record of Linji*.[561] Huangbo was third in the lineage of Chan masters descending from Huineng. The Huangbo literature is a set of records of the sayings of Huangbo in lecture and in conversation with his monks. The principle recorder of these materials was Pei Xiu, who says that he interviewed Huangbo in 843 and in 849. Here you have the first of these two interviews, the second[562] being the *Wan Ling*

---

[560] Huangbo's name was Xiyun, though he is commonly referred to by the name of his monastery's mountain location, Mt. Huangbo. His monastic honorific name was Duanji.

[561] The Chinese texts are numbers 2012 and 1985, respectively, in Junjiro Takakusu and Kaigyoku Watanabe, eds., *Taisho Shinshu Daizokyo* (Tokyo: Taisho Issaikyo Kankokai, 1924-35).

[562] See John Blofeld's book in the suggested readings at the end of this chapter for a translation of this work.

Record, excerpts from which you have read above. It is probable that some of the passages are apocryphal additions made in later centuries by other authors.[563]

I have selected the Huangbo simply because it is a fine Chan text. Pei Xiu gives a summary of its message in his preface:

> One who would explain it does not set up ideas or concepts, does not set up sects or ideologies, and does not open up any ways into it. It is just what is right before us. As soon as cogitations occur, one errs.

Huangbo was the teacher of Linji, who becomes a major figure in East Asian religious history. A Chan sect of the Japanese derivation of his name has millions of adherents in Japan today, the Rinzai sect. The tale of his enlightenment, section 48 of *The Record of Linji,* is translated below. The intriguing origin of this text can be found in the book by Albert Welter in the list of suggested readings at the end of this chapter.

---

[563] For more on this, please see Dale Wright's 2004 article in this chapter's list of suggested readings.

454

Huangbo Xiyun's Essential Teachings of the Transmission of the Mental State[564]

The Master told me, "The buddhas and all the sentient beings[565] are of only one mental state, and there is no other

---

[564] For the term *xin* (mind, heart, mental state) I often use the translation "mental state" instead of term ordinarily used "mind" because it more precisely captures Huangbo's meaning. In most English translations of Buddhist texts "mind" is used with confusing results. As we will, see "mental state" renders the meaning clear. In some places, where a more reifying sense is appropriate, I also use the translation "mind." In the case of the title of this reading, Huangbo isn't speaking about transmitting his mind to another person but rather causing another person to come to share the same mental state (or to have a mental state of the same type) as Huangbo's. There are other places in the text where recognizing that *xin* can mean "mental state" as well as mind and where we would be confused without doing so.

The mental state here is the state where one's mind no longer has any mental states. That seems incoherent, but look at it this way. "Mental state" can have two meanings: particular thoughts or overall state. The title means the second. The overall state of mind here is the state in which there are no particular conceptualizations, no thoughts, but just pure and calm consciousness.

Consider the following illustration. Suppose some neuropsychologists are studying a subject's brain states as they correspond to his mental states. They record brain state A as corresponding to the subject's desire for ice cream. They record brain state B as corresponding to his feeling lonely. They record brain state B as corresponding to his remembering to take something off of the stove. Finally, the subject engages in meditation and, although conscious, has no particular mental state whatsoever. "My mind was perfectly still. I wasn't thinking anything," he later reports. How shall the neuroscientists record his brain state's correspondence? "Well, he had no mental state. Or, his mental state was that he had no particular mental states." By further analogy, consider a pond with various patterns and shapes of wave – various states. You record these in detail. Finally, the pond becomes perfectly still. What state is it now? It is in the state of having no states! There is no incoherence here. Just an equivocation as we learn to see a domain in a new way.

[565] "Sentient beings" is the Buddhist term used to refer to any conscious being which is not a buddha.

dharma.[566] This mental state has no beginning from which it comes. It cannot be created or destroyed. It is not blue or yellow. It has no form or characteristics. One doesn't categorize it as existing or not existing. One doesn't determine its age. It is neither long nor short, neither big nor small. It transcends all determination, language, evidence and distinctions. When you confront substance, there it is. But as soon as you let thoughts move, you go astray. Like an empty void, it has no delimitation and cannot be quantified. Just this one mental state - this is buddhahood.

"A buddha and the sentient beings are not at all different. However, sentient beings are attached to phenomena and seek it externally. In seeking, they lose it. This is to take buddhahood to look for buddhahood and to use mental states to get hold of that mental state. Even if they exhaust themselves for an entire eon, they will never be able to get it. They don't know that if they let thoughts subside and put their cogitations from their minds, buddhahood will show itself before them. This mental state itself is buddhahood. Buddhahood is the sentient beings. When it is the sentient beings, it is not diminished. When it is a buddha it is not enhanced.

"When it comes to the six perfections[567] and the many practices and merits as numerous as the Ganges, what you originally have is sufficient, so don't artificially try to enhance it. When you come across a cause to do so, then engage in them. When the cause is gone, then be still. If you are not certain in your belief that this is buddhahood, and you prefer to be attached to phenomena, cultivations, and practices in order to seek merit, then all this delusional thought will be a diversion from the Way.

---

[566] "*Dharma*" (*fa*) means both thing and the Buddhist teaching. Huangbo makes use of this ambiguity in many places in the text and so I will leave it untranslated throughout in order to let this ambiguity come through. It never represents a pernicious ambiguity but rather a subtle play on words.

[567] *Liudu.* These are six goals of religious self-cultivation in Mahayana Buddhism: generosity, moral conduct, patience, vigorous effort, meditation, and wisdom.

456

"This mental state is buddhahood. There is no other buddhahood, and there is no separate mental state. This mental state is clear and pure. It is like a void, not having a phenomenal appearance. When you set thoughts in motion by means of mental states, then you diverge from the substance of the dharma and become attached to phenomena. But there has never been a buddhahood that was attached to phenomena. To practice the six perfections and the myriad practices in order to become a Buddha is gradual. But there has never been a gradual buddhahood. Just become enlightened in this singlular mental state, and then there won't be even a few dharmas[568] that you can get at. This is real buddhahood.

"A buddha and the sentient beings are of one mental state without any difference. It is like an empty void in which there is no admixture and nothing wrong. It is like the sun's rotation which illuminates the world. When the sun rises and lights up the world, the empty void cannot be lighted up. And when the sun sets and darkens the world, the empty void cannot be darkened. Dark and light alternate with each other, but the nature of the empty void is still and unchanging. The mental states of a buddha and of all sentient beings are also like this. If you see buddhahood as the characteristics of pure, shining, and wise, and you see sentient beings as the characteristics of muddled, benighted, and samsaric,[569] then you who make this analysis will not attain enlightenment, even after as many eons as there are sands of the Ganges because you are attached to characteristics.

"This one mental state in which not even the slightest dharma to be got at - this mental state is buddhahood. If today's students of the Way do not awaken to the substance of this

---

[568] "*Dharmas*" here is ambiguous between "teachings" and "things." If the mind is perfectly calm and devoid of conceptual activity then although one remains conscious, one will apprehend no things. By the same token, neither will the Buddhist teachings, by nature gradual and conceptual, be the object of this mental state.

[569] This pertains to *samsara*, the alternation between birth and death suffered by beings who have not reached nirvana.

mental state, then they will produce mental states on top of it and seek buddhahood outside of it, attaching themselves to phenomena and cultivating the practices. All of this is a bad dharma and not the way of enlightenment.[570]

"Making offerings to the buddhas of the ten directions[571] is not as good as making offerings to one man of the Way who has no mental states. Why? Because the one who has no mental states is without all those mental states. The substance of suchness[572] is like wood and stone inside. It doesn't move; it doesn't stir. Outside, it is like an empty void with no bounds or obstructions. It has no subjective aspect or objective aspect, no phenomenal appearance, and no way of being obtained or lost. Those who make haste do not dare enter this dharma. They fear they will fall into the void with nothing beneath them upon which to stay fast. They look over the precipice and withdraw. This is so for all those who seek through cognition and perception. Those who seek through cognition and perception are like the hairs. Those enlightened to the Way are like the horns.[573]

"Manjusri represents the principle, Samantabhadra the activity.[574] 'Principle' means the principle of real emptiness

---

[570] There is a certain mental state which is devoid of conceptual activity; it is an enlightened mental state. Buddhists who do not grasp this mental state may form concepts of various kinds in a vain attempt to get at it and to reach enlightenment. Notice that Huangbo is saying that standard Buddhist religious practices are a "bad *dharma*." (Here Huangbo uses "*dharma*" in the sense of "teaching;" recall that the term can mean either a teaching or an object. These practices require various conceptual activities of the mind, and so they get on no closer to the state where the mind is free of conceptual activity.

[571] The "ten directions" are up, down, north, south, east, west, northwest, southwest, northeast, and southeast – in other words, "everywhere."

[572] Suchness (*ruru*) is the way things are in themselves. It cannot be expressed or subjected to concepts, so the term "such" is used.

[573] A common Buddhist analogy, the hairs on an animal being many and the horns few.

[574] Manjusri: the *bodhisattva* of wisdom. *Bodhisattvas* are enlightened people who have vowed to save all other sentient beings before entering their final nirvana. Samantabhadra represents practice, Avalokitesvara

458

without obstruction. 'Activity' means the activity that is separate from phenomena and inexhaustible. Avalokitesvara is the Great Compassion. Mahasthama represents the Great Wisdom. Vimalakirti represents the Pure Name. 'Pure' refers to the nature and 'name' to the phenomenon. The nature and phenomena are not different, so it is called 'pure name.'

"What the *bodhisattvas* represent is possessed by all people. It is not separate from the one mental state. Awaken to it and there it is. Today students of the Way don't become enlightened by turning to what is in all of their own mental states but instead grasp for objects and cling to phenomena external to their mental states. They have all turned their backs on the Way.

"Sands of the Ganges - the Buddha said of them, 'If the buddhas, *bodhisattvas*, Indra[575] and all the gods walked across them, the sands would not enjoy it. If cattle, sheep, reptiles and insects walked upon them, the sands would not resent it. Jewels and perfumes the sands do not pine for. For the stench and vileness of excrement the sands have no dislike.'

"This mental state is the mental state without mental states.[576] It is separate from all phenomena. Sentient beings and

---

(Guanyin, who would become enormously popular in East Asian Buddhism) of compassion, and Mahasthama of power and wisdom. Vimalikirti is the lay Buddhist depicted in the *Vimalikirti Sutra.*

[575] A Hindu deity.

[576] Here is a passage in which shows that *xin* is sometimes has the sense of "mental state." If it is translated as "mind," the passage is flatly incoherent. Commonly translated "no-mind," *wuxin* is better understood as "no mental states." The Chan Buddhist tries to calm his mind so that conceptual activity ceases. There is left a mental state but a peculiar one which is this state of lacking any conceptual activity. The mind persists, of course, which is why "no-mind" is a misleading translation.

Consider again a pond with various ripples, waves and disturbances on its surface. These are states of the pond. When the lake is perfectly calm, it can be said to have no state at all. It can also be said that its state is that it has no states of the aforementioned types, namely describable features which involve distinctions and activity. Calmness involves lack of distinctions and lack of activity, so it is a second category of state. To call it "a pond state that is without pond states" is a bit confusing but can be

the buddhas are not distinct. If only you can be without mental states,[577] then you reach the goal. If students of the Way do not right away get rid of mental states, then after all the eons of cultivating the practices, in the end they will not attain the Way. Entangled in the Three Vehicles' meritorious practices, they won't make any breakthrough.[578] Yet, realization of this mental state can be gradual or abrupt. There are those who hear the dharma and in a moment's thought attain the absence of mental states. There are those who reach the ten beliefs, ten stages, ten practices and ten merits and then attain the absence of mental states. Whether by lengthy or short attempt, they

---

rendered coherent. To call it "a pond which is not a pond" simply cannot. This is why *xin* should not be translated as "mind" in this type context in Chan texts but as "mental state." The pond analogy is appropriate, since Chan meditation involves the quieting of the mind such that the brain waves subside. It is a state of mind without the high frequency brain waves, and ordinary mental states are made of such brain waves.

The ordinary mental states with which we are familiar are particular conceptual and intensional states – states of mind in which the mind's concepts are meant to refer to things and to describe them truly in ways subject to language and communication. The mental state associated with Chan meditation, on the other hand, does not involve any of these ordinary mental states. It is therefore understandable that one might describe it as "a mental state without mental states" and then refine this locution by adding that it is a mental state free of conceptual mental states. To reify the term into "mind" causes more confusion.

The usual translation of *wuxin*, "no mind" causes more confusion. Using it, we would have to countenance the notion that the goal is not to have a mind. This makes no sense. Chan Buddhists in meditation are conscious and certainly have minds. What they have is a certain mental state in which all mental states associated with higher-order conceptual activities are absent. It is one and the same mind which has or does not have these various mental states. There is not a plurality of minds.

The translation of *xin* as "mental state" is therefore more accurate and less confusing and obscure, even if somewhat stilted and less mellifluous.

[577] Of course, this does not mean to be stupid or unconscious but to meditate so that your mind is perfectly calm and devoid of thoughts even while you are conscious.

[578] For the meaning of the "Three Vehicles" see the chapter on Chinese Madhyamaka, footnote 395.

attain the absence of mental states. There is nothing to cultivate or realize. Truly there is nothing to attain. This is really the truth and not empty talk. To attain it in one moment's thought or to attain it with the ten stages of the *bodhisattva*, the merit acquired is exactly the same. Nor is there any shallow or deep to it. It's just that one involves eons of bitter toil.

"To do good and to do evil are both to be attached to phenomena. Being attached to phenomena and doing evil, one winds up going through rebirths. Being attached to phenomena and doing good, one winds up going through bitter suffering. So, it's not as good as realizing, as soon as you hear about it, how to grasp the fundamental dharma. This dharma is just a mental state. Outside of this mental state there is no dharma. The mental state itself is something that is without mental states and yet is not devoid of mental states.[579] If we grasp that this mental state is without mental states, the mental state is thus established as real.

"A tacit reconciliation[580] suffices. All the thoughts and ideas are done away with. Thus, we can say that the Way of language is cut off and the place where the mental events keep going comes to an end. This mental state is originally pure and clear. Buddhas and men all have it.[581] Beasts and worms, as well as buddhas and *bodhisattvas*, are of one substance without

---

[579] If the important mental state in Chan to which Huangbo refers as the key to enlightenment is simple consciousness without the admixture of the manifold mental states generated by conceptual activity, then it is independent of those conceptual mental states and separable from them. Yet, it may also be mixed with them. Meditation is the process of letting them subside so that only that non-conceptual mental state remains.

[580] The term is *moqi*, tacit tallying an implicit understanding, or silent recognition. The idea is this: Imagine that you were a jigsaw puzzle piece and you were able to fit yourself silently and perfectly together with a piece with which you belong in order to form a whole and to reveal something. This is very close to the meaning of *moqi*.

[581] The special mental state of conscious awareness without conceptual activity is always present underneath the overlay of the busy plethora of conceptual mental states. Meditation therefore uncovers a mental state that has always been present by dispelling the conceptual mental states.

distinction. It's only the deluded making of distinctions that creates karma of the various kinds.

"At the ultimate and fundamental level of buddhahood, there really is not one thing.[582] There is an empty, far-reaching, quiescent and pure clearness - simply a wondrous, peaceful joy. When you enter deeply into enlightenment, what is right before you is it, perfectly fulfilled, complete, with nothing lacking. Even if you have perfectly mastered each and every stage of the *bodhisattva*'s progression to buddhahood, at the moment of realization, you will realize that all along your buddhahood could never have had a single thing added to it. You see that the meritorious effects of many eons are the illusions of a dream. This is why the Buddha said, 'In complete enlightenment I really attained nothing. If I had attained something, then Dipankara Buddha would have given a prophecy about me.'[583] He also said, 'This dharma is of one level, having no higher or lower. Its name is enlightenment.' For such a fundamentally pure mental state, all the sentient beings and buddhas, the mountains and rivers of the world, that with characteristics and that without, the entire world in all ten directions, everything is of one level, and lacking in the characteristics of self and other.

"This fundamentally pure mental state always shines everywhere from its perfect clarity. Mundane people do not

---

[582] Here we find a very strong Buddhist metaphysical claim. Notice, however, that in meditation the meditator is doing without conceptual mental states and cannot posit the existence of anything, even though he is fully conscious. One might say that the Buddhists mistake this failing to posit the existence of anything with a confirmation that nothing exists. Moreover, since this mental state is blissful and enlightening according to Buddhists, it is understandable that they would accept its metaphysical point of view uncritically. A more critical Buddhist point of view would take notice of the fact that accepting the reality of the many things of the world and accepting that Chan meditation is enlightening are mutually consistent positions to hold. Most Buddhists, however, seem to hold the more radical view, aligning themselves with the Madhyamaka view that everything is empty of inherent reality.

[583] A reference to *The Diamond Sutra*. Dipankara Buddha was supposed to be a Buddha existing long before Sakyamuni, the Buddha of our epoch.

awaken to it, recognizing only seeing, hearing, feeling and cognition as mental states. Because seeing, hearing, feeling and cognition cover it up, they do not perceive the essentially clear basic substance. If only you could right away have no mental states, the basic substance would make itself present, like the sun revolving and ascending into the void, shining everywhere, in all ten directions and without limits or obstructions. Therefore, for you students of the Way who only recognize seeing, hearing, feeling and cognition as a way of proceeding forward, when you empty yourselves of seeing, hearing, feeling, and cognition, your train of thought will be cut off and you will have no place to get through. You have only to recognize the basic mental state in the same place as seeing, hearing, feeling, and cognition and that that basic mental state is not only seeing, hearing, feeling, and cognition, and yet is not separate from them. You have only not to let seeing, hearing, feeling, and cognition give rise to points of perceptions and analysis, not to let thoughts start moving upon seeing, hearing, feeling, and cognition, and not to seek a mental state separate from seeing, hearing, feeling, and cognition, nor cast seeing, hearing, feeling, and cognition off in grasping the teaching. Not treating them as identical or separate, not abiding with them or staying attached to them, one is thoroughly self-possessed and there is no place where the Way is not.

"When people of the world hear it said that the buddhas transmit a dharma about a mental state, they all say that over and above that mental state there is a dharma to learn which can be realized and grasped. So, they use their mental states to go after this thing, not knowing that a mental state just is the thing to be learned and vice versa. You can't take mental states and go looking for the mental state. After ten million eons the day will still not have come. It doesn't even come close to doing without mental states right away, which is the fundamental thing to be learned.

"It is like a warrior with a pearl on his forehead who goes out looking for it. He heads in every direction but cannot obtain it. When a wise man points it out to him, he then sees for himself the very pearl that had been there all along.

"Therefore, you students of the Way misperceive your fundamental mental state and don't recognize it as buddhahood. So, you go out looking for it, doing the meritorious practices in order to realize it gradually. If you keep going after it for eons, you won't achieve the Way. It doesn't even come close to right away doing without mental states and knowing with certainty that all things fundamentally have nothing that can be taken as real and nothing that can be gotten at, nothing that stays or abides, nothing subjective or objective.

"When you don't set into motion delusory thoughts, then you realize enlightenment. When you realize the Way, you realize the fundamental mental state is buddhahood. Eons of meritorious practices are actually specious cultivations. Just as the warrior, when he found his pearl, found a pearl that was originally on his forehead not because of the efforts to go out and look for it.

"Thus, the Buddha said, 'In my perfect enlightenment, there was nothing that I achieved.' Fearful people didn't believe him, and that's why he drew upon the five perceptual modes in which we perceive and the five languages that are spoken.[584] But it was true, not false. It was the first truth.

"As a student of the Way, one should not have any doubts about the four elements constituting one's person.[585] There is no self in the four elements. A self doesn't control them. Therefore, we know that one's person has no self and no controller.

"The five *skandhas* constitute the mental states. But the five *skandhas* have no self and no controller. Therefore, we know that these mental states have no self and no controller. The same holds for the six sense faculties, the six types of perception and the six types of consciousness, which arise and

[584] In other words, the Buddha used symbols and language to guide people along who could not go directly to perfect enlightenment.
[585] These were earth, water, fire, and wind.

cease in concert. The eighteen sensory domains are empty. Everything is empty. There is only a fundamental mental state which is vast and pure.

"There is sensuous eating and there is wise eating. For a body of the four elements, the ills of hunger are bad. To give food accordingly, without giving rise to covetous attachment, is called wise eating. But to lasciviate in flavors and deludedly to make distinctions only seeking to suit one's mouth without deciding that one has had enough is called sensuous eating.

"*Sravakas* are prompted by the voice to become enlightened.[586] That's why they're called "*sravakas*." But they don't understand their own mental states. From the teaching of the *sravakas* arise concepts. Whether it is by contact with deities or by auspicious signs or spoken transmission that they hear of enlightenment and nirvana, it will be three eons before they attain the Way of buddhahood. All this is how it is with the Way of hearing the voice. So, they are called '*sravaka* buddhas.'

"Just individually and suddenly understand your own mental state as all along having been buddhahood. There is nothing that one can obtain; there is no practice to be cultivated. This is the unexcelled Way. This is a Tathagata[587] Buddha.

"Those who study the Way just need to avoid the slightest reifying thought which makes a separation from the Way. With every moment's thought let there be no phenomena. With every moment's thought let there be no intentions. That is buddhahood.

"If you students of the Way want to become buddhas, then for all the Buddha's teachings, study is of no use. Only

---

[586] *Sravakas*, literally "voice hearers," follow the Buddhist teaching. According to Huangbo, this requires mental states and it is therefore inferior to Chan.

[587] The "thus come," fully enlightened Buddha. The idea behind the term is that we can only point to the Buddha and say that he is thus as he is because his enlightened state is beyond the conceptual distinctions necessary to any description.

study how to do without seeking and without clinging. With seeking gone, mental states will not arise. With clinging gone, mental states will not cease. Not arising, not ceasing – that is a Buddha. The eighty-four-thousand teachings aimed at the eighty-four-thousand delusions are just an edifying transformation that draws the entrance closer. At bottom, there are no such things. Doing away with them is the teaching. One who knows how to do away with them is a buddha. But in doing away with all delusions, there is nothing one can attain.

"If you who study the Way want to know the essential secret, then cling to nothing beyond the mental state. To say that the dharma body[588] of the Buddha resembles an empty void is like saying that the dharma body is just emptiness and emptiness is just the dharma body. Often people say that the dharma body is in an entirely empty place or that emptiness contains the dharma body within it. They don't understand that the dharma body is just emptiness and emptiness is just the dharma body. If we fix our terms, there is an 'empty void,' and the empty void is not the dharma body. And if we fix our terms, there is a dharma body, and the dharma body is not the empty void. However, when you aren't forming a concept of emptiness, emptiness is the dharma body. And when you aren't forming a concept of the dharma body, the dharma body is emptiness. Emptiness and the dharma body lack any distinguishing characteristics. A buddha and sentient beings lack any distinguishing characteristics. Samsara and nirvana lack any distinguishing characteristics. Delusion and enlightenment lack any distinguishing characteristics.

"Separate from all characteristics is the Buddha. The ordinary person grasps for objects. The man of the Way grasp for mental states. But when mental states and objects are both put from one's mind, that is the true dharma. To put things from one's mind is fairly easy, but to put mental states from one's mind is extremely difficult. A man won't dare to put his

---

[588] *Dharmakaya*, the ultimate nature of the Buddha.

mental states from his mind, fearing to fall into emptiness without anything to hold onto. They don't understand that emptiness is at bottom not emptiness. It is only one true dharma realm.

"This enlightened consciousness has no beginning or end and is coeval with the empty void. It isn't subject to arising or cessation, to nothingness or being, to defilement or purity, to noise nor silence, or to youth or old age. It has no separate location, no inside or outside, no dimension or shape, no image or sound. One cannot look for it or seek it. It cannot be contemplated with wisdom or grasped with language, mastered with objects or reached by meritorious deeds. The buddhas, the *bodhisattvas* and all wriggling creatures that possess consciousness all alike share this nature of great nirvana. This nature is just the mental state, the mental state is just buddhahood, and buddhahood is just the dharmas. With a moment's thought departing from what is real, all your concepts will become delusional. You cannot seek the mental state by means of mental states. You cannot seek buddhahood by means of buddhahood. You cannot seek the dharma by means of the dharma.

"Therefore, students of the Way, you should right away be without mental states. A tacit reconciliation is enough. In forming delimitations in that mental state you thereby miss the mark. Using the mental state to transmit the mental state – this may be taken as the correct view. By all means do not go after objects outside of it. To mistake objects for the mental state is to mistake a thief for your son.

"Since we have desire, anger, and ignorance, we set up abstinence, calm, and wisdom. Fundamentally, there is no delusion. So, why is there enlightenment? This is why Bodhidharma said, "The Buddha explained all the teachings in order to do away with all mental states. If one has no mental states, what use are all the teachings?" From the standpoint of a Buddha of the original kind, one doesn't stay attached to a single thing. It is like the empty void. Although you adorn it with innumerable gems and jewels, in the end they cannot abide.

"The nature of a buddha is like the empty void. Although you adorn it with innumerable points of merit and instances of wisdom, in the end they cannot abide. On the contrary, they would conceal the fundamental nature, which would become invisible. All the impure dharmas are constructed from mental states. When you meet up with them, objects exist. When you have no objects, they do not exist.[589] From the standpoint of a pure nature, one can't form a concept of objects. It is said, 'Meditation and wisdom are how the mirror functions in particular ways' and 'Make your vision, hearing, sensation, and cognition calm and lucid.' Such concepts formed from the standpoint of objects are only supposed to be explained to people of middle and lower roots.[590] If you would make a direct apprehension, then you shouldn't form concepts such as these. All of these objective dharmas' existence or non-existence implies some principle of existing and not existing. But if you do not to take a view of dharmas as existing or not existing, then you will see the dharmas.[591]

On the first day of the ninth month, the Master told me, "From the time Bodhidharma arrived in China, he only explained a one mental state and only transmitted one dharma. He used buddhahood to transmit buddhahood, not explaining any other buddhahood. He used the dharma to transmit the dharma, not explaining any other dharma. This dharma is one which cannot be explained. This buddhahood is one which cannot be grasped. It is an originally pure mental state. There is only this one fact. Anything in addition to it is unreal.

"Prajña is wisdom. This wisdom is a fundamentally mental state with no characteristics. The ordinary people don't take the Way. They only gives in to the six senses and follow

---

[589] Here Chan's basis in Yogacara's mind-only position is apparent.
[590] "Roots" refers to potentials for enlightenment.
[591] This ambiguates between "then you will perceive the teaching" and "then you will perceive things as they are."

the six sense fields. Students of the Way, if you think for one moment's thought in terms of samsara, you fall into the way of Mara.[592] If for one moment's thought you give rise to the various views, you fall into heretical ways. To opine that there is arising and to seek cessation is to fall to the way of the *sravakas*. Not to believe that there is arising but to believe that there is cessation is to fall to the way of the *pratyekabuddhas*.[593] Things fundamentally do not arise and do not cease. Don't begin to have dualistic views. Neither dislike nor like. All the various things are only one mental state. Then you achieve the Buddha's vehicle.

"Ordinary people all give rise to mental states in response to objects and, in response to mental states, to likes and dislikes. If you would be without objects, then put these mental states from your mind. When these mental states are put from your mind, then objects will be empty. When objects are empty, then mental states will cease. If you don't put these mental states from your mind and still try to do away with objects, then objects cannot be done away with. This will only increase your consternation.

"Therefore, the myriad things are only mind, and mind cannot be got at. So, what do you seek? People who study prajña do not opine that there is a single thing that can be got at. They do away with their ideas of the Three Vehicles, there being only one real truth which cannot be verified or gotten at. To say, "I can verify it" or "I can get at it" is to set yourself above other people. The monks who waved their robes and left in the *Lotus Sutra* were all such disciples.[594] That is why the Buddha said, "In the substance of enlightenment, there was nothing obtained, but only a tacit reconciliation."

"If an ordinary person coming near to the end of his days would only observe that the five *skandhas* and four

---

[592] Mara is the Buddhist demon who, through temptation, torment and deceit, tries to get aspirants to enlightenment to lose their way.
[593] *Pratyekabuddhas* attain a certain level of enlightenment on their own without a teacher
[594] Huangbo is referring to doctrinal disputes among the three vehicles.

elements are devoid of any self, that the true mental state is devoid of any characteristics and neither comes nor goes, that its nature did not come at the time of birth, will not leave at the time of his death, but is placidly and completely still with the mental state and object as one - if he could only do this, it would immediately and suddenly happen. He would no longer be bound by the three periods[595] but would be world-transcending man. You would be altogether unable to find the slightest inclination in him. If he saw the various buddhas of excellent characteristics coming to welcome him and grasping before him in their many kinds, he would have no thought of following along. If he saw evil characteristics appearing before him in their many kinds, he would have no thought of being horrified by them. He would just put mental states from his mind, at one with the *dharmakaya* and at rest in himself. This is the important point."

On the eighth day of the tenth month the master told me, "Now regarding the illusory city, the two vehicles, the ten stages of the *bodhisattva* and other such kinds of enlightenment and subtle enlightenment are all teachings established provisionally in order elicit people's interest. This is the illusory city. When we speak of the treasure's place, by 'treasure' we mean the nature of fundamental buddhahood in the true mental state. This treasure does not belong to the determinations of your conceptual predispositions.[596] You cannot fabricate it. It is devoid of buddhahood or sentient-being-hood. It has no subject or object. Where is there a city? You may say, that's the city of illusion, but where is the treasure's place? The treasure's place cannot be pointed out. If you could point it out, then it would have a location. It

---

[595] I.e., the past, present and future.
[596] *Qing*, cognitive or conceptual predispositions, refers to the conceptual scheme with which we experience reality and which comprises a host of mental states which realize the concepts. (See also footnote 339 in the chapter on Xunzi.) Meditation is the difficult activity of not allowing these predispositions to have their usual effects on one's mental state, such that one remains conscious but without cognitive activity.

470

wouldn't be the real treasure place. I say it is nearby and nothing more. You cannot describe it with language. But its actual substance - when you can reconcile yourself to that, then that's it.

"Icchantikas[597] are those whose faith is incomplete. Any being of the six realms, including those of either vehicle, who does not believe he has incipient buddhahood is called an 'icchantika with his good roots cut off.' *Bodhisattvas* are those who have deep faith that Buddha's teaching is real but don't see that there is a Mahayana and a Hinayana or that a Buddha and sentient beings have one and the same nature in the dharma are called "icchantikas with good roots." Those who for the most part attain enlightenment by hearing the spoken teaching are called *sravakas*. Those who become enlightened by observing the cause and effect are called *pratyekabuddhas.* Those who become buddhas but not by becoming enlightened in their own mental state are called *sravaka* buddhas.

"Most of you disciples of the way become enlightened by being taught the dharma. You do not become enlightened by the mental dharma. Even after eons of practice you will not realize this fundamental buddhahood. Those who become enlightened by the teaching of the dharma and not by means of the mental state place too little emphasis on the mental state and too much on the teaching. They go chasing after clods and are oblivious to the fundamental mental state. If only you will only reconcile yourselves to the fundamental mental state, you will see no use in seeking the dharma. This mental state is the dharma.

"Most ordinary people take objects as obstructions to mental states and things as obstructions to principles. They often try to get away from objects in order to ease their mental states and block out things in order to preserve principles. They

---

[597] These are figures in Buddhist soteriology – *icchantikas, sravakas* and *pratyekabuddhas.* Icchantikas have a stained nature and cannot become enlightened. *Pratyekabuddhas*, as noted earlier, attain a certain level of enlightenment on their own without a teacher, while *sravakas*, as noted earlier, follow the Buddha's teaching.

don't realize that it is mental states that obstruct objects and principles that obstruct things. If they would only allow their minds to be empty, then objects would be empty. If they would only allow principles to become still, then things would be still. Don't misuse your mind.

"Most ordinary people don't dare empty their minds. They fear falling into the emptiness and don't realize that their minds are fundamentally empty. The ignorant do away with things but not mental states. The wise do away with mental states but not things.

"The mental state of the *bodhisattva* is like an empty void. He casts off everything. The merit he accrues he does not cling to. In this there are three kinds of casting off. The casting off of everything – inner, outer, bodily and mental - like the void in which there is nothing to hold on to or cling to. Then, one acts in accord with things and follows along with circumstance, subject and object both put from one's mind. This is great casting off. When one both follows the Way in displaying the virtues and also one returns and casts off the merit with a mental state devoid of ambition, this is mid-level casting off. When one widely cultivates the many virtues with an ambition but hears the dharma and understands emptiness and therefore is not attached, this is small detachment. Great casting off is like a flaming lamp in front of oneself, so that one won't lose sight of enlightenment. Mid-level casting off is like a flaming lamp at one's side; some things it lights up and some it leaves dark. Low-level casting off is like a flaming lamp behind one, so that one doesn't see the pitfalls.

"Therefore, the mental state of a *bodhisattva* is empty. He has cast everything off. His past mental states cannot be gotten at. This is the casting off of the past. His present mental states cannot be gotten at. This is the casting off of the present. His future mental states cannot be gotten at. This is the casting off of the future. These are known as the casting off of the three periods.

"Ever since the Tathagata bequeathed the dharma to Kasyapa, with a mental state one makes the impression of a seal

472

upon another's mental state.[598] Then there is no difference between the one mental state and the other. If the seal were made in emptiness, then it would not amount to anything legible. If the seal were made in things, then it would not amount to a teaching. So, with a mental state one makes the impression of a seal upon another's mental state, and then there is no difference between the one mental state and the other. Making the impression and being impressed both involve a difficult reconciliation. So, those who attain this are few. Nevertheless, the mental state is no mental state at all and obtaining it is not obtaining it at all.

"Buddhahood has three bodies.[599] The *dharmakaya* is explained as the fact of the pervasive emptiness of its nature.[600] The *sambhogakaya* is explained as the fact that all of it is pure.[601] The *nirmanakaya* is explained as the facts about the six levels and various practices.[602] The *dharmakaya* – when you explain this teaching, you can't use language, speech, images or writing in order to go after it. There is nothing subject to explanation or demonstration. Its self-nature is empty and pervasive and nothing more. That is why it is said, "There being no dharma that can be explained is called 'explaining the dharma.'"[603] The *sambhogakaya* and the *nirmanakaya* take their appearance according to the circumstance. The teachings that can be explained also according to events respond to your roots in taking up their manifestations. None of them are the real teaching. Hence it is said, 'The *sambhogakaya* and

[598] A reference to the story of Kasyapa silently receiving the silent transmission of enlightenment from the Buddha.
[599] I give the names of these bodies in Sanskrit translation because this has been so common in Western textbooks in Buddhism.
[600] The "real-teaching body" noted earlier. This is the content of the wisdom supposedly achieved in Buddhist enlightenment. A metaphysical sense: the way the world really is.
[601] The "enjoyment body." This is the Buddha's enjoyment of his wisdom.
[602] The "physically appearing body" of the Buddha.
[603] This is a play on term "*dharma*": (1.) thing, reality; (2.) Buddhist teaching. It might be translated "There being nothing that can be explained is called 'explaining things.'"

nirmanakaya are not real buddhas and are not the ones who explains the *dharma*.'

"That which is called 'unifying' is a single wondrous clearness that gets divided into the six elements. The single wondrous clearness is the one mental state. The six elements are the six sense faculties. Each of these six elements comes together with its defilement. The eyes come together with shape, the ears with sound, the nose with smell, the tongue with taste, the body with feeling, and the cognition with things. In the midst of these there arise the six perceptions, making eighteen realms. If you understand that the eighteen realms are without objective reality, you will fuse the six elements into a single wondrous clearness. That the single wondrous clearness is the mental state - you students of the way all know this. But you can't help forming conceptions of the single wondrous clearness and the six elements. As a result you are put in bondage by things and do not reconcile yourselves to the fundamental mental state.

"When the Tathagata appeared in the world, he wanted to explain the true teaching of the One Vehicle.[604] But then, sentient beings would not have believed it and would have slandered him and been drowned in a sea of suffering. But if he had said nothing at all, then that would have been uncharitable and he would not have been able to pervade the subtle Way among the people. So, he set up the expedient means of speaking of Three Vehicles. These vehicles have degrees of greatness and their accomplishments degrees of shallowness and depth. None of them is the fundamental teaching. So, it is said, 'There is only One Vehicle. If the Way is divided into two, then it is not the real one.' So, in the end he could not elucidate the teaching of the one mental state. This is why he asked the monk Kasyapa to sit with him and receive the one mental state. Without words he explained the teaching. This single branch of the teaching gave rise to

---

[604] In contrast to the various special teachings and practices grouped into distinct vehicles, Chan's tacit reconciliation is the One Vehicle.

different offshoots. Only those who are capable of this tacit reconciliation reach the abode of the buddhas."

I asked, "What is the Way like? How should one cultivate the practices?"

The Master said, "What kind of thing is the Way that you would want to cultivate the practices?"

I asked, "What sort of Chan meditation and study of the Way have the masters of various regions transmitted?"

The Master said, "Talk that attracts people of poor roots - you can't rely on it."

I asked, "If that is talk that attracts people of poor roots, I haven't had an opportunity to consider the teaching for people of good roots."

The Master said, "If they are people of good roots, where would there be anyone for them to follow? Turning within themselves, they can attain nothing, so how much less will there be a teaching that hits the mark? You don't see it in what teachers call a teaching for how can you make a teaching out of that?"

I asked, "If it is so, is nothing worth trying to follow?"

The Master said, "That would save you some mental effort."

I asked, "If so, then we cut all of it off and eliminated it. But it can't just be nothing."

The Master said, "Who taught you it was nothing? Who was he? You go ahead and follow him."

I asked, "If there is nothing to follow, why do you still say that nothing is cut of?"

The Master said, "If you don't follow, you'll have repose. Who taught you to cut anything off? Look at the empty void before your eyes. How can you create or cut off that?"

I asked, "This teaching – if one could attain it, would it be like emptiness?"

The Master said, "At various times I have explained emptiness to you as being suchness or as being difference. I've spoken in this way from time to time. And you've gone ahead and formed concepts of it."

I asked, "So, on that point, some should not form concepts as people do?"

The Master said, "I can't stop you. And concepts follow upon conceptual predispositions. When conceptual predispositions arise, then suchness is shut off."

I asked, "So, should one therefore let no conceptual predispositions arise?"

The Master said, "If you don't let conceptual predispositions arise, then who will teach you what is so?"

I asked, "Why have you said I was mistaken whenever I've asked you something?"

The Master said, "So, you're a man who doesn't understand what is said. What mistakes?"

I asked, "So far the many things you have said were all repudiations. We haven't yet had an exposition of the true teaching."

The Master said, "In the true teaching there is no confusion, but your question itself gives rise to confusion. What true teaching are you looking for?"

I asked, "Since this question itself gives rise to confusion, how will you answer it?"

The Master said, "You just take things and look at them with perspicacity, regardless of other people." He also said, "They are like mad dogs which bark whenever something moves. When it's only the wind blowing the grass or trees they're still no different."

Huangbo said, "This Chan School of ours, throughout its transmission, has never taught people to seek knowledge or concepts. 'Study the Way' is only a turn of phrase used to draw them in at first. But the Way cannot be studied. In fact letting conceptual predispositions persist and studying concepts create an illusory Way.

"The Way has no location. It is what is called the Mahayana mental state. This mental state is not inside or outside or in between. It truly has no location. It is most important that you do not produce knowledge or concepts. I

476

explain this only because you are now preoccupied by the determinations of your conceptual predispositions. When the determinations of your conceptual predispositions are exhausted, then your mental state will not have a location.

"This Way is a natural reality and fundamentally without a name or words. It is only because people of the world don't understand and deludedly locate it in their conceptual predispositions that the buddhas came to explain how to break this habit. Being afraid that you and others wouldn't understand and using discretion, they named it 'The Way.' You mustn't hold onto this name and give rise to concepts. That's why it is said, 'When you get the fish, forget about the trap.'

"When the body and mental states are at their natural ease you will reach the Way and understand the mental state. You will reach the fundamental source and therefore be called monks. This result of being a monk derives from putting a stop to cogitations and is not achieved by study. You now take hold of mental states in order to seek the mental state.[605] You rely on other schools, intending to get it by studying. When will you succeed?

"The ancients were very keen. As soon as they heard one utterance, they gave up studies. Thus, they are referred to as men of non-action and repose in the Way who have given up study. In current times, people only want more knowledge and more concepts. They conduct broad searches for the meaning of the scriptures, calling this "engaging in cultivation and practice." They don't know that more knowledge and more concepts become obstacles. Just knowing more, they are like giving a child cheese-milk to eat whether he digests it or not. That is how it is for students of the Way in all Three Vehicles. Every single one of them is someone with indigestion. They are completely captivated by samsara. Suchness has nothing to do with this. Thus it is said, 'In my Lord's arsenal there is no such sword.' All the concepts they have ever taken

---

[605] This means engaging in the intellectual activity of studying Buddhist concepts in order to attain a non-conceptual mental state.

in should be completely cast away and replaced by emptiness without any more distinctions. This is the empty *tathagatagarba*. This *tathagatagarba* hasn't even a speck of dust in it. This is why the Lord of the Dharma who destroys reification appeared in this world and said, 'During my time with Dipankara Buddha, there were not even a few *dharmas* that I could get at.' This utterance is simply meant to portray your perceptual distinctions, knowledge and concepts as empty. Only one who does not cling to inner and outer perceptions is one for whom nothing is the matter. The system of teachings of the Three Vehicles have medicines specific to particular conditions. They were explained when fitting and established temporarily. Each one is different from the others. If only you could understand, you would no longer be deluded. The most important thing is not to come across a certain teaching for a certain condition and, preferring to hold only to it, to produce concepts of it. Why is this so? Because in truth there was no fixed teaching that the Tathagata could have taught.

"Our school doesn't discourse on these matters. If you only know how to let mental states subside and be at rest, you won't have any use for cogitating all the time."

I asked, "Given everything you have said, this mental state is buddhahood. But we haven't inquired into which mental state is buddhahood."

The Master replied, "How many minds do you have?"[606]

---

[606] Here we see Huangbo play on the ambiguity in the word *xin* which does not come through in English. The questioner is asking about mental states (*xin*), asking, "Which *xin* (mental state) is buddhahood?" Huangbo replies, "How many minds (*xin*) do you have?" The sarcastic and intentional misinterpretation of the question is his effort to get the questioner to stop thinking about mental states, since that is necessary to attaining a mental state devoid of cognitions. It's a typical example of a Chan master using language to try to force an interlocutor to attain the desired mental state which cannot be reached by ratiocination.

478

I asked, "Is it after all that the ordinary mental states are buddhahood or is it the enlightened mental state that is buddhahood?"

The Master replied, "Where are these ordinary and enlightened mental states of yours?"

I asked, "Well, now, in the Three Vehicles the ordinary and enlightened mental states are described. Why do you say it isn't so?"

The Master replied, "In the Three Vehicles it is distinctly described. I tell you ordinary and enlightened are illusions. But you don't understand. In your attachment to reification, you take what is empty and make it into something real. How couldn't that be illusion? It is illusion, so it obscures your mind. You should do away with the ordinary and the enlightened. Outside of that mental state there is no buddhahood. When Bodhidharma came from the west he simply pointed out that for all human beings, all of one's substance is buddhahood. You don't get it. Attached to ordinary and attached to sagely, you go outward at a gallop. Again, you obscure your own mind. So, I tell you this mental state is buddhahood. When a moment's perceptions arise, then you fall into distinctions. The beginningless past is no different from the present. There are no different things. This is why it is called 'Perfect Enlightenment that Establishes Equivalency'."

I asked, "You said 'when...then.'[607] With what rationale?"

The Master said, "Why do you look for rationales? When you have rationales, then your mental state becomes various and sundry."

I asked, "You said, 'The beginningless past is no different from the present.' What is the reasoning behind that?"

---

[607] You can find three instances of the 'when...then' construction in the last two pages of text. Their structure is 'when you do A, then you will be in state B,' where state B is either enlightenment or delusion.

The Master said, "It is only because you seek of your own accord that you make a distinction between them. Where is there a difference?"

I asked, "Since the two terms do not differ, why do you still use them in your explanations?"

The Master said, "If you don't bring up ordinary and sagely, who will speak of 'when...then' to you? 'When...then' would no longer be 'when...then,' and your mental state would no longer be mental states. When you keep your mind in the middle, then you will put both of them from your mind.[608] Where will you keep searching for them?"[609]

I asked, "Delusion can hide this mental state from oneself. You haven't yet taught us how to eliminate delusion."

The Master replied, "The arising and elimination of delusion are themselves delusions. Delusion has no real root but takes its existence from the making of distinctions. If you would only be done with the essences of the two stations of ordinary and sagely, you would naturally and without delusion find the resolution. Even if you still wanted to destroy them, there wouldn't be a single thread of them to get a hold of. This is called 'I cast them away with my two arms and thereby must attain buddhahood.'"

I asked, "If there is nothing to get a hold of, then what is transmitted?"

The Master said, "With the mental state the mental state is transmitted."

---

[608] Notice that in this sentence Huangbo uses a "when...then" construction in order to explain getting beyond this type of thinking. His point seems to be the following: *when you stop thinking in terms of 'when...then' then you will get closer to enlightenment.* This is neither incoherent nor even self-defeating advice. In order to fulfill the advice the aspirant need only stop thinking in terms of 'when...then'. He needn't keep the advice's 'when...then' structure in mind while doing so. Perhaps you have heard it said that the command "Do not think of elephants" is self-defeating. It is not. In order to obey it, one need only turn one's mind's attention to something besides elephants and let it dwell there.

[609] Here "them" refers to ordinary and sagely, and "in the middle" refers to the middle between those two.

480

I asked, "If the mental state is mutually transmitted, then why do you say there are no mental states?"

The master said, "When you don't apprehend a single thing, this is called transmitting the mental state. If you get this mental state, that's the lack of mental states and the lack of things."

I asked, "If there are no mental states and no things involved, then what do you mean by 'transmitted'?"

The Master replied, "You have heard talk of transmission of a mental state and taken it to refer to something that can be gotten at. This is why the Patriarch said, 'When you have gotten the nature of this mental state, you can explain it as incomprehensible. Keen understanding finds nothing it can get at. When you get at it you don't say you know.' If I taught this to you, how would you handle it?"

I asked, "Spread before our eyes is vacuous emptiness. Is that not an object? How are you not indicating an object in order to get a glimpse of this mental state?"

The Master replied, "What sort of mental state could I teach you to see in an object. Even if you saw it, it would be only the mental state as reflected in objects. Like a man using a mirror to reflect his face, he can discern his features clearly in it, all along it would only be an image. What has this to do with your issue?"

I asked, "If I proceed by means of reflections, when will I get a glimpse of it?"

The Master said, "If you pursue means, then these will always be fake things. How could there be a time when you would understand? You ignore others telling you to open your hands like a man who has nothing. You wear yourself out talking about innumerable things."

I asked, "Do those who understand recognize that the reflections are not the things?"

The Master said, "If there are no things, what use are reflections? You shouldn't be talking in your sleep."

Entering the hall, the Master said, "Having one hundred or more kinds of knowledge isn't as good as not seeking. That is the best. Men of the Way are people who have no issue.[610] Reality has nothing to do with the many mental states and there are no concepts that can describe it. There is no issue. Dismissed!"

I asked, "What is worldly truth?"[611]

The Master replied, "What's the point of explaining such creeping weeds! How can we discuss what is fundamentally pure with bogus words? Just being without any mental states is what we mean by 'undefiled wisdom.' Every day whether walking or standing, sitting or lying, and in every word you utter, in your comportment toward things just do without clinging to their existence. When you speak or blink be utterly without defilement. You are now in the later days of the Dharma. Most of you students of Chan are attached to all the sounds and forms. Why don't you be like me and let each mental state be empty and be gone, gone as if it were a rotten log or a rock, gone as if it were cold ashes or a dead fire? Whenever there is something to deal with, respond accordingly. Otherwise, in the end you will be tormented by Yama. Just do without reifying things or treating them as nothing, with a mental state like the sun, always orbiting in the void, brilliant by nature, shining without shining. This is a feat of no small effort but when you reach this point you will have nowhere to drop anchor and then you will be walking with the buddhas. Hence, 'You should by abiding nowhere give rise to the mental state.'[612] This is your pure *dharmakaya*. It is called perfect enlightenment. If you don't get the idea, then even with all your knowledge gained from study, your strenuous cultivations, and your extreme austerities you will not be cognizant of your mind. Utterly heretical practices! You will certainly join Mara. If you cultivate practices like this, what

[610] No issue: *wu shi*, meaning no problem, nothing to attend to, take care of or worry about. Even in modern Chinese a similar phrase, *meishi*, is used casually to mean "no problem."
[611] For the "worldly" (or "conventional") truth, see footnote 443.
[612] A passage from *The Diamond Sutra*.

benefit will come of it? Zhi Gong said, 'Buddhahood is a creature of one's mental state. How can it be sought in texts and writings?'

"Through your study of the Three Ranks, the Four Fruits, and the Ten Stages of a *Bodhisattva*, you fill your mind with them. This is only to sit between ordinary and enlightened. You will not see the Way and that the various practices are impermanent. This creates a samsaric teaching. 'Its energy used up the arrow falls back down. Life after life goes by, each unsatisfactory. You strive to measure up to the Gate of Non-Action and Genuine Characteristics of a Buddha. With one leap you could enter the Buddha's land.' But you aren't that sort of person. You want to go through the way set up by the ancients for broadly studying known concepts. Zhi Gong said, 'If you do not meet an enlightened and brilliant master, you will have taken the Mahayana medicine in vain.'

"If you would now only study how to do without mental states at all times, whether you're walking, standing, sitting or lying down, then in time you would certainly attain the real goal. With the quantity of power you have, you aren't capable of sudden transcendence. But after three, five, or ten years, you would certainly advance, going forward naturally. But since you're not like that, you have to grasp onto mental states by studying Chan and the Way. What has the Buddha's teaching to do with that? That's why it is said that what the Buddha set forth was intended to convert people. It was like taking yellow leaves to be gold in order to stop a child's tears. It certainly wasn't the truth. Anyone who takes it to be the real goal is not a member of my school. Moreover, what does it have to do with your fundamental substance? This is why the *sutras* say, 'There isn't even the slightest *dharma* that one can get. This is perfect enlightenment.' If you can get the intent of this, then you will see that the way of the buddhas and the way of Mara are both mistaken.

"The fundamentally pure and gleaming world is devoid of characteristics such as square and round, big and small, long and short. There are no outflows,[613] no actions, no ignorance and no enlightenment. You must discern that there is not one thing, nor any ordinary people or buddhas. The innumerable worlds are but foam on the sea. All sageliness and wisdom but strokes of lightning. None is anywhere near as real as the mental state. The *dharmakaya*, from ancient times until now and among the all the buddhas and patriarchs, is one. Where is it lacking even one whit? Even if you can get the intent of this, you must still exert all of your energy. This life is leaving. When we breathe our last, it is not guaranteed that we will breathe again."

I asked, "The Sixth Patriarch couldn't read *sutras* or books. How did he attain the robe and become a patriarch? Xiu sat above 500 people. As a teaching master, he could lecture on thirty-two *sutras* and commentaries. Why didn't he get the robe?"

The Master said, "Because he had conceptual thoughts, he took there to be things. He took what was practiced and what was realized as literally so. This is why the Fifth Patriarch entrusted it to the Sixth Patriarch. For the Sixth Patriarch at that moment there was a tacit reconciliation, and he attained the secret transmission of the Tathagata's deepest intent. This is why the teaching was entrusted to him. You don't see it in this way: The fundamental teaching of the teaching is a non-teaching. A non-teaching teaching is still a teaching. Now that the non-teaching teaching has been transmitted, how can anyone take the teaching to be a teaching teaching?[614] Those

---

[613] A technical Buddhist term referring to the persistence of desires for external things which cause rebirth.

[614] This passage is not completely translatable because it plays on homonym "*fa*": *dharma*, teaching, thing. In order to let you see the ambiguities, let's put the ambiguous usages in italics and the usages meaning "teaching" in regular font: "The fundamental *dharma* of the *dharma* is that there is no *dharma*. The *dharma* of there being no *dharma* is a *dharma*. Now that the *dharma* of there being no *dharma* has been transmitted, how can anyone take the dharma to be a dharma of a dharma?" The idea is that there really is no Buddhist teaching and the various things in the world do not really

who get the intent of this are what we call 'monks' and are good at the practices.

"If you don't believe this, then what about the following? The monk Ming travelled to the summit of Dayu Mountain to visit the Sixth Patriarch. The Sixth Patriarch then asked him, "What are you after in coming here? Do you seek the robe[615] or the teaching?" The monk Ming said, "Not the robe. I've come only for the teaching." The Sixth Patriarch said, "Just for a moment, put your thoughts aside. Give no consideration to good or evil. Ming then complied with these words. The Sixth Patriarch said, 'Don't think of good. Don't think of evil. Right at this moment, go back to the countenance you had before the monk Ming's father and mother were born.' With this utterance, Ming immediately had a tacit reconciliation. He then made obeisance and said, "I am like a man who drinks water and knows for himself how cold or hot it is. I have wasted thirty years of work with the Fifth Patriarch. Today I do away with the errors of the past.' The Sixth Patriarch said, 'Precisely. Now you understand that the First Patriarch came from the west to point directly at the human mind. The seeing of its nature and the attainment of buddhahood do not lie in words or discourses. How could you not see it?'

"Ananda asked Kasyapa, 'Besides the golden robe, what did the World Honored One transmit to you?' Kasyapa exclaimed, 'Ananda!' Ananda replied, 'Yes?' Kasyapa said, 'Throw down the flagpole outside out gate.' This was this sign that the First Patriarch gave. Ananda had waited on the master for 30 years. Because he had taken in too much knowledge and wisdom the Buddha admonished him, saying, 'You can study wisdom for 1,000 days, but it won't be as good as studying the

---

exist. This might seem less odd when you consider that a meditator in the mental state Huangbo says is devoutly to be sought for does not conceive of any such teaching or things.

[615] For a while after Hui Neng received the robe making him Sixth Patriarch, it was said that his enemies sought to take it from him.

Way for one day. If you do not study the Way, it's even hard to drink one drop of it.'"

I asked, "How can I make it so that I don't fall into having graded levels?"

The Master said, "Always eat without chewing a single grain of rice. Always walk without setting your foot on a single piece of ground. Then, there won't be any characteristics of self and so forth. You will always be unseparated from mundane affairs, but you won't be deluded by the various objects. Then, you will be called a self-possessed person.[616] And with every single moment, do not perceive any characteristics. Do not recognize any past or present or the three temporal periods. The past isn't gone, the present doesn't abide, and the future will not come. Placidly sit upright, accepting what life delivers to you without being attached to it. Then, you may be called free. Make effort! If there are a thousand or ten-thousand people in this school, only three or five will ever obtain this. If you don't take this as the real matter, then the day will come when calamity befalls you. As long as you make sure you put in enough effort in this life, then how will calamity befall you in eons to come?"

from *The Record of Linji*

When the Master [Linji] was beginning his residence in Huangbo's assembly, his conduct was quite sincere. The head monk therefore praised him, saying, "Although he is young, he's different from the rest." So, he asked him, "How long have you been here?"

The Master replied, "Three years."

"Have you been for an interview yet?" the head monk asked.

---

[616] "Self-possessed" translates *zizai*, literally "located in/with oneself." It means confident, self-assured, or autonomous. See footnote 466.

"I don't go for interviews," said Linji. "I don't know what to ask."

"Why don't you go ask the chief monk of this temple what the greatest significance of the Buddha Dharma is?"

The master then went and asked. But before he could finish his utterance, Huangbo hit him. When the Master came back, the head monk said, "How did your conversation go?"

"I asked the question, but before I could complete my utterance the Master hit me. I don't understand."

"Just go ask again," said the head monk.

The Master went and asked again, and again Huangbo hit him. In this way, he asked three times and was hit three times. He went to the head monk and told him, "It was so compassionate of you to have me go question the Master. Three times I asked and three times I was hit. I regret that I am obstructed by karma from understanding his point. At this point, I'm going to go on leave."

"If you're going away, you should take your leave from the Master," said the head monk.

The Master bowed and withdrew. The head monk went ahead of him to see Huangbo and told him, "The young one who has been questioning you is very much of the Dharma. When he comes to take his leave from you, use skillful means in sending him along. With future breakthroughs he will become a fine, big tree which will provide cool shade for the people of the world."

When the Master came to speak with Huangbo, Huangbo said, "You mustn't go anywhere but to the river in Gaoan to see Dayu. He will certainly explain things to you."

The Master went to Dayu. Dayu asked, "Where do you come from?"

The Master said, "I come from Huangbo's place."

"What did Huangbo have to say?"

The Master said, "Three times I asked him what the greatest significance of the Buddha Dharma is, and three times I got hit. I don't know whether I was at fault or not."

Dayu said, "Huangbo is such a grandmother that he took great pains with you, and you come here asking whether you were at fault or not?!"

With these words the Master experienced great enlightenment. He said, "So there wasn't much to Huangbo's Buddha Dharma after all!"

Dayu grabbed him and said, "What a bed-wetting little devil! Coming here asking whether you're at fault or not! And now even saying that there's not much to Huangbo's Buddha Dharma! What sense did you make of it? Speak! Speak!"

The Master punched Dayu three times in the ribs. Dayu let go of him and said, "Your master is Huangbo. It's not my affair."

Linji left Dayu and returned to Huangbo. Huangbo saw him coming and asked, "This guy! Coming and going, coming and going! When does it ever end?"[617]

"It's[618] thanks to your grandmotherly heart," said the Master. He then paid his respects and stood in attendance.

"What did Dayu have to say?" The Master related the preceding conversation to him and Huangbo said, "If only that guy would come here! I can't wait to give him a good smack!"

The Master said, "Why wait? Here's a taste right now!" said the Master and gave Huangbo a slap.

"What a lunatic, coming back here and pulling the tiger's whiskers!" said Huangbo.

The Master yelled and Huangbo said, "Attendants! Get this lunatic out of here and take him to the monks' hall!"

Later, Weishan related this to Yangshan, saying, "Was Linji then indebted to Dayu or indebted to Huangbo?"

---

[617] Huangbo is lamenting Linji's seeming to bounce back and forth between masters as a sign that he has failed to understand Chan. Perhaps after he utters this, Huangbo recognizes Linji's enlightened countenance.

[618] "It" refers to Linji's enlightenment, which he can see that Huangbo recognizes. This is a case of what we saw referred to in the *Huangbo Xiyun's Essential Teachings of the Transmission of the Mental State* as a "tacit reconciliation."

Yangshan replied, "He not only stepped on the tiger's head but also took a hold of the tiger's tail."

Suggested Readings

Blofeld, John, *The Zen Teaching of Huang Po on the Transmission of Mind* (New York: Grove Press, 1958)

Cheshier, William L., "The Term 'Mind' in Huang Po's Text *Huang Po Ch'uan Hsin Fa Yao*," *Inquiry* 14(1971): 102-112

Cleary, Thomas, *Introduction to Chan Buddhism* (Amazon Digital Services, 2014)

Davis, Joshua Carl, *Metaphysics and the Meaning of Life: Towards a Philosophy of Zen Buddhism* (Milwaukee: Three Brothers Press, 2010)

Dumoulin, Heinrich, *Zen Buddhism: A History, Volume I: India and China*, James W. Heisig and Paul Knitter, trans. (Bloomington: World Wisdom, 2005)

Grigg, Ray, *The Tao of Zen* (New York: Tuttle, 1994)

Hagen, Steve, *Why the World Doesn't Seem to Make Sense* (Sentient Publishers, 2012)

Heine, Steven, *Zen Skin, Zen Marrow: Will the Real Zen Buddhism Please Stand Up?* (Oxford: Oxford University Press, 2008)

Izutsu, Toshihiko, *Toward a Philosophy of Zen Buddhism* (Boulder: Prajña Press, 1978)

McRae, John, *The Northern School and the Formation of Early Chan Buddhism* (Honolulu: University of Hawaii Press, 1986)

McRae, John, *Seeing Through Chan* (Berkeley and Los Angeles: University of California Press, 2003)

Rosemont, Henry, Jr., "Is Zen Buddhism a Philosophy?" *Philosophy East & West* 20(1970): 63-72

Rosemont, Henry, Jr., "The Meaning is the Use: Koan and Mondo as Linguistic Tools of the Zen Masters," *Philosophy East & West* 20(1970): 109-119

Ryan, James A., "Zen and Analytical Philosophy," *The Eastern Buddhist* 31(1998): 25-39

Suzuki, D. T. *An Introduction to Zen Buddhism*, various editions.

Suzuki, D. T., *Essays in Zen Buddhism* (New York: Grove Press, 1994)

Welter, Albert, *The Linji Lu and the Creation of Chan Orthodoxy: The Development of Chan's Records of Sayings Literature* (New York: Oxford University Press, 2008)

Wienpahl, Paul, "Ch'an Buddhism, Western Thought, and the Concept of Substance," *Inquiry* 14(1971): 84-101

Wienpahl, Paul, "On the Meaninglessness of Philosophical Questions," *Philosophy East & West* 15(1965): 135-144

Wright, Dale S., *Philosophical Meditations on Zen Buddhism* (Cambridge: Cambridge University Press, 1998)

490

Wright, Dale S., "The Huang-po Liturature" in Dale S. Wright and Steven Heine, eds., *The Zen Canon: Understanding the Classic Texts* (Oxford: Oxford University Press, 2004), pp. 107-136

Yampolsky, Philip, *The Platform Sutra of the Sixth Patriarch* (New York: Columbia University Press, 1978/2012)

Ziporyn, Brook, "The Platform Sutra and Chinese Philosophy," in Morten Schlütter and Stephen Teiser, eds., *Readings of the Platform Sutra* (New York: Columbia University Press, 2012), pp. 161-187

About the Author-Translator

James A. Ryan has taught philosophy at Georgia State University and Huron University College. He has a B.A., an M.A., and a Ph.D. in philosophy and an M.A. in Religious Studies with a concentration in East Asian Buddhism. He has published about a dozen articles in philosophy on moral theory, Chinese philosophy, and epistemology.

65248328R00279

Made in the USA
San Bernardino, CA
29 December 2017